THE INDEX
OF
Scharf's History
of
Baltimore City and County

: : : MARYLAND : : :

COMPILED BY

Bill & Martha Reamy

HERITAGE BOOKS
2012

HERITAGE BOOKS
AN IMPRINT OF HERITAGE BOOKS, INC.

Books, CDs, and more—Worldwide

For our listing of thousands of titles see our website
at
www.HeritageBooks.com

Published 2012 by
HERITAGE BOOKS, INC.
Publishing Division
100 Railroad Ave. #104
Westminster, Maryland 21157

Originally published 1992, 1993

All rights reserved. No part of this book may be reproduced or transmitted in any form or by any means, electronic or mechanical, including photocopying, recording or by any information storage and retrieval system without written permission from the author, except for the inclusion of brief quotations in a review.

International Standard Book Numbers
Paperbound: 978-1-58549-213-8
Clothbound: 978-0-7884-3409-9

INTRODUCTION

In 1881, Thomas J. Scharf published his *History of Baltimore City and County*. This single volume was a monumental effort to chronicle the development of the region; its political and economic structure; social life; institutions; and the individuals behind them. The work became the prototype for other mass produced local histories throughout the United States.

Thomas Scharf organized his history by subject which paralleled the progression from pre-settlement to approximately 1880. Within these chapters he elaborated on the more important events, individuals, and institutions. An example of this is the chapter on "Commercial Industries and Manufactures." Scharf begins with the development of a tobacco industry and concludes with the "Manufacturing Industries of Baltimore" as delineated in the 1880 census. In between are sub-chapters on every important industry or manufacturing enterprise to be found in the region, along with those individuals responsible for their founding and expansion. He used this scheme with all of the other fifty-eight chapters whose subject manner ranged from topography, local governments, participation in the various national wars, cultural life, religious denominations, etc.

What made the book unique was Thomas Scharf's inclusion of genealogies of those whom he considered the prominent members of the community. Often these genealogical and biographical sketches included steel engravings of the individual and sometimes his places of residence. This mammoth undertaking required 938 pages of text to which was added an index and the list of illustrations.

In 1971, *The History of Baltimore City and County* was reprinted by the Regional Publishing Company. In reprinting Scharf's history the publisher split the volume into two parts, provided a new introduction, and included a "rearranged" index. The original index followed the table of contents scheme, whereby, to find an individual church you first looked under the heading - Religious Denominations, then the individual denomination where the church would be listed alphabetically with the page(s) where the entry appeared. In the reprinted volume, churches were listed both by denomination and the name of the individual church.

Although the rearranged index makes it easier to locate people, places, and things it does not correct the original which is inadequate. This becomes readily apparent to anyone using the volumes for genealogical research. Scharf's index listed under the subject heading - "Biographical Sketches" only the name of the individual treated. As a result, a researcher would have to know that his ancestress had married into that person's family in order to find her. Women are not the only people who are missed in Scharf's index. There are valuable lists of individuals - privateer owners in the War of 1812, sheriffs, members of the Baltimore City Council, but they are omitted from both the original and the reprint's index. People are not the only ones who are overlooked in the two indexes. In both the original and reprint edition's index the only entry for the Abbott Iron Company is page 427. However, this company is also mentioned on pages 264 and 509. The same is true of some of the smaller industries and placenames.

As a result the uninitiated will overlook much valuable information using either of the above indexes. Armed with the knowledge that both the original and the newly arranged index contained serious omissions, Bill and Martha Reamy re-indexed the reprinted volumes. In providing a new index they not only found what had been omitted, but improved upon what had been overlooked. The index that follows contains not only the names of countless men and women, but cross references to these women under their maiden name as well. It will become readily apparent to anyone who compares the number of pages of the reprinted edition's index and this volume that a significant amount of people, places, and events were excluded by Thomas J. Scharf in his original volume. The index that follows corrects these shortcomings and increases the value of both the original and reprint editions for both the genealogical and historical researcher.

Waipahu, Hawaii,
February 1991   Thomas L. Hollowak

ABBOT, ---, Dr. 665
ABBOTT, ---, Mr. 276
E. A. 292
Edwin A. 177, 194, 195, 234
Horace 292, 354, 427, 463, 466, 890, 925
Thomas M. 794
Abbott & Lawrence 276
Abbott Iron Co. 264, 427, 509
Abbottstown Preparatory College (PA) 235
ABBY, Sarah 426
ABELL, ---, Mr. 620, 623, 624
A. S. 369, 446, 506, 508, 609, 617, 619, 622, 817, 887, 905
Arunah S. 617, 621
C. 576
Caleb 622
Edwin F. 444, 484, 623
George W. 444, 623, 887
Mary (FOX) 623
Robert 622
Walter R. 623
William E. 263
Abell Block 286, 623
Abell Building 413, 414, 624
ABERCROMBIE, D. 794
William H. 156
Aberdeen 351
ABEY, Elizabeth F. 880
Jacob 880
Sarah (SHEPHERD) 880
Abingdon, Harford Co. 575
Abington 311, 918
ABRAHAM, J. J. 487
ABRAHAMS, Hannah (WOOLEY) 386
J. J. 189
John J. 303, 440, 463, 487
Joseph 386
Margaret E. (LITTIG) 386
Tabitha (SMITHURST) 386
W. 487
William 386
William H. 303, 465
Woodward 303, 386, 598
Woodward, Mrs. 602
Abrahams & Ashcroft 138
ABRAMS, J. J. 365
Academy of Music 673, 697
Accokeek Furnace 424
ACHENBACH, --- 675
ACHEY, Frederick 242, 243, 253, 484
ACKERMAN, George 794
ADAIR, Robert 60, 67, 726, 794, 814, 816, 819, 921
Thomas B. 234
W. R. 680
ADAMS, ---, Mr. 628
---, Mrs. 569

ADAMS, A. A. 694
Alvan 359
Benjamin F. 254
Bill 58
C. C. 521
Charles C. 888
Edwin 693, 695
Eliza 227
G. F. 553
G. J. 696
George 253
George F. 558, 561, 563, 567, 794, 874
Henrietta C. 230
Henry C. 233
Henry P. 838
Herbert B. 233
J. 628
J. F. 515, 831
Jacob 247, 298, 372, 439, 461
John Q. 166, 447
John Quincy 659
John T. 729
Richard 919, 920
Richard W. 463
S. H. 456, 515, 831
Samuel 69
Samuel H. 178, 210, 509
William 414
Adams & Co. 360
Adams & Davidson 263
Adams Express Co. 144, 286, 358, 359, 360, 516
Adamstown 342
ADDISON, ---, Capt. 91
---, Rev. Dr. 878
Eleanor 879
George C. 189, 465, 484, 794
Joseph T. 156
Robert 794
Samuel S. 487
W. Meade 729
William 190
William E. 231
William Meade 794, 892
ADELON, Piere 100
Adelphi Theatre 694
ADLER, A. S. 747, 841
Abraham 149
Charles 447
Daniel 359
Admiralty Court 707
ADREON, ---, Col. 496
Christian 92, 495
Christopher C. 156
Harrison 156, 493, 494, 495
William 495
William T. 156
Adreon House 584
ADRIAN, William 794
Advent Mission Chapel 526

Advocate 627
ADY, --- 147
 Ed. H. 369
 Edward H. 814, 894, 900
Ady's Hotel 147
Aesop 638
Aetna Glass-Works 402
African Bethel Meeting-House 568
African M.E. Church 584, 798, 822, 909
African M.E. Zion Church 794
African Methodist Church 581
African Protestant Church 212
AGASSIZ, Louis 656
Aged Men's Home 242, 595
Aged Women's Home 595
AGNEW, Edward 794
 Thomas A. 449
AGNUS, Felix 611
Agricultural & Mechanical Association 885
Agricultural Aid Society 411
Agricultural Fair Grounds 887
Agricultural Society of Baltimore County 818
AHERN, ---, Rev. Father 933
 John 465, 488
AHL, Peter 343
AHREN, John 537
AHRENS, Adolph 794
Aigburth Vale 887
AIKEN, ---, Dr. 659
AISQUITH, ---, Capt. 93, 94
 Edward 91, 194, 794
 William 72, 74, 75, 205, 244, 779, 794
Aisquith Street 769
Aisquith Street German Reformed Church 572
Aisquith Street Presbyterian Church 546, 547, 549, 805
AITKEN, Andrew 732, 740, 794
AIVEY, John B. 156
AKEHURST, Charles 917
 William 855
ALARD, Thomas B. 794
ALBAN, William A. 870
 Zachariah 815
Alban Family 870
ALBAUGH, E. W. 194
 Edward 256
 Edward W. 194
 Elizabeth (PETERS) 689
 J. W. 675
 John W. 693, 694
 John William 689
 Mary (MITCHELL) 689
ALBERS, Solomon G. 299
ALBERT, A. J. 697, 698, 887
 Augustus 251, 358, 728
 Augustus J. 155

ALBERT, J. T. 880
 Jacob 254, 313, 439, 461, 484, 794
 Michael 468
 W. C. 494
 W. J. 365
 William J. 139, 146, 195, 466, 516, 794
 William J., Mrs. 604
ALBERTINE, ---, Miss 695
 Alberton 407, 830, 832, 833
 Alberton Manufacturing Co. 408
 Alberton Mills 408, 409
ALBERTSON, Isaac 488
ALBINO, ---, Rev. Father 938
ALBINSON, John 794
Albion 615
ALBRIGHT, John 250
 Philip 346
ALCOCK, Edward J. 616, 794
 James 291
ALDERCISE, William 246
ALDRICH, Jonathan 561
ALDRIDGE, A. 523
 Hattie W. 912
ALER, Reuben 189, 794
ALEXANDER, --- 202, 521, 934
 ---, Dr. 212, 728, 741
 ---, Mr. 273
 ---, Prof. 649
 A. 892
 Ashton 470, 734, 735, 741, 742, 824
 C. 102
 Charles 99
 F. W. 156
 H. Eugene 156
 Henry 433, 455
 John H. 648, 794
 Joseph 202
 Lawson 77
 Mark 38, 70, 74, 77, 194, 205, 244, 392, 544, 779
 Mary 829
 R. G. 156
 Robert 40, 60, 67, 69, 71, 72, 76, 196, 521, 707, 726, 732, 819
 Thomas S. 149, 194, 195, 794
 W. 95, 269
 William 194, 255, 729, 794
Alexander, Browne & Co. 433
Alexandria 354
Alexandria & Georgetown Navigation Co. 480
Alexandria Junction 342
Alexius, ---, Brother 938
ALFRED, Edwin H. 253
ALGIE, William G. 156
ALGIER, Catherine (FOWBLE) 867
 George 867
 Henry 867
 Mary (FOWBLE) 867
ALGIRE, Jacob 855

All Saints' Episcopal Church 911
All Saints' P.E. Church 524
All Saints' Sisters 525
Allan Line 303, 306, 380
ALLARD, Thomas B. 156
Alleghany Coal-Mine Railroad
 Company 314
Alleghany Valley Railroad 345
ALLEN, ---, Mr. 579, 645
---, Rev. Mr. 521
A. G. 615
B. 102
Benjamin 100
Bennet 904
Bennett 704
Bryan 95
E. E. 577
Edward 432
Edward P. 627
Edwin F. 156
Ethan 639, 862, 865, 867
George 794
Henry A. 236
Ira M. 557
J. C. 568
James 249, 569, 733
Jeremiah 100
John 794, 919, 920
John W. 608, 609
Joseph H. 156
Michael 727
N. D. R. 872
Owen 456
Paul 613, 615, 642, 643, 644, 654, 794
R. D. 249
Richard M. 738
Robert 737
Robert D. 794
Sidney S. 156
Solomon 190, 374, 577
W. 831
William 255
William F. 233
William H. 156, 443, 896
Zachariah 449
Allen Colored Methodist Mission 581
Allen's Mill 816
ALLENBAUGH, Charles T. 156
ALLENDER, ---, Dr. 742
Joseph 187, 251, 734, 742, 794
W. T. 916, 917, 924
Walter T. 488, 813, 820
ALLISON, ---, Dr. 224, 545
---, Rev. Dr. 794
Amos 244
Hector 544
Patrick 74, 544, 547, 665
Philip 472
Robert D. 658

ALLSTON, Henry 794
Allston Co. 509
ALMEYDA, Joseph 112
ALMONY, A. C. 873
 Harry 867
ALNUTT, E. S. 447
 George R. W. 659
 James W. 458, 465
Alpha Lodge No. 11, Independent Order of Mechanics 837
Alphonus Hall Building Association, Nos. 13, 14 & 15 509
ALRICKS, Francis W. 140, 193
 Hermanus 89
 Jane 702
 Thomas P. 188, 189
ALSOP, George 765
 Altamont 342
ALTER, Adam 247
ALTMAN, Nehemiah 573
ALTMAYER, Simon 589
ALTVATERS, ---, Misses 569
ALTVATOR, E. W. 916
ALVEY, Richard H. 136
Amateur Journal, The 640
AMBACH, David 448, 841
AMBROSE, Paul 653
AMELUNG, Frederick L. E. 794
 J. L. E. 298
 J. P. W. 794
 John Frederick 402, 794
 Sophia 794
Amelung, John Frederick & Co. 402
American Bank 473
American Baptist Publication Society 564
American Building 286, 509, 608
American Church Monthly, The 627
American Colonization Society 567, 568, 712
American Democrat, The 630
American District Telegraph Co. 509
American Engineer, The 641
American Farmer 493, 609, 614, 751
American Farmer & Rural Register 614
American Fire Insurance Co. 379, 487, 491
American Gas Coal Co. 509
American Graces 821
American Gynecological Society 744
American Hotel 262, 516, 517
American House 516
American Journal of Dental Science 651
American Journal of Medical Sciences 700
American Journal of Obstetrics 739
American Law Journal 644
American Life & Trust Co. 480

American Magazine of Foreign Literature 648
American Manufacturing Co. 509
American Marine Insurance 480
American Monthly Magazine 651
American Museum 616, 691
American Nautical Gazette, The 635
American Observer 756
American Patriot & Fell's Point Advertiser 614
American Philosophical Society 732
American Rapid Telegraph Co. 509
American Register 648
American Republican 624
American Review of History and Politics 648
American Riflemen 669
American Society for the Promotion of Domestic Manufactures 393
American St. Cecilian Societies 673
American Telegraph Co. 507
American Towing Co. 509
American Turf Register & Sporting Magazine 493, 616, 850
American Union Telegraph Co. 508
American Whig 616, 625
American Whig Review, The 629
American, The 656, 798, 804
AMES, ---, Bishop 576, 579, 580, 837, 902
A. H. 576
E. R. 794
Shadrach 99
Ames M.E. Church 580, 803
Amethyst 616
AMEY, Henry 92
Joseph H. 256
Amicable Permanent Land Co. 509
Amicable Society 679
Amicitia Lodge No. 44, Knights of Pythias 874
AMMIDON, J. C. 838
AMODIO, --- 673
AMOS, Alfred P. 813
Berry 720
Corbin 742
John 249, 463
Rachel 874
AMOSS, Alfred P. 814
Corbin 188, 189
AMY, C. L. 870
ANAN, E. J. 127
ANDERSON, --- 694
---, Capt. 432
---, Dr. 741
---, Mr. 682
Abraham 728
Addie 691

ANDERSON, Andrew 342
Benjamin 911
Benjamin T. 813
C. W. 911
Charles W. 908
Clifford C. 155
David 241, 794
E. F. 498
E. W., Mrs. 597
Franklin 866, 867
G. W. 911
George L. 877
Henry 249
Henry P. 156
J. E. 508
J. G. 247
James 741, 871, 911
James E. 637
James H. 872
James M. 155, 193, 484, 740, 742
James M., Mrs. 155, 156
John 77, 244, 911
John W. 872
Joseph 432, 794
Joshua 871
Juliet E. 871
Rebecca 879
Richard 794
S. M. 902
T. D. 838
T. W. 549
Thomas 911
William 311, 592, 871
William A. 877
Anderson & Lanier 655
Anderson Family of Va. 655
Anderson Riot 694
Anderson's Hill 905
ANDOUN, ---, Mr. 219
Joseph H. 195, 242
Oliver 246
ANDRE, Gregorious 95
Gregorius 269
ANDREW, ---, Gov. 790
ANDREWS, ---, Capt. 670
---, Dr. 731
---, Lt. Col. 671
---, Mr. 354
Emily Roseville (SNOWDEN) 669
Ephraim 731, 794
George 252
George W. 740
J. Snowden 668
James 433
John 574, 860, 861, 910
Mary C. (LEE) 671
R. Snowden 364, 444, 670
Richard Snowden 669
T. P. 669
Thomas 730, 794
William E. 156

Andrews Chapel of the M.E. Church South 929
Andrews' Maryland Battery 670
ANDRIES, J. L. 543
ANDROS, Edmond 195
ANGELE, James 77
ANGELL, ---, Mrs. 682
 James 608
 John 254
ANGUS, J. 103
 John 100
ANNAN, ---, Mrs., Dr. 617, 650
 A. M. F., Mrs. 625
 R. 551
 Robert 355
 Samuel 737
Annandale 846
ANNANDER, Thaddeus 542
Annapolis 704
Annapolis & Elkridge Railroad 358, 856
Annapolis & Potomac Canal Company 313, 314
Annapolis Junction 342
Annapolis Presbyterian Church 547
Annapolis Road 936
Anneslie 891
ANSPACH, ---, Mr. 631
 Frederick R. 794
 Henry N. 794
ANSTADT, P. 569
ANTHONY, J. P. 573
 Mark 539, 794
Anti-Democrat 612, 800
Antietam 73, 135
ANWANDER, Thaddeus 542
Apollo Hall 154, 680
APPEL, Christian 762
 Henry 156
Apple Alley 535
APPLEBY, ---, Mr. 637
 B. 569
APPLEGARTH, N. J. 442
APPLETON, C. H. 470
 Charles G. 469
 Georgina L. F. 794
 Virginia 770
 W. S., Mrs. 595
 William H. 589
 William S. 854
 William Stewart 794
Appleton's Cyclopaedia 647
APPOLD, ---, Messrs. 579
 George 212, 365, 404, 494, 794
 George J. 302, 441, 484
 George S. 466
 Samuel 302, 469, 487
Appold M.E. Chapel 579
Apprentices' Library Association 179, 625

AQUARONI, Augustus 544
AQUILLA, Samuel 880
ARAGO, M. 621
Arbiter Hall No. 3 263
Archconfraternity of the Holy Family 541, 542
Archepiscopal Library 667
ARCHER, --- 166
---, Chief Justice 699
---, Judge 816
 J. 741
 J. J. 887
 J. P. 362, 365
 James J. 114
 John 224, 741, 742
 R. Harris 734
 Robert 738
 Robert H. 114, 362, 742
 Stephenson 600, 794
 Stevenson 712
 Thomas 741
Argonauts of California 674
Argus, The 821
Aristocratic Monitor 628
ARKINSON, William C. 231
Arlington 357, 834, 836, 851
Arlington & Pimlico Branch of Western Maryland Railroad 834
Arlington & Pimlico Railroad Co. 352
Arlington Mill 412
ARMACOST, Jabez 813
 James T. 156
 Lewis 156
 Richard 817
 Thomas 872
Armacost Family 869
ARMISTEAD, ---, Col. 267
---, Maj. 89
 Christopher Hughes 794
 G. 268
 George 91
Armistead Monument 213
ARMITAGE, Benjamin 244
 James 142, 153, 193
ARMOR, George F. 156
ARMOUR, Charles Lee 127
 David 794
ARMSTRONG, --- 300
---, Gen. 86
 Alice 595
 Andrew 299
 Anne 596
 D. S. 814
 G. 550
 George B. 794
 H. L. 255
 Hugh 817
 J. 95, 269
 James 84, 89, 184, 249, 483, 547, 794

5

ARMSTRONG, James Dunn 245
  James L. 487
  James S. 487
  John 545, 547, 861, 862
  John A. 600
  Robert 234
  Robert C. 487
  Robert G. 469, 794
  T. 582, 794
  Thomas 184, 359, 414
Armstrong, Cator & Co. 286, 414, 415, 416
Armstrong, James & Co. 184
Army of the Potomac 610, 611
ARNDT, John 655
ARNEST, John 742
ARNOLD, --- 780
  ---, Gen. 79
  A. B. 745
  Abram B. 738, 746
  E., Mrs. 603
  Elizabeth 645
  George Joseph 695
  George W. 247
  Harry E. 936
  J. 579
  Thomas R. 855
  W. H. 149
  William R. 581
Arnold & Co. 505
Arnold's Olympic Theatre 695
ARTAUD, Theodore 156
ARTHUR, Benjamin 828
  Hugh 794
  James 241
  Mary J. (JORDAN) 871
  Richard 871
  T. S. 616, 617, 625, 649, 675
  Timothy Shay 650
  W. W. 191
Arthur's Home Journal 650
ARUNDEL, ---, Lord 527
Asbestos Grange No. 172, Patrons of Husbandry 832
ASBURY, --- 794
  ---, Bishop 47, 575, 862, 867
  ---, Mr. 574, 581
  Francis 574, 575
Asbury Building Association No. 3 509
Asbury Church 922
Asbury College 646, 881
Asbury M.E. Chapel 580
Asbury M.E. Church 580
ASBUTY, ---, Mr. 580
Ascension, Church of the 524
Ascension, P.E. Church of the 264, 522, 589, 641, 642, 802, 861
ASHBRIDGE, Catherine S. 922
ASHBURNER, John 432
Ashburner & Place 432

ASHBY, P. A. 641
ASHER, William 927
Ashland 26, 30, 347, 876, 877, 885
Ashland Division No. 10, Sons of Temperance 828
Ashland Factory 408
Ashland Furnace 18, 346
Ashland Iron Co. 882, 885
Ashland Iron Furnace 806
Ashland Iron-Works 876
Ashland Manufacturing Co. 408, 828
Ashland Permanent Building & Land Co. 509
Ashland Ridge 14, 19
Ashland Square 94, 281, 933
Ashley Hall 896
ASHMAN, George 518, 519, 818, 857
ASHTON, ---, Rev. Mr. 526
ASKEW, Jehu 638
  Jehu B. 194
  Jonathan 77
Aslington Presbyterian Church 937
Assembly Rooms & Theatre Tavern 226
Assembly-Rooms 265, 549, 591, 672, 680, 745, 849
Assistance Fire Co. of Philadelphia 241
Associate Reformed Church 549, 551
Associate Reformed Presbyterian Church 551
Associated Evangelical Churches 590
Associated Fire Insurance Company 245
Associated Firemen's Insurance Co. 484, 491
Associated Methodist Churches 583
Associated Presbyterian Reformed Chapel 552
Associated Press 610, 611
Association for the Improvement of Colored People 227
Association for the Improvement of the Condition of the Poor 754
Astor 515
Astor House 515, 516
Astor Mutual Building Association 509
Asylum for the Blind 475
Atamasco 862
ATCHISON, W. 103
Athenaeum 120, 261, 560, 667, 672, 680
Athenaeum Building 651, 658, 659, 660
Athenaeum Club 668
Athenaeum, The 617, 649
Athenian Society of Baltimore 393

Athenry, ---, Lord 705
ATHERTON, ---, Mr. 681
Athol 398, 459, 460
ATKINHEAD, John 156
ATKINSON, ---, Bishop 523, 774
  Archibald 738
  George 251
  Henry B. 740
  Isaac 188, 251, 484
  J. E. 743, 745
  James E., Mrs. 596, 605
  Joshua 251
  Joshua J. 794
  Josuah 189
  Samuel E. 191
  T. C. 649
  T. E. 742
  T. Edmonson 596
  Thomas 523, 839
  William G. 442, 502
  William L. 156
  William S. 468
ATKINSTON, Thomas 522
Atlantic, Gulf & West India Transit 357
Atlantic & George's Creek Consolidated Coal Co. 467, 509
Atlantic & Pacific Telegraph Co. 509
Atlantic Building Association 509
Atlantic Fire & Marine Insurance Co. 468
ATLEE, Washington L. 748
ATLEY, W. 268
Atonement Mission Chapel 524
Atonement P.E. Chapel 526
ATWELL, H. 873
  John 688
Auburn 906
AUDET, Joseph 102
AUDETT, Joseph 102
AUDOUN, Joseph H. 152, 153, 156, 728
  Lewis 465, 580
  Louis 469
AUDUBON, J. J. 786
AUGS, --- 842
AUGUSTINE, Henry 794
AULL, Elizabeth 762
Aurora Permanent Building & Savings Association 509
AUSTEN, ---, Mrs. 909
  George 909
  M. P. 874
  Philip H. 745
AUSTIN, Charles C. 861, 865, 867
  Edward 883
  George 909
  John 558
  Theodore G. 465
Avalon 852

Avalon Iron-Works 425
AVERY, F. C. 502
AVISSE, Charles 247
Avondale 357
AX, Christian 469, 494
AXER, John 156
AYDELOTTE, W. J. 847
BAARTSCHEER, William 188, 439
BABADE, Peter 234
BABB, John D. 157
  Peter 795
Babcock 91
BABCOCK, John 518
Babcock & Wilcox 426
BACHE, ---, Prof. 358
  Richard 606
Bachelors' Club of Wednesday 674
BACHER, T. H. 77
BACHMAN, Marcus 573
BACHMANN, ---, Rev. Mr. 605
Back River 311, 811, 926, 929, 931
Back River Lower Hundred 70, 71, 812
Back River Neck 926, 931
Back River Upper Hundred 70, 71, 519, 812, 857
BACKUS, ---, Rev. Dr. 775
  J. C. 549, 556, 838, 902
  John C. 546, 547, 548, 551
BACON, --- 37, 518
  Benjamin 772
  Elizabeth 907
  John 814, 894, 907, 911
  L. W. 552
  Lewis M. 912
  Priscilla 772
  Temperance 911
Badders' Tavern 905
BADEN, William E. 817
BADER, Dominic 91
  Dominick 381
  Margaret 381
BADIN, Stephen Theodore 532
  Stephen V. 234
BAER, ---, Dr. 549
  ---, Miss 271
  Charles W. 442
  E. 604
  Edward R. 157
  Elizabeth A. 229
  George H. 444, 502
  Jacob 92
  James S. 157
  John 578
  Michael S. 188
BAETJER, Annie 739
  Henry 739
BAGGS, J. F. 586
BAGLEY, J. E. 350
BAGNEL, Margaret 873
BAHN, John E. 870

BAILEY, A. H. 743
  Edwin 794
  Elisha 250
  George W. 253, 830
  Godfrey 818
  John 519, 872
  Oswell 253
  Thomas 77, 188, 554, 814
  W. 873
  William H. 254
BAILOR, Jacob 343
BAILY, ---, Mr. 362
  Gamaliel 616
  George 402
BAIN, ---, Mr. 507
  George W. 190
Bain Telegraph Line 504
BAIRD, ---, Mr. 271
  E. Thompson 548, 719
  Thomas D. 271, 719, 794, 795
  William S. 636
BAKEMAN, Edward W. 157
BAKER, ---, Dr. 745
  ---, Mr. 399
  ---, Rev. Mr. 822
  Anna (DODSON) 460
  Ashly Lee 460
  B. N. 397, 460
  Benjamin 251, 642
  Bet. 460
  C. J. 459, 595, 602
  C. J., Miss 595
  Charles 253, 795
  Charles E. 459, 460
  Charles J. 125, 140, 155, 193, 354, 415, 450, 458, 459, 460, 461, 469, 577, 585, 596, 601, 633
  Charles J., Mrs. 156, 600
  Charles, Mrs. 155
  David 249
  Desolate 552
  Elizabeth (BOSSEMAN) 460
  Francis Asbury 523
  Frank M. 460
  Frederick 101
  G. G. 578
  George 194
  George B. 149, 460
  George S. 252, 470
  H., Mrs. 595
  Henry J. 460, 794
  Henry S. 870
  Isaac 872
  Jane (JONES) 460
  John 355, 421, 519, 927
  John J. 157
  John L. 191
  Mary H. 460
  May 922
  Richard J. 398, 460, 487
  Samuel 736, 737, 742, 753, 796

BAKER, Samuel G. 796
  Samuel George 624
  Thomas B. 244
  Titura 866
  W. S. G. 359
  William 192, 244, 281, 351, 450, 460, 484, 727, 741, 795, 814, 837
  William G. 595
  William George 194, 479, 593, 795, 827, 890
  William J. 193
  William S. G. 887
  Zebedee 866
Baker, H. J. & Bro. 460
Baker, R. J. & Co. 398, 399
Baker, William & Son 439
Baker & Bro. 460
Baker Bros. 262
Baker Bros. & Co. 460
Baker Bros. Chemical Works 926
Baker Circle 281
BALCH, ---, Rev. Dr. 521, 847
Bald Hill 925
BALDERSON, Hugh 795
  Jacob 795
  Josiah 122, 728
BALDERSTON, Eli 249
  Ely 439
  Hugh 248, 249
  Jacob 241
  John C. 447
  O. H. 222
  William H. 740
BALDESTON, Jacob 240
BALDWIN, ---, Miss 755
  ---, Mr. 881
  A. S. 916
  C. C. 412
  C. W. 578
  David 470
  E. F. 543, 675
  Elizabeth Jane 458
  John 100, 241, 755, 908
  L. P. 577
  O. P. 624
  Oliver P. 636, 820
  Philemon P. 458
  Robert T. 187, 288, 446, 447, 508, 509, 831
  Robert Turner 458
  Summerfield 412, 466, 502
  Summerfield, Mrs. 604
  Thomas 795, 813, 814
  Thomas P. 795
  W. H. 448, 487
  W. Hy. 441
  William H. 155, 412, 464, 473
Baldwin & Myer 458
BALE, William 814
BALL, Dabney 587, 794
  David 487

BALL, Edward H. 817
  George 921
  John 157
  John W. 469
  Robert 50
  Walter 189, 192
  William 244
  William D. 934
Ball's (Mrs.) Coffee House 224
BALLA, Charles T. 288
BALLARD, H. E. 680, 850
BALLENGER, Jacob Lewis 197
BALLOCH, James 153, 157
BALLOU, Moses 590
BALSON, O. P. 889
Baltic Perpetual Building Association 510
BALTIMORE, ---, Lord 766, 858, 916, 919
Baltimore & Boston Steamship Line 302
Baltimore & Bremen Line 306
Baltimore & Catonsville Passenger Railway Co. 368, 821
Baltimore & Catonsville Railroad 815, 820
Baltimore & Cuba Copper-Smelting Co. 422
Baltimore & Cumberland Valley Railroad 356
Baltimore & Delta Narrow-Gauge Railroad 815
Baltimore & Delta Railroad 354, 359, 916, 917
Baltimore & Drum Point Railroad 357
Baltimore & Fell's Point Directory 433
Baltimore & Frederick Town Turnpike Co. 182, 368, 509
Baltimore & Hall Springs Railway Co. 183, 370, 510
Baltimore & Hanover Railroad 356, 370, 379, 815, 854, 868, 869, 870
Baltimore & Harford Turnpike Co. 510
Baltimore & Havana Steamship Co. 475
Baltimore & Havre-de-Grace Turnpike Co. 182, 510
Baltimore & Liberty Turnpike Co. 510
Baltimore & Ohio Junction 354
Baltimore & Ohio Railroad 131, 144, 147, 148, 180, 182, 183, 231, 254, 272, 279, 283, 284, 286, 303, 304, 305, 306, 314, 315, 316, 317, 318, 319, 320, 322, 324, 338, 350, 352, 355, 361, 379, 380, 385, 387, 391, 406, 446, 450, 475, 476, 502,

Baltimore & Ohio Railroad (cont'd) 503, 508, 590, 635, 646, 669, 693, 697, 700, 713, 725, 770, 789, 791, 807, 809, 815, 820, 832, 846, 848, 854, 879, 887, 891, 908, 935
Baltimore & Patomic Railroad 346
Baltimore & Peabody Heights & Waverly Passenger Railway Co. 368
Baltimore & Philadelphia Steamboat Co. 510
Baltimore & Phoenix Shot-Tower Cos. 480
Baltimore & Pikesville Horse Railway 834
Baltimore & Pikesville Railroad Co. 370
Baltimore & Port Deposit Railroad Company 314, 348
Baltimore & Potomac Navigation Co. 480
Baltimore & Potomac Railroad 284, 351, 352, 354, 356, 380, 703, 820, 829, 839, 935
Baltimore & Powhatan Railway Co. 510, 815, 832
Baltimore & Randallstown Horse Railroad Co. 370, 831
Baltimore & Reisterstown Turnpike Co. 182, 370, 510, 856
Baltimore & Savannah Steamship Co. 302
Baltimore & Susquehanna Co. 343, 355
Baltimore & Susquehanna Railroad 314, 344, 347, 507, 648, 891
Baltimore & Susquehanna Steam Co. 510
Baltimore & Susquehanna Tide-water Canal Co. 183
Baltimore & Swann Lake Passenger Railway Co. 359
Baltimore & Washington Railroad Co. 324
Baltimore & Washington Turnpike Company 314
Baltimore & Yorktown Turnpike Co. 182, 509
Baltimore Academy 225, 238, 261, 608
Baltimore Academy of Medicine 739, 744, 745
Baltimore Academy of the Visitation Library 667
Baltimore Advertiser, The 636
Baltimore Advertiser & Price Current 612
Baltimore African Academy 225
Baltimore Agricultural Aid Society 155
Baltimore Agricultural Society 916

Baltimore American 498, 610, 611, 612, 615, 635, 647, 650
Baltimore American & Daily Advertiser 609
Baltimore and Norfolk Line 301
Baltimore Anthracite Coal Mine 391
Baltimore Association for the Improvement of the Poor 593
Baltimore Association of Firemen 240
Baltimore Athenaeum 613
Baltimore Bank-Note Reporter 628
Baltimore Baptist Association 558
Baltimore Baptist Church 553
Baltimore Baptist Church Extension Society 563
Baltimore Bee 637
Baltimore Board of Trade 440
Baltimore Book 649, 650
Baltimore Brick Manufacturing & Exporting Co. 418
Baltimore Bridge Co. 425, 510
Baltimore Bulletin 624
Baltimore Butchers' Hide, Tallow & Cattle Association 381
Baltimore Butchers' Hide & Tallow Association No. 1 510
Baltimore Calf's-Hide Association 510
Baltimore Canal Company 313, 314
Baltimore Car Wheel Co. 460, 509
Baltimore Cemetery 245, 277, 362, 510, 932, 933
Baltimore Chariot Co. 362
Baltimore Charleston & Havana Line 302
Baltimore Choral Society 672
Baltimore Christian Advocate 631, 637
Baltimore Christian Association 153
Baltimore Chrome Works 510
Baltimore Chronicle 654
Baltimore Church News 642
Baltimore City & County Almshouse 743
Baltimore City & County Almshouse Hospital 899
Baltimore City College 226, 227, 229, 265, 680, 754, 803, 856
Baltimore City Fertilizing Manufacturing Co. 510
Baltimore City Guards 668
Baltimore City House of Refuge 820
Baltimore City Loan & Annuity Association 381
Baltimore City Mission M.E. Church 579
Baltimore City Passenger Railway Co. 352, 362, 364, 366, 509, 809
Baltimore City Rifles 668
Baltimore City:
  Assessments 1729 - 1881 186
  Board of Health 182
  Boundaries, Wards 62
  Census of 1800 174
  Census of 1810 174
  Census of 1880 180, 185
  Commissioned Officers 1861 - 1865 156
  Constitutional Convention Members 1776-1867 194
  Council Members First Branch 1797 - 1881 187
  Council Members Second Branch 1797 - 1881 192
  Creation of Wards 121
  Electors 1789 - 1881 195
  House of Delegate Members 1776 - 1880 194
  Jail Wardens 1827 - 1881 202
  Jails 200
  Market Houses 205
  Mayors 1797 - 1881 187
  Old City Hall 176
  Police Department 196
  Population 1730 to 1880 185
  Property Values 1729 - 1881 185
  Public School Buildings 230
  Registers 1797 - 1881 193
  State Senators 1776 - 1881 193
  Tide Elevations 196
  US Senators 1796 - 1867 195
  Voter Registration 122
  Ward Boundaries 179, 180
  Ward Division 116, 172, 174
  Water Department 218
Baltimore Clipper 624
Baltimore Club 481
Baltimore Co. 424, 425
Baltimore Coal Co. 391
Baltimore Coal Tar & Manufacturing Co. 510
Baltimore College 225, 652, 700, 724, 744, 770
Baltimore College of Dental Surgery 738, 744, 745
Baltimore College of Dental Surgery Library 667
Baltimore College of Physicians & Surgeons 637
Baltimore Constitution 627
Baltimore Copper Co. 812
Baltimore Corn & Flour Exchange 442
Baltimore Cotton Manufactory 407, 432
Baltimore Counterfeit Detector 625

Baltimore County Advocate, The 628, 900
Baltimore County Agricultural Association 845
Baltimore County Agricultural Society 818, 842, 883
Baltimore County Grange No. 13 917
Baltimore County Herald 815, 899, 901, 902
Baltimore County Union 749, 815, 898, 900
Baltimore County Whig 855
Baltimore County:
  Almshouse 751, 841, 934
  Clerks 1659-1871 814
  Collectors of Taxes 814
  Court Bailiffs 814
  Deputies 814
  Electors 1789 - 1881 195
  Horse Guards 817, 885, 900
  House of Delegates Members 1659-1880 818, 819, 820
  Judges 1851-1867 814
  Judges of Orphans' Court 1777-1881 814, 815
  Population 815
  Press 815
  Registers of Wills 1771-1881 814
  Sheriffs 814
  Surveyors 814
  Treasurers 1851-1881 813
  Troop 817
  US Senators 1796 - 1867 195
  War of 1812 93
Baltimore Daily Advertiser 608
Baltimore Daily Commercial 624
Baltimore Daily Intelligencer 608
Baltimore Daily News 628
Baltimore Daily Repository 608
Baltimore Daily Sun 622
Baltimore Daily Transcript 616
Baltimore Daily Whig 625
Baltimore Dancing Assembly 175, 678, 679, 680
Baltimore Dispatch, The 637
Baltimore Dry-Dock & Warehouse Co. 303
Baltimore Dry-Dock Co. 303, 510
Baltimore Eastern Savings Institution 463
Baltimore Economical Association 393
Baltimore Economical Soup Society 593
Baltimore Elevator Co. 380, 510
Baltimore Elocutionist, The 641
Baltimore Episcopal Methodist 636
Baltimore Equitable Society 483, 491, 510

Baltimore Evening Bulletin, The 636
Baltimore Evening Post & Mercantile Daily Advertiser 614
Baltimore Evening Star 608
Baltimore Exchange Company 175, 176, 437, 440
Baltimore Express 617
Baltimore Eye & Ear Institute 747
Baltimore Female College 226, 233, 629, 802
Baltimore Female College Library 667
Baltimore Female Orphan Asylum 594
Baltimore Fire Department 242, 244
Baltimore Fire Insurance Co. 382, 483, 491, 770, 796
Baltimore Fire-Engine & Wharf Lottery 244
Baltimore Flag 631
Baltimore Flint Glass Co. 402
Baltimore Free School 224
Baltimore Gas Co. 476
Baltimore Gas-light Co. 686
Baltimore Gazette 261, 617, 644, 798
Baltimore Gazette Publishing Co. 510, 633
Baltimore General Advertiser 608
Baltimore General Dispensary 747, 770
Baltimore Glass-Works 402
Baltimore Harmonic Society 672
Baltimore Herald 641
Baltimore Homoeopathic Medical Society 756
Baltimore Hose Company 253, 773
Baltimore Hospital 755
Baltimore House 464, 737
Baltimore House of Industry 826
Baltimore Hydraulic Cement Pipe-Works 510
Baltimore Illustrated Times & Local Gazette, The 631
Baltimore Independent Blues 668
Baltimore Independents 668
Baltimore Infirmary 737, 747
Baltimore Insane Asylum 927
Baltimore Institute of Architects 668
Baltimore Insurance Co. 298, 480, 482
Baltimore Intelligencer 616
Baltimore Invincibles 669
Baltimore Iris 616
Baltimore Item, The 638
Baltimore Journal of Commerce 637
Baltimore Kaleidoscope & Weekly Express 617
Baltimore Law Transcript, The 637
Baltimore Lead Works 421
Baltimore Library 659, 680

Baltimore Library Association 659
Baltimore Library Company 651, 659, 679
Baltimore Liederkranz 605
Baltimore Life Insurance Co. 459
Baltimore Literary & Religious Magazine 617
Baltimore Locomotive-Works 426
Baltimore Manufacturing Co. 407
Baltimore Marine Sectional Dock Co. 303
Baltimore Market Journal, The 642
Baltimore Mechanic & Literary Gazette 627
Baltimore Mechanical 668
Baltimore Medical Association 739, 745, 746
Baltimore Medical College 739
Baltimore Medical Journal, The 637
Baltimore Medical Journal & Bulletin 739
Baltimore Medical-Surgical Journal & Review 613
Baltimore Messenger 627
Baltimore Minerva & Emerald 613
Baltimore Monthly Budget 624
Baltimore Museum 265, 500, 680, 689, 691, 692
Baltimore Musical Association 672
Baltimore Olio & American Musical Gazette, The 628
Baltimore Opera-House 696
Baltimore Oriole Celebration 449, 697
Baltimore Orphan Asylum 231, 594
Baltimore Pathfinder, The 628, 629
Baltimore Pathological Society 744
Baltimore Patriot 498, 609, 650
Baltimore Patriot & Evening Advertiser 612
Baltimore Pearl Hominy Co. 510
Baltimore Permanent Building & Land Society 510
Baltimore Permanent Museum 692
Baltimore Phoenix & Budget 625
Baltimore Plow Co. 510, 852
Baltimore Post & Transcript 616
Baltimore Presbytery 551
Baltimore Price-Current 630
Baltimore Price-Current & Counterfeit Detector 616
Baltimore Price-Current & Weekly Journal of Commerce 630
Baltimore Privateer 625
Baltimore Public Ledger, The 630
Baltimore Republican 615, 616
Baltimore Retort & Fire-Brick Works 510
Baltimore Rifle Company 668
Baltimore Rifle Target Shooting Co. 510

Baltimore Rosine Association 253
Baltimore Sans-Culottes 668
Baltimore Savings 473
Baltimore Savings, Loan & Trust Co. 510
Baltimore Savings-Bank 404, 718
Baltimore Scheutzen Society 668
Baltimore Screw-Dock Co. 303
Baltimore Sheep Butchers' & Wool-Pulling Association 510
Baltimore Sheep Butchers' Loan Association No. 1 510
Baltimore Spy 616
Baltimore Steam Packet Co. 389, 509
Baltimore Steam Sugar Refinery 418
Baltimore Steam-Boiler Works 426, 429
Baltimore Stethoscope, The 631
Baltimore Stock Board 479
Baltimore Stock Exchange 482
Baltimore Stock Exchange Building Co. 510
Baltimore Stock-Yard Co. 340, 380, 446
Baltimore Sun 610, 612, 616, 619, 620, 621, 622, 623, 624, 628, 639, 649, 709, 887
Baltimore Telegraph 609, 610
Baltimore Theatre 681, 685
Baltimore Theatre & Circus Company 690
Baltimore Times 613
Baltimore Title Co. 510
Baltimore Town East 70
Baltimore Town Hundred 71
Baltimore Town West 70
Baltimore Town:
   1752 Drawing 58
   First Commissioners 54
   List of Lot Owners 53, 54
   Survey 57
Baltimore Turngemeinde 605
Baltimore Type Foundry 615
Baltimore Typographical Union 624, 802
Baltimore Underwriter, The 636
Baltimore United Fire Department 240, 241, 249
Baltimore Volks-Freund, The 642
Baltimore Warehouse Co. 406, 462, 510
Baltimore Water Company 214, 217, 375, 694
Baltimore Water Stock 218
Baltimore Water-Works 213
Baltimore Wecker, The 630
Baltimore Weekly Messenger 612
Baltimore Weekly Sun 622

Baltimore Window-glass, Bottle &
   Vial Works 460
Baltimore Window-Glass Works 402
Baltimore Yearly Meetings 588
Baltimore Young Men's Paper 613
Baltimore, Calverton & Powhatan
   Railway 369, 370, 820, 834
Baltimore, Carroll & Frederick
   Railroad Co. 355
Baltimore, Catonsville & Ellicott
   Mills Railway Co. 369, 509
Baltimore, Chesapeake & Richmond
   Steamboat Co. 510
Baltimore, Hampden & Towsontown
   Railway Co. 359
Baltimorean 635, 638, 639, 654
BALTZELL, ---, Dr. 741
   Jacob 796
   Jacob B. 253
   Mary 796
   Philip 795
   Thomas 796
BAMBERGER, James A. 251
   William W. 157
BANCROFT, George 723
BANDEL, A. J. 190
   Andrew J. 190
   George S. 190, 795
   Leonard J. 190
BANDELL, Lemuel J. 250
BANDLE, George 252
   John 252
   William 249
Bank of Baltimore 450, 455, 769,
   770, 802, 808, 809, 810
Bank of Commerce 451, 465, 469
Bank of Hagerstown 310
Bank of Maryland 283, 449, 450,
   452
Bank of Maryland Mob 784
Bank of Maryland Riot 243
Bank of the United States 452,
   453, 454, 455
BANKARD, Caroline A. (HORN)
   775
   Caroline Lincoln 775
   Catherine (DILL) 774
   Charles H. 157
   Charles Sumner 775
   Clara Virginia 775
   Edgar Howard 775
   Elizabeth Dill 775
   Florence Reppert 775
   H. N. 775
   Henry Nicholas 774, 775
   J. J. 155, 276
   J. J., Mrs. 155, 156
   J. W. 380
   Jacob 380
   Josiah 157
   Margaret Snodgrass 775

BANKARD, Mary Ann
   (SNODGRASS) 774
   Mary Regina 775
   Nicholas Dill 774
   Peter 774
   William 380
BANKERD, J. 191
Bankers' & Brokers' Telegraph Co.
   509
*Bankers' Magazine & State Financial
   Register, The* 628
BANKHEAD, Belle 834
   Emma 886
Banking-House 853
BANKS, ---, Gen. 133, 135, 136, 139,
   199, 632
---, Mayor 499
---, Mr. 889
   Andrew 820, 855, 856, 857
   D. B. 254
   Daniel B. 794, 856
   Jacob 380
   Margaret S. 856
   Margaret Sherwood (WHITELOCK)
   856
   Nathaniel P. 133
   Nicholas 48
   R. T. 165
   Rebecca E. (GODWIN) 856
   Robert R. 222
   Robert T. 177, 187, 357, 728
   William Emmet 847
BANKSON, Elizabeth 795
   John 82, 795
BANNISTER, Aaron 560
   James 559
BANSEMER, G. A. 489
   W. B. 593
   William G. 600
BANTZ, John 795
   William 795
Baptist Black Rock Meeting-House
   866
Baptist Church, Alexandria, Va. 564
Baptist Church, Lynchburg, Va. 556,
   564
Baptist Church Extension Society
   556, 563, 564, 567, 568
Bar Library 667
BARBER, Aseneth 490
   John G. 157
   Thomas 372
BARBOUR, ---, Mr. 359
   B. Johnson 847
   James L. 488
BARCLAY, J. H. 569
   Robert 647
Barclay & Hasson 383
Bare Hill Copper-Mines 772, 839,
   842
Bare Hills 25, 26, 30, 31, 772, 843

13

BARGER, Peter 253
BARID, Thomas D. 226
BARKER, Daniel 565
  Enoch M. 560
  Ephraim 254, 559, 690
  Francis M. 563
  William R. 351
BARKLEY, Hugh 658
BARLING, Joseph 189, 190, 249, 795
  Thomas 392
BARNABY, Elias 192, 432, 795
BARNARD, ---, Gen. 492
---, Very Rev. Father 534
  C. P. 515
  Daniel P. 189
BARNDOLLAR, William P. 442
BARNDY, ---, Mrs. 99
BARNES, --- 223, 859
  A. W. 241
  J. H. 838
  J. T. M. 187
  James 112
  John 480
  John H. 194, 195, 362
  L. P. 249
  Lucian 689
  Mary 878
  Robert C. 157
  Samuel 189, 192, 251, 463, 612, 615, 896
  William P. 251
  Winston 466
BARNESTON, Ann (DODSON) 460
  Joseph 460
  Barnesville 342
BARNET, L. M. 583
  William 255
Barnet's (Mr.) Assembly-Room 680
BARNETT, William 189, 192
BARNETTE, D. P. 820
BARNETZ, ---, Mr. 568
  Covington D. 370
BARNEY, --- 104
---, Capt. 105
---, Com. 795
---, Commodore 88, 91, 116, 483
---, Lt. 318
  Ann 795
  J. 439
  James H. 125, 155
  John 74, 84, 194, 480, 593, 795
  John H. 192, 311, 816
  Joshua 82, 88, 99, 103, 104, 168, 850
  L. 439
  Margaret 796
  Mary (CHASE) 613, 794
  Rebecca 795
  William 38, 99, 783, 899

BARNEY, William B. 84, 194, 498, 794, 795, 796
  William Chase 628
  William H. 497
Barney, John H. & Co. 312
Barney & Hollins 433
Barney Street 769
Barney's Stage-office 312
BARNHAM, John 741
BARNHART, Anna (DELTERER) 485
  Elizabeth 485
  John 485
  Sarah 900
BARNITZ, Charles A. 343
  Covington D. 194
BARNS, Robert 298
BARNUM, Ann (KIRBY) 795
  D. 253, 515
  David 311, 514, 516, 795, 796, 928
  E. Kirby 796
  Jenus 795
  P. T. 690, 693
  Zenus 345, 346, 351, 355, 362, 363, 369, 507, 516, 846, 932
Barnum & Co. 516
Barnum's Hotel 129, 142, 493, 514, 515, 642, 796, 804, 850, 851
BARON, Seth 433
Barons of Baltimore 195
BARR, Daniel 191
  David 526
  John T. 394, 547
Barracks, Frederick 689
Barracksville 342
BARRALL, Charles 613
Barre Street 769
BARRET, William 189
BARRETT, --- 684
  Gregory 157
  John 47, 149
  John M. 795
  William 242
Barrett's Delight 877
BARRI, George W. 190
BARRIER, P. 103
BARRINGTON, Frank 673
BARRISTER, T. Lewis 524
BARROLL, Barrister 707
  Benjamin C. 465, 932
  James 265, 266, 439, 461, 463, 464, 470
BARRON, Daniel 264
  James 254
  John 190, 193, 194, 195
BARROTTI, Felix 795
BARROW, Alex. 796
BARROWS, ---, Rev. Mr. 920
  Elisha P. 471
BARRY, ---, Capt. 114
  George 795

BARRY, J. B. N. 362
James 83, 293, 298, 482, 483
John J. 190
John L. 246, 795
Lanvale 173
Lavallin 247, 248, 795
Matilda 796
R. C. 200
Richard 461
Robert 298
Robert C. 195, 903
Standish 77, 83, 188, 238, 246, 795, 796, 814
Swallen 83
William F. 794
William R. 487, 600, 601
Barry & Hurst 414
Barry Cole & Barry 298
Barry's (Dr.) School 233
BARTELL, Chr. 605
Christopher 194, 605
BARTH, L. 540
Barthe & Lafitte 439
BARTHOLOMEE, Theodore M. 157
BARTHOLOMEW, ---, Mr. 681
B. J. 515
BARTHOLOW, A. J. 191
E. M. 523
BARTLETT, ---, Mr. 219, 919
Aley (ROBINSON) 406
Alice Riggs 406
Amanda Sallie (GRIFFITH) 406
D. L. 415, 447, 448, 469
Daniel 426
David L. 426, 441, 446, 464, 831
Elizabeth 406
George 302, 406, 407, 466, 471, 794
George Burnap 406
George W. 406
George Washington Burnap 406
Harry Griffith 406
John T. B. 813
Joseph T. 935
Julia E. (PETTIBONE) 426
Louisa (STOCKBRIDGE) 426
Lucretia 406
Rebecca C. 406
Sarah (ABBY) 426
Susan 406
Susan (SWIFT) 406
Vashtie (ROBINSON) 406
Vashtie Rebecca 406
W. E. 889
William 406
William E. 193
Bartlett Family 588
Bartlett Robins & Co. 299
BARTLEY, --- 686
BARTO, Charles H. 157
BARTOL, ---, Judge 150, 199, 200
James L. 139, 164

BARTOL, James Lawrence 717
BARTON, ---, Mr. 635
H. E. 484
Henry E. 255
Ida 834
Matthew H. 874
Molly Jane (STANDIFORD) 874
Stephen 886
Steven 814
Thadius J. 688
Thomas 555
William 917
BARTOW, Evelyn 523
BASEMAN, A. W. 817
John 815
Mary 886
Vachel W. 814
BASFORD, Thomas 581
BASH, Henry M. 485
John H. 447, 473
BASIL, John 271
Basin, The 287, 288, 299
BASSELL, Theodore 74
BASSERMAN, A. 590
BASSETT, Martha 47, 202
BASSEY, Jesse 71
BASSFORD, Sarah L. 229
Bassher, Thomas C. & Co. 427
BASSHOR, T. C. 467
Thomas C. 177, 473
BATCHELOR, Josh. F. 245
BATEMAN, --- 693
---, Judge 898
A. W. 717, 794
Alfred 814
B. 252
Clara V. 886
Henry 693
Henry L. 794
John 36
BATES, --- 682
D. W. 584, 902
David A. 509
J. W. P. 746
James 263, 462, 472, 484, 488
L. 350
L. W. 583, 584
W. H. 249
BATHURST, Thompson 438
BATTEE, Dennis H. 414
Richard R. 190
BATTEN, William 55
Battery Square 90
Battle Monument 243, 252, 265, 267, 268, 269, 726, 766
Battle Monument House 137
Battle of Antetiam 810
Battle of:
    Bladensburg 685, 771, 773, 868, 907
    Brandywine 863, 916

15

Battle of: (cont'd)
  Bridgewater 895
  Camden 773
  Cedar Run 670
  Chancellorsville 671
  Chippewa 895
  Eutaw 863
  Eutaw Springs 872
  Germantown 852, 916
  Mechanicsville 670
  Mine Run 671
  North Point 685, 771, 773, 808, 824, 843, 853, 907, 913
  Sailor's Creek 923
  Stony Creek 895
  Trenton 916
Battle on the Delaware 863
Battle-Ground M.E. Church South 933
BATZLER, John F. 446
BAUDLE, Michael 249
BAUER, John 605
BAUGHER, Joseph 190
BAUGHMAN, Francis M. 194
  Frederick 317
  Jacob 886
  John 193
  John W. 498
  S. 268
Baughman's Valley 873
BAUGHNER, Josiah L. 795
BAUM, Christian 250
  Christina 84
BAUSH, A. 874
BAUSMAN, ---, Rev. Mr. 521
  John 247
BAWDEN, J. H. 463
BAXLEY, A. Willis 745
  Elizabeth 583
  George 188, 240, 250, 251, 483
  J. Brown 740
  John 250, 456, 575, 795
  Mary 795
BAXTER, James 251
  Joseph 814
  Joseph P. 256
  Joseph V. 242
  Roger 533
  William 38
Bay Line 284, 302, 315
Bay Line of Steamers 799
Bay View 277, 351
Bay View Asylum 354, 603, 635, 927, 929, 934, 935
BAYARD, James A. 166
  R. B. 494
  Thomas F. 656
BAYER, B. 540
BAYLE, Letitia 594
  Thomas 920

BAYLEY, ---, Archbishop 235, 236, 540, 597, 889, 929, 937
  H. J. 193
  Henry 153
  James F. 935
  James R. 794
  James Roosevelt 529
  John 780
  Josiah 714, 715
  Thomas 921
Bayley, R. P. & Co. 446
Bayley & Burns 649
BAYLISS, J. L. 468
  James 468
  John R. 250
BAYLOR, Charles G. 629
Baylor, C. G. & Co. 629
BAYLY, Richard P. 795
  Thomas M. 556
BAYNARD, Eliza 594
BAYNE, George 887
  Lawrence P. 126
  William 408, 832
BAYNES, James 603
Bayview Grist & Saw-Mills 869
Bayview Station 355
Bazaar 559
BEACH, ---, Mr. 635
  Betsy Ward 394
  S. W. 549
  Thomas J. 616
BEACHAM, ---, Mr. 293, 363
  F. Stanly 157
  James 301, 393
  John 241, 795
  John S. 489, 794
  John T. 488
  Samuel T. 489
  Silas 190
Beacham's, P. Ship Yard 293
BEAGUE, Thomas 246
BEALE, ---, Mr. 207
  David J. 550
  Solon 153, 627
  William E. 190, 795
BEALL, ---, Maj. 85
  E. S. 459
  George T. 193
  W. 102
BEALMEAR, J. F. 415
BEAMER, Henry 189, 471
BEAMS, William 741
BEAN, Joseph H. 523
BEANES, William 741
BEANS, ---, Dr. 741
  William H. 194
Beantown 354
BEAR, ---, Prof. 845
Bear Creek 92, 93, 811, 927
BEARD, ---, Dr. 731
  Alexander 592

BEARD, Mary 421
 W. 70, 730
Beard's Mill 862
BEASLEY, Frederick 520
 H. L., Miss 649
BEASLY, Frederick 595
BEASTEN, Charles 472
BEASTON, ---, Rev. Mr. 658
 Francis 658
BEATLEY, Robert S. 210
BEATSON, George H. 550
BEATTIE, --- 781
BEATTY, --- 434
 Charles A. 741
 George 614
 J. 873
 James 192, 600, 769, 796
 Joseph 394
 William H. 484, 937
BEAUMONT, ---, Mrs. 684
 John 820
Beaver Dam 15, 19, 876
Beaver Dam Marble Co. 421, 510
BECK, A. 597
 Barbara 423
 John M. 487
BECKER, ---, Bishop 889
 Christian L. 572, 795
 Thomas A. 534, 538
Becker Bros. 372
BECKET, J. W. 581
BECKETT, Thomas 795
BECKLEY, ---, Mrs. 602
 Jacob 814, 815, 869
 R. T. 855
Beckley Paper-Mills 869
Beckleysville 869
BECKLY, Henry 247
BECKWITH, Sidney, Sir 87
Beda, ---, Sister Superior 928
BEDELL, Gregory T. 796
Bedford, ---, Duke of 858
BEDFORD, Gunning S. 250
 J. R. D. 817
 John D. 814
 John R. D. 369, 902
Bedford & Morton 298
BEDINGER, Henry 822
Bee-Hive Building Association No. 2 510
Beech Hill 650, 852
BEECHER, Henry Ward 633
BEELER, R. F. 342
BEEMAN, James 187, 592
BEESE, Claudius 298
BEESTON, Francis 247, 532
 J. 534
 T. V. 95, 269
BEHAIM, Martin 655
BEHAN, ---, Rev. Father 933
BEHRENS, J., Mrs. 603

BEHRENS, S., Miss 603
Behrens, John & Co. 372
BEIL, John 468
Belair 359, 848, 898, 918, 926
Belair Academy 898
Belair Avenue 896
Belair Market 207, 501
Belair Road 881, 890, 910, 917, 918, 930, 932
Belair Road Fire Company 818
Belair Turnpike 926, 929
Belfast 876, 877, 883
Belfield 351
BELGER, ---, Maj. 885
BELL, --- 611
 A. Graham 233
 C. 95, 269
 Charles 737
 Ephraim 195, 795, 820
 Ephram 195
 George 759
 Henry 578
 James 252
 John 127, 519
 John H. 191
 Judith Carey 71
 Richard 251
Bellaire 331, 336
BELLAMY, ---, Dr. 544
Belle Grove 824
Belle Isle Iron Co. 925
Bellinger & Son 262
Belmont 515, 516, 614
Belmont Place 887
BELT, ---, Capt. 103, 104
 Catherine (DULANY) 904, 906
 George G. 463
 Horatio 904
 J. 102
 James 101, 593
 John 99
 S. Sprigg 441, 442, 459, 794
 T. H. 192
 Tobias 298
 Walter 592, 795
Belt, The 64
BELTS, Solomon 298
Beltsville 342
BELTZHOOVER, Daniel 795
 George 418, 796
Beltzhoover's 513
Belvidere 59, 61
Belvidere Bridge 217
Belvidere Hill 768
Belvidere Land & Loan Co. 510
Belvidere Land Improvement & Building Association 510
Belvidere Street (York) Fire Company 240
Belvidere Theatre 501
Bench & Bar Review, The 641

BEND, ---, Dr. 557, 756
---, Rev. Dr. 520, 734, 911
Joseph G. J. 658, 795
Joseph J. G. 520
Mary (BOUDINOT) 795
William B. 252, 782
BENDER, Daniel 192
Davis 189
Benedict 88, 90
BENEDICT, ---, Father 826
Beneficial Savings Fund Society of Baltimore 472
Benevolent Society 521
BENEZETT, S. 103
BENJAMIN, H., Miss 603
Park 628, 650, 651, 795, 863
BENNET, Enoch 263
Patrick 526, 532
W. 628
BENNETT, -- 195
--- 703
B. F. 698
Benjamin F. 484, 697
E. W. 191
F. W. 468, 487, 794
F. W., Mrs. 600
James Gordon 293
Mary 472
Matthew 120, 234, 532
Patrick 169, 239, 461, 545, 734
Richard 818
Thomas B. 795
William P. 830
Bennett, F. A., Messrs. & Co. 516
BENSON, Arthur W. 501
B. F. 584, 902
Benjamin S. 667
Elijah 867, 869
Frank 869
George W. 210
James 592, 795
Joshua L. 869
Margaret (FOWBLE) 867
Oregon R. 820
Richard 187
Benson Family 869
BENT, G. R. 153, 154
BENTALOU, P. 239
Paul 82, 83, 118, 238, 269, 298, 592, 729, 795
Bentalou Street 769
BENTEEN, F. D. 795
BENTHALL, William 222
Bentley 347
BENTLEY, Ann Owens (LATY) 429
Anna 429
C. W. 870
Charles Williams 429
George Washington 429
Robert S. 187

Bentley Springs Lodge No. 138, A. F. & A. M. 870
Bentley's Springs 429, 870
Bentley's Springs Lodge 873
Bentley's Station 870
BENTON, Benjamin 202
James 911
John 911
Benton's Ferry 342
BENTZINGER, ---, Capt. 785
Benwood 331, 334, 336, 342
BENZEN, Valentine 149
Benzinger, Eschback & Co. 217
BENZINGER, Mathias 368, 472, 487
Matthias 794
BERAN, Charles F. 745
I. L. 594
BERESFORD, --- 87
BERG, John 558, 562, 628, 630, 889
BERGER, A. J. 855, 866
BERGSTEN, Nicholas A. 741
BERKELEY, ---, Gov. 891
William 639
Berkeley Guards 791
BERKEMEIER, August 194
BERKLEY, Edwin 413
BERLAND, Richard 432
Berlin 342
Berlin Building Association 510
BERNARD, --- 683
---, Mrs. 687
Caroline Richings 696
Joab 63, 813
BERNEY, L. 447
BERRIEN, --- 122
BERRY, ---, Mr. 418
Benjamin 84, 89, 187, 188
Clark, Mrs. 202
Eliza 598
Eliza E. 596
G. R. 191
George R. 126, 194, 205, 484
Henry D. 193
J. S. 576
J. Summerfield 820
Jeremiah 223
John 47, 91, 188, 202, 253, 254, 420, 462, 470, 709, 795, 816
John B. N. 488
John S. 148, 149, 180, 195, 596, 820, 825, 903
John S., Mrs. 596
John W. 207, 582, 795
N. E. 365
Redmond 261
S. 369
Thomas L. 253
Berry, J. B. N. & A. L. 264
Berry's Hill 709
BERRYMAN, H. 855
Rozella 927

BERRYMAN, Silas 830
BERSCH, Bernard 891
BERY, Adolph 157
BESCHTER, J. W. 540
BESSE, C. 102
BESSICK, J. L. 149
BEST, H. 577, 597
  Hezekiah 577
BETCHLER, John A. 929
Bethany Baptist Chapel 566
Bethany Baptist Church 641
Bethany College 591
Bethany Independent Methodist Church 585
Bethel Church 303
Bethel Colored Methodist Church 581
Bethel M.E. Church 580
Bethlehem Greene Church 590
BETTS, Charles M. 157
  Frank K. 930
  Lucy (CORSE) 930
  Solomon 261, 455, 470
BETTY, William 65
Beulah Encampment No. 30, I.O.O.F. 832
BEVAN, C. F. 598
  Charles F. 738
  Richard 188, 192
  Samuel 564, 794
Bevan & Son 542
BEVANS, --- 513
  C. F., Mrs. 602
  Isaac H. 795
  James H. 721
BEYER, Louis 157
Bias Lodge No. 23 of Heptasophs 837
BIAYS, ---, Lt. Col. 87
  Frank S. 157
  James 84, 92, 170, 209, 215, 241, 246, 251, 252, 299, 463, 484, 547, 826, 827
  Joseph 118, 170, 172, 173, 187, 188, 192, 214, 215, 238, 246, 461, 483, 795
  William J. 157
Bibbins Family 927
Bible Times, The 631
BICKLEY, Samuel 759
BIDDERSON, John S. 162
BIDDINGER, Levi 830
BIDDISON, John S. 815, 820
  Thomas C. 927, 929
BIDDLE, --- 88
  Catherine 803
  Edward 803
  Edward B. 795
  Elizabeth 795
  J. S. 427
Bidwell & Spalding 689

Biene von Baltimore, The 642
BIER, Jacob 461, 795
Bier's (Mr.) Assembly-Room 680
BIERBOWER, Lemuel 193, 260
Big Falls of the Gunpowder 874
Big Gunpowder Falls 517, 857
Big Gunpowder River 910
BIGELOW, E. D. 441, 442, 487, 577, 600
  Edmund D. 502
  Horatio 782
  Waldo O. 157
BIGGER, Gilbert 238, 795
BIGGS, C. F. 586
  Joshua 488
  William 380
BIGHAM, Benjamin 577
  John 471, 549
BILLINGS, John S. 233, 746, 747
BILLINGSLEA, Chapman 847
BILLINGSLEY, Charles B. 916
  F. 38
  J. 38
  William 917
BILLOPP, Thomas 919
BINAU, John 157
BINDER, Louis 157
BINES, William 264
BINGHAM, John 484
BINION, Thomas 251
BINNEY, J. G. 561
BINYON, ---, Mr. 219
  Thomas 157
  Thomas W. 157, 246
BIRCKHEAD, ---, Dr. 796
  Augusta LeRoy 892
  F. Harrison McEvers 892
  Huch 394
  Hugh 439, 501, 795
  Jane 796
  Lennox 892
  Solomon 316, 456, 470, 742, 796
BIRD, ---, Capt. 95
  ---, Col. 848
  Henry 547
  J. Edward 587
  William E. 578
Bird River 311, 811, 916, 923, 924, 925, 931
Bird-in-hand 311
BIRELY, L. A. 828
BIRKETT, Thomas 830
BIRKHEAD, Solomon 824
  Thomas H. 741
BIRMINGHAM, Luther M. 872
BIRNEY, ---, Col. 144
BIRSTALL, John 764
BISHOP, ---, Mr. 275, 407, 622
  ---, Rt. Rev. 532
  Anna 680
  David E. 794

BISHOP, Elijah 255
  George W. 191, 728
  H. 569
  H. C. 525
  John L. 157
  John T. 190
  Robert 921
  William 189
BISSE, Claudius 592
BISSELL, William 641
BITTER, Christian 157
BITTING, ---, Rev. Dr. 573
  C. C. 563, 564
BITZLER, Henry 404
BIXLER, David 462, 569
  William Tell 194
BIXTER, S. A. 247
BLACK, A. L. 604
  George W. 742
  James 795
  Jeremiah S. 166
  John 463, 935
  Millard Scott 446
  R. W. 578
  Samuel 252, 488
  Black Ball 770
  Black Bear, Sign of 312
  Black Bear Inn 513
  Black Hawk 899
  Black Horse 311
  Black Oak 342
  Black River 424
  Black Rock 27, 776, 869, 895
  Black Rock Baptist Church 558, 559
  Black Rock M.E. Church 869, 883
  Black Rock Road 866, 869
  Black Rock Run 869
  Black-Snakes 787
BLACKBURN, ---, Rev. 647
  Cyrus 603
  Cyrus, Mrs. 604
  Edwin 449
  J. C. 138
  John C. 189, 190
BLACKFORD, Eugene 836
  William H. 489
BLACKINSTON, George N. 77
BLACKISTONE, James T. 600
BLACKMER, Salisbury 100
BLACKSTONE, --- 726
BLACKWELL, Francis 298
  G. 102
Blackwood's Magazine 715
BLADEN, ---, Gov. 519
  Thomas 195, 858
Bladensburg 311, 342
BLAINE, ---, Mr. 499
BLAIR, --- 102
  Eliza Violetta Howard (GIST) 71
  F. P. 264

BLAIR, Francis P. 71, 127, 722
  James 189, 207, 254
  Montgomery 71, 127, 142, 162, 272, 722
  W. J. 916
BLAKE, B. 442
  Dorothy 706
  George A. 484, 935
  Henry 706
  J. D. 187
  John R. 193, 194
  John W. 219
  Joseph 358
  S. V. 579
  Samuel Vinton 795
  Thomas 358
BLAKELEY, Mathew 759
BLAKENEY, A. R. 795
  Abel R. 189, 190
BLAKENY, A. R. 189
BLAKISTON, D. C. 847
BLAKISTONE, Nathaniel 195
BLANCHARD, E. Wyatt 162, 190, 794
  Elizabeth (PHILPOTT) 863
  George R. 509
  John T. 863
  W. 690
BLAND, ---, Judge 934
  Chancellor 795
  John R. 448
  Sarah 795
  Theodoric 84, 203, 729
  Theodorick 89, 194, 343, 712, 729, 796
BLANEY, Mary 911
BLANFORD, David 190, 251
BLASON, William F. 253
BLATCHLEY, Bobert G. 817
BLEDSOE, A. T. 636, 657
  Albert T. 675
  Albert Taylor 637
  Jesse 71
  Sarah Howard (GIST) 71
BLENKINSOP, P. 613
BLENNERHASSET, --- 781
BLINSENGER, George F. 256
BLISS, Horace 795
BLISSETT, --- 682, 683, 684, 686
BLOCK, Furman 506
  John 740, 794
  M. O. 795
BLOMFIELD, John 48
Blood-Tubs 631, 787
Bloomingdale Insane Asylum 893
Bloomington 342
BLOXHAM, Winsboro 796
Blue Ball 817
Blue Mount Road 907
Blue Ridge 324, 357
Blue Stocking 432

BLUMENBERG, Leopold 157, 794
BLUMENTHAL, George 630
Blumenthal, Messrs. & Co. 630
BLUMFIELD, Francis 608
BLUMHARDT, Charles 597
BLUNT, Ellen Key 145, 616
Board of (Baltimore) County Commissioners, 1851-1877 812, 813
Board of Health 733
Board of Missions 879
Board of Police 801
Board of Police Commissioners 635
Board of Relief 242
Board of School Commissioners (Baltimore County) 1853-1880 813
Board of Trade 440, 770
Board of Trade Library 667
Board Tree 342
BOARDMAN, Mary Anna 654
BOARMAN, Benjamin W. 898
  Isabel 898
  Jane C. 898
  Jane C. (JAMISON) 898
  Robert Raphael 898
Bochemic Workingmen's Permanent Building Association No. 1 510
BODE, Conrad 908
Bodkin 17
Bodkin Creek 862
Bodkin Point 77, 812
BODLEY, Thomas 77
BOEHM, Charles T. 464, 471
  Martin 573
BOEHME, Charles 571
BOETTGER, Conrad 157
BOGARDUS, ---, Mr. 621
BOGART, E., Miss 617
BOGGS, Alex. L. 246
  Alexander L. 795
  Caroline 854
  J. Green 218
  Samuel S. 795
  Sarah Jane 854
  William 854
BOGUE, Henry 472
Bohemia Manor 41, 527
BOHLKIN, D. A. 821
BOHN, Charles 84, 192, 250, 461, 852
  Jacob 515
Bohn & Slingluff 852
BOISLANDRY, R. C. 298
BOISSEAU, David 545, 547
BOKEE, George M. 193, 357
BOKER, Melissa 596
BOLASKIE, Henry 795
BOLGIANO, John 162, 190, 367
  Joseph A. 887
BOLLMAN, Herman 263
  Thomas 795

BOLLMAN, Wendell 137, 357
Bollman, Wendell & Sons 210
BOLTE, Henry 796
  John 439
BOLTON, Henry 641
  Hugh 190, 192, 241, 242, 249, 365, 794
  Hugh W. 484
  John H. 157
  William H. 193
Bolton Building, Land & Savings Society 510
BOMBAUGH, C. C. 636, 696
BONAPARTE, --- 574
---, Madame 770
  Charles J. 938
  Elizabeth (PATTERSON) 925
  J. N. 680
  Jerome Napoleon 795
  Susan 795
  Susan A. 795
BOND, ---, Dr. 736
---, Judge 164, 200
---, Miss 594
---, Mr. 494
---, Rev. Dr. 902
  A. J. 555
  B. 269
  B. F. 927
  Benjamin 519, 921
  Christina 596
  Eleanor 786, 863
  Eli S. 870
  G. M. 191
  G. Morris 194
  George 65
  H. Lennox 130, 165
  Hannah 921
  Hugh L. 140, 145, 364, 729, 753
  Hugh Lennox 717
  James 73, 191, 193, 288, 795
  James H. 362
  John 60, 432, 861, 912, 922
  Mary 863
  Peter 38, 89, 247, 248, 519, 819
  Priscella 921
  R. 95
  Richard 433, 863
  Ross 872
  Samuel 38
  T. E. 785
  Thomas 222, 486, 519, 728, 753
  Thomas E. 192, 233, 576, 631, 636, 637, 736, 737, 738, 744, 745, 753, 794, 937
  Thomas J. 434, 439
  W. T. 873
  William 921
Bond Guards 821
Bond's Pleasant Hills 49
BONE, William 191

BONIFACE, Charles 694
BONIFANT, ---, U. S. Marshal 132
  Washington 129, 729
BONM, Anthony 465
Bonn, A. & J. 154
Bonnie Brae 534
Bonnie Brae Cemetery 820
BONSAL, Louis 762
  Stephen 441, 494
BONSALL, Louis 886
Booker's Neck 303
BOOL, H. W. 690
BOONE, Charles H. 157
  Edward B. 538
  Thomas 55
  W. M. 409, 839
  William M. 600, 603, 698, 794
BOONEHORN, --- 263
Boonsborough Turnpike Co. 310
BOOSE, Peter 572
BOOTH, -- 397
  --- 687, 691, 693, 694
  Abraham 250
  Emma M. 925
  George 241
  George W. 157
  J. B. 694
  J. Wilkes 151
  John Wilkes 695, 933
  Junius Brutus 796, 933
  Margaret (CURRY) 771
  Washington 195, 488, 497, 498, 688, 689, 771, 851
  William 771
BOOTHBY, Edward 818
BOOZE, Thomas 126, 194, 354
BORCHERS, C. 572
BORCK, Edward 157
Border State Perpetual Building Association 510
BORDLEY, --- 698, 703
  Beale 814, 921
  J. B. 60, 726
  John Beale 704
  Stephen 704
  Bordley Family 927
BORING, ---, Mr. 55
  John 54, 55, 56
BOSE, William 440, 609, 610, 672, 794
BOSLEY, ---, Capt. 907
  ---, Mr. 861
  Amon 879, 906
  Amos 905
  Ann (CRADOCK) 861
  Bertha A. (BROWN) 884
  Caleb 379
  Daniel 192, 884
  Daniel Webster 884
  Dorcas 884
  Eleanor (ADDISON) 879

BOSLEY, Eleanor Gorsuch 884
  Elijah 911, 914
  Eliza 379
  Elizabeth 913, 914
  Elizabeth A. 884
  Ezekiel 913, 921
  G. M. 369, 817, 818, 898, 902
  George M. 887
  Grafton M. 896
  Grafton N. 369
  Greenbury 795
  Hannah 913
  Hannah (HUGHES) 913
  James 71, 73, 372, 824, 872, 913
  James B. 188
  John 137, 813, 820, 908, 913, 914
  John C. 912
  John E. 884
  Joseph 877, 884, 912
  Josephine 884
  Joshua G. 877
  Joshua Gorsuch 884
  Joshua M. 636, 817
  Laura V. 913
  Lydia 921
  Maria Louisa 884
  Martha Rebecca 884
  Martha S. (GORSUCH) 884
  Mary 884
  Mary (ENSOR) 884
  Mary (PEARCE) 913
  Mary E. 884
  N. M. 885
  Nicholas 913
  Nicholas M. 379
  Nicholas Merryman 879, 884
  Rebecca 879
  Rebecca (MARSH) 906
  Rebecca Cole 884
  Samuel W. 884
  Sarah 913
  Sarah Ensor 884
  Thomas C. 812, 884, 912
  Thomas Cole 884
  Walter 38
  William 438, 813
  William P. 913
Bosley Family 858, 884
Bosley M.E. Church 883
BOSMAN, Edward 911
  James 911
BOSS, John 252
BOSSE, Anton 468
BOSSEMAN, Elizabeth 460
BOSSOM, Abraham 815
BOSTON, J. E. H. 367
  John E. 368
  John E. H. 467
Boston Museum 696
Boston Patriot 612
Boston Steamship Line 300, 404

BOSWELL, ---, Dr. 71
  L. W. 414
  Marriott 194, 200
BOUCHER, Jonathan 658
  S. T. 102
BOUDINOT, Mary 795
BOUGHMAN, George 576
BOUGHTON, --- 676
BOUIC, W. V. 600
BOUIS, ---, Mr. 692
BOULDIN, ---, Capt. 361
  Alexander J. 190
  Jehu 92
  John 796
  Owen 190
  Susie S. 272
  William 251
BOURDILLON, Benedict 518, 519, 857
  Benjamin 920
BOURDILON, ---, Rev. Mr. 519
Bouring's Landing 77
BOURKE, Thomas 757
BOURNE, George 614
  Thomas 741
BOUTWELL, George S. 146
BOVIE, ---, Rev. Father 928
BOWDITCH, E. W. 747
BOWDOIN, George E. 442, 462
  Graham 441
  W. G. 474, 475
BOWEN, ---, Capt. 668
---, Rev. Mr. 590
  A. J. 637
  Benjamin 369, 422
  C. J. 636
  Charles H. 157, 190
  Charles J. 157
  Henry L. 814, 815, 898, 902
  J. S. 834
  Jesse N. 193, 194
  John 73, 83, 519, 795
  John A. 903
  Joseph F. 898
  Joseph S. 898
  Levi 795
  Levi K. 129, 498, 876
  Reese 38
  Samuel 255
  Samuel W. 255
  Susannah 795
  William 369
Bowen, Sellers & Co. 649
Bowen Family 927
BOWER, Daniel 856
  Martin 249
  William 902
BOWERMAN, R. W. 256
  Richard N. 157
BOWERS, ---, Capt. 267, 795
  D. P., Mrs. 693

BOWERS, Edward C. 202
  J. F. 255
  James W. 465
  John 446
  Thomas 794
  William 263
Bowers' Lot 827
BOWERSON, Levi 254
BOWERSOX, George W. 836
BOWIE, --- 223, 851, 859
  ---, Capt. 352
  ---, Gov. 352, 357, 358, 367, 627
  ---, Miss 773
  ---, Mr. 353
  Alice (CARTER) 353
  J. Oden 162
  John 500
  Kitty B. (DUCKETT) 351
  Mary (BROOKS) 351
  Oden 114, 165, 195, 351, 352, 367, 847, 851
  Owen 350
  R. S. 190
  Richard 742
  Robert 195
  Robert W. 313
  Thomas F. 351
  W. W. 846
  W. W. W. 351
  Wallace A. 157
  Walter 351, 848
  William 351
  William D. 351
  William Duckett 351
Bowie 354
Bowie Family 773
Bowie Junction 353
BOWIN, William 100
BOWIS, Simon S. 465
BOWLEY, Ann 795
  D. 101, 102, 103
  Daniel 79, 100, 101, 168, 193, 203, 224, 392, 452, 674, 727, 779, 795, 816, 845
  Elizabeth 795
  Mary Hollins 770
  Richard 795
  William L. 770
  William Lux 374, 375
Bowley Street 769
Bowley's Wharf 257, 287, 300, 372, 432, 433, 441, 770
BOWLING, R. R. 281
BOWLY, Daniel 58, 845
  J. Hollins 505
BOYCE, ---, Mr. 822
  Benjamin 921
  James 390, 391, 488
  John 212
  Roger 814, 909, 910, 921
BOYD, ---, Capt. 113, 499

BOYD, ---, Dr. 432, 731
 Andrew 795
 F. H. B. 190, 794
 Francis H. B. 244
 Isaac L. 157
 James 113, 114, 592, 903
 James H. 898
 John 68, 69, 70, 72, 74, 442, 488,
  547, 549, 690, 727, 730, 732, 759,
  760, 794
 John C. 484
 Joseph C. 466, 795
 Joseph H. 190
 Mary 795
 R. E. 495
 Reuben T. 582
 S. G. 359
 Samuel 189, 192, 255, 667, 795, 934
 Sidney 582
 William 418
 William A. 194, 205, 484, 794
 William B. 255
Boyd, John & Co. 431, 740
Boyd, Peter & Co. 262
Boyd's 342
BOYER, ---, Mr. 672
 David H. 251
 John W. 250
 Roger 102
BOYLAN, Thomas 516
BOYLE, --- 104, 769
 ---, Capt. 111
 ---, Mr. 781
 ---, Rev. Mr. 842
 C. 674, 692
 Daniel 796
 Francis 236
 George 263
 H. 394
 H., Mrs. 594
 Hugh 234, 261, 464
 James 191, 231
 Joseph M. 255
 Thomas 107, 112, 249, 457, 592,
  795
 William H. 157
 William K. 582, 796
Boys' Home 697
Boys' Home Society 154, 600
Boys' School of St. Paul's Church
  890
Boys' School of St. Paul's Parish
  Library 667
BRACKEN, John 250
BRACKENRIDGE, A. 892
 H. M. 253
 W. D. 887, 891
 William D. 818
BRADDOCK, --- 37, 38
BRADENBAUGH, A. E. 586
 Charles 795

BRADENBAUGH, J. F. 600, 604
 Jacob F. 603
BRADENBOUGH, John 246
BRADFORD, ---, Gov. 139, 140, 141,
  142, 145, 147, 148, 149, 633, 790,
  887
 ---, Governor 498, 499
 ---, Maj. 217
 A. W. 195, 281, 359, 814, 825, 934
 Anthony 519
 Augustus W. 128, 137, 139, 195, 498
 Augustus Williamson 138
 C. H. 125
 Charles H. 139
 Elizabeth (KELL) 139
 Emeline K. 139
 G. W. 142
 Jane 596
 Jane B. 139
 John 464
 Lizzie 139
 Samuel Webster 139
 Thomas Kell 139
 W. 498
 William 920, 921
 William J. A. 628
Bradford & Cooch 439
BRADHURST, B. 101
BRADLEY, Joseph H. 846
 Samuel 813
 Stephen J. 600
 W. E. 250
BRADSHAW, John J. 157
 Richard 189, 690
BRADY, E. J. 543
 Edward 841
 J. Frank 191
 J. W. L. 370
 James W. 157
 Samuel 162, 187, 189, 795, 818, 820,
  887, 905
 William J. 193
Brady's 342
BRAGG, William F. 157
BRAMDT, Jacob 478
Branch Bank of the U.S. 437
BRANCKER, J. S. 195
BRAND, ---, Mrs. 595
 Alexander 794
BRANDAN, G. H. 570
 J. H. 830
BRANDAU, Christian 936
BRANDAW, Jacob 157
BRANDT, Frederick H. 795
 Herman C. G. 233
 Jacob 288, 851
 Brandywine 354, 359
 Brandywine Creek 311
BRANNAN, John 241, 577
BRANNON, Benjamin 74
 John 462

BRANSON, ---, Capt. 361
  Baltis 245
  J. P. 253
  Joseph 188, 253, 761
BRANT, Robert J. 816
BRANTLY, ---, Dr. 567
---, Rev. Dr. 565
  W. T. 565
BRANTZ, ---, Capt. 217
---, Mr. 349
  Lewis 288, 348, 393
BRASHEARS, William 157
  Z. D. 794
BRATT, Samuel 578
BRAUN, F. W. 548
BRAUNS, F. L. 372
BRAY, ---, Rev. Dr. 920
  Thomas 657
BRAZER, Samuel 612, 795
BREANTLY, William T. 562
BRECHARD, ---, Mr. 689
BRECK, Joseph 122, 189
BRECKENRIDGE, ---, Gen. 335, 336
---, Mrs. 795
  A. 886
  Henry M. 194
  John 547
  John C. 127, 136, 795
  R. J. 902
  Robert J. 147, 548, 617, 795
  Breckenridge Raid 335
BRENGLE, Lawrence J. 165
BRENNAN, Charles C. 236
  M. J. 536
BRENNER, ---, Rev. Mr. 578
BRENT, ---, Miss 599
  Arthur E. 903
  Robert J. 195, 794
  William 786
BRERETON, Sally (MARSHALL) 449
  Thomas 449, 482, 795
BRESEE, Alfred A. 490
  Edward L. 490
  Emma (PATTERSON) 490
  John 490
  Louisa (KLECKNER) 490
  Mary E. (PASSANO) 490
  May 490
  Oscar F. 489, 490
  Stuart 490
  Winston 490
BRESEWOOD, Thomas 814
BRESSE, ---, Mr. 490
  Aseneth (BARBER) 490
BREVETT, John 188
BREVITT, John 233
  Joseph 595
BREWER, ---, Mr. 640
  Anne W. (DORSEY) 640

BREWER, Bessie Worthington 640
  Edward D. 640
  Eke 639
  Eliza A. (RAWLINGS) 639
  Eliza R. 640
  George G. 795
  James B. 639
  James R. 162, 195, 635, 636, 640, 729
  James Rawlings 639
  John 639
  Joseph 639
  Nicholas 191, 600
  Rachel 639
  Sarah (RIDGELY) 639
  William 639
BREWERTON, ---, Capt. 289
---, Col. 131
---, Lt. Col. 292
  Henry 795
  Brewerton Channel 289, 290
BREWSTER, George 617
BRIAMANT, P. 101, 103
BRIAN, Daniel 99
  James 795
  John H. 157
  Laura D. 231
  Marion A. 157
BRICE, --- 521
---, Judge 714
---, Miss 904
  B. W. 147
  David 658
  George H. 162
  Henry 95, 188, 254, 438, 462, 469, 470
  J. 102
  James E. 796
  John 457, 458, 470, 795
  John H. 879
  John, Mrs. 594
  N. 470
  Nicholas 452, 458, 459, 709, 712, 824
  Brice Estate 877
  Brick Church 354
  Brick Co. 510
BRICKMAN, A. O. 588
  Arthur O. 157, 571
BRIDDELL, Thomas 593
BRIDE, James 157
  Bridewell 342
BRIDGATE, Benjamin C. 814
  Bridge (Gay) Street Fire Company 240
  Bridgeport 347
BRIDGES, John C. 155, 365, 603
  Stephen L. 157
  William 155, 462, 469
BRIEN, James 298
BRIGGS, O. W. 560

BRIGGS, S. S. 242
BRIGHT, ---, Miss 595
BRIGNOLI, --- 673
Brilhart's 347
BRIM, Henry 425
BRINCKLEY, Joseph B. 601
BRINGHAM, Thomas 95
BRINKETT, William 559
BRINKLEY, J. B. 488
  Joseph B. 459
  Thomas B. 362
BRINKMAN, Edward 929
BRINTON, David 311
BRISCOE, ---, Mr. 300
  ---, Senator 721
  Alexander M. 157
  J. H. 613
  James T. 358, 526
  John H. 745, 814
  S. 84
BRISSON, Robert 100
Bristol College 865
BRISTOW, ---, Secretary 494
Bristow Station, Battle of 897
BRIT, Elizabeth 583
BRITTON, Abraham 71, 72
  F. 889
  Nicholas 71
Broad Street Theatre, Philadelphia 696
BROADBENT, Stephen 796
  William 892
BROADDUS, William F. 561
BROADFOOT, Joseph O. 157
BROADHEAD, J. C. 506
BROADHURST, ---, Mrs. 682
BROADUS, William F. 555
Broadway 342
Broadway & Locust Point Steam Ferry Co. 510
Broadway German M.E. Church 576, 577
Broadway Institute 570
Broadway M.E. Church 580
Broadway M.P. Church 584
Broadway Market-House 208
Broadway Parks 278
Broadway Presbyterian Church 548, 550
Broadway Savings-Bank 472, 473
Broadway Theatre, New York 688
BROCCHUS, Perry E. 795
BROCK, Jonathan 363, 365, 366
BROCKY, Athalinda 896
BROME, John M. 359
BROMELY, Joseph 38
BROMWELL, ---, Bishop 863
  John A. 157
  William 192
BROOK, Clement 74
BROOKE, ---, Col. 95, 96, 97

BROOKE, A. 94
  B. F. 576
  Clement 727
  Edward 100
  Frank 247
  George G. 586
  John B. 127
  John D. 794
  R. T., Mrs. 604
  Roger 845
  William P. 351
Brooke Family 588
BROOKER, ---, Capt. 87
Brooklandville 817, 834, 905
Brooklandwood 877, 905
Brooklyn 358
Brooklyn Tabernacle 889
BROOKS, ---, Mr. 225, 362
  Albert J. 157
  Benjamin 351
  C. C., Mrs. 598, 600
  Charles 877
  Chauncey 189, 330, 331, 354, 363, 364, 365, 404, 440, 471, 604, 846
  Edward F. 579
  Elizabeth 351
  George W. 190, 191
  Henry P. 157, 190
  Isaac 502, 604, 675
  James D. 191
  John 249
  John T. 252
  M. Alice 604
  Mary 351
  N. C. 223, 460, 625, 659
  Nathan C. 226, 465, 649
  Walter B. 463, 487, 501
  William 193, 195
  William K. 233
Brookwood 911
BROOME, R. G. B. 825
BROSIUS, F. 540
BROTHER, ---, Mr. 426
BROUGHAM, --- 693
  John 694
BROUGHTON, Joseph D. 794
BROUMEL, James 191
BROWER, Henry 374
BROWLEE, Arthur 65
BROWN, ---, Capt. 114
  ---, Dr. 732
  ---, Mayor 129, 130, 133, 136, 137, 468, 789, 790, 791
  ---, Mr. 316, 608, 628, 827
  A. 483, 568
  A. G. 469
  Abel 38, 860
  Albert M. 813, 814, 876
  Alexander 179, 252, 316, 317, 318, 439, 452, 457, 458, 470, 474, 475, 665, 795, 796

BROWN, Alexander D. 851, 877, 905
Amos 244, 470
Ann 843
Aquila 482
B. Gratz 71, 165, 166
Banjamin 816
Bernard 737
Bertha A. 884
Charles 434
Charles J. 157
Charles M. 855
Cornelia 213
D. T. 893
David 172, 173, 241, 249, 587, 935
David M. 462
David Paul 142
David R. 276
David U. 484
Dixon 239
E. 302
Edward 817
Elias 819, 820, 843
Elisha N. 252
Elizabeth 795
Ettie D. 927
F. G. 599
Frank 794
G. 547
G. J. 84
G. W. 729
Garret 463, 876
George 176, 179, 189, 315, 316, 317, 318, 324, 355, 404, 439, 457, 458, 464, 474, 475, 545, 547, 550, 593, 595, 658, 665, 732, 733, 734, 735, 736, 742, 770, 795, 824, 887, 921
George I. 665
George J. 91, 343, 461
George S. 276, 302, 458, 461, 470, 474, 547, 603, 698, 828
George Stewart 475
George W. 125, 126, 157, 222, 232
George W., Mrs. 598
George William 125, 126, 137, 138, 141, 184, 187, 195, 199, 667, 717, 729, 788
George, Mrs. 593
Gideon 255
Gustavus 740
Gustavus Richard 741
Harriet (EATON) 475
Henry 61, 263
I. A. 569
Isabella 475, 550, 828
J. H. 365, 602
J. Harman 550, 794
J. Harman, Mrs. 156
J. Harmon 602, 728
J. Harmon, Mrs. 155, 596
BROWN, J. N. 205
J. Wilcox 441, 449, 458, 482
J. Wilson 446
Jacob 569, 727
James 247, 474, 795
Jane S. (WILSON) 770
Jeremiah 884
Joe 252
Joel 877
John 59, 170, 173, 201, 247, 418, 483, 540, 544, 545, 587, 632, 727, 908, 921
John A. 474, 795
John Dixon 795
John M. 249, 549
John N. 153, 155, 545, 547
John S. 189, 190, 255, 292, 469, 794
John T. 189, 484
John W. 157
Joseph 189, 372, 794
Josiah 187, 795
Levi K. 497
Levin 525
M. J. 442
Matthew 592
Mollie E. 877
Morgan 740, 742
Moses 795, 819, 861
Obadiah B. 567
R. 916
R. H. 234
Rachel 596
Robert 70
Robert D. 471
Robert P. 595, 770
S. T. C. 847
Samuel 246, 547
Samuel J. 795
Sarah 795, 884
Sidney Buchanan 665
Simon 506
Stewart 188, 234, 298, 439, 456, 474, 547, 601, 795, 796, 824
Susannah D. 843
T. W. 918
Thomas 193
Thomas J. 190
Thomas R. 825
V. J. 462
Valentine 795
W. H. 465
William 89, 92, 200, 247, 248, 474, 519, 573, 796, 816, 843
William A. 795
William D. 144
William H. 157, 484, 740
William R. 157
Brown, Alexander & Sons 53, 438, 474, 550, 604, 665
Brown, H. & Co. 102
Brown, John A. & Co. 474

Brown, Shipley & Co. 324, 474
Brown, William & James & Co. 474
Brown, William H. & Brother 264, 265
Brown, William H. & Co. 402
Brown & Brune 876
Brown Brothers & Co. 474
Brown Brothers' 253
Brown Chemical Co. 402
Brown Family 843
Brown Mansion 176
Brown Memorial Church 475
Brown Memorial Presbyterian Church 550
Brown Memorial Presbyterian Mission Chapel 552
Brown's Hill 775
BROWNE, ---, Dr. 637
  B. B. 745
  B. F. 525
  Charles 433
  Elisha N. 470
  James 818
  John 76
  William 233, 470
  William Hand 233, 637, 656, 657
BROWNING, John H. 188
  Louisa 229
  Warfield T. 191
  William H. (G.) 363
  William S. 189, 200, 364, 366, 465
BROWNS, Adam 871
BROWNSON, Nathan 74
BRUCE, John M. 157, 191
  Joseph R. 263
  Robert 163
  Upton 188, 593
  William 549
Bruce Family 750
Bruelot's Assembly-Rooms 680
BRUETTING, George W. 157
BRUFF, Eleanor (MORSELL) 413
  J. D. 936
  James M. 795
  James W. 414
  John W. 413, 414
  Joseph 413
  Joseph E. 413, 414
  Sallie J. (FLOYD) 413
  Thomas 413
  Thomas C. 813, 886, 902
  William 225
Bruff, Faulkner & Co. 410, 413, 624
Bruff, John W. & Co. 413
BRUN, Theodore 263
BRUNDAGE, William 399
BRUNDIGE, James 577
  Thomas V. 577
Brundige, Vose & Co. 439
BRUNE, F. W. 439, 887, 914
  Fred. W. 795

BRUNE, Frederick W. 470, 794, 795
  Frederick William 659, 795
  John C. 130, 137, 194, 288, 351, 365, 418, 440, 594
  John Christian 795
  John W. 795
  W. H. 365
  W. H., Mrs. 602
  William F. W. 137
  William H. 483
  William H., Mrs. 598
Brune, F. W. & Sons 195
  Foulke & Co. 433
Brune & Dannemann 372, 439
BRUNER, D. 253
BRUNNER, Andrew B. 157
  David 523
  William Stevenson 609
BRUNT, R. 576
BRUSCUP, Thomas 191
BRUSH, Charles W. 629
Brush Electric Light Co. of Baltimore 502
BRUSTER, James 902
BRUTE, ---, Father 235
  Simon G. 235
  Simon Gabriel 234
BRYAN, --- 766
  Arthur 765
  James 127, 892
  Nicholas 813
  William Sheppard 195
Bryan, T. A. & Co. 396, 397
BRYANT, Gridley 317
Bryant, Stratton & Sadler's Business College 237
Bryantown 898
BRYARLY, Robert 38
BRYDEN, ---, Mr. 238, 239, 678
  James 312, 795
  William 592
Bryden's 513
Bryden's Fountain Inn 215, 261
Bryden's Hotel 215
Bryden's Inn 197, 454, 456, 658
Bryden's Tavern 433
BRYLEY, George 911
BRYNON, John 100
BRYSON, William J. 205
BUCHANAN, --- 521
  ---, Capt. 668
  ---, Dr. 51
  ---, ex-President 154
  ---, Miss 651
  ---, Mr. 60, 299, 434, 628, 882
  A. 101, 102, 103, 728
  Andrew 38, 60, 69, 71, 72, 73, 75, 78, 192, 193, 205, 244, 249, 298, 431, 455, 520, 521, 545, 679, 719, 726, 728, 733, 795, 814, 819, 934
  Ann (MC KEAN) 795

BUCHANAN, Arch. 101
　Archibald 69, 77, 194, 795, 921
　Charles 162
　Charles A. 137, 195, 820, 903
　Edward 120
　Eleanor (ROGERS) 719
　Elizabeth 795
　Franklin 114, 719
　G. 101, 102
　George 37, 50, 51, 56, 101, 173,
　　187, 521, 719, 729, 731, 732, 733,
　　734, 741, 795, 815, 819
　George D. 549
　H., Mrs. 796
　J. 102
　J. A. 84, 547
　J. S. 77, 678
　James 97, 101, 102, 425, 433, 794,
　　795, 892
　James A. 77, 83, 84, 86, 89, 173,
　　187, 195, 214, 215, 216, 265, 266,
　　267, 393, 456, 470, 545, 592, 699,
　　723, 795, 826
　James E. 794
　James H. 880
　James M. 133, 195, 493, 717, 718,
　　719, 819
　Laetitia (MC KEAN) 732
　Ld. (Archibald) 205
　Lloyd 778, 795, 819
　Robert 70, 78, 196, 392, 707, 779
　Robert C. 114
　S. 189
　Thomas 313
　Thomas McKean 796
　W. 707, 728
　William 51, 59, 69, 71, 72, 73, 170,
　　215, 425, 519, 544, 545, 547, 719,
　　728, 795, 796, 814
Buchanan & Hughes 432
Buchanan & Young 298, 433
Buchanan's Wharf 261, 287, 418
BUCHTAR, John 246
BUCK, Benjamin 71, 120, 189, 241,
　249, 796
　Benjamin C. 440
　Dorcus 795
　George 246
　George W. 246
　J. M. 586
　John 120, 249, 459, 816, 923
　John M. 578
　John S. 879
Buck Creek 743
Buck Eye 342
Buck Town 311
Buck's Range 77
BUCKEY, Samuel 264
BUCKINGHAM, J. S. 679
BUCKLER, ---, Dr. 288, 899
---, Mrs., Dr. 596

BUCKLER, John 700, 701, 720, 737,
　756, 795
　L. N. 256
　Riggin 745
　Thomas H. 287, 417
　William 432, 487, 547
BUCKLEY, David Z. 157
　J. J. 761
　M. Brooke 349
　Thomas 242, 263
　Victor 879
BUCKMAN, David 887
　Esther 887
　S. J. 892
　Washington 836
BUCKMILLER, Elizabeth Ann 392
　Robert S. 392
BUCKNER, ---, Mr. 51
　William 50, 53
BUDEKE, George H. 231
Buena Vista, The 628
Buerger Schuetzen Association 807
BUFFINGTON, J. 102
BUFFURN, J. 252
BUHRMAN, E. 875
BULL, ---, Mr. 630
　B. H. 576
　Edmund 255, 624, 794
　Emanuel 872
　George W. 902
　Isaac 911
　Jacob 920
　John 102
　John E. 488
　John W. 157, 877
　Nicholas 871
　Pamelia 627
　Randolph 157, 795
　William 276
Bull & Sewell 515
Bull Fountain 276
Bull's Head 513
BULLETTE, L. D. 830
BULLIS, Charles J. 923
BULLOCK, ---, Mr. 494
　---, Rev. Dr. 146
　J. J. 151, 549
　John S. 191, 193, 494
BULTER, ---, Gen. 499
BUMGARDNER, Joseph 149
BUNBERRY, ---, Capt. 91
BUNBURY, Mons. S. 592
BUND, Gustav Adolph 605
BUNKER, George 592
BUNN, Gilbert 836
BUNNICKE, George 605
BUNTING, John 190, 193
　Spencer J. 191
BUNZIE, ---, Prof. 267
BURBAG, John E. 149
BURBING, Thomas 482

BURBRIDGE, Emma 646
BURCH, Marion K. 483, 598
  Thomas B. 177, 191, 193
BURCHELL, Thomas 560
BURGAN, Daniel S. 813
Burgen Family 927
BURGER, Andrew J. 820
BURGESS, ---, Mr. 567
  C. W. 193
  Caleb W. 466
  Hugh 373, 375
  John 373
BURGOYNE, Henry A. 869
BURK, David 246
  Henry 157
  Nicholas 248
BURKARD, Peter J. 446
BURKE, ---, Col. 136
  ---, Mr. 86, 219
  A. J. 193, 872
  Andrew J. 190
  B. 380
  Charles 693, 695
  David 84, 89, 188, 192, 246, 459
  Eliza 432
  I. C. 569
  Nicholas 92, 795, 814
  P. B. 359
  W. L. 814
Burke Family 886
Burke Street 769
BURKHARDT, N. 605
BURKHART, N. 570
BURKHEAD, Samuel 921
  Solomon 736
BURKHEIMER, William 597
BURLAND, Richard 569, 727
BURNAP, ---, Dr. 648
  G. W. 795
  George 590
  George W. 647, 664
BURNE, ---, Dr. 741
  James 39
BURNELL, John 100
BURNES, John 892
BURNESTON, I. 233
  Isaac 393, 407, 461, 469, 470, 575, 735, 795, 826
  J. 95, 269
BURNET, D. S. 591, 795
BURNETSON, Isaac 244
BURNETT, E. 237
  Joseph P. 794
  S. 826
  Samuel 469
BURNEY, C. 866
  Clotworthy 867
  R. 866
BURNHAM, Enoch 794
  William H. 157
BURNISTON, Isaac 203

BURNS, Allan 755
  Allen 737
  Elizabeth (HIGHLAND) 472
  Francis 189, 448, 463, 471, 472, 794, 795
  Frank 487
  John 814
  Mary E. (RUDDACH) 472
  Richard 872
  Robert D. 464
  William 880
  William F. 390, 478, 501
  William Findley 471
  William H. 877
  William M. 463
Burns, Francis & Son 472
Burns, Russell & Co. 472
Burns & Russell 472
BURNSIDE, ---, Gen. 142
Burnside's Bridge 810
BURR, --- 710
  ---, Mr. 816
  Aaron 644, 781
BURREL, Charles 796
BURRELL, Charles 493
BURROUGH, Edward E. 740
  Horace 740
BURROWS, Frederick M. 157
  J. L. 564
  John 100
BURT, ---, Dr. 549
  A. P. 367
  Alfred P. 194, 367
  N. C. 548
BURTON, Aaron 737
  George W. 489
  J. Wolf 820
  Mary K. 886
  W. H. 688
  William E. 688
  Burton 342
BURWELL, P. L. 390
  William M. 612
BUSBY, David T., Mrs. 596
BUSCH, Abraham 255
BUSEY, E. F. 586
  William M. 488
BUSH, Benjamin B. 814, 815
  Charles 836
  James 690, 916
  Stephen C. 870
Bush Creek Forge & Mill 425
Bush River 816, 918, 923
Bush River Bridge 130
Bush River Iron-Works 425
Bush River Upper Hundred 910
Bush Town 311
BUSHELL, ---, Prof. 638
BUSHEY, William 855
BUSK, Ellen 522
  Jennie 673

BUSK, John 615, 794
BUSSEY, Jesse 728
  Robert H. 877
  Sallie E. 877
BUTCHER, Alexander 559, 560
Butcher's Hill Building Association No. 3. 510
Butchers' & Drovers' Gazette 641
Butchers' Association of Baltimore 380, 800, 804
Butchers' Building Association No. 1 510
Butchers' Hide & Tallow Association 381
Butchers' Loan & Annuity Association 381
BUTLER, --- 166
---, Gen. 131, 146, 278, 632, 791
---, Lord 391
  Abraham 553
  Ann 795
  B. F. 141
  Benjamin F. 147
  Chester 391
  J. G. 722
  J. W. 152
  John L. 391
  Martha A. 753
  Samuel 292, 303, 463
  Samuel F. 814, 894, 898
  Thomas 753
  William E. 753
  William H. 821
  William O. 123, 753
  William Ormond 753
Butler 26, 27, 869, 876, 877, 883
BUTT, Caleb 836
BUTTERFIELD, David G. 821
BUTTON, James 812
  William 814, 815, 927
BUZBY, D. T. 441
  David T. 466, 489
BYARD, P. 95, 269
BYERLY, George 77
BYNES, Samuel 249
BYNS, James 100
BYRA, Francis Otway 795
BYRD, Harvey L. 642, 738, 739
  J. C. 95, 269
BYRNE, Thomas V. 793
  William 795
BYRNES, Samuel 439
BYRON, R. 106
BYRORN, Bernard M. 234
CABANEL, --- 676
Cabin Creek 303, 310
CABOT, ---, Mr. 747
CADDEN, Charles W. 161
  J. W. 839
CADWALLADER, ---, Gen. 131, 133, 885

CADWALLADER, George 132
CAIN, Alexander 101
  Joshua 877
CAIRNS, Samuel 184
CALANDRIA, Anthony 825
CALDER, Charlotte 873
  George E. 873
  James 797, 871, 872
  John 911
  Margaret 873
  Margaret (BAGNEL) 873
  Mary 873
  Sarah 872, 873
  William 157
CALDWELL, ---, Capt. 99
---, Mr. 392
  John 797
  S. G. 254
Caledonian Church 549
CALHOUN, ---, Brigade-Maj. 94
---, Mayor 174, 175, 734
  Ann 796
  Charles 149
  James 70, 71, 73, 74, 75, 76, 77, 78, 79, 80, 83, 84, 118, 170, 172, 173, 187, 192, 196, 214, 216, 239, 244, 265, 266, 392, 407, 432, 452, 482, 520, 545, 547, 728, 733, 736, 780, 796, 797, 814, 824, 885
Calhoun, James & Co. 100
Calhoun Street 769
California 358
CALLAHAN, Martin 157
  Samuel G. 879
CALLAWAY, Charles M. 796
CALLENDER, James Thompson 781
CALLIS, George R. 190, 191
CALLON, ---, Mr. 361
CALLOW, William 139, 364
Calvary Cemetery 534
Calvary Church 523
Calvary M.E. Church South 568, 586, 587, 589
CALVERT, ---, Miss 774
  Benedict 702
  Benedict Leonard (4th Lord Baltimore) 50, 195
  Caldwell C. 586
  Cecilius 66
  Cecilius (2d Lord Baltimore) 41, 195
  Charles 50, 51, 195
  Charles B. 145, 503, 845, 846, 847
  Charles (3d Lord Baltimore) 195
  Charles (5th Lord Baltimore) 195
  Charles (6th [sic: 5th] Lord Baltimore) 702
  Frederick 42
  Frederick (6th Lord Baltimore) 195
  George 40, 702, 845
  George H. 609, 613

31

CALVERT, George Henry 647
 George (1st Lord Baltimore) 195
 George, Sir 39
 Joseph 45
 Leonard 33, 34, 195, 639, 931
 Philip 35, 195
 Rosalie Eugenia 702
 Rosalie Eugenie 353
Calvert City Springs 213
Calvert Family 702
Calvert Hall 122, 530, 541, 938
Calvert Station 347
Calvert Street 727
Calvert Street Baptist Church 561
Calvert Street House 559
Calvert Street Railway Station 216
Calvert Street Station 345
Calvert Sugar Refinery 418, 419
Calvert Universalist Church 797
Calverton 16, 64, 834, 840, 935
Calverton Almshouse 827
Calverton Asylum 935
Calverton Heights 841
Calverton Hotel 517
Calverton Mill Race 217
Calverton Mills 407
Calverton Road 935
Calverton Road Stock Yards 380
Calverton Stock & Droveyard Co. 840
Calverton Stock-Yard Co. 446
CALVIN, Patrick 575
Calvin's Stone Tavern 759
Calvinistic Baptists 559
CALWELL, James 298
 James S. 641
 Thomas 77
CAMAN, Robert Nathaniel 797
CAMBRELENG, ---, Mr. 652
Cambria Co. 341
Cambridge 310
Camden Station 139, 141, 146, 147, 150, 331, 342, 789, 790, 792, 793
Camden Street 769
Camden Street Military Hospital 636
Cameron 342
CAMERON, ---, Secretary of War 132
 D. 162
 Daniel W. 820
 J. D. 368
 J. Donald 346
 Simon 345
CAMP, William 84, 89, 459
Camp Bradford 141, 846
Camp Chase 142
Camp Parole 153, 342
Camp Relay 131
CAMPANIUS, --- 33, 34
CAMPBELL, ---, Capt. 103, 779

CAMPBELL, ---, Col. 880
 ---, Miss 871
 ---, Mr. 781
 ---, Mrs. 595
 Alexander 591
 Archibald 172, 214, 239, 291, 452, 453, 454, 796
 B. U. 234, 252, 474, 797
 Bernard U. 627
 Bernard W. 659
 Catherine 879
 D. 103
 Edward S. 930
 George A. 260
 J. M. 77, 523
 J. Mason 126, 198, 702, 703, 914
 James 72, 100, 470, 547, 738, 797
 James Mason 796
 John 850
 John P. 552
 John S. 194
 John Turfman 796
 Mary W. (CORSE) 930
 Rebecca 797
 Robert 364
 Ross 487, 796
 Thomas M. 253
 Thomas W. 260
 W. H. H. 855
 William 797, 845
Campbell, Ritchie & Co. 438
Campbell, Ross & Co. 832
Campbell Family 588, 839
Campbell's Slave Jail 139, 144
CAMPER, Charles 157
 John E. 821
 Thomas 413
CANBY, ---, Gen. 164
 E. K. 635, 797
 James 279, 595, 797
 Samuel 279
 Thomas Y. 466, 467, 488, 489
 Thomas Y., Mrs. 604
 W. 365
 William 598, 602
CANFIELD, Ira C. 602, 796
 W. B. 549
 William B. 153, 469, 546, 547, 550, 599, 838
CANNON, ---, Mr. 223
 Clayton 467
 Duncan B. 880
 James 796
 John 432
 Louisa 155, 156
Cannon Bennett & Co. 262
CANTEL, John B. 157
CANTER, I. W. 586
 Isaac W. 586
Canterbury, Archbishop of 918

Canton 29, 56, 90, 122, 132, 150, 284, 303, 347, 349, 350, 354, 426, 525, 879, 926, 927, 928, 929
CANTON, Ed. 796
Canton Branch Point 937
Canton Co. 277, 354, 355, 362, 387, 429, 460, 501, 510, 797, 849, 926, 928, 935
Canton Ferry 340
Canton Fire Company 818
Canton Forges 427
Canton House 797
Canton Iron-Works 321
Canton M.E. Church 580
Canton Market-House 208
Canton Park 277
Canton Race Course 850
Canton Racetrack 122
CANTRILL, William 39
Cape Charles 39
Cape Henry 310
CAPELENO, Antonio 269
CAPITO, Susan L. 771
CAPLES, Jacob L. 903
  Rosalie 908
Capon Road 342
CAPPEAU, Joseph 418, 797
  Sarah Ann 418
CAPRICE, Joseph 251
CAPRON, Horace 845
  R. J. 370
  Richard J. 887
CAREW, Nicholas Hachett 424
CAREY, Archibald 71
  George 253, 488
  J. E. 438
  James 118, 155, 169, 170, 173, 187, 188, 200, 374, 431, 447, 452, 456, 469, 470, 482, 488, 604, 658, 747, 826
  James, Mrs. 604
  John 102, 568
  John E. 197, 252
  John L. 194, 394, 610, 659
  Joseph W. 251
  Lott 567, 568
  S. 438
  T. 103
  Thomas I., Mrs. 604
  Thomas J. 488
  Thomas K. 447
  William M. 846
  Wilson M. 796, 846
Carey & Tilghman 433
Carey Howe & Co. 263
CARGILL, John M. 581
CARL, Louis A. 157
CARLING, Michael 469
CARLISLE, Grafton D. 141
  Hugh 919
CARLYLE, ---, Mr. 653

CARMAGH, John 911
CARMAN, ---, Mrs. 71
  Charles 174
  George H. 816, 817
  John 797
  Phineas 797
  Samuel 782
  William 89
Carmelite Chapel 544
Carmelite Convent 597, 598
Carmelite Nunnery 786
Carmelite Nuns 802, 807
CARMICHAEL, --- 136
  ---, Lt. 135
  Richard B. 600, 722
  Thomas H. 199, 200
  William 280, 380, 381, 813, 834
CARMON, George H. 813, 814
  Newton 101
CARNAGHAN, James 246
CARNAN, Charles 797, 860
  Charles Ridgely 819
  Christopher 864
  Maria North 864
Carnass Scrutiny 77
CARNES, Edward 76
CARNEY, James 236
CARNIGHAM, James 824
CARNIGHAN, James 457
CARNIN, Chois 58
Caroline Street M.E. Church 579
Caroline Street Permanent Building Association No. 1 510
Caroline Street Station 578, 580
CAROTHERS, Peter 255
CARPENTER, ---, Mr. 632
  L. B. 579, 796
  W. H. 675
  William 65, 190, 237, 649
  William H. 140, 508, 612, 625, 628, 631, 633, 649, 650
  William Henry 649
Carpenter's Association 433
CARR, A. 299
  Dabney S. 188, 497, 498, 797
  G. W. H. 237
  J. 672
  James 256, 790
  James E. 187, 200
  Robert H. 155
  Robert H., Mrs. 156
  Wilson, Mrs. Dr. 156
Carr, Horner & Co. 624
CARRERE, John 482, 532
CARREY, James 82
Carriage & Toy Co. 510
CARRIERE, John 298
  L. 588
CARRIGAN, James 404
CARRINGTON, Eugene 821
  Isaiah 841

CARRISS, Sampson 796
CARROLL, --- 261, 698, 703
---, Archbishop 235, 382, 533, 534, 679
---, Bishop 225, 535, 595, 684
---, Gov. 662, 752, 792, 912
---, Messrs. 516
---, Miss 796
---, Mr. 57, 59, 373, 402
---, Rev. Dr. 224
---, Rt. Rev. Bishop 534
Albert H. 370, 839
Annie E. 844
Aquilla 797
C. 850
C. R. 680, 850
Charles 42, 48, 49, 50, 51, 53, 54, 67, 69, 79, 117, 157, 168, 193, 202, 237, 312, 314, 315, 316, 317, 318, 374, 418, 421, 432, 521, 532, 679, 680, 705, 706, 708, 796, 797, 826, 882, 887, 908
Charles of Carrollton 515, 526, 530, 534, 535, 541, 600, 650, 705, 706, 712, 797, 821, 848, 882, 908
Charles of Duddington 909
Charles R. 796
Clare (DUNN) 705
D. H. 870, 889
Daniel 49, 51, 74, 118, 310, 431, 527, 705, 796, 908
David 50, 370
David H. 489, 837
David S. 839
Dorothy 705
Dorothy (BLAKE) 706
Elizabeth 821
Henry 796, 876, 908, 909
Henry Hill 796, 909
James 50, 127, 149, 188, 192, 193, 200, 217, 253, 254, 290, 351, 455, 469, 470, 504, 520, 658, 796, 797, 814, 819, 820, 826, 903, 921
John 157, 234, 527, 530, 531, 532, 594, 658, 705, 707, 776, 854
John B. 246
John H. 819
John Henry 706
John K. 190, 193, 728
John Lee 166, 195, 793, 847, 851
John N. 820
Judith (CARTER) 796
Julia Ann (STEVENSON) 842
Louisa (TILGHMAN) 909
Margaret (TILGHMAN) 707
Mary (HILL) 909
Mary (WINCHESTER) 909
Mary B. (STERRETT) 909
Mary Clare 706
Mary Lee 796
N. M. 580

CARROLL, Osborn 880
Rachel 796
Rebecca (THOMPSON) 909
Richard 188, 458, 470, 593, 796, 797
Robert Goodloe Harper 796
S. J. 354
Sallie 842
Samuel S. 483
Samuel Sterrett 909
Sarah A. 909
Sarah A. (ROGERS) 909
St. John 472, 796
Thomas 797
Thomas K. 498
Thomas King 195, 497, 842
William P. 149
William Sterrett 909
Carroll, Tasker & Co. 424
Carroll Estate 887
Carroll Family 907, 909
Carroll Hall 507
Carroll Hall Building 631
Carroll M. E. Chapel 855
Carroll Manor 375, 535, 871
Carroll's Island 705
Carroll's Run 214
Carroll's Woods 846
Carrollton 820, 825
Carrollton Hotel 515, 679
Carrollton Manor 777
Carrollton Savings & Loan Association 510
Carrollton Viaduct 319
CARRUTHERS, J. 678
John 455
CARRVELL, Charles 846
Howard 846
CARSON, ---, Mr. 831
Anne 770
David 166, 465, 577, 796
Elijah 250, 255
George 462
J. E. 586
Joseph 255, 796
Richard 79, 172, 173, 392, 483, 796
T. E. 586
Thomas J. 796
Thomas M. 579
W. K., Mrs. 604
Washington K. 604
William 469
Carson, William & Company 261
Carson & Bryan 931
CARSTON, Isaac 77
CARTER, --- 59, 698
---, Mr. 454, 633, 703
A. M. 152, 155, 601
A. Robert 187
Alexander M. 550, 551
Alice 353

CARTER, Bernard 191, 195, 501, 701, 702, 723, 914
  Bernard Moore 702
  Charles H. 353, 702, 796
  Dennis 140
  E. F. 145
  Edward F. 633
  H. H. 353
  J. P. 830
  J. W. 587
  James H. 481
  John C. 157
  John F. 202
  John G. 817
  John H. 797
  John M. 195, 834, 903
  Joseph F. 157
  Judith 796
  King 353, 702
  Mary B. (RIDGELY) 703
  Robert 702, 733
  Rosalie Eugenia (CALVERT) 702
  Rosalie Eugenie (CALVERT) 353
  W. 586
Carter & Co. 633
Carter & Neilson 633
Carter Family 702
Carter's Delight 49, 168
Cartwill Creek 311
CARUNCHIO, Victor 826
CARUSI, ---, Mr. 680
CARVER, William 877
  William V. 797
CARY, James 58
  Richard 70
  William F. 153, 155, 796
  Wilson M. 820
CASE, Eliphalet 506
CASENORE, Stephen 482, 483
CASENOVE, Stephen 796
CASHMYER, Henry 191, 193, 194
CASKERY, Bernard 189
CASPARI, Charles 740
  William 740
CASPEAR, ---, Mr. 263
CASS, Lewis 123
CASSADY, Francis Stansbury 796
CASSARD, George C. 157
  Gilbert 249, 797
  John 488
  Lewis 577, 797
  Louis R. 157
  Thomas 489, 887
CASSATT, --- 350
  A. J. 346
CASSELL, ---, Capt. 275
  James 796
  Louisa 834
  William H. 276, 834
CASSIDY, Luke 472
CASTELLO, James 252

Castlehaven 309
CASWELL, ---, Gov. 773
  Richard 72, 819, 921
Catawba College 840
Catch Church 932
CATE, Ammon 462
CATHCART, ---, Mr. 498
  A. Roszel 487
  J. M. C. 872
  John 249
  R. 498
  Robert 363, 364, 366, 497
  William H. 193, 472
Cathedral 80, 530, 534, 803, 808
Cathedral Cemetery 272, 534, 536
Cathedral of the Roman Catholic Church 672
CATHELL, Joseph 908
Catholic Almanac 648
Catholic Mirror, The 629
Catholic Monthly Magazine 613
Catholic Register, The 641
Catholic Tract Society of Baltimore 537
Catoctin Mountain 324, 341
CATON, Edward 822
  Elizabeth 802, 821
  Elizabeth (CARROLL) 821
  Emily 803
  Louisa 821
  Louise 796
  Mary 821
  Richard 172, 298, 313, 386, 407, 452, 658, 796, 797, 802, 803, 808, 811, 821, 825, 845
Caton, R. & Co. 432
Catonsville 26, 820, 821, 823, 824
Catonsville Avenue 936
Catonsville Library & Literary Association 821
Catonsville Lodge No. 164, Good Templars 821
Catonsville Military Institute 151
CATOR, Benjamin F. 155, 415, 488, 796
  Franklin T. 415
  George 415
  James H. 415
  John 188
  R. W. 448
  Robinson W. 415, 441, 464
CATTELL, ---, Mrs. 71
Cattle Market 207
Cattle Show & Agricultrual & Horticultural Exhibition 846
Caucasian 633
CAUGGHEY, Benjamin 255
CAUGHEY, Charles M. 641
  Michael 189, 192, 796
  N. W. 536
CAUGHY, S. H. 458, 484

CAULFIELD, R. 102
 Robert 100, 101
 Thomas W. 157
CAULK, James I. 191
 James T. 191
CAULP, William 187
Causeway Mission M. E. Church 576
Causeway Mission Society 576
CAUSICI, --- 266
CAUSTEN, Isaac 298
CAVANAGH, Patrick 526
CAVATES, James A. 193
CAVEN, Joshua 836
Caves 30, 705, 706, 707, 854
CAWTHORNE, William 920
CAZANAVE, ---, Mr. 82
CAZE, J. 103
CECIL, Martha Ann 373
Cecil County Railroad Company 314
Cedar Creek 336, 342
Cedar Grove Church of the U.B. 869
Cedar Heights 937
Cedar Hill Cemetery Co. 510
Cedar Point 879
CELESTE, ---, Madame 694
Centennial Building Association No. 1 510
Centennial Grange No. 161, Patrons of Husbandry 904
Centennial Hill 275
Centennial M.E. Church 580
Central Course 818
Central Cross-Town Railway 370
Central High School 754
Central M. E. Church 586
Central M. E. Church South 586
Central Mutual Building Association 510
Central National Bank 468
Central Police Station 133, 137
Central Presbyterian Church 420, 548, 549, 599, 754
Central Presbyterian Church Mission 552
Central Race Course 849, 850, 851
Central Savings 473
Central Savings-Bank of Baltimore 469, 473
Central Union Permanent Building Association 510
Centre Fountain 214
Centre Lodge No. 40, I.O.O.F. 894
Centre Market 89, 173, 174, 501, 540, 592, 593, 667, 682
Centre Market Space 149, 467
Centre Market-House 84
Centreville 32, 717, 930
CHABOT, G. H. 796

CHABOT, J. H. 610
CHADWICK, ---, Capt. 103
 G. 102
CHAIDS, P. 252
CHAILLE, Peter 252
CHAIMIER, Daniel 814
CHAISTY, E. 534
 E. F. 272
 Edward J. 162, 194
CHALMERS, --- 682
 George 707
 James 432
 John 89, 797
 William 92, 189
Chamber of Commerce 439
Chamber of Commerce Building 440, 442, 443, 444, 669
CHAMBERLAIN, J. E. M. 743
 John 432, 910, 921
 Joseph 101
 N. H. 590
Chamberlain's Tavern 250
CHAMBERLAINE, Samuel 66
CHAMBERS, Daniel 470
 E. F. 128, 846
 Ezekiel F. 128, 313
 J. Wesley 738
 John Thomas 797
Chambers Family 717
Chambersburg 356
CHAMBLISS, ---, Mr. 559
 Joseph E. 558
CHAMIER, Daniel 38, 67, 76, 200, 796, 910
Champion Lodge No. 84, Knights of Pythias 839, 840
CHANCE, ---, Bishop 536, 933
 J. J. 537
CHANCELLOR, ---, Dr. 753
 C. W. 193, 288, 495, 825
 Charles W. 191, 494, 751, 752
 Elizabeth (EDWARDS) 751
 Fannie L. (POUND) 751
 Leah Seddon 753
 Martha A. (BUTLER) 753
 Mary (TALIAFERRO) 753
 Mattie Butler 753
 Philip Stanly 753
 Sanford 751
Chancellor's Point 310
Chancellorsville, Battle of 897
CHANCHE, ---, Bishop 236
 John Joseph 235, 236
Chandlee 446
CHANDLEE, H. P. 579
CHANDLER, ---, Mr. 747
 Benjamin 249
 D. T. 796
 George 433
 H. G. 195
 H. J. 562, 870, 874

CHANDLER, John 861
  Joseph R. 667
  Kennard, Mrs. 598
  Lewis 380
CHANDLEY, John H. 157
CHANEY, ---, Rev. Mr. 579
  Louis 157
  R. G. 237
  William 157
  William H. 157
CHANFRAU, ---, Mr. 656
CHANNING, J. 103
  T. 103
  William Ellery 589
Chapel of Visitation Convent 544
CHAPELLE, P. L. 536, 938
CHAPMAN, ---, Mayor 135, 140, 145, 147, 148, 150, 151, 177, 200, 220, 272, 499
  ---, Rev. Mr. 874
  Allan 302
  Allan A. 440
  Allen A. 125, 484, 485
  Belle 830
  D. C. 487
  David P. 113
  F. 604
  George 251, 252
  J. J. 153
  John 402
  John G. 359, 845
  John L. 163, 190, 498
  John Lee 140, 141, 146, 149, 187, 200, 219, 222, 270, 357, 497
  N. F. 830
  Robert 519
  Robert B. 830
  W. H. 575, 579
  William A. 222
CHAPPELL, J. M. 256
  John 582
  P. S. 616
  Philip S. 194, 466, 488, 489, 796, 797
  Samuel M. 256
CHAPPELLE, P. L. 855
  P. S. 367
Chaptico 720
Charitable Marine Society 592
Charity Lodge No. 124, A. F. & A. M. 873
CHARLES, Daniel 797
Charles Street Avenue 886, 887, 892, 896
Charles Street Bridge 218
Charles Street M. E. Church 575
Charlestown 309, 342, 351
Charlotte Hall 911
Charlotte Hall Academy 878
CHARLTON, ---, Capt. 65
  Arthur 65

CHARLTON, Edward 65
  Francis 238
  Henry 65
  J. W. 584
  John 65
  Thomas 65
CHARTERS, Thomas 759
CHASE, --- 698, 723
  ---, Capt. 432
  ---, Judge 588, 709, 712, 727, 781
  ---, Mr. 816
  Algernon 796
  Charles 462
  Charles M. 255
  Daniel 796
  George B. 243, 255, 256
  George R. 242
  H. 734
  H. H. 465
  Hannibal H. 190
  Jeremiah 194
  Jeremiah T. 71, 75, 76, 77
  Jeremiah Townley 69, 71, 72, 76, 194, 707, 797, 819
  John 112
  John H. 157
  Mary 794
  Parson 58
  R. 37
  Richard 768
  S. P. 145
  Salmon P. 142
  Samuel 61, 76, 116, 193, 194, 206, 209, 461, 519, 521, 613, 704, 706, 707, 708, 709, 710, 711, 728, 780, 794, 797
  Samuel W. 933
  Thomas 37, 67, 205, 519, 521, 526, 858
  Thorndick 120, 461, 592
  Thorndike 84, 86, 89, 192, 216, 251, 299, 796
  Wells 465
Chase's Hill 113
Chase's Station 927
Chase's Wharf 129
CHATARD, ---, Dr. 532, 600, 742
  ---, Mrs. 595
  Jane 594
  P. 734, 786
  Peter 734, 735, 824
Chatard Building 746
CHATEAU, Louis M. 505
Chatham, ---, Earl of 674
Chatham Street 769
Chatsworth 49, 50, 51, 729, 856, 857, 862
Chatsworth Independent Methodist Church 584, 585
CHAUNCEY, ---, Mr. 362
CHAYTOR, ---, Capt. 86

CHAYTOR, James 112
Chazik Amuno 589
Cheapside 287, 769
CHEATHAM, John 758
CHEERU, Lorana D. 749
Cheese Joe 802
CHEESEBOROUGH, Robert C. 796
CHEFFELLE, J. S., Miss 596
  Judith 596
Cheltenham 603
Chemical & Fertilizer Exchange of Baltimore City 397
Chemical Co. of Canton 460
Chemical Exchange 401
CHENET, Lewis S. 523
CHENEWITH, Arthur 836
CHENOWETH, Ferdinand 157
  Isadora 927
  Lillie R. 916
CHENOWITH, Richard P. 262
Chenowith M.E. Chapel 580
Cherry Hill 354
Cherry Point 310
Cherry Run 342
Cherry-Stone Light-house 310
Chesapeake & Delaware Canal 309, 313, 341, 442, 447
Chesapeake & Ohio Canal 284, 313, 314, 315, 325, 388, 389, 725, 794
Chesapeake & York River Steamboat Co. 771
Chesapeake Artillery 897
Chesapeake Bank 451, 880
Chesapeake Bank Building 472
Chesapeake Bank of Baltimore 463, 469
Chesapeake Chemical Works 852
Chesapeake Guano Co. 510
Chesapeake Marine Railway & Dry-Dock Co. 510
Chesapeake Riflemen 669
CHESNUT, William 155, 366
Chester 351
CHESTER, S. K. 694
Chester Creek 311
Chester Creek Railroad 350
Chester River Steamboat Co. 303, 510
Chester Street M.E. Church 577
Chestertown 32, 309, 691, 717, 899
Chesterwood 604, 927
CHESTNUT, William 262, 440, 441, 442, 796
Chestnut Grove 908
Chestnut Grove Presbyterian Church 904
Chestnut Hill 914
Chestnut Hills 33
Chestnut Ridge 14, 19, 30

Chestnut Ridge Baptist Church 552, 553, 554
Chestnut Street Theatre, Philadelphia 683
CHESTON, ---, Mr. 407
  G. 369
  Galloway 139, 232, 288, 358, 440, 464, 466, 472, 488, 746, 747, 797, 937
  Galloway, Mrs. 596
  James 217, 358, 470
CHETWYND, William 424
CHEVERUS, ---, Bishop 527
  ---, Dr. 235
  ---, Right Rev. Dr. 532
CHEVES, ---, Capt. 361
CHEW, ---, Lt. 897
  Benjamin 100, 863
  Charles R. 902
  H. B. 64
  Henry B. 902
  James W. 729
  John H. 488
  Margaret 863
  S. C. 743, 937
  Samuel 365, 587, 745, 754, 796, 797
  Samuel C. 745
  William B. 369
Chew Family 904
Chew Street Bochemic Building Association No. 1 510
Chewsville 357
CHEYNE, Roderick 921
Chicago Times 633
Chickering Pianos 674
CHIFFELLE, Thomas P. 217
  Thomas R. 932
Chilberry 43
CHILCOAT, Aquilla 820, 855
  F. A. 814
  George 855
  John 877
CHILD, Francis J. 233
  G. G. 597
  Samuel 796
  William 439, 470, 589, 796
  William J. 797
CHILD(S), Samuel 189
Children's Aid Society 154, 601
Children's Aid Society of Baltimore 599
Children's Magazine 654
CHILDS, ---, Miss 576
  A. 576
  A., Mrs. 576
  George W. 271
  Henry 112
  J. W. 585
  Jesse D. 157
  John D. 877
  Nathaniel 251, 816

CHILDS, William 470
CHILTON, ---, Mrs. 606
China Hall 573
CHIPCHASE, James 524
CHIPPENDALE, --- 693, 694
CHISOLM, J. J. 745
CHITTY, --- 726
CHOAT, Edward 559
CHOATE, E. W. 820
  Edward 519
  Edward S. W. 488, 830
Choice, The 49
Choptank River 309
Chrighton's Distillery 213
Christ Church 138, 522, 523, 526
Christ Church Episcopal Church 720
Christ Church Orphan Asylum 720
Christ Episcopal Church 911
Christ P. E. Church 521, 524, 544
CHRISTIAN, Lulu 927
  Samuel 106
Christian Advocate 753
Christian Brothers 537, 538, 541
Christian Church 591, 592
Christian Family Magazine 625
Christian Review, The 630
Christiana 311, 875, 881
Christiana Creek 311
CHRISTIE, Arthur 148
  Charles 814, 921
  Gabriel 497, 498, 797
  James 47, 76
  John 73, 76
  Robert 69, 814
  Christina 64
CHRISTOPHER, Elisha 886
  N. 194
  Z. W. 157
CHRISWITH, Arthur 374
CHROM, Bernard 281
Chronicle 615, 795
Chronicle of the Times 613
Chronotype, The 636
CHURCH, E. F. 900
  E. I. 578
  R. J. 485
  Royal W. 157
Church Bridge 918
Church Hill 425
Church Home 748
Church Home & Infirmary 389, 526, 738
Church of Our Saviour P.E. 524
Church of the:
  Ascension 586
  Covenanters 551
  Disciples 926
  Holy Communion P.E. 861, 867
  Holy Cross 526
  Holy Evangelists 526

Church of the: (Cont'd.)
  Holy Innocents 526
  Holy Trinity P.E. 524, 861
  Messiah 522
  Most Holy Passion 826
  Rock of Ages 525
  Sacred Heart 855, 891
Church Times, The 647
Church's Creek Landing 310
Churchman 654
CIAMPI, A. F. 538
Cincinnati Enquirer 633
CINNAMOND, George R. 465
Citizen, The 616
Citizens' Bank 451, 796
Citizens' Fire Insurance Co. 723
Citizens' National Bank 379, 409, 451, 462, 469
Citizens' Passenger Railway Co. 367
Citizens' Permanent Building, Savings & Loan Co. 510
Citizens' Railway Co. 510
Citizens' Security & Land Co. 510
City & Hampden Railroad Co. 362
City Agent, The 631
City Bank 310, 450
City Bank of Baltimore 461
City Block Ferry & Towing Co. 292
City College 800
City Dock 208
City Gas Co. of Baltimore 502
City Guards 854
City Hall 179, 212
City Horse Guards 770
City Hospital 738, 748, 823
City Hotel at Annapolis 904
City Library 667
City Mills 216
City of Baltimore Association No. 2 510
City Passenger Railway Company 182, 183, 278, 757
City Point 146
City Reform Association 787
City Spring 213, 287, 834
City Trust 473
Civil Rights Bill 499
CLABAUGH, E. A. 465, 851
CLACKNER, Joseph 796
CLAGETT, Hezekiah 797
  Joseph L. 745
  Levi 95, 269
  Samuel A. 193
  Zachariah 741
Clagett, Hez. & Son 438
CLAGGETT, --- 521
  ---, Bishop 520, 522, 773, 911
  Charles 797
  Eli 461
  Hezekiah 456
  Joseph 499

CLAGGETT, Thomas J. 521
  Thomas John 860
  William Brewer 796
CLAIBORNE, --- 32, 34, 39, 40
  ---, Capt. 35
Clapboard Meeting-House 868
CLAPP, L. W. 739
CLAPPER, Andrew 461
Clare Mont 705
Claremont & Farley Nursery 929
CLARIDGE, Henry 256
  Joseph S. 157
CLARK, ---, Gov. 744
  ---, Mrs. 709
  Benjamin 189
  Benjamin J. 255
  Bernhard 466, 487
  Charles 212
  Charles H. 190
  Daniel 703, 721
  David 38
  Edward L. 191, 579
  Frank P. 485
  Frederick 560
  Gabriel D. 362, 367
  George 38, 797
  George B. 896
  George R. 364
  H. D. 591
  Henry 447
  J. B. 441
  James 118, 190, 249, 446, 484, 797, 850
  James C. 303
  James R. 441, 466, 484
  John 274, 462, 466, 577, 692, 796, 882
  Joseph 246, 251, 252
  Levin P. 218
  Lucretia E. 555
  Mathew 549
  Matthew B. 463
  Nelson 797
  Nelson, Mrs. 564
  P. R. 301
  Ray S. 796
  Sophia 596
  Stephens 797
  T. S. 579
  William 311, 312
  William H. 796
  William R. 790
  Wilson, Mrs. 556
Clark Combination Lock Co. 510
CLARK(E), James H. 188
CLARKE, ---, Mr. 682, 781
  ---, Mrs. 47
  Barnibe 65
  Charles L. 194
  Daniel 796
  James 70, 169, 246, 298, 452, 820

CLARKE, James C. 820
  James H. 89, 246, 667
  James R. 149
  John 592
  John S. 693, 695
  John Sleeper 695
  Jonathan 100
  Joseph F. 636
  Powhatan 229
  Samuel F. 233
  W. B. 611
  William B. C. 797
  William F. 536, 538
Clarke Bridge Co. 425
CLASSEY, James 256
Classical & English Seminary 233
CLAUSS, Joseph 542
CLAVY, James L. 157
CLAXTON, ---, Mrs. 595
  Alexander 797
  Cornelius 797
CLAY, Henry 120, 122, 138, 503, 543
  Henry Mrs. 71
Clay Island 310
Clayite 625
CLAYLAND, Thomas E. 796
Clayland, Dobbin & Co. 609
Claymont 351
CLAYPOOLE, Septimus 796
CLAYTON, --- 122
  Ann 821
  James W. 796, 797
  John W. 922
  Joseph 922
  Moses 568
  S. S. 841
  Sarah 922
  Thomas S. 922
  Wells 925
CLEAVER, ---, Rev. Mr. 874
CLEMENT, Ruth 772
  Samuel 772
CLEMENTS, Adron 846
  Joshua 77
  William M. 342
CLEMM, J. 95, 269
  John R. 157
  Maria 796
  W. T. D. 832, 909
  William 82, 214, 244
CLEMMENTS, Andrew 202
CLEMMS, William 727
CLENDINEN, Jane (DASHIELL) 744
  William H. 463, 744
  William Haslett 797
CLERK, James H. 188
Clerks of Circuit Court 729
Clerks of City Courts 729
Clerks of Court of Common Pleas 729

Clerks of Superior Court 729
CLEVELAND, A. J. 673
  H. W. 502, 508
  Henry W. 505
CLEVER, C. 572
CLIFF, ---, Mr. 263
CLIFFE, George 659
  Henry 690
Clifford 907, 908
CLIFFORD, Jennie 688
Clifton 231, 232, 277, 834, 842, 926, 930
CLIFTON, ---, Mr. 317, 403, 687, 694
  Arthur 673
  James 102
CLINE, Christian 252
CLINGHAM, William 555
Clinical Society 739
CLINTON, DeWitt 715
Clipper Mill 837, 870
Clipper Mills 275, 409, 836
Clipper Park 836
CLODDIS, Joseph 249
CLOKE, James 191
CLOPPER, --- 214
  Andrew 77
  Peter 592
CLOUD, Charles 617
  Charles F. 256, 615, 630, 728
  Jessie 797
  R. 617
  Robert M. 615, 630
Cloud & Pouder 616
CLOUSE, John Baptist 540
Clover Hill 64, 896
CLUNET, Victor 487
CLUTZ, Jacob A. 570
Clymalira M.E. Church 908, 909
COAKLEY, George W. 914
  P. H. 480
COAL, Samuel Stringer 432
Coal Run 345
COALE, ---, Mr. 612
  ---, Rev. Dr. 828
  Abraham G. 189
  Cassandra (CORSE) 930
  E. J. 672, 680
  E. P. 613
  Edmund J. 399
  Edward J. 58, 247, 265, 266, 593, 616, 797
  George B. 484
  George H. 675
  Isaac 488, 603, 826
  Isaac, Mrs. 604
  James Carey 195, 303, 304, 441, 466, 488, 494, 826
  James Cary 495
  James J. 548
  John 797

COALE, John H. 157
  Rachel 554
  S. S. 730, 733
  Samuel Stringer 74
  Susan 930
  Thomas 149, 170, 291, 519, 554
  William 730, 797
  William A. 828
  William E. 127, 157, 826
  William Elias 826
  William R. 624, 635
Coale, E. J. & Co. 613
Coale, Isaac P. & Bro. 149
COATES, John 466, 757, 796
  L. R. 739
Coates & Glenn 262
COATS, George W. P. 368
  John 65
  Michael 575
COBB, Daniel 313, 439
  Howell 847, 894
COBERTS, Jacob 571
COBURN, Thomas 191, 194
COCHRAN, ---, Mr. 262
  Charles 797
  James E. 386
  Morris 796
  S. M. 194
  Samuel H. 193
  T. J. 386
  Thomas J. 125, 385, 796
  William H. 797
Cochran & Co. 386
COCHRANE, ---, Admiral 88
  Alexander 111, 112
  John S. 157
  S. M. 465
  William 77
COCKBURN, --- 85, 87, 88
  ---, Admiral 85, 86, 87, 90, 642
COCKE, James 265, 266, 735, 736, 737, 742, 797
COCKEY, ---, Mr. 844
  Anna Olevia 843
  Charles 796, 817, 843
  Charles F. 842
  Charles Thomas 843, 844
  Edward 71, 76, 195, 728, 819
  Edward A. 843, 866
  Edward Augustus 843
  Elizabeth (FOWBLE) 867
  Elizabeth (SLADE) 843
  Ellen 843
  George B. 902
  J. C. 189
  J. F. 879
  J. G. 817
  John 54, 55, 56, 71, 72, 74, 515, 797, 843, 861
  John C. 817
  John G. 466

COCKEY, John T. 797
Joseph 852
Joseph F. 797
Joshua 867
Joshua F. 812, 814, 877
Joshua F. C. 879
Mary 797
Mary Ann (WORTHINGTON) 843, 864
Mary F. 852
Prudence (GILL) 843
Ruth 862
Sarah 843
Susan 70
Susannah D. (BROWN) 843
Thomas 55, 128, 861
Thomas B. 63, 843, 864
Thomas Beal 843, 844
Thomas Beale 843
Thomas Deye 797, 819
Thomas R. 869
Urath 843
Urath (COCKEY) 843
Urath (OWINGS) 843
Urith 843
Urith (COCKEY) 843
Urith (OWINGS) 843
Urith Cromwell 843
William 519, 843, 857
William Brown 843
William H. 902
Cockey Family 858, 877
Cockeysville 13, 19, 20, 30, 55, 64, 130, 178, 346, 347, 628, 790, 817, 818, 873, 876, 877, 878, 879, 880, 884, 891, 893, 900
Cockeysville Lodge No. 80, I.O.O.F. 874
COCKRAN, F. S. 787
S. Morris 152
COCKRILL, James J. 750, 796
Thomas 246
CODLING, John 813
Codorus Mills 346
COELKE, ---, Capt. 298
COFFAY, John F. 191
Coffee House 392, 606, 681
COFFIN, ---, Mrs., Capt. 577
G. A. 576
William H. 225
COFIELL, N. Frank 869
COGGESHALL, --- 107, 112
COGGINS, Harry 157
Thomas 153
Cogley's 342
COHEN, B. I. 672, 680, 850
Benjamin I. 253, 439, 480, 688, 796, 797
Benjamin L. 797
Bernard 841
E. P. 440

COHEN, Israel 245, 480, 481, 675, 697, 796
J. I. 190, 192, 240, 241, 439, 484, 890
J. J. 672
Jacob I. 113, 188, 189, 254, 343, 479, 483, 501, 796
James I. 349
Joshua I. 120, 659, 824
Joshua T. 745
Kitty 797
Mendes I. 194
Mendez 483
Mendez I. 254, 796
Moses 841
Cohen, Messrs. & Brothers 479
COIT, C. P. 829
COKE, --- 726
---, Bishop 575
Thomas 574
COKER, Abner 797
Cokesbury College 575, 679
COLBURN, ---, Dr. 521
A. W. 746
Cold Harbor, Battle of 897
Cold Spring 907
Cold Spring Hotel 361, 369
COLE, --- 208
---, Capt. 103, 104
---, Dr. 565
---, Mr. 615, 616
A. G. 486
Abraham 120
Abraham G. 189
Abraham S. 462
B. F. 256
Benjamin F. 813
C. M. 189
Charles R. 880
Edwin 424
Elizabeth 883
George 797
George B. 471, 484
Isaac 564, 874, 905
Jeanette 834
John 672, 673
L. M. 342
Mollie P. 877
Roswell L. 348
Samuel 250, 797
Samuel S. 732
Sarah (PRICE) 883
T. 102
Thomas 48, 49, 102, 246, 592, 883, 884
W. D. 855
W. H. 191
William 38, 193, 253, 298, 439, 483
William E. 63, 124, 189, 787
William H. 189, 497, 498, 550, 624, 796

COLE, William J. 189
  William P. 161, 797, 855, 866
  William R. 508
Cole Family 843
Cole's Addition 49
Cole's Harbor 48, 49, 50, 54, 56, 57, 59, 203
Colegate's Creek 926
COLEMAN, ---, Mr. 362
  ---, Rev. Mr. 865, 911
  C. R. 458
  Erastus 515
  F. W. 515
  George 911
  George A. 178, 194, 367
  John 797, 861, 911, 920
  Joseph 261
  R. B. 515, 516
  Robert H. 740
  Thomas 861
Coleman, Nicholas & Co. 433
Coleman & Stetson 516
Coleman & Taylor 427
COLES, William P. 596
COLFAX, Schuyler 147
COLGATE, Charles E. 157
  Clinton G. 508
  John 57
  Richard 55, 57, 818, 819, 921
  Thomas 57
COLLANE, John 759
College of Dental Surgery 801
College of Medicine of Maryland 736
College of Physicians 738
College of Physicians & Surgeons 738, 751
College of St. James 180
COLLET, John 48
COLLETT, John 814
  Nicholas R. 877
  Stephen 871
COLLEY, John W. 178
COLLIER, George 78
COLLINGS, Robert 102
Collington 354
COLLINS, ---, Capt. 84
  ---, Mr. 432
  J. A. 576
  James 343
  James L. 465
  S. 189, 192
  Sally N. 854
  Samuel 818
  Stephen 194, 547, 658, 659
  William 95
  William E. 194
  William H. 128, 138, 191, 691
  William Handy 797
COLLISON, William 153
COLMAN, ---, Rev. Mr. 589

COLONEY, J. B. 796
  Josiah B. 157
Colonial Spring 275
Colored M.P. Church 584
Colored M.P. Israel Church 584
Colson's Glue-Factory 422
COLSTOCK, S. A. 837
COLSTON, Frederick M. 476
COLT, ---, Mr. 507
  R. C. 393
  R. L. 437
  Rosswell L. 298
  Roswell L. 316, 343, 438, 470, 547, 796
COLTON, ---, Mr. 363
  Cora Lee 635
  Elizabeth (MOORE) 634
  George 194, 200, 210, 634, 635
  Hannah More 635
  John 634
  Luther F. 635
  Lydia Jane (HAMILTON) 635
  Wesley Hamilton 635
  William 189, 190, 193, 251, 601, 796
Columbia 816
Columbia Building Association No. 5 510
Columbia Street M.E. Church 577
Columbian College 556
Columbian Democrat 616
Columbian Fire Company 240, 241, 242, 251, 484, 583
Columbian Riflemen 668
Columbian University 556, 562
COLUMBUS, Christopher 277, 887
Columbus Statesman 619
COLVER, Stephen 797
COLVIN, --- 718, 841
  Daniel 735, 796
  Patrick 796
  Rachael 233, 254
  Richard 247, 796
Colvin Institute for Girls 233
COMEGYS, C. 249
  Cornelius 89
  E. Glanville 936
  John 265, 266, 736, 797
  John G. 252
  William 249
COMFORT, ---, Mr. 576
COMLY, ---, Mr. 842
Commercial, The 638
Commercial & Farmers' Bank 450, 451, 805, 852
Commercial & Farmers' National Bank 451, 461, 469
Commercial Bank of Baltimore 473
Commercial Buildings 497
Commercial Calendar 613
Commercial Chronicle 615

Commercial Chronicle & Daily Marylander 615
Commercial College 799
Commercial Exchange Co. 515
Commercial Fire Company 244
Commercial Mutual Building Association 510
Commercial Register 629
Commercial Savings Institution 473
Committee of Health 733
Committee of Observation 765, 910
Committee of Observation for Baltimore County 844
Committee of Vigilance & Safety 770
Communicator 636
Companion 608
Companion & Weekly Miscellany 616
COMPTON, Barnes 825
 John 244
 Robert 560
 William E. 146
COMSTOCK, ---, Judge 434
CONAIN, Louis 796
CONANT, Catharine 430
 Sallie (WINSLOW) 430
 Samuel W. 430
CONARD, Annie C. (CORSE) 930
 Calvin 930
CONAWAY, Carvel 241
Concert Hall 667, 680
Concordia German Assoc. 695
Concordia Opera-House 496, 695, 841
Concordia Society of Baltimore 510
CONDEN, James 737
CONDIFF, William 303
CONE, --- 684
 J. M. 889
 Joseph 254, 888
 Joseph M. 362
 Spencer H. 555, 613
Conewago Falls 343
Congreave Family 774
Congress Hall 432, 514
CONGREVE, William 774
CONINE, A. B. 576
 W. C. 207
 W. C., Mrs. 276
 William C. 796
CONKLIN, William H. 463
CONKLING, John A. 818
 W. H. 303
 William H. 485, 548, 796
CONN, Daniel 84, 89, 188, 202, 459
 Hugh 544
 Martin 815
 William 191
 Connecocheague 82

CONNELL, John 56
Connellsville Co. 337
Connellsville Railroad 337
CONNELLY, --- 30
 Daniel 526
 William Montague 637, 638
CONNER, ---, Gov. 142
 Charles A. 161
 James 120
CONNIFF, Hettie 886
Connocacheague Bank 310
CONNOLLY, Dixon 916
 Edward 484
 J. F. 189
 John B. 421
 John F. 190, 421, 796
 Michael 191, 272
CONNOR, Daniel 797
 James 877
 Michael 877
 Rebecca 797
 Robert 856
 Thomas 202
CONOLLY, John B. 178
CONOWAY, William E. 157
CONRAD, J. S. 745, 825
 Julius 605
 L. L. 370
 P. M. 856
Conrad Hill Gold & Copper Co. of N.Y. 771
CONRADI, F. A. 590
CONRADT, G. J. 673
 George M. 157
CONREY, Henry S. 830
Conrordia Club Library 667
CONROY, George 236
Conservative Churchman, The 641
Consolidated Co. 344
Consolidated Gas Co. , 501, 510
Consolidated Real Estate & Fire Insurance Co. 468, 510
Consolidation Co. 390
Consolidation Coal Co. 389
CONSTABLE, A. 463
 Albert 348, 701, 717, 718, 720, 797, 896
 Charles 58
 George 796
CONSTANCE, John 540
CONSTANTINE, Daniel 193
Constitution Lodge No. 78, I.O.O.F. 828
Constitution, The 629
Consular Convention 295
Consuls at Baltimore 195
Consumers' Mutual Gas-Light Co. 501
CONTEE, Benjamin 118
 Charles Snowden 669
 John 114

Contee's 342
Continental Hotel 152, 517
Continental Telegraph Co. 509
Convalescent, The 635
Convent of the Visitation 528, 598, 676
CONWAY, --- 687
　Fred. B., Mrs. 694
　James 149
　John N. 194, 231
　John R. 365
　Martin F. 190
　Robert 92, 252
　T. 103
　Thomas 101, 251
Conway Street 769
COOBES, James 252
COODE, John 704
COOK, ---, Capt. 361
---, Lt. 318
　A. 189
　Adolphus D. 834
　Albert S. 233
　C. E. 254
　Charles 246
　Cornelius 856
　Frederick 193
　George 850
　George T. 636
　Isaac P. 153, 154, 469, 578, 599, 728, 830, 892, 902, 933
　J. F. 191
　James H. 157, 190, 193, 194, 796
　James M. 797
　John 554, 908
　John F. 610, 796
　Richard K. 95
　S. G. B. 817
　W. 187
　W. I. 638
　William 207, 375, 559, 920
Cook, J. & Co. 614
Cook & Randall 484
Cook's Branch 854
Cook's Cotton Factory 262
COOKE, --- 521
---, Mr. 262, 684, 690
　Anthony L. 253
　George 99
　H. W. 351
　James 99
　Mary 397
　W. H. 548
　William 192, 214, 215, 216, 372, 439, 450, 452, 464, 470, 658, 797
　William H. 157
COOKMAN, Alfred 576
COOKSEY, R. K. 95, 269
COOLEY, Thomas M. 233
COONAN, J. V. 187
COONEY, P. 241

COONEY, Patrick 241, 463
COOPER, --- 686, 687
---, Brig.-Gen. 796
---, Miss 756
---, Mr. 321, 684
　Abraham S. 869
　Alfred S. 161
　Catherine (GILL) 756
　Edward K. 398
　Elizabeth 202
　G. W. 577, 579
　H. A. 190, 192
　Hannah 926
　Hugh A. 125, 126, 189, 303, 796
　Isaac 320
　J. Campbell 629
　James 876
　James M. 796
　John 38, 870, 932
　John H. 193, 194
　John H. L. 927
　John W. 157
　Lehman A. 797
　Nathan 100
　Nathaniel 100
　Nelson 815
　Peter 320, 427, 928
　S. B. 252
　S. H. 856
　S. S. 873
　Samuel 235
　Stephen 38
　Thomas 38, 192, 756, 813
　Thomas A. 255
　William 298
　William M. 442
　William O. 580
Cooper Forges 427
Cooperman, Zach. & Co. 298
COOPPENIDER, George T. 571
COPELAND, Philip D. 820
Copley 919
COPLEY, Lionel 195, 918
Copley Parish 518
COPPER, Norris 100
COPPREICE, Joseph 241
Copus' Harbor 54, 59
CORBAN, Nicholas 518
Corbett's 347
CORBIN, William 99
CORCORAN, Thomas 797
　William Wilson 769
Corcoran & Riggs 506
Corcoran Art Museum, Washington 676
CORDELL, E. F. 745, 746
　Eugene F. 742, 743
CORDEY, Thomas 919
CORIELL, Isaac 193
CORKRAN, Benjamin W. 579
　Charles 601

CORKRAN, F. S. 124
  Francis S. 127, 129, 497, 498
  William 497, 498
CORMAN, George H. 813
Corn & Flour Exchange 441, 882, 927
Corn Exchange Bank of Baltimore 459
Corn Exchange Buildings Co. 441, 443, 510
CORNEL, Ezra 503
CORNELIUS, J. W. 902
  Joseph 519
  Nicholas 797
  Richard 464
CORNELL, E. 506
  Ezra 502, 507
CORNER, ---, Mrs. 595
  George 577
  George W. 469, 580, 604, 747
  James 438, 463, 577
  James L. 439
  S. R. 442
  Solomon 470, 484
Corner Hill & Sharp Streets Building Association No. 2 510
CORNIGHAN, James 556
CORNMILLER, Philip 89
CORNTHWAIT, John 244, 252, 587, 796, 797
  Mary 796
  Thomas 251, 252
  William 241, 251
CORNWALEYS, ---, Capt. 34
CORNWALLIS, ---, Gen. 79
  Early 104
CORPONI, --- 678
Correspondent 654
CORRICK, George 817
CORRIE, --- 720
  James 261, 298, 522
  Peter 202
CORRIGAN, O. B. 841, 938
  Owen 538
CORRY, James 592
CORSE, ---, Gen. 923
  Annie C. 930
  Carrie D. 930
  Cassandra 930
  Deborah S. (SINCLAIR) 930
  Elizabeth 930
  Esther Sinclair 930
  Frank 930
  George F. 930
  Harry C. 930
  James Rigby 930
  John 930
  John M. 930
  Lucy 930
  Mary W. 930
  Robert S. 813

CORSE, Robert Sinclair 930
  Susan (COALE) 930
  William 929, 930
Corse, William & Sons 930
CORWIN, --- 122
COSKERY, ---, Father 529
  ---, Rev. Dr. 932
  ---, Vicar-General 540
  H. B. 539, 542, 544, 597, 822, 882, 938
  Henry B. 534, 938
  Henry Benedict 236, 534, 796
  Oscar J. 738
Cosmopolite, The 636
COST, John L. 157
COSTAGGINI, --- 537
COSTAGIANI, --- 539
COSTELLO, J. I. 252
COSTOLAY, Patrick J. 472
COTHUS, William H. 797
COTTERELL, Henry W. 797
Cotton Plant 809
Cotton-Press Co. 510
COUDEN, Benjamin 871
COULSON, ---, Capt. 83, 668
  ---, Madame 673
  George 249
  John 189
  John B. 157
  Thomas 82
Coulson's Glue-Factory 265
COULTER, ---, Dr. 730, 741
  Alexander 77, 357, 433, 797
  George T. 842
  Hannah Mifflin 357
  John 116, 118, 170, 173, 187, 194, 195, 461, 733, 734, 735, 742, 796, 797, 824
  Mary 595, 796
  Mifflin, Mrs. 596
COULTHARD, James 592
Council for Plantations 767
COUNCILMAN, J. B. 836
  J. T. 813, 834
  James B. 850
COUNSELMAN, J. H. 796
  Jacob 190
  Thomas H. 157
  William H. 202
County Committee of Observation 862, 863
COUREY, John F. 898
COURSEY, Henry 36
  Wesley B. 813, 936
Court-House Hill 768
Court-House Point 300
COURTENAY, A. M. 580
  David 547
  David S. 551
  Elizabeth J. 797
  Henry 797

46

COURTENAY, Hercules 70, 173,
   545, 796, 797, 885
  Mary 797
  Robert 298
  Sarah 796
  William 797
COURTNAY, Hercules 239
COURTNEY, ---, Rev. Father 892
  David 545
  E. S. 234
  Enoch S. 440, 598
  Hercules 74, 187, 482, 519, 728
  J. A. 152
  James A. 152, 157, 253
  Mary 382
  Michael 382
  Patrick 796
  Thomas 382
COUSER, S. L. M. 577
COUSIN, ---, Mr. 262
  John 263
  John M. S. 797
COUSINS, Philip 571
COUTH, William S. 759
Cove Point 309
Cove Street 548
Covenanters 549
COVER, John 355
COVINGTON, --- 85
COWAN, Alexander 921
  William H. 247
COWARD, W. 103
  William 101
COWELL, Joseph 687, 688, 690
COWEN, John K. 446, 723
COWLES, ---, Col. 576
  Henry M. 231
  Wesley 462
COWLING, Agnes Maria (ONION)
   922
  Edward 922
COWMAN, Emma 230
  John G. 449
  John P. 757
  Martha A. 757
COWPLAND, William S. 796
Cox 354
COX, ---, Miss 678
  ---, Rev. Mr. 521
  Abraham 911
  Amos 817
  C. 95, 269
  C. C. 195, 600, 624, 625
  Catherine 796
  Christopher C. 149, 157, 675
  Hester 185
  Isaac 185
  J. H. 95, 269
  James 73, 77, 244, 254, 455, 547,
   554, 779, 796
  James B. 846

COX, James E. 845
  James H. 190, 615
  John R. 190, 191, 465, 603
  Joseph 470, 917
  L. J. 442
  Larkin 249
  Louisa (GITTINGS) 917
  Luther J. 362, 441, 464, 582
  Maria 583
  Melville B. 616
  Nathaniel 194
  S. K. 586, 587
  Samuel K. 636
  Walter 264
  William T. 855
Cox & Boyce 391
Cox & Frazier 402
Cox's Creek 309
COXE, A. Cleveland 523
COXON, George 927
COY, Andrew M. 250
COYNE, Thomas 797
CRABB, Richard S. 782
CRACK, Henrietta 797, 817
CRACOCK, Ann 861
CRADDOCK, ---, Dr. 731
  ---, Rev. Mr. 730
  John 819
  Thomas 734, 815, 818
CRADOCK, ---, Dr. 862
  Agnes Walker 842
  Ann 841, 861, 864
  Ann (WALKER) 862
  Ann (WORTHINGTON) 858, 861,
   862
  Arthur 842, 860, 861, 864
  Catharine (RISTEAU) 858
  Catherine 841, 864
  Catherine (RISTEAU) 842
  Catherine Julia 842
  Elizabeth 861
  John 70, 71, 728, 842, 858, 860, 861,
   862, 864
  John C. 73
  Katharine 861, 862
  Katherine 796
  Katherine (RISTEAU) 863
  Mary 861
  Sallie (CARROLL) 842
  Stevenson 842
  Thomas 71, 223, 741, 796, 834, 841,
   842, 858, 859, 860, 861, 862, 863,
   864
Cradock Family 858
CRAFT, Charles H. 796
  J. 576
  J. C. 190
CRAFTON, Mark 192, 253
CRAGER, Peter 380
CRAGG, Mary H. 485
CRAGGS, R. 252

CRAGGS, R. D. 241
  Robert 241
CRAIG, J. 95, 269
  John 100
  John A. 887
  John D. 393, 667
  John T. 562
  Joseph 255
  Thomas 233
CRAIGE, Robert 101
CRAIGHILL, ---, Col. 291
  ---, Maj. 290
  W. P. 210, 289
  Craighill Channel 289, 290, 307
CRAIN, P. W. 351
CRAM, Omer P. 157
CRAMPTON, ---, Mr. 918
  S. W. 526
  Savington W. 919
  Cranberry 342
CRANCH, ---, Judge 647
CRANDALL, Adam 253
CRANE, ---, Capt. 305
  ---, Col. 624
  ---, Dr. 902
  ---, Rev. Mr. 521
  A. F. 604
  A. F., Mrs. 595
  A. Fuller 302, 600
  A. Fuller, Mrs. 595
  Andrew F. 603
  B. Frank 255
  Banjamin 796
  E. E. 240
  E. F. 558
  James C. 559, 561
  John 244
  Thomas R. 600, 817
  William 469, 559, 561, 567, 568, 796
  Craney Island 293, 310
CRAVEN, H. S. 304
CRAWFORD, ---, Dr. 741
  Alfred 797
  Francis 911
  John 734, 735, 736, 742, 797, 824
  R. K. 190
  W. H. 448
  William 281, 439, 463, 464, 466
  William A. 488
  William C. 489
  William H. 467, 577
  William J. 157
  Crawford & Berry 263
CRAY, Frederick 471
CREAGER, Francis M. 157
CREAGH, John 189
  Peter 423
CREAMER, David 616, 650
  Joshua 189
  Thomas 250, 728

CREERY, Hans 74
  William R. 272, 641, 870
  William Rufus 796
  Creery Mounment 272
  Creighton & Woodville 439
CRESAP, --- 66
  ---, Col. 859
  Michael 651
  Thomas 65
  Thomas, Col. 37
CRESSWELL, J. A. J. 494
  James 38
CRESWELL, John A. J. 145
CRICHTON, ---, Mr. 441
  W. 302
  William 155, 162, 440, 441, 442, 796
CRISE, John L. 275
  Crise Fountain 274
  Crisfield 310
CRISFIELD, J. W. 600
  John W. 145
CRISP, Richard O. 358
CRITTENDEN, J. J. 127
  John J. 122
CROCKER, Charles W. 157
  E. 152
  Emanuel 153
  Samuel G. 442
CROCKETT, Benjamin 100, 796
  J. 101
  John 45, 100
  R. 101
  Crockett & Harris 402
CROFTON, ---, Capt. 95
CROGGS, William 246
CROMER, Thomas W. 190, 366
CROMIO, A. 103
  S. 103
CROMWELL, --- 114, 115
  ---, Dr. 741
  Edith 70
  Gabriel 903
  John 55, 56, 734, 741, 753, 797, 824, 861, 862
  Joseph 288, 519, 867
  Joseph W. 864
  Mary 864
  Mary (CRADOCK) 861
  Mary (OWINGS) 862
  Nathan 38, 70, 195
  Richard 71, 74, 456, 488, 518, 728, 796, 839, 843, 862
  Stephen 72, 796, 861, 864
  Thomas 780
  Urath (OWINGS) 862
  William 71, 73, 859
  Cromwell Family 843
  Cromwell's Bridge Road 886
CRONEY, John W. 189, 190
CRONHARDT, Charles 468
CRONIMILLER, P. 252

CRONIMILLER, Philip 251
CRONIN, Martin 264
CROOK, Charles 797, 923
  Columbus S. 488
  F. A., Mrs. 596
  Frances A. 600
  Francis A. 483, 577, 596, 604
  Francis A., Mrs. 604
  Joseph 921
  Walter 246, 368, 690
  William 449
  Crook & Duff 262
  Crook's Mill 923
  Crooked Billet Wharf 311
CROOKSHANK, C. 101, 103
CROPPS, --- 720
  Mariona 202
CROSBY, Josiah 77
  Kirk 828
CROSMORE, Alfred 917
CROSS, Alexander H. 114
  Andrew B. 153, 617
  D. W. 834
  Frances E. 852
  George R. 149
  John 65, 249
  John M. 233
  Lewis 246
  R. J. 486
  Richard 262
  Richard J. 189
  Thomas 814
  Trueman 114
  Valentine 870
  William H. 202
Cross Street M.E. Church 580
Cross Street Market 207, 339
CROUCH, David 157
  Elizabeth 582
CROUT, H. 191
  Hezekiah 190, 191, 796
  John E. 815, 855
CROW, John T. 797
  Mary E. (OWENS) 797
CROWDER, ---, Mr. 758
  John 759
CROWE, A. D. 551
  John 346
CROWLEY, ---, Mr. 362
  F. C. 126, 219
  Frederick C. 194
  W. S. 362, 365
  William S. 190, 193, 796
Crowley, Hobitzell & Co. 219
Crownsville 342
CROWTHER, Isaac 813
  John 813, 877, 879
CROXALL, ---, Mr. 571
  C. 224
  Charles 768, 796
  James 71

CROXALL, L. 77
  Richard 796
  Robert 424
  Thomas 77
Crozer Theological Seminary 566
CROZIER, John R. 847
CRUMP, Alfred 253
CRUSE, Christopher 796
  Engelhard 767
  Henry 202
  Henry Stansbury 797
  Jacob 796, 797
  Mary 770, 797
  P. H. 680
  Peter H. 609, 680
  Peter Hoffman 642, 652
  Rosina 796
CRUTCHFIELD, ---, Col. 671
  A. F. 635, 639
  S. 670
  Crutchfield Bros. 637
Crystal Coal Oil-works 265
Cub Hill 916, 921
CUDDY, Michael 535, 796
CUGLE, ---, Mr. 515
  Edwin 797
  John 488
  Cugle & Frost's Inn 513
  Cugle's Tavern 207
Cugly 743
CULBERTSON, Cyrus D. 157
CULBRETH, M. R. 449
CULLEY, Langly B. 255
Culley's Ship Yard 293
CULLIMORE, William 690
  William H. 157
CULLINGS, Nelson 820
CULLINGTON, Anna 834
  James 688
CULLUM, John 189
CULLY, L. B. 394
Culturist, The 628
Cumberland 342, 792
Cumberland & Pennsylvania
  Railroad 389, 390
Cumberland Academy 721
Cumberland Bank 450
Cumberland Bank of Alleghany 310
Cumberland Railroad Co. 344
Cumberland Street Baptist Church,
  Norfolk, Va. 556
Cumberland Valley Railroad 345
CUMMING, James 77
CUMMINGS, J. 627
  J. P. 194
  John 877
  Robert 71
  S. H. 579, 641
CUMMINS, ---, Bishop 525
  Alexander 463
  George D. 274, 522

CUMMINS, George L. 222
  J. P. 256
  John P. 255, 256
  Jonathan P. 157, 796
Cummins' Memorial P.E. Reformed 525
CUMMISKEY, Eugene 796
CUMMISKY, Eugene 190
CUNINGHAM, George A. 190
CUNNINGHAM, Briggs S. 446
  D. H. 101
  George A. 190
  George W. 193
  J. E. A. 889
  James 251, 537, 538
  John 459, 592
Cunningham Hall 525
CUREAU, Richard 482
CURLETT, John 467, 469, 599, 604, 697
  John G. 272
CURLEY, ---, Mr. 678
  Henry R. 187, 462
  James 188, 194
  Joseph H. 465
  William E. 830
Curley, James W. & Co. 852
CURRAN, James 222
CURREY, James H. 157
  Samuel 797
CURRY, Jackson 908
  James H. 745, 746
  Margaret 771
CURSON, R. 101, 678
  Richard 102, 679
Curson, R. & Co. 102
CURTAIN, Thomas 188
CURTEAN, Thomas 463
CURTICE, James 463
CURTIN, ---, Gov. 129, 789
CURTIS, Alfred A. 534
  John 867
  Levi 813
  Samuel 911
  William 555, 816
  William H. 820
Curtis' Creek 375, 937
Curtis' Creek Iron-Works 425
CUSHANE, John 740
CUSHING, --- 122
  Caleb 127
  David 271
  F. W. 350
  John 252, 258, 263, 471, 484
  Joseph 128, 188, 194, 225, 254, 439, 470, 596, 796, 797
  Joseph M. 195, 471
  Richard C. 157
  Wiley E. 604
CUSHMAN, Charlotte 691, 693
CUSTER, Charles S. 149

CUSTIS, ---, Mr. 849
  Daniel Parke 743
  Francis 707
  George Washington Parke 82
  Peggy 743
  Wilson Parke 743
Custom-House 496
CUTAIAR, Francis 288
CUTLER, Pliny 928
CUTTING, John 396
CUYLER, J. M. 360
  R. L. 368
Cylburn 773
CYPHUS, --- 202
Cypress Point 358
CYTMIRE, Chris. 37
CZACKERT, Peter 540
CZVITKOVICZ, Alexander 540
D'Arbel & Co. 425
D'ARCY, --- 425
  Henrietta 770
  Maria 770
D'Arcy & Didier 439
DABNEY, Frederick 669
DADE, ---, Maj. 887
DAGG, ---, Dr. 567
DAGGETT, ---, Bishop 586
  D. S. 587
DAIGER, M. A. 190
DAIL, Daniel 240, 241
DAILEY, Jesse 870
Dailey, Massey & Maupin 263
DAILY, ---, Mr. 261
  George 550
  George W. 637
  Jesse 814
  S. T. W. 577
Daily Advertiser 796
Daily American Times 629, 630
Daily Argus 615
Daily City Item, The 628
Daily Evening Chronotype 636
Daily Evening Gazette 625
Daily Exchange 631, 632, 633
Daily Gazette 633
Daily Globe 630
Daily Intelligencer 616
Daily Laborer, The 636
Daily Morning News, The 629
Daily Press 629
Daily Register, The 630
Daily Republic 630
Daily Republican 615
Daily Workingman, The 641
DALCHO, Frederick 432, 732
DALE, Edward C. 349
  J. McGrego 911
  John 921
DALL, Austin 488
  Carrie H. 202
  James 452, 454, 470, 589, 798, 828

DALLAHIDE, Francis 818, 819
DALLAM, E. B. 440
  F. J. 189
  Francis I. 189
  Francis J. 483
  H. Clay 195, 210, 494, 831
  J. Wilner 798
  John 411
  Richard 921
  William 814, 921
DALLAS, G. M. 122
Dallas Street M.E. Church 575, 580
DALLEY, Jacob 262
DALLUM, Francis J. 798
DALRYMPLE, E. A. 523, 654, 828
  John 247, 433
  William F. 471, 797
  William H. 797
DAME, William M. 524
DAMER, Thomas Staford 673
DAMERTE, John 102
DAMES, Charles 817
DAMMANN, F. William 472
  William F. 472
DAMPHOUX, ---, Father 235
  Edward 235, 236, 798
  J. B. L. E. 536
DAMPMAN, William 922
Dan's Mountain 388
DANABURG, Philip 149
DANAKER, John J. 188
  O. A. 193
Dancing Assembly Rooms 594
DANDERS, Benedict J. 188
DANEKER, John F. 157
  John J. 728
  William H. 157
DANELS, Bolivar D. 194, 728
  John D. 797
DANENHAUER, Henry 542
DANESON, William 246
DANIEL, ---, Dr. 749
  J. Townsend 157
  John D. 112
  O. 102
  William 195
DANIELS, Cassandra W. 902
  L. D. 250
  Walter 902
DANNELS, Bolivar D. 797
  J. D. 798
DANSKIN, Wash. A. 592
  Washington A. 157
DANT, Knowles 65
Danville, Hazelton & Wilkesbarre Railroad 345
Danville Theological Seminary 550
DARBY, Benjamin 577, 797
  Benjamin F. 578
  D. 102
  John 65

DARBY, Philip 448
  Robert 38
DARE, G. H. 745
  George H. 746
DARLEY, --- 682
  Moses 70
Darley Hall 49
Darley Park 536, 817, 932
DARLINE, Moses 520
DARLING, F. T. 194
  Henry 187
Darlington 930
Darlington Court House 897
Darly Hall 168
Darly Park 370
DARNALL, Eleanora 527
DARNELL, Henry 103
Dartmouth, Nelson & Co. 637
DASH, John M. 253
DASHIEL, J. F. 128
DASHIELL, Alice 522
  Alice Ann 744
  Benjamin 101
  C. 103
  Eleanor Virginia 744
  George 522, 592, 744
  George W. 298
  George Washington 744
  Henry 298, 744
  James 744
  Jane 744
  Jane (RENSHAW) 744
  John H. 152
  Joseph 100, 744
  Julius 920
  Levin 592, 744
  Louisa Maria 744
  Louisa T. 744
  Louisa Turpin (WRIGHT) 744
  Mary 298
  Mary (LEEKE) 744
  Mary Leeke 744
  Matilda D. 744
  May Leeke 744
  Nicholas Leeke 744
  R. 102
  R. L. 576
  Robert 99, 103, 744
  Thomas 744
  William 730
  William Augustine 798
DASKIN, Michael 921
DAUGHERTY, Thomas 580
DAUSCH, Michael 539
DAUSHIN, W. A. 262
DAVENPORT, ---, Miss 693
  A. H. 694
DAVEY, ---, Capt. 112
  A. W. 261, 432
  Alexander W. 76
  Hugh 798

DAVEY, William 312
DAVID, ---, Father 535
  John B. 234
  David Reus Permanent Loan &
    Savings Co. 510
  David's Fancy 49, 50, 59
DAVIDGE, ---, Dr. 753
  ---, Prof. 748
  F. H. 660, 665, 675
  Francis H. 192, 609, 613, 615, 629, 680, 798
  John B. 735, 736, 737, 742
  John Beale 735
  John Beall 798
DAVIDSON, Andrew 432
  Henry J. 502
  J. 102
  James 95, 741
  John 798
  R. C. 412
  William 298, 463
  William J. 397
Davidson, John & Co. 101
DAVIE, ---, Mr. 296
  Allen J. 616
DAVIES, ---, Col. 113
  ---, Mayor 113
  Daniel 616
  J. C. 680
  J. G. 680, 850
  Jacob G. 120, 123, 187, 205, 288, 439, 493, 680, 798, 850
Davies & Fulton 433
DAVIS, --- 34
  ---, Dr. 741
  ---, Mr. 323, 558, 652
  A. Bowie 847
  Alfred H. 253
  Allen Bowie 846
  Augustus G. 509
  Charles S. 241
  D. 95, 269
  Daniel 559, 560
  David 95
  Edwin R. 194
  Elder 558
  Elijah 741
  Eliza J. 231
  Ella V. (MOWELL) 880
  Frank E. 207, 579
  Fred. 255
  Frederick 255
  George A. 178, 189, 190, 193, 471, 797
  George L. L. 651
  George Lynn Lackland 797
  Hannah 772
  Henry 525, 834, 836, 855
  Henry G. 389, 830

DAVIS, Henry Winter 127, 132, 133, 142, 145, 146, 400, 498, 499, 719, 775, 787, 798
  J. G. 394
  J. N. 902
  Jacob C. 217
  James Stewart 99
  Jarrett 841
  Jefferson 140
  John 213, 216, 252, 298, 553, 554, 797
  John C. 342
  John F. 190
  John W. 136, 157, 194, 198, 199, 200, 242, 342, 604, 728, 729
  Laura 871
  Noah 568
  Phineas 322, 326, 343, 798
  Robert W. 790
  S. 102
  Samuel 544
  Sturgis 820
  T. Sturgis 905
  Thomas H. 157
  William 251, 838, 921
  William H. 157
Davis, Mayer & Co. 389
Davis & Gartner 322
Davis' Flour-Mills 817
DAVISON, William 488
DAWES, James 456, 459, 798
  Rufus 613, 647
  Samuel 264
DAWN, Edward 817
DAWNES, Jesse 741
DAWSON, ---, Capt. 108
  Frederick 348
  John 65
  Joseph 101
  Joseph M. 695
  Philemon 798
  Philip 452
  Thomas 65
  William 592, 798
Dawson, William & Co. 372, 438
DAY, Edward 921
  Elizabeth 920, 922
  Gideon 577
  H. J. 584
  Horace H. 508
  Ishmael 148, 797, 798, 922
  John 921
  Mary 655
  Nicholas 45, 920
  O. F. 551
  Samuel 920
  Stanley 638
  W. Y. 923, 925
Day Star 717
Day's Church 910
DE BALL, William 814

DE BAR, Ben 689, 696
DE BLEQUER, J. Benel 102
DE BUTTS, Elisha 736, 737, 742, 753, 798, 845
  G. 733
DE CARNAPS, James 432
  Jasper 432
DE CASTRO, Paul 715
DE CHARLIER, Charles L. 157
DE CORSE, Alphonso 929
De Courcey Family 843
De Courcy Family 717
DE COURSEY, W. H. 847
DE DYCKER, John 541, 542
DE FORD, Charles D. 798
DE FORREST, Gussie 688
DE GARMENDIA, C. G. 302
DE GHEQUIER, A. 397
DE GOEY, William 363, 364, 366
DE GRASSE, --- 769
---, Admiral 80
DE HAAS, A. P. 433
DE KALB, --- 769
---, Baron 274
DE LA CORTE, A. 195
DE LA LAUM, Arne 80
DE LA ROCHE, George F. 298
DE LA ZOUCH, ---, Sailing Master 91
DE LACERE, ---, Miss 708
---, Monsieur 708
DE LAMAR, Jose 237
DE LAUZUN, ---, Duke 80
DE LEON, ---, Messrs. & Co. 636
DE LOUGHERY, Susannah 798
DE LOUGHREY, Edward 189
DE MARCHI, Joseph 539
DE MEZOLLA, E. 195
DE MURGUINDO, P. 155
DE MURGUIONDO, Prudencio 195
DE NEUVILLE, --- 676
DE PERRIGNY, George 658
DE ROCHAMBEAU, ---, Count 80
DE RONCERAY, ---, Mr. 673
DE ROSE, Edward 390
DE SELDEN, --- 694
DE SOUZA, Sully 195
DE VALIN, Laura V. 229
DE VERE, William T. 158
DE VRIES, --- 33
De Witt's Coffee-house 169
DE YOUNG, John 911
DEAGLE, Simon 592, 798
DEAKINS, William 298
DEAL, Charles 798
DEALE, James F. 191
DEAN, Edwin 693
  Julia 693
  William 125, 140, 162, 193, 797
  William A. 210
DEANE, ---, Capt. 77

DEANS, ---, Rev. Mr. 816, 859
  Hugh 909, 910, 920
DEARDORFF, Elizabeth 852
DEARING, John 48
  Redman 56
DEAVER, Emanuel K. 253
  John 70, 225, 244
DEBARK, T. 102
DEBOIS, James 565
DEBRULER, ---, Mr. 921
DEBRUTON, William 921
DEBUS, Henry 836
Decatur Street 769
DECKER, Frederick 728
  George 89, 172, 187, 216, 247, 393, 456, 461, 470, 569, 826
DECKMAN, E. J. 566
Declaration of Rights 707
Decorative Art Society of Baltimore 675
DEEMS, Hugh 920
  Jacob 92, 207, 253, 667
  James M. 157, 666, 673
Deep Point 60, 171
Deep Run 311
Deer Creek 526, 816, 871, 898, 909
Deer Creek Hundred 812
Deer Park 342
DEFORD, B. F. 404
  Benjamin 128, 302, 394, 403, 404, 466, 550, 603, 797, 798
  Thomas 404, 447, 448, 458, 473
DEGEN, A. V. 605
DEGGES, William H. 114
DEIBEL, George 605
  Hy. 605
DEIBLE, Peter 465
DEITCH, John 70
  Lewis 550
DEITER, Jacob 432, 569
DELACOUR, James 545, 547
DELANTY, William 190
DELANY, Daniel 904
Delaplaine's Repository 648
DELAPORTE, Elizabeth 798
  Frederick 798
DELAROCHE, Paul 675
Delaware, Lackawanna & Western Railroad 345
Delaware & Hudson Canal Co. 391
Delaware & Maryland Railroad 348
Delaware College, Newark 865
Delaware Hundred 70, 71, 812, 859
Delaware Junction 351
Delaware Railroad 357
DELISLE, M. 104
Dell, The 275
DELLINGER, Adolphus 253, 776
  Catharine (MC MURRAY) 776
DELOUEL, ---, Father 536
DELOUL, ---, Father 235, 236

DELOUL, Lewis Regis 236
  Louis Regis 235
DELOZIER, Daniel 497, 498, 798
Delphian Club 612, 613, 642, 643,
  644, 649, 712, 765
DELPRAT, John C. 372
DELPRATT, John C. 439
Delta 359
DELTERER, Anna 485
  George Philip 485
DEMARE, --- 102
DEMENT, ---, Lt. 670
  William F. 669
Dement's Battery 897
DEMITT, Richard 798
Democratic Herald 617
Democratic Sentinel 627
DEMONDIDIES, ---, Mr. 518
DEMOSS, John 911
DEMPSEY, Owen 453
DENHAM, G. W. 688
DENIER, Lydia 688
DENISON, A. W. 165
  Andrew 493
  Andrew W. 157, 797
  Charles W. 627
  I. M. 365
  Isaac M. 193
  John M. 142, 256, 798
  Marcus 126, 152, 153, 193, 194,
    484, 797
  Robert 137
DENKIN, William N. 798
DENMEAD, Abram 247
  Adam 128, 222, 247, 303, 364, 365,
    485, 667, 798
  Talbot 797
  Talbott 303, 524, 600
Denmead, A. W. & Son 150
Denmead, W. Iron-Foundry 212
Denmead Wharf 293
DENNIS, George R. 847
  Henry 101, 525
  Jacob 798
  Littleton 313, 709
  Oliver 190
  Peter 525
DENNISON, R. M. 903
  Robert M. 820
  T. H. 870
  William 147
Dennison Post No. 8, G.A.R. 837
DENNY, Elizabeth 863
  Israel 202, 799
  James W. 231
  R. A. 439
  William 252
DENSON, Isaac M. 192, 195, 205,
  364, 368
  Isaac N. 255
DENT, John F. 721

DENT, Mary 397
  William H. 742
Deptford 70
Deptford Fire Company 240, 241,
  242, 246, 247, 484
Deptford Hundred 169, 171, 172
Der Demokratische Whig 625, 626
Der Deutsche Correspondent 625,
  626, 627
DERALIN, Hugh 246
DERAMPLE, John 519
DEROME, --- 675
DESHON, ---, Mr. 86
  C. 438, 470
  Christopher 592
  Daniel 100
DESK, M. 95, 269
Despard Coal Co. 389
DESPEAUX, Joseph 798
  Joseph P. 158
DEVENEY, John 158
DEVERE, William 255
DEVINE, George W. 534
DEVON, William H. 237
DEVRIES, Christian 414, 448, 455,
  456, 487, 489
  H. O. 855
  Harry 414
  William 128, 155, 205, 414, 797, 846,
    847, 851
  William R. 414
Devries, William & Co. 409, 410,
  414, 868
Devries Stephens & Thomas 263
DEVRIESE, William 368
DEW, James C. 84, 249
Dewee Family 899
DEWEY, Orville 590
DEWLEY, ---, Capt. 106
DEXTER, Charles H. 158
DEYE, Penelope 519
  Thomas Cockey 38, 69, 70, 71, 72,
    75, 76, 194, 798, 819, 821, 863
Deye Family 843, 862
DIBELIUS, Franz 605
DICK, A. D. 902
  Thomas 38
  William 224
DICKENS, Charles 695
DICKER, Frederick 70
Dickerson 342
DICKEY, Charles E. 368
  W. J. 820
  William A. 828
  William J. 828, 829
DICKINSON, A. E. 563
  Bittingham 798
  Brittingham 76, 519
  Daniel S. 147
  Edward 246
  John S. 442

54

DICKINSON, Mary, Sister 599
 S. 301
 William 498
Dickinson College 577
DICKMEYER, Christian 870
DICKSON, ---, Dr. 547
 ---, Rev. Dr. 546
 C. 155, 600
 Cyrus 549
 I. N. 855
 Isaac N. 488
 J. N. 855
 John 246
 John T. 746
 Thomas 84, 101, 192, 432, 459, 547, 734
 Dickson Family 588
DIDIER, --- 425
 Edmund 536, 537, 538
 Henry 461, 798
 Henry A. 489
Die Gartenlaube 655
Die Geschaeftige Martha 625
Die Katholische Volks-Zeitung 640
DIEFFENBACH, C. H. 740
DIEHL, ---, Mr. 631
DIELMAN, ---, Mr. 673
 Henry 673
DIETER, --- 925
DIETZ, Charles 157
DIFFENDERFER, Daniel 798
 Michael 76, 798
 Peter 84
DIFFENDERFFER, Charles 188, 240, 241, 246, 593, 798
 Daniel 89, 246, 569
 E. 241
 John 249, 299, 439
 John A. 246, 484
 M. 572
 Michael 168, 169, 170, 192, 197, 224, 241, 244, 246, 483, 572
 O. 488
 Peter 89, 187, 246, 569, 572
 Robert C. 362
DIGGEN, Ignatius 849
DIGGS, Beverly 298, 798
 John 53
 John R. 189
 Richard H. 194
DIKE, John H. 791
Diligence 49
Diligent Line 312
DILL, Catherine 774
 Eraza 190
DILLEHUNT, John G. 193
DILLEHUNTY, ---, Lt. 318
DILLET, ---, Father 235
 ---, Rev. Mr. 235
 M. 234
DILLON, James 92

DILLON, John 250, 592
 Michael 592
DIMAN, J. Lewis 233
Dime Savings-Bank of Baltimore 469
DIMMICK, J. 141
DIMOCH, ---, Col. 669
DIMOND, Francis 628
DINGLEY, Elijah 898
DINNIES, Annie P. 628
DINSMORE, Patrick 475
DISHON, John C. 816
DISNEY, John 190, 253
 Oliver M. 190
 Owen 351
Dispatch 616
DITTMAN, John H. 158
DITTMAR, Charles 191
DITTY, C. Irving 825
DIVER, William 158
DIVERS, Ananias 923
 Anauias 921
Divers' Island 923, 925
Dividing Creek 303
DIX, ---, Gen. 137
 ---, Maj. Gen. 137
 Benjamin F. 488
 J. F. 487
 J. Franklin 466, 467, 473, 489, 550, 551
 John A. 139
DIXON, --- 201
 ---, Mr. 831
 Ann 871
 Ann (STEELE) 871
 Basil S. 358
 James 893
 James B. 456
 Jeremiah 66
 John 246
 John A. F. 190
 John B. 449
 John G. 92
 Robert 871
 Thomas 170, 194, 202, 238, 407, 727, 893
 William T. 447, 448, 466, 489
Dixon & Carson 550
DIXSON, Anthony 65
 Benjamin 65
 Thomas 733, 814
DOANE, ---, Bishop 888
 A. Sidney 506
 John 550
DOBAKER, Adam 797
DOBBIN, ---, Judge 177, 664
 Archibald 92, 798
 G. 609
 George 459, 798
 George W. 130, 195, 232, 659, 675, 717, 729, 746, 817

55

DOBBIN, Joseph T. 610
R. A. 798
Robert A. 440, 609, 610, 798, 817
Thomas 609, 610
Dobbin, Murphy & Bose 610
DOBLER, Mary 569
T. 190
DOBSON, George H. 158
J. A. 191
Susie 821
Dobson, John A. & Co. 446
DOCHEERSB, Greenbury 312
DOCWRA, Edwin H. 798
DODDRELL, James C. 403
DODGE, Augustus W. 158
 Daniel 555, 557, 560
 G. R., Mrs. 597
 George R. 136, 199, 200, 466, 469, 797
 William 846, 847
 William E. 462
DODSON, ---, Mrs. 460
 Ann 460
 John W. 158
Doe Gully 342
DOEK, George 102
DOERKSON, Jacob 573
DOGAN, Edward 37
 Frederick, Mrs. 213
DOGGETT, D. S. 636
DOHME, Charles E. 740
 Lewis 740
DOLAN, ---, Father 536
 ---, Rev. Father 933
 James 236, 529, 535, 536, 540, 601, 627, 797, 932, 938
 Lawrence 114, 798
Dolan Institute 536
Dolan's Orphans' Home 601
DOLCH, John 605
DOLFIELD, Alexander Y. 468
DOLL, --- 723
 Penfield 602, 603, 797
DOLPHIN, Francis 798
Dolphin Street Presbyterian Church 550
DOMEIER, ---, Mr. 568
Domestic Telegraph Co. 509, 510
DON, O'Connor 705
DONALDSON, --- 521
 Alexander 70, 79, 453
 Caroline 798
 Frank 701, 742, 745, 828, 899
 Gideon 54
 J. I. 463
 J. J. 298, 824
 J. L. 84
 James 592
 James Lowey 269
 James Lowry 114, 194, 798
 Jane 808

DONALDSON, John 244, 298, 665, 798
 John I. 188
 John J. 459, 659
 John Johnston 797
 John Lowry 95
 John M. 628
 John T. 189
 Joseph 547, 798
 Lowry 808
 Samuel 234
 Samuel J. 189, 298, 470, 797
 Sidnor S. 194
 Thomas 797
 William 736, 737, 742
Donaldson, Alexander & Co. 432
Donaldson & Burgee 408
DONAVAN, M. W. 191, 740
DONAVIN, M. W. 193, 194
 Matthew W. 178
DONE, John 757
 John H. 798
Donegal Presbytery 544
DONELAN, ---, Rev. Mr. 534
 J. P. 627
 John 236
 John B. 537
DONELLAN, Thomas 74, 798
DONELLY, Catharine 212
DONELSON, --- 124
DONN, J. W. 550
DONNELL, --- 521
 ---, Judge 773
 ---, Messrs. 578
 Ann 798
 J. S. 850
 James S. 798
 John 84, 215, 216, 298, 375, 437, 438, 439, 450, 461, 798
 John S. 680
 Joseph 798
 William 390
Donnell, John & Sons 279
Donnell Mansion 596
DONNELLY, --- 202
 Daniel 466, 472, 489
 James 187
DONOGHUE, William J. 158
DONOHUE, Denis 195
 James 580
DONOVAN, ---, Mr. 494
 Joseph 255
 Joseph S. 189, 798
 M. W. 495, 587
 Simpson K. 636
Donovan's "nigger jail" 633
Donovan's Slave Jail 144
DOOLITTLE, James R. 165
DORBACKER, William 798
DORGAN, Gustavus A. 484
Dorgans & Bailey's Ship Yard 293

DORITY, Joseph 101
DORNIN, ---, Commodore 139, 144, 151
DORSEY, --- 425, 707
---, Col. 46
---, Mr. 47, 299, 434
---, Prof. 737
Alexander 482
Algernon S. 158
Allan, Mrs. 155, 156
Anna 649, 650
Anna H. 628
Anne W. 640
B. J. 830
Basil 798
C. O. 856
C. S. W. 850
Caleb 424, 855
Charles S. W. 464
D. B. 616
Daniel 516
Dennis B. 581, 582
E. 826
Edward 640, 818, 860
Edwin 576
Elijah 70
Elisha 910
Elizabeth 889
Enoch 889
Ezekiel 241, 463
Flora 866
Francis 519
George W. 815
Greenbury 45, 261
James T. 193
John 44, 61, 74, 76, 80, 102, 223, 392, 425, 521, 798
John A. 797
John G. 372
John H. 254
John Hammond 757, 819, 921
Joseph 516
Josiah 100
L. W. 146
Michael 255, 262, 441
Nicholas 71, 120
Owen 233, 250, 456, 575, 814
Rebecca (WORTHINGTON) 640
Richard 245, 640, 798
Robert 74
Samuel 425
Thomas 61
Thomas B. 194, 729, 861
Thomas Baker 798
Thomas Beale 712
Vincent 921
Walter 456, 728
William H. 461, 471, 826
William P. 358
Dorsey, John & Co. 101, 102
Dorsey Family 773, 858
Dorsey's 342
Dorsey's Furnace 424
DOSH, J. H. C. 798, 830, 889, 928
Doub's 342
Double Pipe Creek 357
Double-Pumps 631
DOUD, Mark J. 793
DOUDLE, Michael 343
DOUGHADAY, John 38, 867
Richard 77
DOUGHERTY, --- 212
Benjamin F. 161
Caleb 201, 202
Charles 938
Charles M. 155, 472, 778, 840, 847, 937
Daniel 201, 202
Edward 817
J. 236, 840
J. J. C. 495
John 247, 248, 534, 539
John J. 536
M. 421
Theophilus F. 483
Dougherty & Woods 418
Doughoregan Manor 526, 534
DOUGHTERY, Adelaide 834
John G. 540
Susie 886
DOUGLAS, --- 680, 684
George 192, 438
Stephen A. 127, 846
Douglas, R. H. & W. 438
Douglas Institute 152
DOUGLASS, --- 292
---, Col. 774
---, Gen. 95
Ellen 774
R. H. 372
Richard Henry 383, 384
William 383
Douglass Institute 745
DOUTY, Joseph 101
DOVE, Milton C. 158
Dover M.E. Chapel 866
Dover M.E. Church 883
Dover Road 854, 865, 869, 883
DOWELL, Francis 253
DOWIG, George 569
DOWLING, C. 544
Edward 276, 729
DOWNES, Stewart D. 261
DOWNEY, John 191
DOWNING, ---, Mr. 217, 508
DOWNS, Abraham 872
Charles 158
Samuel 911
DOYLE, ---, Mr. 456, 685
J. 434
James 212, 236
James A. 488

DOYLE, William J. 442, 890
DRAHLEY, H. W. 365
DRAIHS, F. R. 264
DRAKE, Samuel G. 761
DRAKELEY, Henry W. 603, 797
DRAKELY, Henry W. 155, 190
DRAPER, William 730
DRECHLER, J. 597
DRESSEL, Werner 697
DREW, Frank, Mrs. 691
DREYER, W. A. 469
DRILL, ---, Mr. 354
  J. M. 604
  James M. 600, 603
DRINKHOUSE, E. J. 617
DROKENBROT, H. 597
Drovers & Mechanics' National
  Bank 451, 468, 469
DROWLEY, F. C. 190
Drug Exchange 449
Druid Hill 26, 806, 909
Druid Hill Avenue National
  Building Association 510
Druid Hill Avenue Permanent
  Building Association 510
Druid Hill Building Association No.
  2 & No. 3 510
Druid Hill Lake 274
Druid Hill Park 22, 26, 28, 31,
  132, 219, 220, 272, 273, 274, 275,
  353, 406, 697, 719, 807, 834, 842,
  853
Druid Hill Permanent Building &
  Savings Association 510
Druid Lake 219, 221
Druid Lodge No. 53, Knights of
  Pythias 837
Druid Mills 275, 409, 410, 836
Druid Park Heights 834
Drum Point 310, 358
Drum Point Harbor 359
Drum Point Railroad Co. 358
DRUMGOLE, Edward 575
Dry Tortugas 632
DRYDEN, Ann Elizabeth 801
  James 432
  Joshua 189, 190, 253, 418, 462, 576,
  797, 801
  Joshua R. 149
  Samuel 252, 263
DRYER, John H. 572
DRYSDALE, Thomas 77
DU BOISE, ---, Gen. 923
DU BOURG, ---, Father 235
  Lewis 235
  William 235
  William Valentine 234
DUBERNAT, John A. 298
DUBOIS, John 234, 235
DUBOURG, ---, Mr. 527
  ---, Rev. Father 535

DUBRENIE, ---, Vicar-General 855
DUBREUEL, F. C. 102
DUBREUIL, Armande 229
DUBREUL, ---, Rev. Dr. 538
  Joseph Paul 797
DUBRUEL, Joseph Paul 236
DUCAND, William 639
DUCATEL, ---, Prof. 628, 660, 845
  Edine 798
  Edmund 824
  Julius T. 402, 613
  Philip 740
DUCKER, Anna K. (SANDERS) 868
  George Ephraim 868
  Harry H. 868
  Harry T. 868
  J. 868
  Jeremiah 868
  Julia 868
  Julia Ann (FISHER) 868
  Ducker & Howard 868
  Ducker & Reister 868
DUCKET, --- 851
DUCKETT, --- 848
  Baruch 351
  Judson M. 816
  Kitty B. 351
  Richard I. 741
  Richard J. 741
Duddington 909
DUDROW, Charles E. 158
DUER, Adgate 836
  John 252, 459, 523, 798
  John, Mrs. 156
  Samuel 190, 193, 270, 441
  Thomas 252
DUFF, --- 684
  ---, Mr. 687
  ---, Mrs. 687
  Henry 797
  Kennedy 508
DUFFIE, Cor. R. 798
Duffield's 342
DUFFY, ---, Capt. 792
  ---, Mr. 680
DUGAN, Cumberland 89, 192, 194,
  215, 249, 298, 368, 459, 472, 798,
  938
  Cumberland, Mrs. 798
  Frederick J. 188
  George 798
  Pierre C. 600
  Dugan's Wharf 215, 263
DUGDALE, William 550, 604
DUGGAN, F. P. 887
  Francis P. 837
DUHURST, Henry P. 242, 484
  Henry P. (C.) 245
DUKE, A. W. 193
  Basil 253
  William 932

DUKEHART, ---, Mr. 484
 Henry 246, 569, 797
 J. 192
 John 188, 190, 222, 243, 244, 245, 260, 366, 484, 593, 797
 John M. 797
 Joseph K. 241
 Robert W. 797
DUKER, Otto 597
Duker, Otto & Bro. 264
DULANEY, --- 698
 Bladen T. F. 158
 Grafton L. 798
Dulan(e)y's Bridge 910
Dulan(e)y's Valley 18, 28, 30, 817, 877, 903, 904, 905, 906, 907, 911, 912, 916, 917
Dulan(e)y's Valley & Sweet Air Turnpike 912
Dulan(e)y's Valley & Towsontown Turnpike 912
Dulan(e)y's Valley Road 886
Dulan(e)y's Valley Turnpike 876, 898, 908, 913, 917
DULANY, --- 223, 703, 859
 Catherine 904
 Daniel 69, 704, 705, 706, 708, 798, 848, 904
 Grafton L. 928
 H. R. 191
 H. Rozier 191
 John M. 191
 Lloyd 904
 Mary 904, 905
 Mary (GRAFTON) 904
 Rebecca 904
 Rosier 708
 Walter 894, 904, 910, 912
Dulany Family Graveyard 904
DULHAIER, Henry 642
DULHAUER, Henry 608
DULIN, A. F. 751, 797, 842
DUMASTE 102
Dumbarton 837
Dumbarton Farm 892
DUMPHY, Richard G. 161
DUNAHUE, James 298
DUNAN, Adolphus 690
 Winfield S. 397
DUNBAR, ---, Col. 37
 ---, Dr. 660
 ---, Prof. 899
 George T. 252, 461
 J. R. U. 523
 J. R. W. 600, 624, 797
 John R. W. 751, 786
 William Graham, Mrs. 595
DUNBOYNE, ---, Lord 753
DUNCAN, ---, Rev. Dr. 672
 ---, Rev. Mr. 261
 Charles V. 158

DUNCAN, David 158, 242, 246
 J. M. 420
 James 592
 John 251, 758
 John M. 467, 549, 614, 737
 John Mason 551, 798, 854
 John McKim 122
 Joseph W. 488
 Margaret 476
 William 298
Duncan's Ship Yard 293
DUNDON, Michael 194
DUNDORE, Henry 241
DUNGAN, A. S. 934
 S. 855
DUNHAM, ---, Admiral 111
 Jacob 252
Dunham & Sons 674
DUNK, Peregrine 99
DUNKEL, ---, Dr. 735
 George A. 470
Dunkers 591
DUNKIN, J. McKim 798
DUNLAP, Albert 158
 C. Lewis 488
 Charles 165, 191
 G. W. 798
 John 605
 R. W. 548, 549
 S. B. 931
 Silas G. 550
 William 608, 798
Dunlap's Maryland Gazette 608
DUNMORE, ---, Lord 530
DUNN, Charles 207
 Clare 705
 J. 95, 269
 James 189
 Jane Bermingham (FITZ RICHARD) 705
 O'Connor 705
 Robert 38
DUNNING, Halsey 550, 797
 M. M. 149, 202
 Dunnington 797
DUNNINGTON, T. 659
 W. A. 462
 William A. 659
 William P. 372
DUNNOCK, Samuel R. 190
DUNWOODY, Robert 188
DURAND, Charles 158
Durand, James & Co. 102
DURANG, Edward F. 270
Durang Brothers 685
DURBIN, ---, Rev. Dr. 575
 John P. 443, 460
DURHAM, D. 101
DURKEE, Pearl 249
 Robert A. 624
DURLIN, Elijah S. 561

DUROCHER, Auguste H. 797
DURST, Elizabeth 155
  John W. 255
DURWIN, J. P. 576
DUSHANE, John 394, 471, 484, 516
  N. T. 128, 190, 194
  Nat. T. 190
  Nathan F. 63, 256
  Nathan T. 158, 201, 798
  Valentine 188, 189, 254, 516
Dutch Stone Church 866
Dutchess County Academy 891
DUTTON, John 189, 246
  Norris B. 158
  Robert 253, 463
DUVALL, --- 848
  ---, Mr. 225
  Charles 351
  Edmund B. 324
  Evans 879
  Gabriel 711
  Grafton 742
  Henry 191, 193, 193, 358
  Marcus 130
  Thomas H. 255
  Washington 600, 824
Dwerhagen & Groverman 298
DWYER, --- 684
  Catharine 212
DYE, Thomas Cockey 40
DYER, H. Page 488
  John M. 380
  Leon 380
  P. 855
  W. B. 252
  William 433
  William B. 91, 188
  William R. 251
Dymer's Creek 303
DYR, Phoeby 797
EADES, ---, Mrs. 604
EAGER, Ruth 863
Eager Street 769
Eager Street Building Association No. 6 510
Eagle Artillery 744
Eagle Brewery 931
Eagle Loan & Building Association 510
Eagle of Freedom 609
Eagle Rifle Corps 817
EAKIN, ---, Mr. 311
EARECKSON, Edwin 740
  Robert 125
EARLE, ---, Capt. 103
  A. B. 563
  James 101
  James T. 846, 847
  John 100
  Samuel 757
  Thomas 77

EARLEE, ---, Capt. 104
EARLEY, S. L. 281
EARLY, ---, Bishop 586
  ---, Father 540
  ---, Gen. 335, 899
  ---, Mr. 781
  ---, Rev. Father 938
  Eugene A. 194
  John 538, 882
  Samuel S. 624
EARNEST, Caleb 89
EAST, Caleb J. 830
East Baltimore German Methodist Episcopal Church 405
East Baltimore M.E. Church 575, 586
East Baltimore M.E. Church South 587
East Baltimore M.P. Church 583
East Baltimore Medical Society 739
East Baltimore Permanent Building & Land Society 510
East Baltimore Public Cemetery 934
East Baltimore Special Dispensary 739
East Hundred 812
East Monument Street Permanent Building & Savings Assoc. 510
EASTER, Charles F. 149
  Hamilton 149, 364, 370, 469, 489, 547
  Hamilton, Mrs. 602
  Ira A. 879
  J. H. 149
  John 149
  John B. 667
Easter, Hamilton & Co. 149
Eastern Avenue 926
Eastern Avenue M.E. Church 575
Eastern Avenue Methodist Church 574
Eastern Bank of Baltimore 463
Eastern Boundary Mission 526
Eastern City Spring 280
Eastern Dispensary 748
Eastern Express 386
Eastern Female High School 227, 229, 669
Eastern Fountain 213
Eastern Mechanics' Savings Institution of Baltimore 473
Eastern National Building Association No. 4. 510
Eastern Shore Railroad of Maryland 314, 357
Eastern Shore Steamboat Company 301, 510
EASTGER, Hamilton 488
EASTMAN, Arthur M. 508
  Jonathan S. 798
  L. M. 745, 746

Easton 32
Easton Landing 309
Easton's 342
Eastville Landing 310
EASY, Edward 616
EATON, --- 694
---, Capt. 620
A. H. 237
Charles J. M. 667
Charles J. W. 664
George A. 128
George N. 139, 798
George N., Mrs. 604
Harriet 475
Jeremiah 918
Eaton & Burnett's Business College 237
Eaton & Co. 637
EBAUGH, Conrad 867
Daniel 869
David A. 869
George 816
George W. 869
Sallie A. 820
Servina (FOWBLE) 867
Z. C. 870
EBELING, George W. 820
Ebenezer Baptist Church 555, 556, 559, 560, 561
Ebenezer Colored Methodist Church 581
EBENSEIN, George 929
ECCLES, John 759
Samuel 441
ECCLESTON, ---, Archbishop 236, 382, 529, 530, 534, 536, 537, 540, 541, 542, 647, 798, 835
---, Bishop 937
---, Dr. 533
---, Judge 798
Augusta C. 360
B. J. 600
John 528
John B. 360
John Bowie 717
Samuel 235, 236, 528
ECHBERGER, William 251
ECKER, Samuel 355
ECKERT, Thomas T. 509
ECKES, H. 597
ECKHARDT, William 597
Eckhart Branch Railroad 390
ECKLE, Philip P. 192
EDDIS, ---, Mr. 72
EDDY, ---, Dr. 576
T. M. 928
Thomas 837
Thomas M. 576, 798
EDEN, ---, Gov. 73, 706, 768
Robert 67, 195, 848, 851
William 380, 468, 469

Eden Street Synagogue 588
EDES, ---, Lieut-Com. 798
---, Mr. 612
Benjamin 92, 613, 614, 647, 798
EDGAR, Charles W. 158
John 931
Edgar & Fulton 689
Edgemont 356
Edgewood 351
Edgewood Colored M.E. Chapel 880
EDIE, William A. 549
Edinburg 342
Edinburgh Review 654
EDLEMANN, C. 597
Jacob 597
EDLER, J. E., Mrs. 633
EDMISTON, ---, Mr. 867
William 861, 919
EDMONDS, Samuel 465
EDMONDSON, Isaac 439
John 798
Joseph 487
T. G. 252
Thomas 279, 798
Thomas H. 659
Edmondson Avenue 871
Edmund's Well 275, 276
EDMUNDS, James R. 465
EDWARDS, E. J. 193
Elizabeth 751
J. E. 636
James 118, 169, 173, 187, 239, 247, 452, 572
John 919, 920, 927
John S. 798
Jonathan 548, 551, 590
Joseph 173
Joseph H. 798
Moses 518
Philip 592, 608
R. 271
Robert 250
Samuel 465
Tyron 551
W. B. 576
W. H. 255
W. S. 575, 839
William 189, 249, 250, 592
Edwards, R. & Co. 263
Edwards & Smith 608
EDWINSTON, William 860
EFFINGEN, John R. 579
EGERTON, A. D., Mrs. 156
A. DuBois 155
A. DuBois, Mrs. 155
C. C. 271, 372
Charles C. 250
Charles Calvert 798
Egerton & Keys' Auction Bazaar 137
EGGLESFIELD, George 552, 554

61

EGGLESTON, Joseph W. 191
W. G. 586
EHLEN, Amelia 479
  John F. 194
  John H. 463, 479
EHLER, Louis 830
EHLERS, John D. 158
  Justus H. 830
  Lewis 191, 193
EHRMAN, Charles H. 250
  Lewis 280, 468
EICHELBERGER, Albert G. 886
  Barnet 70, 196
  George M. 882
  Jacob 798
  Jesse 98, 188
  Louis 798
  Martin 249, 545, 569, 572
  Otho W. 487, 798
  William 798
  William George 798
Eichelberger Family 774
Eighth District Colored School Teachers 877
Eighth District School Teachers 877
Eighth District School Trustees 877
Eighth German American Building Association 510
Eighth Synagogue 589
EIHLER, George W. 855
EISELEN, Conrad 592
EISENBRAND, H. 152
  H. E. 246
  H. R. 246
EISENBRANDT, Christian H. 798
Eklo 870
ELBERT, Joseph Sadler 798
ELDER, ---, Mr. 302
  ---, Mrs. 595
  ---, Rev. Father 933
  Alexius 235, 236, 776, 835
  Alexius J. 534
  Alexius Joseph 236
  Allen 798
  B. S. 247
  Basil S. 247, 532, 798
  Charles 863
  F. W., Mrs. 155, 156
  George H. 834
  John 70, 860
  Ruth (HOWARD) 863
ELDERDICE, J. M. 584
ELDRIDGE, Daniel 560
Elevator, The 630
Eleventh District School Teachers 916
Eleventh District School Trustees 916
Eleventh District Teachers of Colored Schools 916
ELI, Hugh 833
ELIOT, ---, President (Harvard College) 232
  Samuel 665
Elk Neck 919
Elk River 79
Elkridge 342, 361, 839
Elkridge Landing 375, 425, 816, 936, 937
Elkton 40, 77, 351
Elkton & Wilmington Railroad Company 314
Elkton Bank 450
ELLENDER, Frederick 249
  George W. 260
ELLENGER, Jacob 469
Ellengowan 882
Ellenham 880
ELLERS, John T. 158
ELLICOTT, --- 937
  Andrew 188, 194, 224, 375, 376, 393, 425, 456, 470, 483, 798
  Andrew T. 252
  Benjamin 192, 245, 252, 386, 393, 407
  Edward T. 798
  Elias 89, 170, 172, 175, 215, 375, 438, 455, 470, 798, 826
  Evan T. 177, 193, 219, 222, 252, 354, 394, 470, 593, 785, 786, 798, 824
  George 217, 375, 434, 798
  Hannah 798
  James 89, 386, 457, 798, 826, 827
  James Brooke 375
  John 178, 310, 374, 375, 798, 847, 851
  Jonathan 215, 216, 375
  Joseph 224, 373, 374, 375, 376, 798
  Judith 798
  Nat. 252
  Nathaniel H. 816
  Samuel 798
  Thomas 205, 217, 244, 253, 298, 310, 316, 317, 393, 456, 461, 470, 826, 827
  William M. 369
  William, Mrs. 596
Ellicott & Co. 374, 375
Ellicott City 15, 24, 25, 342, 375, 376, 407, 798, 820, 821, 822, 830
Ellicott's Mills 147, 214, 217, 318, 319, 320, 321, 323, 361, 375, 770, 856, 879, 893, 894, 936, 937
Ellicott's Wharf 514
ELLINGER, Jacob 446, 468
  William 517
ELLIOT, Joseph P. 747
  Thomas 167

ELLIOTT, --- 85
---, Mr. 271, 359
A. Marshall 233
Andrew 374
E. T. 784
George 253, 871
H. A. 740
Hartman 253
Henry 254
J. 102
J. P. 441
James 872, 911
John 71, 373, 798
Joseph 101, 103, 158
Joseph H. 237
Joseph P. 232, 464
Joseph P., Mrs. 604
Robert 380, 674
Stephen 565
Thomas 168, 174, 206, 292, 361, 592, 728, 784, 872
Thomas A. 815, 908
William 226, 229, 271, 740
William L. 456
ELLIS, ---, Mr. 777, 778
Alexander B. 776
Reuben 798
Thomas 488
Ellisville 833
ELLMAKER, Amos 120
ELLSWORTH, ---, Chief Justice 296
Annie 503
H. L. 502
Elmira & Williamsport Railroad 345
ELMORE, James 380, 463
L. W. 380
ELSEY, Arnold 741
ELSROOD, Michael 889
Susannah 889
ELSWORTH, G. D. 254
ELWELL, ---, Prof. 351
ELY, --- 122
Charles W. 466
Hugh 798, 816, 819, 820
John 363, 836
Ely O'Carroll 49
Elysville 24, 25, 342, 408, 409, 477, 798, 830, 832, 833
ELZEY, Arnold 114, 798
EMACK, C. S. 353
EMBERT, John B. H. 148
Emerald 628, 646, 647, 650
Emerald & Baltimore Literary Gazette 613
EMERICH, Martin 194
EMERICK, W. H. 191
EMERSON, Arthur 582
Sarah 583
EMERY, ---, Mr. 527
E. J. 213

Emery & Co. 616
Emery Street Permanent Building & Loan Co. 510
EMICH, C. V. 449
H. F. 855
Emigsville 347
Emmanuel Episcopal Church 601
Emmanuel Evangelical Association Church 262
Emmanuel German Evangelical Lutheran Church 570
Emmanuel German Reformed Church 573
Emmanuel Lutheran Congregation Cemetery 933
Emmanuel M.E. Church 586
Emmanuel P.E. Church 523, 802, 908
Emmanuel P.E. Reformed Church 252
EMMART, Caleb 820
Gerard 813, 830
EMMENIZER, --- 924
EMMITT, Jacob 343
Emmittsburg 356, 357
EMORY, ---, Bishop 575, 798
---, Mr. 641
---, Rev. Mr. 234
Agnes S. (HALL) 915
Ann (GITTINGS) 914
D. C. H. 362, 798, 814
D. H. 903
Daniel C. H. 465
Frederick 624
J. B. 201
J. K. B. 442
John 856
John B. 465
R. 911
Richard 480, 914
Robert 443
Sabine 798
Thomas 845, 914
Thomas Hall 915
Thomas L. 188, 470
William H. 114, 465
Emory Chapel M.E. Church 868
Emory Family 907
Emory Grove Camp-Ground 854
Emory Grove Station 356, 854
Emory M.E. Church 576, 800
Empire House 263
EMSLEY, Ruth 650
Encyclopaedia Americana 648
ENDICOTT, ---, Governor 396
ENGELHARDT, H. 605
ENGLAND, ---, Bishop 529, 565
John 290, 424, 537
John H. 158
Joseph 37
Joseph H. 593

ENGLISH, ---, Maj. 65
John A., Mrs. 595
Marshal 250
Ned 65
English New Jerusalem Society 588
English-German Schools 228
ENNALLS, A. S. 103
ENNALS, ---, Mr. 225
Andrew Skinner 407, 545
Andrew T. 520
ENNIS, I. L., Miss 603
Joshua 187
Enquirer, The 637
ENSEY, ---, Miss 596
John H. 798
Lot 462, 798, 852
Mary 596
Ensey & Slingluff 852
ENSOR, Abram 798
J. 840
J. Fulton 161
Jacob 840
Jane 880
John 37
John C. 256
John H. 813, 877
John T. 814, 820, 898, 902
Mary 884
Thomas E. 815, 869, 870
William 872
William O. 877
Ensor Family 884
Ensor Orchard 905
Enterprise, The 628, 641
Enterprise Company 641
Enterprise Perpetual Building
 Association 510
ENTWISLE, John Pawson 759
ENTWISTLE, ---, Mrs. 686
Epidemiological Association 751
Epiphany P.E. Church 524, 525
Epiphany P.E. Mission 525
Episcopal Church Home 601
Episcopal Diocesan School 865
Episcopal Methodist 636, 753
Epping 906
Epping Forest 904
Epsom M.E. Chapel 902
Equitable Fire Insurance Co. 404
Equitable Gas Co. 502
Equitable Insurance Co. 802
Equitable Life Insurance Co. 665
Equitable Society of Baltimore 261
ERB, ---, Bishop 573
ERDMAN, A. G. 929
Johannes 929
Peter 927
Erdman Avenue 930
ERHMAN, John 241
ERICH, A. F. 738, 746
Annie (BAETJER) 739

ERICH, Augustus F. 738, 739
Henry C. 158
ERICHSON, W. 195
ERICK, A. F. 745
ERICKSON, Ereck 921
Ericsson 360
Erie Railway Co. 345
ERSKIN, Jonas 64
ERSKINE, --- 703
J. P. 439
ERWIN, Robert W. 737
ESCAVAILLE, ---, Mr. 629
ESCAVILLE, Joseph 798
Joseph B. 191, 193, 269, 270, 798
ESCHBACK, E. R. 155, 572
ESKERIDGE, A. 855
ESMENARD, John Frances 798
ESPEY, William 249
ESSENDER, James 192
Established Church of England 860
ESTE, David Kirkpatrick 702
Louise 702
William M. 150
ETCHBERGER, William 246
ETCHBURG, ---, Capt. 856
ETCHINSON, J. P. 855
ETTER, J. W. 573
ETTING, Hetty 798
Reuben 77, 83, 729
Samuel 438
Solemon 316
Solomon 89, 120, 188, 215, 216, 238,
 239, 252, 318, 438, 439, 455, 456,
 470, 483, 667, 680, 798
ETTINGER, George M. 820
ETZLER, R. F. 442
Eugenie, ---, Empress 773
EULER, Conrad 95
European House 459
Eutaw House 136, 141, 263, 362,
 471, 513, 515, 516, 802
Eutaw Infantry 854
Eutaw M.P. Church 891
Eutaw Paint Co. 510
Eutaw Place Baptist Church 565,
 566, 799
Eutaw Place Square 281
Eutaw Savings-Bank 142, 389, 471,
 473, 794
Eutaw Street 769
Eutaw Street Fire Company 240
Eutaw Street M.E. Church 575
Eutaw Zion's M.E. Chapel 578
Evangelical Association 548
Evangelical Episcopal Church 522
Evangelical Lutheran, The 631
Evangelical Lutheran Church 799
Evangelical Lutheran Church at
 Canton 571
Evangelical Reformed Church 573
EVANS, ---, Capt. 91

EVANS, A. D. 205, 602
  Alexander D. 141
  Amos A. 737
  C. W. 241
  Catharine 376
  Charles H. 158
  Charles W. 241, 376
  Daniel 252
  David 70, 238
  Elias 252
  Elijah 238
  Evan 919, 920
  French S. 129
  George 122
  George W. 158, 836
  Griffith 798
  H. D. 193
  H. W. 254, 372, 393, 439, 680
  H. W. S. 251
  Henry W. S. 251
  Hugh D. 188, 245, 595
  Hugh Davey 521, 627, 630, 798
  Hugh Davy 647, 716
  Hugh W. 343, 456, 498, 798
  J. 95, 269
  J. L. 880
  James 899
  John 190, 432, 798
  Nellie 877
  Nicholas 927
  Oliver 374, 375, 431
  R. H. 932
  Samuel M. 190, 242, 247, 729
  Solomon 880
  T. B. 743, 745
  T. J. 917
  Thomas 241
  Thomas H. 158, 190
  Thomas J. 158
  Thomas R. 158
  William 252, 514, 679, 798
Evans, William & Co. 311
Evans & Cogswell 670
Evans' 513
Evening & Sunday News, The 639
Evening Bulletin 624, 656
Evening Herald 638
Evening Journal 624
Evening Loyalist, The 636
Evening News 624, 635, 640
Evening Picayune & Baltimore Daily Advertiser, The 629
Evening Post 612, 639, 636
Evening Record, The 641
Evening Star, The 635, 637
Evening Times, The 636
Evening Transcript 635, 639, 649
EVERETS, L. H. 96
EVERETT, --- 611
  Edward 127
  F. 597

EVERETTE, L. S. 543
Evergreen 475
EVERHART, George 71
EVERRET, L. 77
EVERSFIELD, ---, Miss 773
EVERSMAN, Frederick 673
Eversfield Family 773
Every Saturday 641
EVITT, Robert 447
EWALT, Samuel A. 191
EWART, R. 103
EWELL, ---, Gen. 671, 923
  J. E. T. 584
EWING, Charles 569
  Ella J. 840
  Frank Kirk 840
  Guy 840
  H. M. 745, 840
  Henry Moore 839
  Henry Purcell 840
  James 99
  Kirkpatrick 839
  Malvina (MOORE) 839
  Margaret Ann (JOHNSON) 839
  N. M. 840
  R. 102
  Samuel 253
  T. W. 617
  Thomas 70, 71, 122
  W. P. 127
  William J. 840
  William P. 129
Excelsior Stove-Works 427
Exchange 151, 437, 634, 650, 785
Exchange Building 437, 438, 440, 493, 507
Exchange Buildings Co. 441
Exchange Hotel 437, 515
Exchange Mutual Permanent Building Association 510
Exchange Permanent Savings & Loan Co. 510
Exchange Place 147
Exchange Rooms 798
Exchange Rotunda 486
Exeter Hall 589
Exeter Street M.E. Church 575
Expectation 923
Experiment, The 616
Exposition Line 312
EYSON, Elisha 245
EYSTER, ---, Dr. 595
  George H. 745
EZEKIEL, --- 662
FABER, John Christian 571
  P. J. 588
FACIUS, ---, Mr. 695
  ---, Prof. 597
  G. 605
  Gustave 572
FAHNESTOCK, Benjamin 253

FAHNESTOCK, Christian D. 462
D. 247, 463, 482
Derrick 852
FAIR, Campbell 522, 641, 642
Samuel 869
Fair Grounds 818
Fair Haven 135, 309, 358
Fair View 351, 353
FAIRBANKS, A. J. 342
Fairbanks' Slave Jail 144
FAIRBURN, Joseph 253
FAIRCHILDS, ---, Mrs. 517
Fairfax Monthly Meeting 884
Fairmont 342
Fairmount Chapel 577
Fairmount Garden 846
Fairmount Water-works 217
Fairview 867
Fairview M.E. Church 909
Faith Chapel Literary Association 552
Faith Presbyterian Chapel 552
FAITHFUL, W. T. 820
William T. 158
FALCON, B. 102
FALCONER, Abraham 298
John 546, 547, 549
FALKENSTEIN, ---, Lt. Gen. 671
FALKERSTEIN, Fred. 605
FALLIER, G. 95, 269
FALLIN, Ira S. 834
FALLON, ---, Capt. 792
FALLS, Abigail 799
Benjamin F. 191
Moor N. 193, 504, 506, 507, 799
Moore 733, 799
Moore N. 465
Stephen W. 814
Falls, Alexander & Co. 359
Falls & Brown 298
Falls of Patapsco 816
Falls of the Gunpowder 881, 894
Falls Road 866, 869, 876, 883, 896
Fallston 924
FALTZ, William 245
Family Magazine 617
Family Visitor, The 654
FANNING, John 100
FARADAY, ---, Professor 508
FARBER, Edwin G. 821
Henry J. 417
FARDY, John T. 799
Fardy, John T. & Co. 145
FARIBAULT, J. 101
Joseph 101
Farley Hall 930
FARLOW, ---, Col. 200
J. T. 192
John T. 193, 199, 200
William G. 233
FARMER, --- 694

Farmer & Gardener, The 614
Farmers & Gardners' Beneficial Society 929
Farmers & Gardners' Society 929
Farmers & Mechanics' National Bank 852
Farmers & Merchants' Bank 450, 451, 459
Farmers & Merchants' National Bank 382, 451, 458, 469
Farmers & Merchants' Retreat 253
Farmers & Planters' Bank 451, 482, 804, 882
Farmers' Bank of Maryland 450
Farmers' Bank of Worcester & Somerset 450
Farmers' Convention 818
Farmington 342
FARNIER, William 380
FARQUAHARSON, Charles 189
FARQUHAR, William P. 758
FARQUHARSON, Charles 190
Farraday & Woodall 303
FARRAN, John 236
FARREL, J. 191
FARRELL, M. 193
William 911
FARREN, ---, Mrs. 693
George 693
FARRETT, F. A. 761
FASTIE, George 917
Fatherland, The 629
FAU, Abram 402
FAULKNER, ---, Col. 791
Alfred B. 414, 449
FAWCETT, George D. 641
FAXON, Eben 155
FAY, G. W. 746
James 158
T. S. 625
Fayette Association of Baltimore City 511
Fayette M.E. Church 804
Fayette Street 769
Fayette Street M.E. Church 576
Fayette Street Station 578
FAYMAN, James D. 158
FEAST, John 191
Louden 202
Nannie 886
FECHTIG, George F. 740
Fedden, J. W. & Co. 641
Federal Fire Company 247, 248
Federal Gazette 493, 612, 644, 712, 903
Federal Gazette & Baltimore Daily Advertiser 608
Federal Hill 256, 262, 287, 288, 292
Federal Hill Marine Observatory 129
Federal Hill Market-House 207

Federal Hill Park 278
Federal Hill Perpetual Building
  Association 510
Federal Hill Steam Ferry Co. 292
*Federal Intelligencer & Baltimore
  Daily Gazette* 608
Federal Meadow 923
Federal Republican 613
*Federal Republican & Baltimore
  Telegraph* 614
*Federal Republican & Commerical
  Advertiser* 613
FEELMEYER, Z. 836
FEIG, George 194
  George A. 191
FEINOUR, Charles 246, 799
  Edward 488
  William 252
FELGNER, Edward Lewis 446
  F. W. 264
Felgner & Co. 264
FELKS, Anne 44
FELL, ---, Mr. 59
  Anne 60
  Edward 50, 54, 55, 56, 59, 60, 206, 373, 518
  William 50, 54, 55, 56, 59, 60, 194, 799
  Fell's Point 47, 424, 548, 577, 579, 687, 733, 740, 757, 760, 761, 780, 793, 799
*Fell's Point Daily Commercial
  Advertiser* 612
Fell's Point Eagle Artillery 669
Fell's Point Fire Company 240
Fell's Point Hose & Suction
  Company 251
Fell's Point Market 206
Fell's Point Savings Institution
  451, 463
Fell's Point Telegraph 609
Fell's Prospect 49, 59, 61
Fell's Swampy Moor 923
Fell's Wharf 299
FELLEN, Augustus 158
FELLMAN, J. R. 630
  John R. 605
FELLMANN, F. R. 605
  John R. 605
Felstone 909
FELTON, Samuel M. 349
Female Charity School 521
Female Grammar School No. 3 740
Female Humane Association 595
Female Humane Association
  Charity School 594
Female Orphan Asylum 261
Female Sunday-school 248
Female Union Relief Association 153
FENBY, Peter 252, 463, 548

FENBY, S. 252
  Samuel 485
  William 813
FENDALL, ---, Dr. 745
  Josiah 195
FENLEY, Peter 188, 189
FENLY, ---, Mr. 441
  Peter 189
FENNEL, --- 682
FENNELL, --- 684
FENNICK, J. R. 850
FENSLEY, William 158
FENTON, A. 488
  Aaron 152, 191, 487, 549
  John J. 194
FENTRESS, W. H. 641
FENWICK, E. 237
  Enoch 594
  Ign. 101
  Martin 737
FERGUSON, ---, Dr. 376
  ---, Mr. 58
  A. D. 190
  Anne 912
  Archibald D. 158
  J. D. 851
  J. Henry 482
  James 298
  John 300, 301
  John F. 202, 799
  Joseph 372
  Levi 917
  Thomas B. 288
  William 37, 77, 464, 550, 838
  William Boyd 271
  William Boyle 799
Ferguson Monument 271
FERK, Stanislaus 822
FERNANDIS, Elizabeth 628
  Henry D. 825
FERNS, John 298
FERRALL, James 251
FERRIS, William 312
FERRY, Dennis 190
  John 191, 195, 231, 465, 487, 818
  Ferry Bar 144, 292, 299, 937
  Ferry Branch 91, 312
  Ferry Branch of the Patapsco 816
  Ferry House 658
  Ferry Point 49, 62, 168
Fertility Farm 907
FESSENDEN, ---, Lt. 318
FESSOP, ---, Mr. 407
FETHERSTONE, Richard 39
FETT, Elizabeth 405
Fetterman 342
FIBBS, John M. 161
FICKEY, F. 365
  Frederick 141, 364, 487, 798
FIELD, ---, Midshipman 91
  George W. 658

67

FIELD, J. K. 691
 John A. 149
 Montgomery 696
 P. S. 828
FIELDING, --- 687
FIELDS, Daniel 847
 James 188, 189, 192, 799
 John W. 367
 Philip 899
 William 148, 592
Fifth Avenue Theatre 696
Fifth Baptist Church 561
Fifth Church of the United
 Brethren 573
Fifth District School Teachers 869
Fifth District School Trustees 869
Fifth German American Building
 Association 510
Fifth German Reformed Church
 572
Fifth Maryland Regiment 369, 771,
 793, 794, 933
Fifth Presbyterian Church 548,
 550, 589
Fifth Regiment 668, 669, 697, 726,
 792
FIGGE, Nelson 841
FILLMORE, --- 122
 Millard 124
FINDLAY, John V. L. 790
FINDLEY, ---, Dr. 129
 Hugh 694
 John 694
 William 694
FINK, Henry 902
 Joseph 465, 487
Fink, Sheetz McSkeny & Co. 418
Finksburg 357, 854
Finksburg Station 854
FINLAY, ---, Mr. 559
 Charles 547
 John 555, 556, 559
FINLEY, ---, Col. 799
 ---, Mr. 348
 David B. 799
 E. L. 361, 394, 738, 786, 827, 850
 Ebenezer 207, 239, 250, 455, 456,
 546, 547, 734
 Ebenezer L. 188, 253, 928
 J. V. L. 723
 John 192, 246, 267, 737
 Thomas 207, 343, 439, 493, 545,
 547, 729
 Washington 497, 498
Finley, Johnson & Co. 630
FINN, William 433
Finn's Bridge 49
FINNEY, William B. 745
Fire-Proof Buildings Co. 510
Firemen's Insurance Co. 226, 483,
 491, 773, 807

FIRK, Joseph 472
First Baltimore Baptist Church 553
First Baltimore Batallion 668
First Baltimore Fire Company 241,
 242, 258, 484
First Baltimore Hose Company 240,
 241, 252, 258
First Baltimore Hose Fire Company
 240
First Baltimore Hussars 770
First Baltimore Light Infantry 668
First Baltimore Sharpshooters 610
First Baptist Church 554, 555, 556,
 559, 560, 561, 563, 564, 566, 568,
 769, 892
First Baptist Church of Augusta, Ga.
 562
First Baptist Church of Philadelphia
 562
First Baptist Church of Richmond
 567
First Christian Church 795
First Colored Baptist Church 567,
 568
First Colored M.P. Church 584
First Congregational Church 552
First Constitutional Convention of
 Maryland 707
First Constitutional Presbyterian
 Church 550, 797
First District School Teachers 820
First District School Trustees 820
First District Teachers of Colored
 Schools 821
First English Lutheran Church 264,
 569, 877
First Evangelical Church 590
First Evangelical Lutheran Church
 571
First German New Jerusalem
 Church 588
First German Reformed 521
First German Reformed Church
 572, 573
First German United Evangelical
 Cemetery 890
First Independent Church 647, 666,
 672
First Independent Unitarian Church
 589
First Lutheran Church 655
First Maryland Artillery 669
First Maryland Cavalry 796
First Maryland Federal Regiment
 818
First Maryland Infantry 796
First Maryland Regiment 798
First Maryland Rifle Regiment 795
First Maryland U.S. Vols. 810
First Maryland Vols. 810
First Mechanical Company 933

First Mine Run 871, 875
First Monumental Co-operative
  Boot & Shoe Manufacturing Co.
  511
First National Bank of Annapolis
  467
First National Bank of Baltimore
  346, 404, 406, 451, 466, 469
First Presbyterian Church 83, 127,
  264, 545, 546, 549, 550, 552, 556,
  665, 729, 794, 801, 805, 834
First Presbyterian Church
  Sabbath-school 548
First Reformed Church 154
FIrst Rifle Regiment 668
First Society of the New Jerusalem
  Church 588
First Spiritualist Congregation 592
First Synagogue 588
First Unitarian Church 643, 647,
  795
First United Presbyterian Church
  549
First Universalist Church 543
FISH, ---, Capt. 112
---, Col. 145, 146
---, Provost-Marshal 633
Virginia 522
William S. 141
Fish Street 568
FISHBURNE, R. B. 187
FISHER, --- 698
 Abraham 149
 Amos 592
 Amy 820
 Charles D. 442, 444, 445, 449, 494,
  502
 Charles D., Mrs. 604
 Edward 189
 Francis A. 412
 Frank 442
 George 855
 George W. 191, 813, 855
 Harry 509
 J. Harmanus 482
 J. I. 466, 887
 James 149
 James C. 502
 James I. 440, 547, 798
 James Isom 383, 384
 James J. 383
 Jane (ALRICKS) 702
 Jehel 487
 Jeremiah 487
 John 244, 264, 355, 432, 457
 Julia Ann 868
 Louise (ESTE) 702
 Richard 484
 Richard D. 449, 464, 471, 604
 Richard D., Mrs. 604
 Richard Douglass 383

FISHER, Robert A. 383, 440
 Robert Alexander 383, 384
 Smith J. 399
 Solon 515
 Sophia M. P. (MOXLEY) 383
 T. 678
 William 194, 466, 481, 702, 799, 890
 William A. 189, 222, 354, 604, 723,
  728
 William Alexander 702
Fisher, Charles & Co. 417
Fisher, James I. & Sons 383
Fisher, R. A. & R. D. & Co. 383
Fisher, Robert A. & Co. 383
Fisher, Wagner & Mackall 383
Fisher, William & Sons 481, 702
Fisher Boyd & Brother 263
Fisher Boyd & Co. 263
Fisher Brothers & Co. 383
Fishing Bay 313
FISHPAW, John 38
FISK, John 592
FISKE, J. D. 191
FITCH, --- 431
 Jonathan 249, 463
FITE, Anna 799
 C. R. 576
 Conrad R. 798
 Jacob 73, 174, 192, 799
 Peter 799
 William 816
FITZ, John 246
FITZ RICHARD, Jane Bermingham
  705
FITZELBERGER, Theophilus T. 690
FITZERALD, John 771
FITZGERALD, Edward 449
 F. B. 365
 George 799
 Margaret (CURRY) 771
 Peter 887
 Richard 771
 Richard B. 771, 799
 Susan L. (CAPITO) 771
 W. B. 191
 W. Bolton 191
Fitzgerald, Booth & Co. 771
FITZHUGH, --- 848
---, Mr. 632
 Daniel Dulany 904, 906
 Daniel Hughes 799
 George 904
 George, Mrs. 904
 H. M. 905
 Henry M. 126, 631, 814, 819
 Mary (DULANY) 904, 905
 Peregrine 355
 William 99, 905
 William H. 114
FITZPATRICK, John 191
 John L. 908

69

FITZPATRICK, Nathaniel 911
T. C. 136
FLACK, ---, Mr. 579
G. W. 252, 253, 484
George N. 488
James W. 368, 484
Thomas J. 484, 799
Flag of Liberty, The 629
Flag of the Union, The 628
FLAGET, ---, Bishop 528, 529
---, Father 535
B. J. 647
Benedict 235
Joseph 234
FLAHARTY, A. Q. 855
FLAHERTY, Edward F. 194, 195
FLANAGAN, ---, Mr. 310
John 432, 799
William 459
FLANNAGAN, Andrew 288
FLANNERY, James J. 202
FLANNIGAN, Andrew 799
William 300
FLAUT, George 538
FLECHTNER, Charles G. 158
FLECKENSTEIN, Louis 158
FLEDDERMAN, H. G. 191, 193
FLEET, Henry 39
Fleet Street 558
FLEEWOOD, Benjamin 95
FLEMMING, James R. 466
John 50
FLETCHER, Patrick 293
Richard 158
Samuel J. 799
FLINN, John 251
FLIPPO, O. F. 838
Floating School 234
Floods & Storms 211
Florida Railroad 357
Flower Mission 552
FLOWERS, Dame Sarah 763
FLOYD, Elijah 413
John 535, 799
John B. 847
Rachel 413
Sallie J. 413
William J. 583, 830
FLUHARTY, Thomas J. 579
William R. 488
FLUMFORD, T. 205
FLYNN, S. A. 301
FOARD, A. K. 489
Benjamin F. 820, 916
Jeremiah 799, 921
May 922
Sylvester 922
Thomas 922
FOCHT, G. R. 855
FOCKE, Frederick 799
FOER, George 418

FOGG, Amos 514
FOLANSBEE, L. T. 264
FOLEY, ---, Rev. Mr. 534
D. J. 155, 395, 448
Daniel J. 469, 472, 484
J. M. 600
John 539, 596, 597, 892
John S. 538, 540
M. 538
Mary J. 395
Matthew 799
T. J. 539
Thomas 236, 534, 536, 596, 597, 798, 826, 892, 938
Foley, D. J. & Bro. 132
FOLGER, ---, Capt. 104
Edward F. 799
F. 102
FOLLANSBEE, ---, Capt. 791
FOLLITT, Peter 765
Folly Inlet 897
FOLSOM, Norton 746
FOLTZ, William 799
FONDER, Richard 466
FONDERDEN, Adam 89
FONEIN, ---, Mr. 291
FONERDAN, John 601
FONERDEN, Adam 82, 173, 187, 188, 194, 206, 225, 244, 456, 457, 459, 727, 799
John 232, 613, 745
John, Mrs. 596
FORBES, J. 102
James 101, 102, 103, 741
James S. 466, 489
M. L. 524
Matthew L. 911
FORD, ---, Mr. 697
Addison K. 440
Charles E. 688, 696
Ebenezer 434
Edmund 814
Elias 696
F. C. 250
George T. 604
Henry J. 611
J. T. 249
John T. 158, 190, 191, 193, 205, 288, 370, 487, 495, 593, 603, 604, 631, 688, 689
John Thomas 820
John Thompson 696
Joseph 72
Joseph O. 441
Sylvester 820
Walter J. 162
William 922
William G. 499
William H. 484
Ford, Messrs. A. J. & Sons 516

Ford's Grand Opera-House 165, 590, 696, 697
Ford's Hotel 516
Ford's Theatre, Washington 696
FORE, Lucy 582
Foreign & Domestic Exchange Institution 473
FOREMAN, David 799
  Edward 786
  Francis 189, 192, 547
  James E. 255
  Valentine 177, 191, 193
Forest, The 881
Forest Street 862
Forest View 835, 836
FORHAN, P. 538
Fork 916
Forks M.E. Church Burials 922
Forks M.E. Meeting-House 922
FORMAN, --- 851
  E. M. 190
  Elizabeth 582
  Evan M. 249
  Ezekiel 845
  H. C. 465
  James R. 582
  T. M. 850
  Thomas 92
Forman Family of Clover-Fields 717
FORNEY, Amelia 443
  J. H. 442
  Jacob 443
  M. N. 484
  Matthias N. 253
  Peter 187, 188, 192, 253
FORREST, --- 691, 693
  Alexander 253
  Edwin 657
  Henry 190, 194
  Mary Leeke (DASHIELL) 744
  Moreau 729, 744
  Uriah 117
Forrest Street Building Association Nos. 6 & 7 510
FORRESTER, ---, Mr. 638
  Allen E. 179, 191, 193, 637
  William 757
FORSET, ---, Dr. 741
FORSYTH, Alexander 432
  W. 514
FORT, Samuel W. 698
Fort Avenue M.E. Church 580
Fort Avenue Permanent Building Association 510
Fort Carroll 130, 289, 290, 291, 927
Fort Covington 85, 90, 91, 97
Fort Defiance 342
Fort Delaware 633
Fort Erie 895
Fort George 88
Fort Gregg 897
Fort Lafayette 630, 632, 698
Fort Lookout 655
Fort Madison 84
Fort Marshall 132, 143, 929
Fort McHenry 289, 290, 291, 611, 630, 632, 633, 635, 642, 685, 698, 726, 749, 792, 793, 846, 853, 862, 885, 887, 899, 907, 921, 924, 927
Fort McHenry M.E. Church 578
Fort McHenry: Civil War 132, 142
Fort Mifflin 78, 83
Fort Monroe 139
Fort Sumpter 897
Fort Warren 632, 698, 844
Fort Warren (Boston) 136, 137
Fort Washington 88, 780
Fort Worthington 132
Fortune 923
FORTUNE, James 799
Forty-sixth Regiment Maryland Volunteer Militia 817
FOSBENNER, Daniel 189
FOSLER, Job 251
FOSS, William W. 487
FOSSET, Thomas 741
FOSSITT, Francis C. 813
FOSTER, Arthur 839
  Edward F. 158
  George 911
  J. 102
  J. N. 194
  J. Nelson 194
  James 38, 92
  John 911
  Jose. 102
  Nelson 194
  Reuben 604
  W. 442
  William 813, 814, 815
  William N. 872
Foster Family 717
Foster's Creek 923
Foster's Hill 923
Foster's Neck 42, 43, 44, 923, 924
FOTHERGILL, ---, Miss 156
FOTTERALL, Edward 519
FOTTRELL, Edward 54, 59, 76, 526
FOUDER, B. 255
  Richard 125, 255
FOUNTAIN, Collin 100
  H. 600
Fountain Hotel 499, 510, 608
Fountain Inn 80, 82, 83, 84, 238, 311, 312, 437, 456, 492, 513, 515, 615, 678, 679
Fourteen Holy Martyrs, Catholic Church of 543
Fourth Artillery 865
Fourth District School Teachers 854

Fourth District School Trustees 855
Fourth District Teachers of Colored Schools 855
Fourth German American Building Association 510
Fourth Mine Run 871
Fourth P.E. Reformed Church 525
Fourth Presbyterian Church 547, 548
FOUSTER, Edward 35
  John 35
FOWBLE, Catherine 867
  Elizabeth 867
  Ellen (WHEELER) 867
  Jacob 247
  John Jacob 867
  Joshua Uhler 867
  Kinsey 241
  Margaret 867
  Mary 867
  Melchor 867
  Nancy (SHAW) 867
  Peter 137, 250, 867, 870
  Servina 867
  Servina (UHLER) 867
  Susan 867
  Thomas 867
Fowble Family 869
Fowblesburg 854, 867
FOWLER, Benjamin 92, 247, 505
  George T. 191
  Isaac J. 255
  Jesse 814
  John H. 441, 467
  Margaret A. 927
  Richard 120
  Robert 441, 799, 820, 856
  Robert E. 516
  Robert S. 799
  William H. 255
FOX, --- 704
  ---, Mr. 896
  C. J. 508
  George 751
  Harriet 751
  John 623, 838, 888
  Mary 623
FOXALL, Thomas 247
FOXHALL, Thomas 456
FOY, Frederick 799
  Gregory 252
  John H. 158
  Peter 251, 252
FRAILEY, ---, Brigade Maj. 94
  Ebenezer 251
  James E. 114
  Leonard 250, 320, 609
FRAMES, James P. 740
FRANCE, ---, Capt. 123
  Charles 149

FRANCE, H. 577
  Jacob 202
  John 190
  Joseph 561, 578, 579, 928
  Spencer L. 799
  Thomas 252
FRANCES, ---, Mr. 433
  Basil 432
FRANCIS, --- 684
  ---, Mr. 682
  ---, Mrs. 682, 684
  Alexander 886
  Charles 887, 922
  Mary, Sister 799
  Franciscan Sisters 890
FRANCISCUS, George 168, 169, 246, 572
  John 188, 246, 593
FRANCK, George 484
  John 195
Franconia 354
FRANK, Alexander 149, 482, 841
  Henry 927
  John H. 793
  Simon 149
  Solomon 448
Frank, Simon & Co. 149
Frank & Adler 406
FRANKE, George 469
Franklin 16, 407, 816, 820, 839
FRANKLIN, ---, Dr. 492
  Benjamin 606
  Fabian 233
  James 38, 74
  John 663
  Thomas 70, 728, 778, 815, 819, 909, 920, 921
  Thomas J. 488
  Walter 912
  Walter S. 877
Franklin Academy 646, 868
Franklin Bank 450, 451, 459, 460, 469, 794, 797, 799, 800
Franklin Building 480
Franklin Co. 828
Franklin Coal Co. of Maryland 390
Franklin College 839
Franklin Fire Company 240, 241, 242, 251, 484
Franklin Hotel 816
Franklin Permanent Building Association 855
Franklin Road 817, 820, 935
Franklin Seminary 646
Franklin Square 279, 548
Franklin Square Baptist Church 152, 563, 564, 566, 567
Franklin Square Building & Loan Association 510
Franklin Square Presbyterian Church 548

Franklin Street 769
Franklin Street M.E. Church 577
Franklin Street Presbyterian
  Church 546, 547, 548, 549
Franklin Telegraph Co. 509
Franklintown 369, 828
Franklinville 828, 916
Frankville 342
FRASER, William 604
FRASHER, John 37, 519
FRAZIER, ---, Capt. 577
---, Lt. 91
---, Mr. 730
  James 101, 192, 205, 251, 264, 485, 592, 799
  John 59, 101
  John M. 155, 194, 799
  Solomon 100, 101, 799
  Thomas F. 246
  William Delisle 99
  William W. 830
Frazier, E. H. & Co. 263
Frazier's Farm 670
FREBURGER, Jacob H. 193
FREDERICK, George 542, 872
  George A. 177, 179, 271, 274
  Jacob 385, 886
  John 830
  John M. 472
  Susannah 874
  William 368
Frederick & Pennsylvania Line Railroad 873
Frederick Arsenal 83
Frederick Avenue M.E. Chapel South 586
Frederick Carl, ---, Prince 671
Frederick City 776, 777
Frederick City Baptist Church 553
Frederick County 70
Frederick County Agricultural Society 847
Frederick County Canal Company 313
Frederick Junction 335, 342
Frederick Republican 808
Frederick Road 896
Frederick Road Fire Company 818
Frederick Street Fire Company 240
Frederick Town 74
Frederick Turnpike 379, 820, 937
Fredericksburg, Battle of 897
FREDET, Peter 236, 799
  Pierre 236
FREE, E. W. 489
Free & Accepted Masons 750
Free Excursion Society of Baltimore 927
Free Sewing-Schools 599
Free Summer Excursion Society 603, 697

FREEBAIRN, Finchete 608
FREEBERGER, J. A. 191
FREEBURGER, George A. 253
  Jacob 191
Freedman's Bureau 150
Freedman's Rest 150
Freedmen's Bureau Bill 499
Freeland 871
FREELAND, John 838
  Peregrine Frisby 742
Freeland Station 869
Freeland's 347, 870
FREEMAN, ---, Rev. Dr. 589
---, Rev. Father 799
  E. D. 370, 829
  Edward B. 820
  W. H. 816, 828
  William H. 348, 667, 876
Freeman, The 641
Freeman's Banner 613, 616
FREESE, A. P. 840
  John H. 433
FREITAG, A. 236
  Augustus C. H. 799
FRELINGHUYSEN, Theodore 122, 503
FREMONT, --- 124
Fremont Savings Institution 465
FRENCH, ---, Capt. 146
---, Gen. 135, 792
---, Maj. 846
  B. B. 505, 506
  Ebenezer 612, 613
  Hannah 799
  John C. 582
  Mary 582
  William H. 799
French & Indian War 769
French Society 796
French Street 573
French Town 59
French's 342
Frenchtown 300, 527
Frenchtown & New Castle Railroad 480
FRERE, --- 676
FRESH, William 896
Fresh Pond 862
FREUND, Jacob 820, 821
  Louis 927
FREUSCH, Adam 799
FREY, Deputy Marshal 202
  Edward S. 799, 937
  J. W. 365
  Jacob 200
  Samuel 187
FRIBOURG, John 433
FRICK, --- 698
---, Dr. 701
---, Judge 138, 799
---, Miss 155, 156

FRICK, ---, Mr. 700
---, Mrs. 156
Achsah (SARGENT) 701
Ann B. 799
Ann Elizabeth (SWAN) 700
Charles 596, 700
Frank 210, 368, 484
George 799
George A. 932
George P. 255, 368, 441, 464, 502
John 244, 265, 266, 799
Mary 596
Mary (SLOAN) 699
Mary L. 596
Peter 173, 187, 197, 238, 239, 455, 569, 572, 699, 799
William 193, 195, 343, 497, 498, 675, 680, 699, 712, 717, 799, 850
William F. 390, 508, 596, 697, 698, 700, 723, 817, 903
William Frederick 699
William T. 509
FRIDENRICK, H., Mrs. 603
FRIDGE, Alex. 252
Alexander 252, 316, 452, 547, 577, 692, 824, 827
Fridge & Morris 439
FRIEDENRICH, A. & L. 149
Abraham 149
Leon 149
FRIEDENWALD, Aaron 738
Jonas 589, 598
Joseph 368, 409, 488, 747, 841, 935
FRIEDMAN, M. 469
Friendly Inn 603
Friends' Discovery 892
Friends' Elementary & High School Library 667
Friends' Meeting House, Lombard Street 261
Friendsbury 460
Friendship 358, 886, 888, 890
Friendship Fire Company 238, 240, 241, 242, 244, 246, 484
Friendship Lodge No. 7, I.O.O.F. 888
FRIES, John 781
FRIESE, Charles 469
Henry F. 799
Philip R. J. 799
FRIEZE, John F. 252, 253
FRIM, William 246
FRINCKE, Charles H. F. 570
FRINGER, Henry 855
Henry L. 488
FRISBY, Richard 89, 267, 461, 799, 845
Thomas 158
FROCK, Joshua 902
FROEHLICH, Hilary 542
FROEHLING, Henry 739

Front Street Theatre 147, 673, 690, 691, 721
Front Street Theatre & Circus 262, 689
FROST, Annie Bates (PEREGOY) 887
Elias W. 887
FRUSH, Jacob 799
W. W. 441
FRY, John 592
Richard 855
Samuel 188
FRYE, Joseph 582
Samuel 418
FRYER, James 155
FUCHS, F. 469
FUGETT, James P. 524
FUGIT, Martin 911
FUGITT, J. Preston 523
FULFORD, Eleanor 799
John 799
Thomas 799
FULLER, ---, Dr. 565, 566
---, Officer 816
Bartholomew 894
John 920
Nancy 368
Nicholas 911
Richard 556, 562, 565, 567, 799
S. B. 350
William 35, 368, 799
Fuller Memorial Baptist Church 566
FULLERTON, Thomas D. 149
William 149
FULTON, ---, Mr. 611
A. K. 675
Albert K. 611
Albert Kimberly 610
Alexander 611
C. C. 505, 507, 508, 610, 611, 612
Charles C. 281, 610, 799
D. C. 585
David 84, 187, 188, 203
Edington 497, 498, 610, 798
Emily J. 799
John L. 548
R. H. 548, 838
Thomas 799, 840, 880
Fulton, Charles C. & Son 610
Fulton, D. & Co. 311
Fulton Lodge No. 21, Independent Order of Mechanics 856
Fulton Station 29
Fulton Street Permanent Building Association 511
FURGUSON, T. B. 698
William B. 190
FURLONG, Henry 577
John 245
McKendree C. 158
William 592

FURMAN, Richard 554
Furnace Creek 358
FURNEVAL, Alexander 799
FURNIVAL, Alexander 72
FURNWAL, Alexander 493
FURSTENBURG, Levi 925
FUSELBAUGH, John 799
Fusselback's Lot 248
FUSSELBAUGH, John S. 249
  W. H. B. 242
  William H. B. 200, 249, 466
FUSTING, ---, Mr. 822
FYFFE, John 873
  Rebecca J. 873
Gable McDowell & Co. 263
GADDES, Alexander 799
  Robert 629
GADDESS, Alexander 317
GADSBY, --- 492, 513
  John 252, 470, 514, 799
  Gadsby's Hotel 311, 312, 469, 470, 514
Gadsby's Inn 492
Gadsby's Tavern 845
GAIL, G. W. 448
Gail & Ax 372
GAINES, ---, Gen. 887
  John H. 568
  Myra Clark 543
GAITHER, Edward 74
  Ephraim 782, 868
  G. R. 523
  George R. 799
  Hannah B. 524
  Joseph 74
  William 782
Gaither's 342
Gaithersburg 342
GAITLEY, John 536
  John T. 540, 938
GALBRAITH, ---, Capt. 530, 779
  ---, Mr. 684
  H. C. 892
  R. C. 154
  William 75
GALE, ---, Dr. 783
  George 117, 118, 452, 453, 454, 600
  Joseph H. 231
  Leonard D. 502
  Levin 66, 452, 652, 799
GALES, Joseph 850
GALLAGHER, ---, Mr. 694
  Albert 834
  F. H. 799
  Francis 158, 194, 799, 876
  Frank 624
  John H. 158
  Leslie 799
  Richard 380
GALLAIT, --- 676

GALLITZIN, Demetrius Augustine 234
GALLOWAY, ---, Mr. 851
  Benjamin 709
  Charles 911
  Mary 911
  Moses 71
  Peter 74
  Samuel 587, 848
  T. K. 814
  Thomas 158, 252, 911
  William 550
Galloway & Wharton 605
Gallows Hill 118
GALT, Peter 92, 251, 252, 593
GAMBLE, ---, Lt. 91
  C. B. 745
  George 158
GAMBRILL, ---, Mr. 837
  Abba 917
  Albert 882
  Charles A. 799, 881, 882
  Eli 918
  Fred. 917
  George T. 442
  Henry 202
  Horatio N. 409, 836
  Lancelot 799
  McGill 882
  Walter C. 917
  William 813, 917, 925
  William, Mrs. 917
Gambrill, C. A. & Co. 882
Gambrill, Sons & Co. 837
Gambrill & Carroll 836
Gambrill's Mills 275
Gambrills 342
Game Cock Hall 917
GAMEN, ---, Mr. 694
Gamewell, J. M. & Co. 260
Gamewell, Phillips, Robertson & Browning 260
GANNON, ---, Mr. 694
GANNT, Edward 741
GANSTER, Nicholas 158
GANTERBINE, J. G. 840
GANTRUM, John 929
GANTT, H. L. 831
GANTZ, Adam 569, 572
GAR, George Bailey 519
GARBER, Uriah 158
Garden Lodge No. 114, I.O.O.F. 929, 931
Garden Street 934
Gardenville 927, 929, 930
GARDINER, Charles 757
  Thomas H. 141, 365
GARDNER, George 188, 189
  George A. 641
  Isaiah 189
  Israel 194

GARDNER, J. S. 586
  James 224, 765
  John 841, 862
  Obediah 592
  Richard F. 158
  Susannah 841, 862
  T. H. 158
  Thomas H. 140
  Timothy 84, 592
  William 288, 463, 548
  Gardner & Yates 392
  Gardnes' Ship Yard 293
GAREIS, John A. 158
GAREY, H. F. 729
  Henry F. 195, 717, 723, 729
  James A. 166, 370
GARLAND, --- 643
  H. M. 628
GARMHAUSEN, Frederick C. 158
GARNER, --- 687
GARNIER, ---, Rev. Mr. 234
  Anthony 235, 534, 535
GARRATSON, Cornelius 779
  Job 779
GARRETSON, Freeborn 43
  Garret 38
  Job 70, 73, 77
GARRETT, --- 791, 890
  ---, Mr. 306, 333, 334, 336, 337,
    339, 341, 471
  Andrew 800
  Elizabeth 799
  Henry 351
  Henry S. 332, 440, 476, 799
  John W. 128, 130, 232, 275, 280,
    303, 331, 338, 340, 342, 404, 440,
    468, 475, 476, 601, 604, 666, 746,
    799, 887, 889
  Martha (HANNA) 800
  Robert 303, 304, 332, 333, 339,
    340, 342, 390, 446, 458, 471, 475,
    476, 508, 509, 698, 799, 800, 851
  Robert, Mrs. 604
  T. 95, 269
  T. H. 463, 602
  T. Harrison 303, 333, 475, 476, 598,
    698
  Thomas 424
  Garrett, Messrs. Robert & Sons 516
  Garrett, R. W. & Sons 410
  Garrett, Robert & Sons 332, 333,
    475, 515, 880
  Garrett Bridge Springs 275
GARRETTSON, Martha 864
  Mary 920
  R. W. 252
GARRICK, --- 683
  Garrison 843, 844
GARRISON, ---, Judge 136
  Cornelius 911
  S. C. 194

GARRISON, Samuel J. 190
  Thomas J. 158
  Garrison Forest 518, 857
  Garrison Forest Grange No. 15,
    Patrons of Husbandry 834
  Garrison Forest Rangers 835
  Garrison Lane Fire Company 818
  Garrison Road 854
GARRITSON, James 850
  Job 814
GARSTON, ---, Capt. 104
  George 101, 103
GARTNER, ---, Mr. 322, 323
GARTS, Catherine 799
  Charles 118, 169, 569, 799
GARTZ, Charles 452
  Gartz, Charles & Co. 418
  Gartz, Leypold & Co. 418
GARY, ---, Mr. 409
  James 408
  James A. 409, 441, 471, 487, 501,
    698, 833
  James Albert 832
  James Alfred 408
  James S. 829, 832
  James Sullivan 408, 800
  John 408
  Pamelia A. 829
  Gary, James S. & Son 408, 832
  Gary Manufacturing Co. 409, 829
  Gas Company 800, 805
  Gas-Light Co. of Baltimore 500, 501
GASKINS, Govert 520
  James R. 241
  Samuel 728
  Samuel S. 799
GASSOWAY, Henry 921
  Thomas 921
  Gaston Gas-coal Mine Co. 390
GATCH, Charles H. 761
  Elizabeth (SMITH) 932
  George 931
  Nicholas 814
  Philip 931
  Thomas B. 817, 927
  Thomas R. 820
  Gatch Family 927
  Gatch's Meeting-House 929
GATCHEL, Elisha 65
  John G. 659
GATCHELL, Jeremiah 799
  Samuel H. 592, 800
  W. H. 211
  William 188
  William H. 136, 141, 189, 198, 199,
    200, 799
GATES, --- 780
  Thomas 915
GATTIE, Catharine 434
GAULT, Cyrus 189, 800
  J. Emory 158

76

GAULT, Matthew 578
  Peter 188
  William A. 600
GAUSE, J. T. 301
GAY, John 518
  N. R. 545, 768
  Nicholas Ruxton 58, 205, 909, 921
Gay Street Bridge 816
GAZAN, Jacob 598
Gazette 630, 631, 634, 635, 650, 810
GEDDES, A. 271
  Alexander 256
  H. 101
  Henry 100
  Mary C. 229
  Robert 613, 740
GEDDESS, James 343
GEDDINGS, ---, Prof. 613
  Eli 755
GEE, Joshua 424
  Osgood 424
  Samuel 424
Geeofarison 424
GEGAN, Joseph 534, 673
GEHRING, Charles J. 158
  J. George 191
GEIST, Martin 877
GELLOTT, John 800
GELSTON, Hugh 176, 274, 695, 799, 800
Gelston Mansion 176
GEMMELL, B. B. 836
GEMMILL, James L. 870
  M. Rankin 908
General Baptists 554
General Church Guild of Baltimore 522
General Society for the Aid of Mechanics Library 667
General Wayne Inn 513, 515
General Workingmen's Sick Relief Union 668
Genius of Universal Emancipation 616, 803
GENT, William C. 812
Gentsville 876
Geographical Centre 64
GEORGE, ---, Mr. 468
  Andrew J. 729
  Archibald 189, 462, 674
  Augustus 675
  Charles W. 487
  Eliza 596
  Elizabeth A. 467
  Elizabeth A. (MANN) 467
  G. W. Russell 467
  I. S. 484
  Isaac 191
  Isaac S. 195, 222, 447, 467
  J. B. 194
  J. Brown 467

GEORGE, James 439, 440, 799
  James B. 193, 362, 467, 799
  Katie B. 467
  Lillie A. 467
  Mary Ellen 467
  Mary Ellen (STEWART) 467
  Mary, Sister 799
  P. T. 448, 484
  Philip T. 382, 464, 851
  Samuel K. 400, 483, 485, 799
  Samuel M. 365
  Sarah Mann 467
  William E. 158, 244, 252, 483
George, G. W. Russell & Co. 467
George, Isaac L. & Son 467
George & Jenkins 382
George Schwerin Building Association No. 2 511
George Washington Building Associations E F G & H 511
George's Creek 388, 389
George's Creek Coal & Iron Co. 511
George's Creek Mining Co. 390
George's Run 869, 870
Georgetown 73, 930
Georgetown Advocate 611
Georgetown College 527, 676, 776, 833
Georgetown College (Ky.) 566
Georgia 168
Georgia (Mt. Clare) 49
Georgia Reverse 168
GEPHARD, C. E. 236
GEPHART, Elinor 582
  John 191, 582
GERE, John A. 578
GERKER, H. 422
GERKIN, John W. 468
GERMAINE, George, Lord 73
GERMAN, Benjamin 190
  Philip 800
German Aged Men's Home 605
German Baltimore Herald, The 628
German Bank, The 468, 469, 852
German Baptist Church 566
German Baptists 591, 592
German Building & Savings Association No. 4 & No. 5 511
German Central Bank 405, 469
German Central Building Association No. 2 511
German Correspondent 629
German Evangelical Emmanuel Church 590
German Evangelical Lutheran Jerusalem Church 929
German Family 927
German Fire Insurance Co. 489, 491
German Guards 669
German Hill Road 926
German Homestead Association 511

German Ladies' Relief Association 593
German Lutheran Church 262, 274, 800
German Lutheran Church at Perry Hall 918
German Mannerchor 668
German Mannerchor Singing Assoc. 695
German Mechanics Library 667
German Methodist Church 822
German Music Society 672
German Orphan Asylum 597, 599, 786
German Presbyterian Church 773
German Reformed Church 212, 571, 800
German Reformed Church on Howard's Hill 572
German Reformed Messenger 900
German Savings-Bank 468, 473
German Society of Maryland 668
German United Evangelical Church 590
German Workingmen's Sick Relief Union 605
German-American Bank 451, 468, 469
German-American Fire Insurance Co. 488, 491
German-American Institute Library 667
Germania Building Association Nos. 15 16 & 17 511
Germania Club 668
Germania Club-House Association 511
Germania Good Will Building Association 511
Germania Lodge No. 31, U.O. Mech. 605
Germania Mannerchor 672
Germania Mechanics of South Baltimore Library 667
Germania Savings Association No. 2 511
Germantown 342, 918
GERMON, Frank W. 231
Geroack & Twinnall 727
GEROCH, ---, Mrs. 800
 George Seigfried 800
GEROCK, ---, Rev. Mr. 568
 S. 102
GERRALD, Thomas 432
Gerrard & Hopkins 433
GERRY, ---, Mr. 296
GERST, Jacob 929
GERWIG, William 820
GESNER, Charles H. 800
GESSE, Peter 592
GETTIER, John T. 191

GETTINGS, ---, Mr. 299
GETTY, G. W. 152
 John A. 226
Gettysburg, Battle of 897
GETZ, Charles S. 693
 Frederick 593
 John M. 191
GEYER, John W. 625
GHENT, John R. 817
GHEQUIERE, ---, Mrs. 595
 Charles 455, 532, 545
 Harriett 594
GHEQUIRE, Charles 298, 433, 483, 800
GHERDLINE, G. C. 929
GHESLIN, R. 742
 Reverdy 741
GHOLSON, John Y. 526
GIBBENS, James 146
GIBBES, R. M. 680
GIBBON, John 38
GIBBONS, ---, Archbishop 236, 537, 538, 540, 543, 776, 826, 832, 841
 ---, Bishop 539, 540, 889
 E. P. 641
 Francis A. 207
 J. L. 902
 James 529, 534, 540, 938
 John S. 836
 Thomas 101
GIBBS, A. C. 358
 J. Willard 233
 Robert Morgan 890
GIBNEY, G. Frank 442
GIBSON, --- 521
 ---, Dr. 755
 A. E. 576, 826
 E. A. 579
 Frederick 523, 914
 George S. 234
 James 95, 577, 672
 John 74, 439, 463, 464, 470, 737
 Lee 849
 Miles 818
 Patrick 455
 Robert 252
 William 62, 74, 158, 173, 465, 520, 572, 734, 737, 742, 799, 814, 824, 845
Gibson, John & Co. 649
Gibson, Messers. & Co. 515
GIDDINS, Thomas 920
GIES, H. Louis 813
 John 855
GIESE, J. Henry 155
GIFFORD, ---, Deputy Marshal 133
 A. 695
 Alex. 255
 Hugh 137, 191, 255
 J. 695
 James J. 688, 696

GIFFORD, Marshal 247
 Thomas 200, 255, 799
GIFFORDS, John 102
GILBERT, A. N. 591
 E. C. 930
 Esther Sinclair (CORSE) 930
 Henry 346
 John H. 730
 Joseph 463
GILCHRIST, William 137
GILDART, ---, Mr. 72
GILDEA, ---, Rev. Mr. 786
 John B. 799
 John Baptist 236, 537, 542
GILDER, ---, Dr. 731, 732
 R. 733
 Reuben 732
GILDERSLEEVE, Basil L. 233, 720
GILDERSLEVE, George 482
GILES, --- 673
 ---, Mr. 816
 Anne 800
 Edward 800
 James 800
 John 53, 290, 587
 John R. 517, 799
 Nathaniel 38
 Rebecca 800
 William F. 131, 729
 William Fell 123, 194, 799
 Giles Family 588
 Giles' Hotel 799
GILETTE, James 158
GILFERT, ---, Mrs. 686
GILL, ---, Miss 594
 C. L. 484
 Catherine 756
 Edward 865
 Eleanor 776
 Elizabeth 863
 Gabriel 170
 George M. 125, 126, 130, 162, 192,
  195, 368, 550, 716, 721, 799, 934
 Jabez 799
 Jabez M. 193
 James L. D. 255
 James S. 487
 John 187, 194, 393, 407, 442, 445,
  470, 502, 508, 817, 857, 863, 921
 Joshua 868
 Mary Ann 799
 N. Rufus 191, 193, 222, 466
 Noah 190, 799
 Patrick 793
 Prudence 843
 R. W. 452, 784, 799
 Richard H. 869
 Sarah (GORSUCH) 921
 Sebastian 790
 Stephen 71, 519, 800, 863, 910
 W. J. 549

GILL, W. L. 799
 William 253
 William D. 449
 William J. 937
 William L. 545, 547, 800
 Gill & Fisher 445
 Gill Family 858, 862
GILLESPIE, J. M. 927
GILLINGHAM, ---, Mr. 348
 Christopher R. 158
 Edward E. 158
 Ezra 799
 Henry R. 158
 James 241, 884
 John 252, 911
 T. 241
 William 252
GILLISS, John P. R. 231
GILMAN, --- 79
 ---, President (Hopkins University)
  232
 Charles 799, 937
 Daniel C. 233
 John H. 800
 John S. 463
 Judson 158, 743, 746
GILMOR, --- 900
 ---, Judge 516
 ---, Mr. 424
 Charles 799
 Harry 141, 147, 150, 200, 899
 Henry 817
 Louisa 799
 R. 86, 850
 Robert 60, 77, 82, 83, 137, 173, 192,
  197, 265, 266, 291, 375, 393, 407,
  433, 439, 440, 452, 454, 470, 545,
  547, 650, 658, 679, 682, 699, 717,
  729, 799, 800, 826, 827, 902
 W. 847
 William 77, 359, 426, 470, 680, 799
 Gilmor, Robert & Son(s) 298, 438
 Gilmor Family 886, 904
 Gilmor House 137, 142, 144, 152,
  516
 Gilmor Street M.E. Church 579
GILMORE, Charles H. 799
 James 190
 William 688
 Gilmore, Meredith & Co. 390
 Gilmore, R. & Sons 372
GILMOUR, James D. 517
 Gilmour, James D. & Sons 516
GILPIN, ---, Col. 498
 A. G. 604
 Charles 498
 Gilpin Canby & Co. 263
GINNODO, John Q. 826
GIRARDIN, ---, Dr. 699
GIRAUD, J. J. 735
GIRAURD, John James 799

GIRD, Henry 608
GIRNAN, James 799
GIRVIN, James M. 488
GISSEL, Christopher 468
GIST, --- 78, 769
---, Brig. Gen. 81
---, Col. 77
---, Gen. 76, 727
---, Maj. 73
Anne (Nancy) 71
C. H. 197
Christopher 51, 53, 70, 71, 519, 857
Cornelius H. 814
Edith (CROMWELL) 70
Eliza Violetta Howard 71
Henry Carey 71
Independent 71
Joseph 73
Judith Carey (BELL) 71
Mordecai 70, 71, 72, 432, 763, 800, 843
Nancy 71
Nathaniel 71, 519
Richard 50, 51, 53, 70, 71, 518, 521, 728, 819
Sarah (HOWARD) 71
Sarah Howard 71
States 71
Susan (COCKEY) 70
Thomas 70, 71, 72, 73, 75, 76, 519, 800
Thomas Cecil 71
Thomas G. 120
Zipporah (MURRAY) 71
Gist Family 858
Gist's Inspection 61
GITTEAU, S. 153
GITTINGS, --- 166
---, Dr. 896, 924
---, Mr. 434, 897
Ann 914
Ann Louisa 885
Anna Sellman 720
Arabella (YOUNG) 917
Archibald 914
Ashel 921
Bettie Bose 917
Charlotte Elizabeth 917
D. S. 916, 917
David S. 917
David Sterett 719, 720
Eleanor A. 718
Elizabeth (BOSLEY) 914
Henrietta 799
Israel 921
J. S. 523, 595
J. S., Mrs. 155, 156, 595, 596
James 69, 70, 71, 73, 75, 374, 719, 800, 816, 819, 917, 921
James C. 463
John 117

GITTINGS, John Beale Howard 917
John S. 128, 162, 189, 192, 346, 351, 463, 480, 718, 719, 799
John S., Mrs. 156
John Sterett 719
Juliana West (HOWARD) 917
Julianna West (HOWARD) 719, 917
Lambert 125, 719, 799
Laura A. (KING) 917
Leila 720
Louisa 720, 917
Margaret West 917
Mary Sterett 720, 917
Polly (STERETT) 719, 917
R. J. 718
Richard 719, 799, 917
Richard J. 128, 195, 723, 814, 887, 903
Richard James 719, 720
Richard T. 917
Thomas 909, 920, 921
Victoria (SELLMAN) 720
Victoria Elizabeth 720
Gittings, Donaldson & Graham 474
Gittings, John S. & Co. 481
GIUSTINIANI, Joseph 539, 600
GIVEN, James G. 855
James J. 820, 855
John S. 820
Given, John & Co. 102
GLANDUT, Leon 195
GLANDYE, Levi 246
GLANVILLE, John W. 190
GLASGO, Nancy 467
GLASGOW, James 734
GLASS, Isaac 190
John 240, 241, 463
GLASSBRENNER, A. J. 506
Glatfelter's 347
GLAZEBROOK, Otis E. 524
GLEESON, John 272
John P. 158
Thomas J. 158
Gleeson Mounment 272
GLEIG, --- 96
---, Rev. Mr. 93
GLEN, Eliza 800
James 158
John W. 800
Glen Burn Corse 930
Glen Ellen 18, 902
Glen Morris 357
Glencoe 347, 880, 883, 907, 909, 916
Glencoe Grange 818, 883
Glencoe Station 908
GLENDY, Elizabeth 800
John 234, 467, 547, 595, 800
William H. 799
Glendy Pesbyterian Graveyard 548
GLENN, --- 521
---, Mr. 785

GLENN, Elias 712, 729, 800
　Elijah 249
　Henrietta R. 364
　John 162, 188, 265, 364, 393, 479,
　　526, 632, 693, 698, 714, 729, 784,
　　786, 799, 800, 822, 845, 846, 850,
　　890
　S. F. 625
　S. K. 691
　Samuel T. 799
　W. R. 237
　W. W. 155, 265, 364, 630, 693, 851,
　　890
　William W. 137
　William Wilkins 632, 800
Glenn & Carpenter 633
Glenn & Co. 632, 633
Glenn Estate 820
Glenn House 429
Glenrock 347
Glenwood 915
GLEYRE, --- 675
Globe Inn 513, 515
GLOSS, John J. 799
GLOSSON, Jacob 189
GLOVER, George H. 307
Glover's Gap 342
GOBRIGHT, J. C. 631
　Lawrence 800
　William H. 630, 635, 799
Gobright, Thorne & Co. 629
GODDARD, --- 708
　---, Mr. 780
　Charles 95, 262, 799
　Giles 605
　Lemuel 800
　Mary 779
　Mary K. 493, 608
　Mary Katharine 606, 800
　William 492, 605, 606, 608, 779
GODEFROY, J. Maximilian 268
　Maximilian 267, 461, 589
GODWIN, ---, Mr. 682
　Rebecca E. 856
Goethe 647
GOFF, Theodore L. 158
GOLA, Charles 673
GOLD, ---, Capt. 299
　Daniel 506
　Elizabeth 382
　Peter 89, 120, 188, 192
Golden Bee-Hive 433
Golden Fan 433
Golden House 513, 514
Golden Lamb 513
Golden Mortar 740
Golden Rule Encampment of the
　Good Templars 856
Golden Sun, The 432
Golden Umbrella 432
GOLDER, Archibald 154

GOLDER, Robert 154
Goldsboro' 347
GOLDSBOROUGH, ---, Mr. 225
　B. 600
　Charles 195, 448, 488
　Charles E. 158
　Edward Y. 729
　G. R., Miss 156
　H. 145
　Henry Holliday 498
　Howes 741
　Mortair 846
　N. 846
　Nicholas 358
　R. H. 313
　Robert 707, 738, 741
　Robert H. 845
　Robert Lloyd 919
　William F. 127
　William T. 123, 799
Goldsborough Farm 935
GOLDSMITH, ---, Dr. 682, 730
　---, Mr. 58
　G. 921
　George 818
　J. 841
　Jonas 598, 841
　R. H. 938
　Samuel 36, 48
　William C. 192, 727
GOLSPEY, Charles 911
GONTRUM, John 927
GONZALES, C. 688
GOOD, James 817
Good Endeavor 923
Good Intent Line 312
Good News 637
Good Samaritan Lutheran
　Congregation 571
Good Shepherd Chapel 526
GOODMAN, ---, Capt. 77
　John S. 691
GOODRICH, James W. 246
　Thomas J. 129
GOODRICK, G. W. 246
　Thomas 246
GOODSHELL, George 190
GOODWIN, ---, Dr. 238, 261
　Charles 459, 523, 799
　Frank 884
　James 911
　Josephine (BOSLEY) 884
　L. 733
　Lloyd 519
　Lyde 172, 439, 498, 728, 732, 733,
　　734, 741, 814, 850
　Lyle 206
　Rachel 911
　Richard B. 799
　William 71, 77, 173, 174, 192, 196,
　　206, 425, 728, 907

Goodwins' Lot 827
GOOLRICK, Peter 738
GORDEN, John 61
GORDON, ---, Capt. 85, 88
---, Mr. 635
A. B. 523
A. M., Mrs. 598
Alexander B. 193
Basil B., Mrs. 596
D. H., Mrs. 598
Henningham 229
Henry Charles 691
James 544
John 55, 77, 99, 779
John M. 456
Patrick 64
Robert 53
GORE, Alverda 854
Charles 812
Christian 812
George 813
Henry H. 855
J. 544
James 799, 856
John F. 856
Samuel 813
William 855
GORGAS, ---, Col. 671
Ferdinand J. S. 745
GORMAN, ---, Mr. 361
A. P. 856
Arthur P. 830
William 819
GORSUCH, --- 92, 93, 208
---, Mr. 248, 876
Benjamin 813, 911
Catherine S. (ASHBRIDGE) 922
Charles 49, 50, 290, 911, 921, 922
Dickinson 818, 875, 877, 881, 883, 912
Edward 875, 881
Edwin A. 922
Eleanor 884
Elizabeth 922
Elizabeth (MERRYMAN) 881
Hannah 922
Hannah Juliet (ONION) 922
Isaac 911
Jane (ENSOR) 880
Jehu 189
John 53, 71, 881
John M. 881
Joseph 922
Joseph H. 922
Joshua 249, 875, 881, 884, 922
Joshua M. 912
Lemuel W. 251
Lovelace 881
Lydia (BOSLEY) 921
Maggie E. (QUINLAN) 922
Malinda 922

GORSUCH, Martha S. 884
Mary 925
Mary (TALBOT) 881
Nicholas 881
Peregrine 189
Rachel 922
Robert 35, 799, 814, 816, 881
Robert M. 158
Sarah 921, 922
Thomas 149, 880, 881, 911, 912, 920, 921, 922, 927
Thomas B. 916, 921, 922
Thomas J. 813
Thomas Talbot 877, 880, 881, 912
U. G. 190, 191
W. H. 761
William G. 251, 255, 762
William S. 927
Gorsuch Family 588, 869, 884, 922
Gorsuch's Mills 869, 871, 872
GORWITZ, Orville 700
GOSDEN, ---, Mr. 673
GOSLAND, ---, Capt. 103
GOSLIN, W. G. 576
GOSLING, Henry 880
GOSMAN, Adam J. 740
GOSNELL, Greenbury 799
Lemuel 205
Lemuel W. 498
Nimrod 830
Peter 519
Gospel Advocate 613
GOSWELL, Peter 857
GOTT, Anna Maria 885
Anthony 38
Jackson C. 488
Samuel N. 885
Gott Family 902
GOTTLIEB, Adam 929
GOTTSCHALK, A. 469
GOUCHER, J. F. 578
John F. 822
GOUDY, Stephen 161
GOUGH, ---, Mr. 574
H. D. 392
Harry Dorsey 800, 819, 845, 934
Henry Dorsey 70, 592
Prudence 800
Gough Street Building Association No. 6 511
Gough's Mansion House 262
GOULD, Alexander 799
James 101, 102
Paul 592
Peter 188, 592
GOULDSMITH, George 818
Samuel 818
GOUTRAM, John 814
GOVANE, James 70, 800, 891
William 778, 819

Govanstown 361, 802, 818, 845, 886, 891, 892, 903
Govanstown M.E. Church 892
Govanstown Presbyterian Chapel 547
Govanstown Presbyterian Church 892
GOVER, E. G. 834
 L. H. 365
 Philip 38
 Samuel H. 488, 799
Governor's Mansion 669
Governors of Maryland 195
GOVETT, William 74
GRACE, Philip 432
 Samuel 252
Grace Episcopal Church 601
Grace M.E. Church 579, 870
Grace P.E. Church 523, 524
Grace Presbyterian Church 552
Graceham 357
GRAF, Frederick 372
GRAFF, Frederick C. 438
 Henry 799
GRAFFLIN, ---, Miss 595
 George 459
Grafton 342
GRAFTON, Mark 188, 190, 254, 462
 Mary 904
 Nathan 188
 Samuel H. 190
GRAHAM, ---, Dr. 730
 David 608
 George R. 158
 Henry G. 158
 James B. 246
 John 432
 John T. 140, 152, 158
 Mary Ann 694
 Samuel 252
 Thomas J. 600
 W. H. 474
 William 225, 288, 474, 577, 799
 William A. 123
 William D. 484
 William H. 464, 475, 501, 604, 675
GRAHAME, William 450, 459
GRAIN, ---, Mr. 685
GRAMMER, ---, Rev. Dr. 598, 891
 Julius E. 522, 739
GRANBY, John 298
Granby Street 769
Granby Street Fire Company 240
Grand Division of Maryland 628
Grand Lodge of Maryland I.O.O.F. 803
Grand Lodge of Odd-Fellows of Maryland 640
Grand National Sangerbund 673
Grand Opera-House 688

Grand Turk 311
GRANE, Herman H. 423
GRANGET, Andrew 571
Granite 24, 830
Granite Presbyterian Church 830
Granite Roofing Co. 511
GRANT, --- 165, 166
 ---, Gen. 147, 163, 164, 335, 771
 ---, Mr. 225
 ---, President 138
 Alexander 212
 Daniel 75, 238, 311, 514, 575, 679, 800
 John 592
Grant & Garretson 432
Grant Building Association 511
Grant House 515, 517
Grant's Assembly-Rooms 658
Grant's Fountain Inn 81
Grant's Tavern 845
GRAPEVINE, Frederick 247
GRASMUCK, ---, Mr. 568
GRASON, ---, Chief Justice 903
 ---, Commodore 99
 ---, Judge 898
 John 688
 Richard 128, 717, 720, 814, 816, 817, 880
 Thomas 99, 103
 William 195
GRASTY, E. H. 927
GRATZ, Benjamin 71
 Charles 800
GRAUE, H. H. 423, 605
 Herman H. 155, 368
Grave Run 869, 870
Grave Run M.E. Church 869
Grave Run Mills 869
Gravelly 43, 918
GRAVENSTEIN, James H. 250
GRAVENSTINE, Joseph H. 242
GRAVER, J. Adams 691
GRAVES, Henry M. 222
 John J. 194, 827, 828
 John James 745
 Robert 252
 Uriel 569
GRAW, Henry 800
GRAY, ---, Dr. 730
 Alexander 921
 David W. 195
 E. J. 579
 E. W. 393
 Edward 470, 471, 653, 816
 Frances 800
 Frederick 471
 G. Farring 158
 George L. 612, 800
 Henry W. 189
 J. W. 902
 James 741

GRAY, John 253, 800
  John F. 749
  John F. F. 886
  John T. 199, 200
  Samuel 519
  William 799
Gray Manufacturing Co. 511
Gray's Ferry 311, 349
Gray's Gardens 433
Gray's Inn 303, 703
GRAYBELL, Isaac 77
  John 855
  Philip 70, 569, 572, 592, 799
GRAYBILL, Jacob 729
  Philip 392, 800, 814
GRAYWORTH, Hugh 38
GREANER, William 799
GREASER, Bernard N. 158
GREASLEY, Jacob 380
Great Cacapon 342
Great Central Basin 18, 19, 30
Great Eastern Building Association No. 6 511
Great Falls of Gunpowder River 816
Great Gunpowder 905
Great Gunpowder Falls 408
Great Gunpowder River 220, 916, 922, 923, 925
Great Valley Baptist Church 553
Great Western Express 360
Great York Street 559
GREBLE, Benjamin 189
GREELEY, --- 166
  Horace 165, 651
GREEN, --- 682
  ---, Mr. 201, 219
  ---, Mrs. 481, 682
  Amon 466
  Amos 799
  C. B. 190
  Caleb 592
  Charles 927
  Charles B. 466
  Duff 616, 624, 636
  George W. 191
  Henry 814
  J. M. 365
  Jacob 190, 249
  James E. 871
  John 99, 189, 192, 902
  John P. 346
  Jonas 545, 605
  Josiah 120
  Lewis F. 548
  Neal 135
  Peter 251
  R. C. 191, 193
  Richard 355, 800
  Samuel S. 191
  Thomas 195, 817

GREEN, Thomas M. 449
Green Family 927
Green Spring 342, 834, 841
Green Spring Branch Railroad 834
Green Spring Hotel 344
Green Spring Junction 347, 356, 357
Green Spring M.E. Colored Church 841
Green Spring Ridge 14
Green Spring Valley 15, 18, 20, 26, 30, 276, 345, 355, 843, 852, 859, 862, 863, 905
Green Street Presbyterian Church 548
Green Tree 608, 642
Greenback Party 638
Greenbury's Forest 862
GREENE, ---, Gen. 78, 80, 81
  ---, Mr. 505
Greene Street 769
Greene Street Presbyterian Church 550
GREENFIELD, A. H. 189, 191, 193, 495, 728
  Aquilla H. 194
  Joanna 878
GREENLEAF, --- 726
GREENLEE, William 65
Greenmount Avenue M.E. Church 578
Greenmount Cemetery 132, 144, 267, 270, 271, 272, 354, 676, 776, 797, 876, 890, 896, 937
Greenmount Cemetery Co. 511
Greenmount Mutual Building Association 511
GREENWAY, ---, Capt. 103
  E. M. 481, 602
  Edward M. 600
  Joseph 101
Greenwood 357, 916, 918
GREENWOOD, George Z. 442
GREER, George 593
  John 78
GREETHAM, William 457
GREGG, Andrew 471, 799
  Athalinda (BROCKY) 896
  David 896
  J. 95, 269
  John 390
  Martha 896
GRENEWALD, Leonard H. 158
GRENVILLE, George 744
GRESSITT, John M. 442
Grey's Hill 33
GRIER, ---, Judge 876
GRIEST, ---, Mr. 291
  Isaac 60, 70, 72, 79, 82, 118, 310
GRIEVES, James 189, 192
  James F. 251
GRIFFIN, ---, Rev. Mr. 534

GRIFFIN, Benjamin 76
  C. M. 585
  Elias T. 497, 498
  Henry W. 579
  Hugh 236
  Hugh F. 236
  Stephen 830
  Thomas W. 139
  William B. 234
GRIFFITH, --- 60, 727
  ---, Mr. 153, 291
  Alicia Brewer 743
  Allen 462, 799
  Amanda Sallie 406
  Ann 884
  Benjamin 59, 70, 72, 74, 76, 196,
    310, 374, 544, 553, 554, 555, 779
  Charles E. 255
  Charles G. 190, 193, 728
  David 743
  Dennis 74
  Elizabeth (DURST) 155
  G. S. 231, 599, 600, 602, 603
  Goldsborough S. 153, 154, 155, 489,
    601, 602, 603
  H. B. 317
  Isaac 884
  J. M. 193
  John 74, 75, 799
  John A. 222, 469
  John J. 262
  John R. 799
  John W. 368
  Lewis 866
  Matthew 246
  Nathan 76, 432, 554, 800
  Patrick 790
  Samuel G. 461, 800
  Samuel K. 814
  Thomas M. 656
  Thomas W. 470, 800
  Ulysses 406
  William 821
  Griffith, G. S. & Co. 154
  Griffith & Cate 262
  Griffith's Bridge 287, 816
GRIFFITHS, Henry 816
  J. 692
  Thomas J. 178
GRIFFY, T. T. 880
GRINDALL, J. J. 190, 193
  Joseph J. 193
GRINNELL, Charles 596
  Charles A. 252
GRINSFELDER, Joseph 484
GRISWOLD, --- 166, 646
  Benjamin B. 526
  Charles 830
  Elias 194
  Rufus W. 651
GROBP, John G. 799

Grocers' Exchange 449
GROE, Ann 594
GROESBECK, William 166
GROFTON, Mc. H. 365
GROGAN, Rebecca 835
GROH, Jacob 193, 194
GRONEBERG, A. E. 469
GROOM, Moses 919, 920
GROOME, ---, Gov. 912
  ---, Mr. 649
  James Black 195
  John 741
  John C. 128, 600
GROOMS, Nanie B. 908
  William 190
GROONER, John C. 364
GROSBENNER, J. J. 573
GROSS, ---, Bishop 540
  ---, Dr. 737, 755
  ---, Mr. 837
  ---, Rt. Rev. Bishop 543
  J. J. 193
  Jacob 690
  John 246
  John J. 189, 690
  Maria 702
  Michael 189
  Samuel D. 748
GROTHE, Franz 605
GROUNDS, Jacob 814
GROVE, Conrad 363
  Conrad S. 365, 366
  Jacob F. 190
  Stephen 247
  Grove Chapel M.E. Church 830
GROVER, Burr H. 158
  Charles 690
GROVERMAN, Anthony 298, 433
GROWTHER, John 912
GRUBB, J. W. 587
  John 253, 254
GRUBER, Jacob 581
GRUNDY, --- 521
  George 215, 250, 298, 454, 455, 520,
    592, 799
  George Carr 800
GRURER, Jacob 255
GUARD, Thomas 576
Guardian & Temperance Intelligencer
  613
GUAY, James 255
  Thomas 255
GUELE, John 149
GUENTHER, J. 597
GUERKE, Ferd. 605
GUEST, J. W. 466
  J. Wesley 462, 489
  John 255
  Samuel 465, 582
  Susan 583
GUESTIER, P. A. 439

GUIDA, John B. 538
GUILD, Edward C. 590
Guilford 622, 623, 804, 887
GUILLEAUME, ---, Prof. 625
GUION, ---, Mr. 318
GUITEAU, J. 902
　R. 799
GUNDY, William 738
GUNNELL, Charles H. 302
GUNNISON, ---, Mr. 787
　William 124, 465
Gunpowder 217, 884
Gunpowder Baptist Church 553, 870
Gunpowder Copper Works 422, 511
Gunpowder Falls 870, 871, 872, 876, 881, 910, 916
Gunpowder Farmers' Club 818, 881, 912
Gunpowder Grange No. 127, Patrons of Husbandry 917
Gunpowder Hundred 918, 919
Gunpowder Lower Hundred 812
Gunpowder Meeting 883
Gunpowder Meeting-House 886
Gunpowder Mill 870
Gunpowder Monthly Meeting 884
Gunpowder Neck 311
Gunpowder Permanent Supply 222
Gunpowder Permanent Water-supply 222
Gunpowder River 218, 220, 696, 815, 886, 904, 918, 919, 920, 921, 922, 924, 926, 931
Gunpowder River Bridge 130
Gunpowder Upper Hundred 70, 71, 812, 910
GUNTHER, Caroline (MENSCHING) 373
　Catherine (UPSHAW) 373
　Conrad 468
　George John 373
　L. A. 281
　L. W. 464, 484, 825
　Ludolph Wilhelm 373
　Martha Ann (CECIL) 373
Gunther & Finks' Furniture-Factory 265
GUNZBURG, A. 588
Gustar Adolph Building & Loan Association 511
Guthrie Family 907
GUTMAN, Joel 605, 841
GUTTROW, Simon 732
GUY, Francis 434, 674
　John 799
　William 799
Guy's 152
Guy's Hotel 516
Guy's Monument House 142, 145, 516

GUYTON, Abraham 911
　Henry 922
　John 911
　Joshua 911
　Sarah 820
GWINN, ---, Mr. 58
　C. J. M. 126, 194, 195, 508, 723
　Charles 438, 799
　Charles J. M. 166, 195, 746, 755
　Charles J. W. 659
　Edward 782
　James M. 149
　William 174
Gwinn's Falls 214
GWINNETT, Button 74
GWYNN, ---, Lt. 318
　---, Mr. 828
　Charles 461
　Charles J. M. 232, 828
　Eleanor 799
　John 457
　Walter 646
　William 116, 265, 266, 393, 456, 457, 470, 500, 609, 612, 642, 645, 675, 679, 684, 692, 712, 734, 736, 799, 800, 812, 890, 911, 928
　William R. 252, 470
Gwynn's Falls 217, 811, 817, 820, 821, 823, 826, 828, 834, 857, 936
Gwynn's Falls Railroad 356
Gwynn's Folly 642
HAANEL, Eugene 158
HAAS, Isaac C. 639
　John P. 495
Habbersett's 513
HABLISTON, Henry N. B. 800
HACK, Andrew 569
　Andrew A. 800
　George W. 158
　Henry C. 158
　Oliver F. 194
　W. A. 192
　William A. 189, 190, 484
　William E. 484
HACKETT, --- 694
　John E. 916
　William 927
HADEL, William 158
HADEN, Florence Eloise 357
HAEFLIGH, Frederick 433
HAELBRAITH, Thomas 250
HAESBAERDTH, John 569
HAESBAERT, J. P. C. 570
HAFKENSCHEID, Bernard 541, 542
Hagar 865
HAGE, William J. 549
HAGER, George W. 189, 801
Hagerstown 671
Hagerstown Bank 310, 450
HAGERTY, ---, Mrs. 595
　J. S. 250

HAGERTY, James S. 367, 467, 579
John 224, 225, 233, 244, 408, 840
HAHN, Edward 380
John 870
HAIG, James M. 137
HAILE, Charles T. 815
Elizabeth 925
Neale 519
Nicholas 519, 857
Susan 925
HAINES, Daniel 883
Eliza M. 852
Levi 840
Mary (PRICE) 883
Nathan 357, 883
Reuben 355
Sophia (PRICE) 883
W. 355
Haines' Bros. 674
HAIR, Francis 911
HALBATE, Henry 432
HALBROOK, Joseph 244
HALCOMB, Chauncy P. 846
Joseph C. 846
HALDERMAN, Ann 862
HALE, Annie D. 916
Cubel 801
Edward Everett 665
Frank X. 534
Thomas 813
HALEY, John F. 506
Thomas 919
HALL, --- 727
---, Dr. 784
---, Mr. 632
---, Rev. Dr. 830
---, Rev. Mr. 822
A. C. 140
Agnes S. 915
Andrew 928
Ann R. 723
Aquila 69, 814
Aquilla 40, 801
Augustus 358
B. W. 845
Blanch 921
Caleb 727
Catherine 864
Clayton C. 489
Edward 728, 814, 920
Edward C. 922
Edwin H. 233
Eliene, Mother 798
Elisha 731
Elisha J. 120, 864
Eliza 922
F. M. 851
Frank M. 851
Georgia T. 927
J. B. 442
J. W. 255

HALL, James 76, 506, 813
John 43, 45, 71, 550, 592, 706, 709,
  728, 814, 818, 819, 910
John E. 644, 782
John H. 189
John T. 158
John W. 255, 466, 501
Joseph 741
Joshua 53, 54, 56, 59, 71, 728
Josias Carvil, Mrs. 801
Levin 592, 801
Lyman 74
Lyman B. 233
Martha 920
N. Taylor 927
Nathan H. 251
Nathaniel 255
Natilla 830
Philip 76
R. W. 736
Rebecca 582
Richard 203
Richard C. 888
Richard W. 737, 742
Richard Wilmot 801
Robert 250
Robert Lyon 922
Samuel 817
Simeon 801
Theodoric B. 158
Thomas 252, 672, 800
Thomas H. 358
Thomas L. 820
Thomas W. 137, 141, 187, 222, 271,
  439, 463, 464, 481, 624, 631, 635,
  637, 723, 915
Washington 265, 266, 723
Hall & Marean 438
Hall & Sellers 605
Hall of Sculpture 675
Hall's Mill 311
Hall's Spring Railroad 815, 890
HALLAM, --- 680
---, Mr. 169, 681, 682, 689
Frank 526
HALLE, James 193
Halle's Folly 49
Hallem & Henry 849
HALLETT, William R. 414
HALLIDAY, G. S. 846
HALLIS, William 35
HALLOCH, William 103
HALLOCK, ---, Capt. 779
Halltown 342
HALSTEAD, --- 122
Haman's Gallows 47
HAMBERT, J. 269
HAMBLETON, Sarah A.
  (SLINGLUFF) 477
Arabella (STANSBURY) 477
Bell 477

HAMBLETON, Bessie 477
  Catharine (OBER) 401
  Clara 477
  Francis H. 477
  Frank S. 477
  Grace 477
  J. A. 482
  J. Douglass 478
  J. Edward 281
  James Douglass 477
  Jesse Slingluff 477
  John A. 401, 477, 487, 852
  John E. 477
  John N. 477
  Kate (OBER) 477
  Mary E. (WOOLEN) 477
  Sallie S. 477
  Samuel 477, 800
  Sarah A. (SLINGLUFF) 852
  T. E. 852
  T. Edward 477
  Thomas B. 194
  Thomas E. 205, 222, 365, 462, 476, 477, 487, 852
  Thomas Edward 852
  Thomas S. 477
  William 477
  William Sherwood 477
Hambleton, John A. & Co. 477
Hambleton & Son 477
Hambleton Hills 477
HAMBLIN, ---, Mrs. 651
HAMER, William H. 564
HAMERICK, ---, Mr. 655
  Asger 232, 666, 667, 673
HAMILL, Carl Webb 430
  Catharine (CONANT) 430
  Charles W. 430
  Elizabeth T. (WELLENER) 430
  Frank Wesley 430
  George Wade 430
  Grace Wellener 430
  Harry Winslow 430
  Hattie Winslow 430
  Robert 430
  William J. 729
Hamill, Charles W. & Co. 430
HAMILTON, --- 166
  ---, Dr. 849
  ---, Gov. 752, 912
  ---, Mr. 51, 271
  Alexander 229, 781
  Charles 800, 887
  Charles R. 194
  Edward 509
  Francis H. 477
  Henrietta 529
  Henry 449
  J. Augustus 886
  J. Douglass 800
  Jehu 190

HAMILTON, John 190, 311, 385, 592, 857
  John W. 158
  Lydia Jane 635
  Patrick 310
  Richard 251
  S. M. 828
  T. B. 194
  Thomas 800
  Thomas H. 191, 194
  William 50, 51, 223, 519, 595, 728, 819, 857
  William Campbell 194
  William H. 191
  William P. 468, 641
  William T. 166, 195, 231, 725
HAMLIN, ---, Mr. 434
  Hannibal 147
HAMMAN, John A. 468
  Michael 255
HAMMER, ---, Mrs. 595
  Augustus 252
  J. E. 151
  James G. 745
HAMMERSLAUGH, V., Mrs. 603
HAMMERSLOUGH, Louis 598
HAMMITT, Thomas P. 158
HAMMOND, ---, Col. 51
  ---, Dr. 848
  Elizabeth 832
  Isaac 73
  J. Pinkney 526
  James 246
  John 51, 168, 169, 520, 569, 709, 864
  John D. 370
  John S. 800
  Lloyd 741
  Mary 864
  Mordecai 38, 70
  Nicholas 757, 845
  Rachel 864
  Rezin 70, 351, 819
  Thomas 253, 358, 818, 819
  W. 205
  William 37, 45, 50, 51, 53, 56, 61, 70, 74, 100, 206, 392, 425, 518, 519, 521, 730, 814, 844, 859
  William A. 360
  William S. 583
Hammond, John & Co. 423
Hammond, Mr.'s Green House 682
Hammond & Newman 372, 438
Hammond Family 843
Hammond's Ferry 82
HAMNER, G. 254
  J. G. 548, 829
  John G. 548
Hampden 409, 410, 807, 836, 838, 839
Hampden Heights 886, 887, 888

Hampden Lodge No. 24, I.O.O.F. 837
Hampden Presbyterian Church 838
Hampden Reservoir 221
Hampshire & Baltimore Coal Co. 511
HAMPSON, A. J. 190, 800
  Isabella 230
Hampstead 867
Hampstead Building Association Nos. 11 & 12 511
Hampstead Hill 87, 89, 90, 276, 559, 620, 782
Hampton 15, 18, 806, 837, 910
Hampton Estate 895
Hampton Reservoir 219
Hampton Roads 632
Hancock 38, 342, 807
HANCOCK, --- 166
  ---, Maj. Gen. 793
  John F. 740
  Winfield S. 151
HAND, ---, Adjt. Gen. 80
  ---, Dr. 813
  E. J. K. 813
  Moses 233, 250, 667
Hand Tavern 513
HANDS, Thomas 717
Hands, W. G. & Co. 825
HANDY, ---, Miss 674
  ---, Mr. 280
  A. H. 127
  George 801
  George D. 919
  George D. S. 920
  Henry 190, 254
  J. 102
  James 100
  Joseph 102
  S. J. K. 191
  Samuel J. K. 497, 498
  Thomas P., Mrs. 604
  Washington R. 745
  William U. 737
  William W. 786
Handy Family 899
HANK, A. S. 575
Hanley & Bansemer 263
HANLON, ---, Mr. 628, 629
  D. H. 628
HANLY, Daniel T. 820
HANN, Albert N. 693
Hann & Owens 693
HANNA, A. B. 800
  Alexander B. 801
  Andrew 244
  Clinton 877
  John 92
  Martha 800
  Robert 359
  Robert B. 263

HANNA, Samuel 249
  Samuel T. 260
Hanna, R. B. & Co. 263
Hannah, R. M. & Co. 307
Hannah More Academy 866, 867
HANNON, John 586
Hanover 342
Hanover Junction 345, 347, 379
Hanover Loan & Savings Co. 511
Hanover Market 173, 174, 206, 245, 432
Hanover Road 868
Hanover Street Fire Company 240
Hanover Street M.E. Church 578
Hanover Street Synagogue 589, 934
Hanover Turnpike 866, 869
HANSEN, William H. 188
HANSER, H. 570
HANSHEWEG, --- 727
HANSLEY, ---, Mr. 843
HANSON, --- 614, 707, 709
  ---, Judge 117, 361, 845
  ---, Mr. 783, 784
  A. C. 613
  Alexander 50
  Alexander C. 801
  Alexander Contee 195, 614, 782
  Andrew 416
  Anthony 251
  Charles W. 801
  Edward 38
  J. M. 581
  James M. 582
  John 101, 102, 614
  John Wells 481
  Jonathan 49, 54, 373, 374
  Mary 56
  Peter 365
  Rebecca (DULANY) 904
  Rebecca Dorsey 801
  Thomas 904
  Thomas H. 466
  W. H. 188
  William H. 176, 189, 463
Hanson's Mill 54, 55
Hanson's Wood Lot 49
HANWAY, Castner 876
  Elizabeth 884
Hap Hazard 49, 168
Hapleford Creek 313
Har Sinai Verein 588
HARBAUGH, ---, Mr. 727
  Leonard 61, 168, 206, 432, 726
HARBERSETT, Henry 801
Harbor Board of Baltimore 181, 288, 662
Harbor Commission 288
Harbor Masters 288
HARBOUGH, Leonard 607
Harbour 424
HARDAN, Samuel 244

HARDEN, Samuel 192, 234, 393, 439, 593, 801
  William 359, 462
HARDER, William 800
HARDESTY, B. McG. 912
  B. McLean 879
  Frank H. 158
  George W. 191
  Henry 248
  S. R. 466
HARDIE, Robert 771, 800
HARDINGE, --- 684
---, Mr. 685
HARDWAY, Vitus 203
HARDY, John 380
  Overton 298
  W. W. 937
HARE, --- 202, 934
---, Col. 132
  Ephraim 838
  George H. 869
  Harewood 931
  Harewood Park 931
  Harford 311
HARFORD, Henry, 6th Lord Baltimore 42
  Henry, Sir 195
  Harford Avenue M.E. Church 578, 800
  Harford Avenue M.E. German Chapel 577
  Harford Baptist Church 553, 554
  Harford County Academy 138
  Harford Road 886, 888, 890, 891, 896
  Harford Town 77
  Harford Turnpike 916, 917, 918, 921, 926, 929, 931
HARGEST, Thomas 886
HARGROVE, John 588, 595
  Samuel 263
  Hargrove Baptist Church 561
  Hargrove Church 588
HARIG, Bernard L. 194
  R. L. 194
HARKER, J. J. 190
  James 262
  John Newton 615
  Samuel 189, 615, 801
  Harker & Lower 615
HARKEY, Joshua 921
HARKINS, George 77
HARKINSON, Charles 688
HARLAN, Calvin 916
  David 465
  Samuel 301
  William H. 231
  Harlem 798
  Harlem Park 279
  Harlem Permanent Building Association 511

Harlem Stage-coach Co. 362, 511
HARLOW, E. H. 523
HARMAN, Charles 39
  George 484
  Jacob 879
  Mary D. 916
  Samuel J. 193
  William 212, 673, 800
HARMAR, Jacob T. 245
Harmon Episcopal Lutheran Sunday-School 855
Harmon's Ferry Road 935
Harmonic Society 673
Harmonic Society of Baltimore 672
Harmony Building Association Nos. 14 & 15 511
Harmony Perpetual Loan & Savings Co. 511
Harnden Express 359
HARNER, David 247
HARNLY, ---, Mrs. 604
HARPER, --- 698, 805
---, Gen. 268
---, Miss 155, 156
  Anna D. 676
  Charles A. 676
  Charles C. 120, 452, 680
  Charles Carroll 194, 801
  Ellen 676
  Emily 600, 777
  John 114
  R. G. 215
  Robert G. 195
  Robert Goodloe 98, 215, 375, 437, 642, 648, 679, 712, 781, 800
  William H. D. 586, 587
  Harper's Ferry 342, 632, 789
  Harper's Ferry Gap 324, 325
  Harpers of New York 646
HARRID, D. 102
HARRINGTON, Elisha 194
HARRIS, --- 59, 166
---, Bishop 579
---, Mr. 356, 481, 627
  Alexander 304
  B. I. 938
  Benjamin G. 145, 441
  Benton 744
  C. A. 675
  Chapin A. 576, 744, 745, 801
  David 91, 206, 250, 452, 454, 470, 658, 679, 801
  Edward 89, 461
  Ephraim 877
  J. Morrison 130, 166, 547, 659
  J. Morrison, Mrs. 604
  J. W. 902
  James H. 745
  John W. 581
  Joseph 194, 801
  Lloyd 53

HARRIS, Mary 744
N. S. 879
Nicholas 658
Richard 800
Runyon 252
Samuel 252, 253, 440, 481, 516, 577, 800, 801
Samuel H. 253
Thomas C. 480
W. D. 251
William 253, 688
William C. 695
William S. 190
Harris, Samuel & Sons 481
Harris' Creek 90, 168, 293
Harris' Creek Bridge 130
HARRISON, --- 101, 849
---, Mr. 60, 206, 207, 318, 321, 892
---, Rev. Mr. 521
Anne R. (WILSON) 770
B. F. 481
Benjamin 72, 149, 891
Benjamin F. 440
C. 101, 103
C. K. 836
Charles K. 846
Clem. 101
Elisha 741
Ella 886
F. 890
Frederick 770, 887, 889, 891
George 830
George L. 303, 483
James 246
James C. 815
John 101
Joseph 801
Nathaniel 891
Olevia 821
Peyton, Mrs. 155, 156, 551
Richard 587, 891
Samuel 800
Thomas 37, 38, 56, 57, 58, 59, 69, 71, 72, 74, 167, 205, 224, 463, 464, 471, 519, 578, 800, 801, 819, 891
W. G. 439
W. H. 524, 602, 617
William 193, 547, 801
William G. 130, 137, 141, 194, 330, 354, 365, 404, 440, 460, 463, 483, 499, 596, 914
William G., Mrs. 595
William S. 439
Zillah (HOPKINS) 891
Harrison, L. & Co. 263
Harrison & Sterett 438
Harrison Building Association No. 9 511
Harrison Permanent Building Association 511

Harrison's Marsh 52, 54, 57, 61
Harrisonburg 342
Harrisonville 830, 832, 893
HARROD, Hannah L. 582
J. J. 616
John J. 582
HARRYMAN, ---, Miss 906
A. 933
Amos A. 813
David 249
George 819, 877, 906
John 120
John G. 158, 442
HART, ---, Governor 223
Anne (Nancy) (GIST) 71
Catherine 774
George M. 506
Henry B. 194
J., Mrs. 600
Jacob 79, 310
John 195
Joseph 249
Lewis 209
Nathaniel 71
Oliver 554
Stephen 35
Hart's Tavern 695
Hartford Baptist Church 553
HARTLEY, Phineas 830
HARTMAN, A. M. 229
Andrew 746
Edward 485
Isaac 472, 489, 938
Isaac P. 800
J. H. 745
Lizzie (SEIDENSTRICKER) 485
Pamela A. 230
Hartman, H. & E. 624
Hartman's W. S. 342
HARTNER, Jacob 362
HARTOGENSIS, H. S. 589
HARTOR, John 741
HARTSHORN, ---, Mrs. 595
HARTSHORNE, Joshua 550
HARTSOG, Henry 263
HARTWAY, Nich. 37
HARTWELL, Thomas 518
HARTWIG, ---, Mr. 568
HARTY, John 244
HARTZ, John 205
T. 589
HARVEY, ---, Mr. 896
Alice L. 927
Andrew 830
Daniel 163, 190, 193
Henry D. 139, 488
J. 241
J. G. 463
J. K. 815
James 462, 471, 800
James W. 800

HARVEY, John K. 814, 869
  Joseph 465
  Joshua 241
  Joshua G. 463
  Thomas 38, 578, 861
  Thomas P. 471
  William 38
  William Charles 800
  William H. 800
HARVIE, ---, Mr. 434
HARWOOD, --- 682, 683
  Henry 89
  James 120, 394, 814
HASHALL, Isaac 896
HASKELL, John H. 546, 547
HASKINS, Govert 461
  Joseph 246, 845
HASKINSON, William 149
HASLAM, John 249
HASLETT, ---, Dr. 731
  ---, Miss 476
  M. 730
  Moses 733, 734, 801
  Robert E. 128, 129
  William 393, 498
HASLUP, J. J. 832
  Lloyd J. 158
HASS, John F. 189
HASSEBACK, John 572
HASSELBACH, John 569
HASSELBOCT, --- 606
  Nicholas 605
HASSENCAMP, Fred. 740
HASSON, A. A. 551
  Joseph 263
HASTINGS, Charles S. 233
  Jonas 298
HASWELL, John B. 177
HATCH, Davis 99
  Samuel T. 190, 195, 487, 800
HATCHER, William E. 563
Hatcher's Run, Battle of 897
HATCHESON, B. O. 800
HATFIELD, ---, Mr. 621
HATHOWER, George 254
HATTER, Charles W. 466
HAUBERT, J. 95
  Michael 92
HAUGH, Henry 158
HAUPI, Horatius H. 800
HAUSER, J. Conrad 573
HAUXTHALL, F. 438
  L. 438
HAVEN, -- 350
HAVENER, J. T. 270
Haverford Road 891
HAVERSTICK, L. M. 900
  Levi M. 161
Havre de Grace 43, 148, 349, 351,
  576, 919
HAW, John 101

HAWKINS, ---, Dr. 879
  ---, Mr. 238, 261
  A. 637
  Amanda (MOWELL) 878
  Ann (WARING) 878
  Annie M. (SHRIVER) 878
  Archibald 250
  Charles 207
  Elizabeth 877
  Elizabeth Bordley 717
  Ernault 717
  Henry 877, 878
  Henry Holland 878
  Henry J. 158
  J. M. 902
  J. W. 873
  James 924
  James L. 120, 316, 343, 459, 850
  Joanna (GREENFIELD) 878
  John 519, 717
  John H. W. 582, 801
  John J. 403
  John W. 880
  John Weems 877, 878, 879
  Jonas Henry 878
  Joseph Mowell 878
  Josias 878
  Josias Henry 877
  Mary (BARNES) 878
  Matthew 717
  Rachel 582
  Samuel 878
  Sarah Ann (WEEMS) 877
  Sarah Elizabeth 878
  Thomas 717
  William 89, 187, 203, 233, 358, 575
Hawkins' Point 289, 292, 309
HAWKINSON, William 801
HAWLEY, Martin 449, 600
  Martin, Mrs. 600
  R. K. 303, 463
HAWTHORNE, J. B. 563
HAY, ---, Maj. 900
  George P. 902
  Jesse 190, 465, 468
HAYDEN, ---, Prof. 656
  H. H. 675
  Horace A. 745
  Horace H. 744
HAYES, John 728
  John S. 927
  Richard 36
  T. W. 870
  Thomas G. 202
HAYFIELD, John M. 812
Hayfields 19, 379, 847, 877, 879,
  884, 885
HAYNE, ---, Maj. 80
Hayne & Croxall 439
HAYNES, T. W. 874
Haynes, D. E. & Co. 446

HAYNIE, Ezekiel 741
HAYS, George P. 153, 548
J. B. 264
James 608
John S. 814, 815
R. C. 442
Robert W. 193, 194
Thomas G. 194
William 741
HAYWARD, --- 375
---, Mr. 219
H. P. 880
Isaac 483
Jacob 250
John 250
Jonas H. 800
William 100, 250
William H. 762, 800
Hayward, Bartlett & Co. 426
HAZARD, --- 33
Hazard Powder Co. 132
HAZELHURST, Andrew 801
Samuel 441
HAZELTINE, Elizabeth (RUTLEDGE) 873
Silas W. 873
HAZELTON, George 251
W. B. 611
HAZEN, H. B. (G.) 194
HAZLEHURST, H. R. 292
HAZZARD, ---, Lt. 318
HEACOCK, Israel R. 830
J. S. 892
HEADINGTON, Daniel 911
HEALD, Howard 255, 256, 487
J. 256
Jacob 256, 463
Jacob H. 800
John 505
John H. 485
John R. 255
W. H. 576
William 288, 466, 471, 800
HEALEY, John 557, 558, 559
HEALY, George 449
John 433, 801, 836
HEAPS, John 934
HEART, William 871
HEAT, ---, Mr. 627
HEATH, ---, Brig.-Gen. 801
---, Judge 699
---, Maj. 94
F. W. 577
H. 455
H. W. 820
J. P. 486
James 800, 819
James P. 614, 801
Levi 920
Levi T. 158
R. K. 827

HEATH, Richard K. 93, 826, 933
Stephen P. 158
U. S. 195, 850
Upton S. 188, 317, 714, 729, 800, 801, 824
HEATHCOTE, John 801
Martin 872
Heathcote & Dall 740
Heathcote & Doll 433
Hebrew Benevolent Society 668, 747, 841
Hebrew Cemetery 934
Hebrew Hospital 589, 747
Hebrew Hospital & Asylum Association 747
Hebrew Ladies' Sewing Society 603
Hebrew Orphan Asylum 265, 841
Hebrew Synagogues 588
Hebron Lodge No. 74, Knights of Pythias 877
HECHT, H., Mrs. 603
Jacob 367, 368
S., Miss 603
HECK, Frederick W. 158
HECTOR, James 236
HEDGES, C. 552
J. W. 840
John W. 580
Peter 250
Thomas 814
HEDIAN, P. J. 629, 800
HEDINGER, Michael 249
HEDRICK, J. W. 873
HEFFNER, Edward 902
HEGTHORP, Edward 246
HEIDE, George 245
HEIDELBACH, J. H. 439
HEIDELBAUGH, Susie 821
HEIER, ---, Rev. Father 570
HEIGH, B. M. 801
HEILEG, William 855
HEILNER, L. 589
HEIM, J. Fred. 927
HEINE, Francis 468
HEINEKEN, C. H. 372
HEINER, Elias 572, 800, 840
HEINRICH, Anthony Philip 673
HEINTZ, F. E. B. 260
HEIRM, Frederick 927
Heise & Doughtery 931
HEISER, Charles 447
HEISKELL, Sydney O. 927
HEISS, I. A. 569
HEITMUELLER, William A. 237
HELDIC, Isaac 149
HELFFENSTEIN, Albert 572
Hell Point 42
HELLER, A. 543
HELLING, Bennet 149
HELLINGS, John 343
HELLWEG, August 469

HELM, Henry 741
  Leonard A. 250
  Mayberry 519
  William O. 255
HELMES, Mayberry 70
HELMPRAECHT, Joseph 541, 542
HELMS, Leonard 253
HELMSLEY, --- 703
HELSBY, Thomas 746
HELVINA, Anna Catherine 879
HEMBY, Darby 921
HEMMETER, J. 605
HEMMINGWAY, Harriet 394
HEMPHILL, Andrew 801
HENCHY, Edward 538
HENCK, J. 153
  Lewis 153
HENDERSON, ---, Mrs. 595
  Andrew F. 483
  Andrew Fisher 300
  Benjamin Franklin 473
  Elizabeth Ellen (JONES) 473
  Gustavus A. 190
  Henry 471
  J., Miss 595
  James A. 195, 603, 800
  John 241, 251, 288, 307, 800
  John W. 158
  Josiah 751
  Robert 76, 79, 168, 292
  Robert G. 251
HENDON, Henry 801
HENDRICKS, John 64
  William H. 908
HENDRICKSON, Charles R. 560
HENDRIX, W. F. 873, 874
  William F. 872
HENEKE, F. W. 372
HENFREY, Benjamin 386, 500
HENING, Lewis 572
  Ludwick 569
HENKEL, Adolph 158
HENKELMAN, Frederick 489
HENKLE, E. J. 358
HENNEBERRY, Richard 242
  Richard F. 191
HENNICH, George 250
HENNICK, John M. 243, 260
HENNIGHAUSEN, F. L. C. 605
  F. Ph. 571
  Louis 605
HENNING, Ludwig 192
HENNINGS, Hy. 605
HENRICKS, Christly 417
HENRIE, ---, Capt. 114
HENRY, ---, Mr. 169, 681, 682, 689, 694
---, Prof. 664
  Charles M. 202
  J. V. D. 584
  John 117, 195, 711, 818

HENRY, John C. 464
  Josiah 801
  P. S. 889
  Patrick 642, 644, 709
  Thomas 158
Henry, Messennior & Zolleckoffer 103
Henry Clay Lodge No. 81, I.O.O.F. 855, 902
Henry Colored M.E. Chapel 584
HENSHAW, ---, Rev. Dr. 866
  J. P. 745
  J. P. K. 801
  J. P. R. 867
  John P. K. 522
Henshaw Memorial Church 526
HENTZE, Frederick E. B. 246
HEOFLICH, Frederick 569
HEPBURN, Stalia 100
  Thomas 433
HERA, E. R. 562, 870, 874
  Edwin R. 158
Herald 637, 638
HERBECH, H. 264
HERBERT, --- 686
  James R. 200, 441, 792
  John C. 324
  Richard 812
Hereford 30, 31, 871, 872, 874
Hereford Farm 885
Hereford Lodge No. 89, I.O.O.F. 874
HERGESHEIMER, Benjamin 149
  Chris. 191
  E. 191
HERING, Ludwig 249
HERMAN, Augustine 35, 40, 41
  Solomon 149
HERMANGE, E. V. 639
Hermange & Brewer 639
HERMANN, ---, Rev. Mr. 573
  C. C. 281
HEROLD, J. B. 191
  John B. 158
HERR, John 345
  Michael 345
HERRING, ---, Mr. 260
  A. 821
  B. W. 197
  George W. 137, 155, 162, 193, 260
  H. 262
  Henry 800
  J. Q. A. 144, 600
  John Q. A. 360, 603
  Ludwick 393, 407, 459
  Ludwig 89, 187, 801, 853
  O. 190, 191
  Rebecca 853
Herring Run 209, 214, 811, 816, 818, 850, 926, 935
Herring Run Driving Park 927
Herring Run Race-Course 794, 848

HERRINGTON, Jacob 911
HERRMAN, J. M. 929
　John M. 927
HERRUA, DeCarriere 103
HERSCH, Charles 569
HERSH, C. H. 801
HERTEL, John 468
HERWIG, C. P. 734
HERZBERG, P. 589
HESPELEIN, John 542
HESS, Emanuel 841
　Marcus 194
　Nathan 800
　Samuel 240
HESTON, Susan (FOWBLE) 867
　William 867
HEUISLER, George A. 189
　Joseph S. 191
HEWES, ---, Mr. 609, 616
　Edwin 442
　John 470, 484, 593, 608
　John G. 441, 465
　Joseph 72
HEWETT, Horatio H. 911
　John H. 613, 616
HEWITT, A. 236
　Caleb 170, 187
　Eli 89, 187, 246
　Elie 247
　Horatio H. 523
　J. H. 649, 650, 673
　John H. 617, 628, 646, 695
　Mary 617
　N. A. 888
　Richard 45, 53
　Thomas 432
Hewitt, John H. & Co. 624
HEWLD, Deitrick 251
HEWLETT, Henry W. 830
　John Q. 128, 471, 484, 800
HEYEN, J. T. 627, 654
HEYER, Sophia 423
Hibernian Advocate, The 625
Hibernian Corps of Union Greens 669
Hibernian Infantry 669
Hibernian Literary Association 641
Hibernian Society 233, 668, 806
HICHBORN, Philip 304
HICKEY, John 235, 534, 538
　John F. 236, 534, 538, 800
HICKLEY, ---, Mrs. 595
　William 463, 690
HICKMAN, ---, Capt. 361
　Charles 800
　George H. 625
　John T. 158
　N. 189
　Nathaniel 728
　Washington 242
　William H. 158

HICKOK, John J. 401
　Mary E. (OBER) 401
Hickory Hill 907
HICKS, ---, Ex. Gov. 142
　---, Gov. 127, 128, 130, 132, 139, 632, 789, 791, 882, 885, 903, 908
　---, Governor 499
　---, Mr. 424
　Abraham 911
　Charles 875
　Gove. 138
　Hooper C. 498
　John 248, 249
　Lewis 568
　Miranda 875
　Sarah 875
　Thomas H. 600
　Thomas Holliday 124, 195, 498, 787
Hicks Hospital 152
HIDDLEMAN, --- 676
HIELBERT, John 256
HIGENBOTHAM, E. 673
　Thomas 298
HIGGINBOTHAM, --- 65
　Charles 65
　Ralph 65, 454, 456
HIGGINS, ---, Mr. 494
　---, Mrs. 212
　Asa 140, 193, 749, 800
　Edward 205, 459, 509
　Edwin 468
　Elisha 592
　Eudora 749
　Eugene 193, 194, 368
　James 750, 800
　Mary A. 749
　S. H. 550
　Stephen 45
　William 246
HIGGINSON, John 45
HIGH, William J. 246
High German Reformed Presbyterian Church 572
High Service 275
High Service Reservoir 220, 221
High St. 137
High Street Baptist Church 561, 566
High Street M.E. Church 578
HIGHAM, John 465
Highland Avenue M.E. Church 927
Highland Park 834, 852, 853
Highland Park Hotel 853
Highland Park Land Co. 723
HIGHLANDS, Elizabeth 472
Highlandtown 277, 926, 927, 928
Highlandtown Fire Company 818
HIGINBOTHAM, R. 252
　Ralph 801
HIGLE, Eliza P. 916
　Samuel 815
HIGNET, John 89

HILARY, ---, Sister 800
HILBERT, John 193
HILDEBRAND, ---, Mr. 731
  George W. 487
  T. 873
HILFERTY, Felix 158
HILGARD, J. E. 288
  Julius E. 233
HILL, ---, Dr. 739
  ---, Mrs. 690
  ---, Rev. Mr. 902
  ---, Supervising Architect 495
  A. P. 670, 897
  Charles C. 351
  D. H. 637
  D. I. 604
  E. J. 821
  J. 102
  John H. 483
  Joseph 38
  Josiah 100
  Mary 909
  Moses 38
  N. S. 342, 442
  Nicholas 698
  S. E. 593
  S. P. 561
  Samuel E. 600
  Stephen 581
  Stephen P. 555, 556
  Thomas 600
  Thomas G. 801
  W. B. 576
  W. S. 637
  William 38
  William B. 369, 600
Hill Street Baptist Chapel 556
HILLARD, Elizabeth 766
  George S. 714, 715
HILLEARY, William T. 158
HILLEBRAND, Charles F. 158
HILLEGAS, ---, Mr. 74
  Samuel 74
HILLEN, Catherine 801
  Charlen 929
  John 62, 77, 118, 170, 187, 206,
    246, 298, 382, 393, 483, 801, 824
  John S. 324
  Solomon 187, 194, 471, 800, 801,
    819
  Thomas 187, 701
  Hillen Family 886
  Hillen Road 891
  Hillen Station 183, 356, 851
HILLIARD, Betsy 801
HILRETH, ---, Mr. 781
HILT, Mary A. 443
HINCKLEY, Isaac 349
HINCKS, Charles D. 569
HINDES, ---, Mr. 164
  M. G. 190

HINDES, Samuel 126, 163, 199, 200
HINDMAN, --- 88
  Jacob 801
  James 455, 470, 800, 824
  W. 850
  William 100, 680
HINDS, Moses G. 465
  Samuel 200
HINE, L. G. 359
HINES, Jesse K. 491
  Samuel 800
  William 911
  William J. 252
Hines' Slave Jail 144
HINKLEY, E. Otis 365
  Edward 801
  Edward Otis 237, 478, 594, 599
HINKS, Charles D. 125, 136, 198,
    199, 200, 415, 441, 800
  Samuel 124, 187, 219, 222, 786
HINTZ, Fred. E. B. 754
  Frederick E. B. 800
HINTZE, ---, Dr. 785
  F. E. B. 188, 190, 193
HIPKINS, F. S. 524
HIPSLEY, E. G. 191, 466, 488
  William H. 158
  William R. 877
HIRES, A. J. 559
HISER, James H. F. 430
HISS, Charles D. 250
  George 892
  Joseph 253
  Philip 577
  Philip Hanson 578
  Phillip 469
  William Henry 935
  William J. 487
Hiss M.E. Chapel 931
HISSEY, William 245
Historical Art Gallery 659
HITCHCOCK, Asael 911
  Fordyce 693
  Isaac 911
  J. Irving 614
  R. S. 548
  Robert S. 158
HOBART, ---, Bishop 654
  Hobb's 342
HOBBS, ---, Mr. 312
  Thomas 310
HOBBY, William 554
HOBITZELL, F. S. 194
  Fetter S. 194
HOBLITZELL, F. S. 938
  Hoblitzell, Crowley & Co. 219
  Hoblitzell, Joseph H. & Co. 219
HOBSON, John E. 487
HOCK, William A. 189
HOCKHEIMER, H. 588
Hockley Furnace 425

Hockley Works 217
HODGE, ---, Dr. 637
  John Blair 637
  Robert 605
  Thomas 919, 920
  William E. 158
HODGEN, James B. 745
HODGES, ---, Rev. Dr. 526, 828
  Benjamin M. 372, 439, 800
  J. S. B. 521
  James 125, 137, 155, 365, 415, 416, 417, 449, 456
  James, Mrs. 155
  John H. 252, 439
  John T. 351
  Joseph C. 158
  Mary Hanson (RINGGOLD) 416
  Robert 416
  William 416
  William Ringgold 416
Hodges & Emack 263
Hodges Brothers 416
HODGKINSON, ---, Capt. 361
HODGSON, Joseph 801
  Robert 312
Hodgson & Nicholson 432
HOECKE, ---, Mr. 568
HOEN, --- 774
  A. 888
  Adolph G. 739
  August 495, 887
  Ernest 488, 495, 605
Hoen, A. & Co. 502
Hoen Building 552
HOENEMANN, H. R. 468
HOERR, John 570
HOEY, John, Mrs. 694
Hoey & Co. 359
HOFF, ---, Rev. Dr. 879
  Adeline (WHITING) 722
  Augustus W. 158
  J. F. 887
  Jacob 280, 381, 722
  John 380
  John G. 902
  S. Emma 722
HOFFACKER, Henry M. 813
HOFFLER, M. 929
HOFFMAN, --- 521, 723
  ---, Mr. 280, 481, 715
  ---, Rev. Mr. 917
  Aaron 576, 728
  Andrew 468
  August 834
  Charles 487, 599
  D. P. 202
  Daniel 247, 593
  David 195, 647, 659, 672, 680, 712, 714, 715, 782, 801, 827
  Deborah (OWINGS) 862
  Dora 155, 156

HOFFMAN, George 158, 265, 266, 316, 317, 318, 439, 470, 520, 801, 824
  George B. 440
  George Frederick 801
  H. W. 498
  Halbet 936
  Henrietta 156
  Henry 801
  Henry W. 129, 130, 497
  Isaac P. 800
  J. S. 241
  Jacob 432, 456, 457, 572
  Jacob V. 241
  John 298, 439, 461, 470, 680, 740, 801, 826
  Louisa 155, 156
  Michael 253
  P. 935
  Peter 118, 167, 187, 197, 213, 224, 238, 239, 245, 470, 483, 545, 572, 593, 594, 699, 727, 800, 801, 862
  Peter B. 816
  Philip Rogers 613
  S. Owings 602
  Samuel 439, 463, 464
  Samuel O. 252
  Samuel Owings 193, 801
  Samuel, Mrs. 155, 156
  Thomas C. 469
  W. E. 191
  W. Gilmor 481
  William F. 870
  William G., Mrs. 595
  William Gilmor 456
  William H. 195, 489, 820, 870, 876
  William J. 158, 870
  William W. 158
Hoffman, Peter & Son 298
Hoffman, W. H. & Sons 870
Hoffman & Co. 629
Hoffman Family 870, 886
Hoffman Street 769
HOFFSTETTER, Lorenz 929
HOFLAND, Thomas R. 625
HOFSTETTER, J. H. 929
Hog Island 473
HOGAN, ---, Mr. 225
HOGARTH, William H. 158
HOGE, Levi 190
HOGG, ---, Mr. 494
  John S. 191, 193, 207, 208, 245, 368, 935
  William 550
Hogg, J. H. & Bros. 934
HOHMAN, Mathias 830
HOHN, E. A. 279
HOJDA, J. 543
HOLBROOK, John 920
  William G. 256

HOLDEN, Catharine (MC
    MURRAY) 776
Ira S. 776
James 820
Mary K. 821
Robert S. 237
HOLEN, Henry 406
Holiday Street Theatre 265
HOLLAHAN, Thomas R. 202
HOLLAND, --- 166
---, Mrs. 673
---, Prof. 276
A. 637
Albert 673
H. 902
Jackson 367
James 368
John 298
John C. 122, 145, 161, 368, 369,
    817, 820
Littleton 247
Nancy (FULLER) 368
Nehemiah 312
HOLLER, --- 689
Holler's Town 689
HOLLIDAY, John R. 814
John Robert 728
W. H. 576, 800
Holliday Street Theatre 517, 680,
    682, 684, 686, 687, 688, 689, 691,
    694, 696, 810
HOLLINGSHEAD, D. A. 549
HOLLINGSWORTH, --- 521
---, Capt. 83
Catharine 45
F. 392
Francis 77
Henry 78, 99
J. 101, 392
Jacob 816
Jesse 60, 167, 173, 194, 197, 213,
    224, 239, 310, 452, 483, 574, 575,
    733, 801
L. 84
Levi 98, 202, 237, 265, 266, 386,
    439, 470, 820
Levy 483
Lydia 786
Rachel Lyde 801
Richard J. 399, 600
Samuel 82, 89, 169, 172, 214, 235,
    238, 239, 267, 298, 433, 454, 461,
    483, 727, 733, 801, 935
T. 214
Thomas 173, 187, 197, 214, 238,
    239, 298, 452, 455, 482, 519, 520,
    801
Thomas E. 727
Valentine 45
Zeb 729

HOLLINGSWORTH, Zebulon 82,
    172, 173, 174, 187, 214, 456, 658,
    679, 712, 801, 845
Hollingsworth, Samuel & Sons 438
Hollingsworth & Worthington 439
Hollingsworth Copperworks 220
HOLLINS, ---, Capt. 135
George H. 800
J. S. 84, 680
J. S., Mrs. 594
J. Smith 187, 479, 890
Jane 801
John 84, 170, 175, 192, 209, 238,
    298, 437, 438, 452, 456, 592, 727,
    801
John Smith 123, 801
John, Mrs. 594
Mary 801
R. L. 393
R. S. 680
Robert S. 345
William 207, 801
Hollins & McBlair 425
Hollins Hall 586
Hollins Land, Homestead & Loan
    Co. 511
Hollins Street Baptist Church 561
Hollins Street Chapel 580
Hollins Street M.E. Church 580
Hollins Street Market 208
HOLLINSWORTH, Jesse 244
HOLLIS, William 919
Hollofields 342
Hollow, The 374
HOLLOWAY, Anna H. (ROSS) 258
Charles B. 261
Charles T. 242, 243, 256, 257, 258,
    260, 264, 818
Edward 800
Eleanor 257
G. N. 465
George N. 158
J. Q. A. 468
John M. 801
John Q. A. 487
Robert 240, 249, 257
HOLLYDAY, John G. 937
HOLMEAD, ---, Rev. Mr. 911
HOLMER, Victor 820
HOLMES, Caroline M. 428
Gabriel 911
J. L. 563
J. M. 584
John 298, 452
John A. 580
John B. 814, 819, 820, 876, 908
Laura J. 908
Lemuel 253
Reuben A. 800
Theodore J. 552
Victor 162, 800

HOLMES, William 890
HOLT, ---, Atty. Gen. 147
  Charles J. 524
  Daniel 549
  John 605, 921
HOLTER, L. 241
  Lewis 189, 241
  Louis 246
HOLTHOUS, F. F. 468
HOLTON, C. A. 800
  Charles A. 158
  H. B. 409, 818, 828
  Hart Benton 829
  Mary (ALEXANDER) 829
  Pamelia A. (GARY) 829
  Thomas 829
HOLTZ, George G. 193
HOLTZMAN, W. 155
Holy Comforter P.E. Church 524
Holy Cross, Catholic Church of 543
  Cemetery of 536, 542, 932
Holy Evangelist, P.E. Church of 525
Holy Innocents P.E. Church 524
Holy Trinity P.E. Church 868
HOLZER, Lawrence 542
HOMANDS, J. Smith 628
Home Building Association Nos. 4 5 6 7 & 8 511
Home Circle, The 636
Home Fire Insurance Co. 488, 491
Home for Aged Women of the M.E. Church 600
Home for Fallen Women 597
Home for the Aged of the M.E. Church 599
Home of Industry 826
Home of the Friendless 231, 253, 596, 599
HOMER, C. C 463
Homestead 64, 881, 886, 888, 890
Homestead Association 511
Homestead Grange No. 170, P. of H. 892
Homestead P.E. Chruch 890
Homestead Village 896
Homewood 887
Homewood Park 890
Homewood Villa 886, 887
Hominy Mill 559
Homoeopathic Dispensary 748
Homoeopathic Free Dispensary of Baltimore City 756
HONEYWELL, Charles B. 253
  Stephen 458
HOOD, Benjamin 357
  Florence Eloise (HADEN) 357
  Hannah Mifflin (COULTER) 357
  J. M. 351, 356
  James 120
  John M. 340
  John Mifflin 357

HOOD, Sarah 357
  Zachariah 67
Hood's Mill 342
HOOE, Robert T. 100
Hooe's Ferry 312
HOOGERWERFF, J. J. 439
HOOGEWERF, Samuel E. 467
HOOGEWERFF, S. M. 484
  Samuel E. 441
HOOGEWORFF, J. J. 372
HOOK, Charles A. 222
  Frederick 801
  Henry 188
  Henry W. 842
  Joseph 192, 207, 247
  Marcus R. 819, 820
  R. B. 222
  R. E. 814, 816, 817
  R. Edwin 902
  Richard W. 814
  William 836
Hook, Richard & Co. 842
Hook Family Burying Ground 842
HOOKER, George H. 151
  Richard 38
  Thomas 38
Hookstown 369, 842
Hookstown Road 818, 853
HOOLMAN, ---, Mrs. 686
HOOPER, ---, Mr. 494, 837
  Alcarus 446
  Henry 101
  James 125, 155, 189, 303, 440, 464, 466, 487, 800, 801
  James A. 441
  James E. 820, 834
  James Edward 446
  John 254
  John G. 194
  Joseph 53, 54, 518
  Robert 222, 364, 365
  Robert H. 641, 642
  Theodore 140, 446, 471
  Thomas 189, 801
  William 249, 251, 471, 800
  William C. 139
  William E. 128, 273, 276, 409, 466, 603, 836, 887
  William Edward 446
  William J. 166, 191, 367, 415, 446, 484, 579, 838
  William John 446
Hooper, William & Sons 409, 838
Hooper, William & Sons Mills 275
Hooper, William E. & Sons 837, 840
Hooper & Sons' Mills 275
Hooper Building 441
Hooper Line 306
Hooper's Straits 39, 310
Hooper's Wharf 445
HOOPES, ---, Dr. 370

HOOPES, David H. 190
  Isaac 254
  William M. 370
HOOS, John 446
HOOVER, Adam 312
  F. 380
  Francis 381, 800
HOPE, W. H. 800
  William 189, 245
  William H. 615
Hope Junior Fire Company 257
Hopeful Baptist Church, Va. 564
Hopewells 905
HOPF, George 158
HOPKINS, ---, Commodore 99
  ---, Miss 774
  Abel J. 813
  David 70, 729, 801
  Eleanor (MORSELL) 413
  Eliz. S. 604
  Elizabeth 48
  Elizabeth (THOMAS) 773
  G. W. 625
  Gerald 70
  Gerard 74, 172, 244, 587, 801
  Gerard P. 470
  Gerard T. 222, 231, 466, 488, 826
  Gerrard 432
  Hannah (TANNEY) 231
  Henry 801
  J. J., Mrs. 605
  Jarrard 275
  Jerrard T. 393
  Joel 252
  John 773, 800
  Johns 128, 220, 233, 277, 345, 358, 365, 404, 440, 466, 468, 484, 588, 596, 746, 747, 800, 801, 825, 846, 895, 926
  Lewis N. 232, 456, 746, 747
  Margaret 772
  Mary Ann 665
  Patience 722
  Richard 74, 740
  Samuel 231, 254, 432
  Sarah 213, 800
  Stephen 891
  T. 368
  W. 365
  W. H. 583
  William 232, 254, 464, 470, 487, 746, 800, 801
  William S. 800
  Zillah 891
Hopkins, Johns, Colored Orphan Asylum 231, 820
Hopkins, Johns, Hospital 232, 279, 445, 746, 824
Hopkins, Johns, University 231, 288, 655, 657, 720, 746, 801, 930
Hopkins, Johns, University Library 667
Hopkins & Brothers 231
Hopkins & Moore 231
Hopkins University 926
HOPKINSON, Francis 801
  Joseph 781
  Thomas 860, 861
HOPPE, C. F. W. 571
  J. 303
  J. Henry 355
  Justus 343, 438, 672
HOPPER, John K. 237
  S. W. T. 600
  Washington 801
HOPPIN, ---, Mr. 621
HORE, E. 268
HORN, Adam 202, 708, 715
  Benjamin 263
  Caroline A. 775
  George L. 449
  J. C. 427
  John V. 820
  John W. 158, 205, 603
  Malinda 202
HORNAGLE, John 255
HORNE, Samuel B. 148
HORNER, --- 136
  E. R. 191, 549
  Eli Ross 487
  F. F. 585
  John 135
  John A. 281
  Joshua 191, 800
  Wilson G. 190
HORNEY, Edward 190, 193
  Stacey 252
Horney & Mead 292
HORRT, August 816
HORST, Ernest 820
HORSTMANN, William 422
HORTON, A. 320
  E. Tudor 625
  H. P. 246
  James 92
HORWITZ, --- 698
  ---, Mr. 702
  B. F. 723
  J. 701
  Maria (GROSS) 702
  Orville 483, 701, 723
HOSHALL, Jacob 813, 870
HOSKINS, John H. 801
  Joseph 433
HOSMER, James R. 158
HOSTETTER, Daniel 120
Hostetter, David's Tavern 312
HOUCK, Annie I. 855
  J. W. 745
HOUGH, R. R. S. 586
  Robert 458, 801

HOUGH, Samuel 458
Hough, Turner & Co. 458
HOUGHTON, ---, Mr. 777
 Caroline (MC MURRAY) 776
 Charles E. 776, 778
HOULE, Louis 158
HOULTON, William 193, 205, 240
HOUSE, C. F. 877
 Samuel 189, 248
 House of Correction 155
 House of Reformation &
  Instruction for Colored Boys 154
 House of Reformation &
  Instruction for Colored Children
  602, 603
 House of Reformation for Children
  404
 House of Refuge 404, 475, 724,
  826, 827, 828, 852
 House of Refuge Library 667
 House of the Good Shepherd 596,
  597
HOUSER, Henry 361
HOUSTON, James 729
 John 74
 Peter 101
 Samuel 113
 Samuel T. 190, 800
HOVENDEN, --- 662
HOWARD, --- 93, 358, 521
 ---, Capt. 114
 ---, Col. 61, 81, 207, 216, 532
 ---, Mr. 632
 ---, Mrs. 695
 ---, President 133
 Alice (MORRIS) 873
 Anne 863
 B. C. 667
 B. C., Mrs. 155, 156
 Beale 801
 Benjamin C. 91, 188, 193, 194, 195,
  316, 672, 748, 758, 800, 824, 881,
  933
 Blanch (HALL) 921
 Charles 38, 136, 141, 198, 199, 200,
  471, 680, 695, 800, 801, 814, 824,
  893
 Charles R. 800, 820, 846, 902
 Charles Ridgely 524
 Charles, Mrs. 155, 156
 Chew 801
 Cornelia A. 800
 Cornelius 59, 801, 814, 819, 857,
  862, 863
 D. 95, 269
 E. H. 641
 E. Lloyd 637, 733, 738, 745, 800
 Edward 519, 925
 Eli D. 218, 219
 Elizabeth 873
 Ephraim 730, 801

HOWARD, Francis Key 137
 Frank Key 141, 145, 190, 631, 633
 George 195, 800, 816, 859, 863
 Govane 892
 Henry 158, 734, 738, 800, 801, 873
 J. E. 680, 727, 845
 J. G. 921
 James 393, 439, 800, 820, 850, 861,
  863, 902
 James C. 298
 Joanna (O'CARROLL) 71, 862
 John 49, 50, 70, 72, 576, 801, 816,
  921
 John Beale 719, 720, 728, 814, 819,
  921
 John Beall 921
 John E. 61, 73, 86, 89, 195, 215,
  263, 280, 393, 454, 592, 680, 800,
  801, 804, 814, 826
 John Eager 59, 62, 89, 114, 193,
  195, 202, 206, 214, 247, 250, 265,
  515, 520, 521, 549, 591, 592, 709,
  736, 800, 801, 844, 845, 849, 859,
  863
 John P. 582
 Joshua 71, 862, 863
 Julia Elizabeth 804
 Juliana West 917
 Julianna West 719, 917
 Lemuel 920
 Margaret 801
 Margaret (CHEW) 863
 Margaret (WEST) 720
 Mark 432
 Philip 863
 Rachel 863
 Robert 189, 192, 205, 281, 288, 391,
  394, 463, 800, 842, 876, 925, 932,
  934
 Ruth 863
 Ruth (EAGER) 863
 Samuel 250, 757
 Sarah 71
 Thomas 921
 Thomas Gassaway 71
 Thomas Gassoway 921
 Violetta 863
 W. Govane 801
 W. T. 641
 William 202, 313, 318, 434, 667, 754,
  793, 801, 891
 William Key 481, 695
 William R. 441
 William T. 745
Howard, Henry & Co. 425
Howard Association 799
Howard Athenaeum & Gallery of
 Arts 695
Howard Bank 451, 465, 469
Howard Engine-House 263
Howard Family 858, 862, 907

Howard Fire Company 240, 241, 242, 254
Howard Fire Insurance Co. 487, 491
Howard Free Church 925
Howard House 515
Howard Land Co. of The City of Baltimore 511
Howard Latin School 721
Howard Relief Building Association No. 5 511
Howard Society 271
Howard Street 769
Howard Street Savings-Bank 465
Howard Street Station 578
Howard's Branch 49
Howard's Hill 206, 216, 225, 575
Howard's Inheritance 862
Howard's Park 61, 80, 214, 786
Howard's Range 816
Howardville 834, 842
HOWE, ---, Gen. 77
---, Lord 779
---, Rev. Dr. 855
HOWELL, D. C. 698, 824, 825
 Darius C. 368
 George 525
 J. B. 464
 John B. 439, 463, 801
 John S. 298
 Louis 801
 Thomas 41, 44, 812, 818
 Thomas, Capt. 42
 William 311
Howell, ---, Messrs. & Bro. 362
Howell, William & Son 439
Howell Brothers, ---, Messrs 251
Howell's Point 309
HOWLAND, Daniel 89, 298, 470, 592, 824
 John D. 800
Howland & Woollen 261
HOWSER, John 246
Hoxley Forge 424
HOY, William F. 855
Hoyt, Henry E. & Co. 635
HUBAL, L. 102
HUBBARD, Ann 522
 Henry A. 149
 Jacob 95
 Joseph 592
 William 188, 192, 225, 463, 667, 824
HUBBELL, Josiah S. 158
HUBBERT, Peter 545
HUBER, Elizabeth 381
HUBERT, Stephen 236
Hubert, ---, Brother 938
HUBIN, William 311
HUBNER, John 362
HUDDLE, Joseph 66

HUDGINS, J. R. 191
HUDSON, D. U. 189
 David W. 189, 202, 255, 800
 Henry N. 627
 I. 102
 Jonathan 61, 68, 74, 76, 206, 392
 Samuel 801
Hudson & Thompson 432
HUEY, Samuel C. 346
HUFFAND, Michael 38
HUFFINGTON, ---, Capt. 112
HUGER, Benjamin 800
HUGG, J. H. 463
 J. W. 194
 Jacob 800
 Jacob W. 194, 463
 John H. 473
 Susannah (JONES) 473
HUGGINS, A. L. 307, 442
HUGHES, ---, Archbishop 529
---, Col. 134
---, Dame 58
---, Miss 822
---, Rev. Bishop 537
 A. W. 873
 Barnabas 205, 244
 C. 680
 Christopher 61, 70, 84, 98, 194, 801, 822
 Daniel 45, 73
 David 519
 Elijah 577
 G. H. 358
 George A. 593
 George W. 358, 876
 H. 102
 Hannah 37, 913
 James 73, 77, 191, 433, 911, 927
 James E. 549
 Jeremiah 614, 801
 John 189, 433, 472, 537, 909
 Jonathan 45
 Joseph 560
 Joseph R. 158
 Kit 607
 Laura Sophia 801
 Nehemiah 877
 Peggy 801
 Priscilla 801
 S. R. 834
 Samuel 76, 79, 100, 193, 216, 424
 Thomas 927
 William 592
 William D. 636, 641
 Zanes 911
Hughes, Christopher & Co. 432
Hughes, John & Co. 310
Hughes & Williamson 392
HUGHLETT, Robert E. 158
 William 464
HULL, ---, Mr. 783

HULL, A. Gerald 749
  George V. 472
  Morris B. 202
  Morris N. B. 934
  Robert 410
Hull Street 769
HULLETT, David F. 158
HULSE, ---, Dr. 730
  Mathew 433
  Matthew 557
  R. 730
HULTON, Levi 312
Humane Impartial Society of
  Baltimore 595
Humane Society 733
HUME, Frank 359
  Thomas 556
HUMES, Thomas 158
HUMPHREY, Ebenezer 253
Humphrey's Creek 96
HUMPHREYS, C. 824
  John 54, 920
HUMPHRIES, ---, Col. 82
  John 919
HUMRICHOUSE, Charles 488
  Charles W. 489
HUNEKE, Peter J. 158
HUNGERFORD, ---, Mr. 647
  Emma (BURBRIDGE) 646
  James 617, 646, 650, 855
HUNT, ---, Gov. 127
  ---, Mr. 219, 425, 486, 837
  G. R. 916
  German H. 441, 489, 831, 838
  Germon H. 155, 446, 448, 469
  H. S. 190
  Henry S. 153, 630
  Jesse 142, 187, 194, 241, 253, 254,
    393, 470, 471, 484, 486, 594, 596,
    785, 800, 827
  Job 801
  Richard 594
  Thomas 911
  William 251, 264, 800, 871, 911
Hunt's M.E. Church 882
HUNTEMILLER, Herman F. 800
HUNTER, ---, Dr. 631
  ---, Gen. 138, 147, 335
  ---, Mr. 910
  Ann 875
  George 592
  John 532, 708
  John F. 205, 210, 222
  John F., Mrs. 155, 156
  Joseph 852
  Peter 872
  Pleasant 128, 488, 812, 813, 814,
    817, 820, 872, 903
  Rebecca A. 382
  T. V. 872
HUNTING, E. B. 281

Hunting Creek 310
Huntingdon 49
HUNTINGDON, ---, Lady 554
Huntingdon Academy 865
Huntingdon Avenue M.E. Church
  578
Huntingdon Riflemen 817
Huntington 64, 801, 888
Huntington Church 888
HUNTMILLER, H. W. 834
HUNTON, Eppa 923
Huntress 616, 630
HURD, Samuel C. 821
HURDLE, Charles 264
HURLEY, Michael 385
HURST, --- 49
  Ann Elizabeth (DRYDEN) 801
  E. 825
  J. 369
  John 57, 203, 205, 414, 448, 576,
    800, 801
  John E. 441, 448, 466, 593
  John J. 800
  William 576, 933
  William R. 600, 800
Hurst, Purnell & Co. 410, 414
Hurst & Barry 414
HUSBAND, A. 253
  Albert S. 158
  Joseph 244
  Thomas 38
  W. 38
  William 244
HUSSEY, A. 241
  Asahael 250
  Ashabel 516
  Ashael 241
  Azalia 500
  Enuion 249
  George 241
  N. 575
  Nathaniel 514
  Paul 99, 101
  William 516
Hussey House 516
HUSTED, Lyman L. 501
  S. L. 501
HUSTER, ---, Mr. 868
HUSTON, ---, Rev. Dr. 830
  L. D. 586, 636, 842
HUTCHINGS, James 76
  William 223
HUTCHINS, Abraham 911
  H. C. 908
  Henry C. 813, 815, 916
  Henry Ross 916
  Horace Walker 916
  Jarrett 916
  Jarrett Eugene 916
  John 801, 814
  Joshua 63, 820, 896

HUTCHINS, Nicholas 875, 876, 910, 911
 Richard 815, 908
 T. S. 137
 Thomas 911, 916
 Thomas T. 820
 William 812, 911
 William H. 820
Hutchins Family 907
HUTCHINSON, E. S. 140
 J. N. 346
 William 202
HUTTER, E. W. 800
HUTTON, Elijah 189, 248, 249
 George D. 728
 James 84, 89, 98, 246, 461
 N. H. 288
 Perry 202, 934
 Richard G. 403
Hutton's 342
HUXFORD, David C. 158
HUXLEY, ---, Professor 232
HUZZA, Columbus 190
HYADES, James 250
Hyatt Mansion 601
HYDE, Edward I. 158
 Emily 916
 Francis 547
 George 800
 George W. 579
 James 191, 193
 Moses 546, 547
Hyde, Bruce & Co. 629
Hyde, Francis & Son 212
Hyde Turbine Soap Co. 511
HYDZ, Maria Louisa 465
HYETT, E. 246
HYLER, J. H 354
HYLLARY, ---, Dr. 741
HYLLORY, William 741
HYNDES, John 728
HYNES, Caleb B. 190, 194
 J. H. 465
 Joshua F. 814
 Joshua H. 190, 465, 814, 820
 Thomas 189
HYNSON, G. W. 241
 John Ringgold 114
 Nathaniel 187, 205, 251
 Stanley 191
 Thomas 416
HYSER, John 801
HYSORE, M. E. 583
HYURNE, --- 81
I.O.R. 928
IDDINS, Frederick 127
IDE, ---, Rev. Dr. 929
Iglehart, James & Co. 722
IJAMS, Alfred 449
 E. E. 855
 William H. 250, 342

Ilchester 15, 24, 25, 375, 410, 541, 821
IMLAY, ---, Mr. 322
 Richard 320, 323
Immaculate Conception Catholic Church 237, 539
Imperial Land & Loan Co. 511
Improved Order of Heptasophs 668
Improved Order of Red Men 761, 762
Independence 342
Independent Blues 771
Independent Building Association No. 6 511
Independent Engine-House 524
Independent Fire Company 240, 241, 242, 247, 248, 484
Independent Grays 669
Independent Methodist Church 801, 890
Independent Methodists 584
Independent Order of Mechanics 855, 869
Independent Order of Odd-Fellows 269, 270, 758, 759, 760, 810, 855
Independent Order of Red Men 762
Independent Order of Red Men Library 667
Independent Practitioner, The 642
Independent Press 625
Independent Riflemen 817
Independent Telegraph Co. 509
Independent Volunteer Company 733
Indian King 432
Indian Queen 311, 433, 513
Indian Queen Hotel 514, 679, 737, 798, 899
Indigent Sick Society 253, 604
Industrial Home 599
Industrial Permanent Building Association No. 3 511
Industrial School Advocate, The 629
Industrial School for Girls 154
Industrial School for Orphan Girls 635
Inebriate's Record, The 641
INGELFRITZS, Jackson 264
INGERSOLL, Elizabeth 462
INGINFRITZ, Daniel 343
Inglehart 342
INGLEHART, Thomas S. 358
Ingles, S. & Co. 102
INGLIS, ---, Dr. 546
 ---, Judge 897
 ---, Rev. Dr. 268
 Charles 801
 Charles, Mrs. 595
 James 545, 547, 594, 801
 Jane 801
 John 247

INGLIS, John A. 440, 598, 728, 801
  William C. 801
INGRAHAM, ---, Prof. 625
Ingraham Chapel 586
INGRAM, Charles 255, 262
Inlan's Choice 77
Inlan's Oblong 77
INLOES, ---, Dr. 263
  Henry 911
  Henry A. 158
  Joshua 174, 187
  William 188, 189, 192, 463
INSKIP, John S. 576
Institute Building 465
Institution for the Colored Blind & Deaf Mutes 601
Insulated Lines Telegraph Co. 508
Insurance Co. of the State of Va. 490
Insurance Co. of the Valley of Va. of Winchester 490
International 515
Inventors' Journal, The 628
Inventors' National Institute 628
Ionic Lodge No. 145, A. F. & A. M. 855
IRELAN, C. Davis 801
  Charles Davis 158
  David 194, 242, 251
IRELAND, David 193
  Isabella C. (JONES) 473
  John 520, 919
  Joseph 741
  William S. 473
Ireland & Potts 432
Iris Lodge of Odd-Fellows 640
Irish-American Citizen, The 641
Iron Hill 35
Iron Hills 33
IRONMONGER, Edmund L. 559
IRONS, Emanuel 190
IRONSTINE, Daniel 880
IRVIN, James H. 202
  Levin 741
  Robert 357, 801
IRVINE, Alexander 470, 801
  Baptist 612
  George 919, 920
IRVING, George C. 369
  Washington 653, 936
  William H. 158
Irvington 820, 825
IRWIN, ---, Gen. 850
  Alexander 253
  E., Miss 605
  James 801
Irwin, George C. & Co. 481
ISAAC, ---, Mr. 894
  Ellen Penny (PHILLIPS) 893
  John T. 830
  Mary R. (WARE) 893

ISAAC, Mattie A. 886
  W. M. 903
  William M. 813, 814, 902
  William Moore 893
  Zedekiah Moore 893
ISAACS, ---, Miss 596
  John T. 830
  John W. 158
  William M. 162
ISGRIG, Mary 883
ISHAM, James 45
Isle of Kent 35
ISRAEL, Arad 814
  Edward 253
  Fielder 471, 551
  John 223
  Stephen G. 194
Itinerant Weekly 616
Itinerant, The 616
ITZELL, ---, Capt. 207
IVES, James H. 191, 193, 495
  William M. 231
JACKINS, Joseph 886
JACKSON, ---, Dr. 741
  ---, Gen. 120, 671
  ---, Miss 569
  ---, Mr. 516, 896
  A. I. W. 189
  A. J. W. 205, 802
  Andrew 124, 147, 643, 712, 753, 869
  Edward 48
  Elijah 740
  H. F. 802
  Harriet (MYERS) 774
  Henry F. 515
  Henry M. 759
  J. Edward 774
  J. J. 675
  James 53, 675
  Joseph 861
  Mary Grant 347
  Melville 774
  Samuel 801
  Samuel Keerl 774
  Stonewall 332, 670
  T. J. 670
  William 192, 246, 456, 457, 919
  William A. 347
  William Myers 774
Jackson Guards 669
Jackson Lodge No. 55, I.O.O.F. 605
Jackson Square 281
Jackson Square M.E. Church 580, 796
Jackson Street 769
Jackson's Bridge 361
Jacksonian & Baltimore County Advertiser, The 903
JACOB, Wesley 927
JACOBI, Charles G. L. 159
JACOBS, J. W. 917

JACOBS, J. W., Mrs. 917
  Joseph W. 253
  William 592
JACOBSEN, Henry G. 372
JACOBSON, Eugene Philip 802
JACQUES, ---, Dr. 741
  John J. 313
JAECKEL, Nicholas 541
JAFFRAY, James 206
  Jos. 102
JAFFREY, James 102, 298
  Joseph 433
JAKES, Henry 802
Jamaica Point 303
JAMART, Lewis A. 194
  Michael 802
JAMES, ---, Bishop 575
  Daniel 462
  Elizabeth (CORSE) 930
  Elizabeth (INGERSOLL) 462
  Flemming 523
  George W. 159
  Henry 252, 462, 463, 494, 501, 698,
    921, 927
  Henry C. 245
  Jesse 102
  Joseph 930
  N. W. 462
  Nathaniel 462
  Samuel 173
  Thomas C. 202
  William 233
  William L. 245
James, Henry & Co. 462
James' Park 77
JAMESON, ---, Dr. 741
  Horatio 737
  Horatio G. 737, 742
  Horatio Gates 755
JAMIESON, Alexander 673
  Joseph 89, 459
Jamieson's Powder-Mills 816
JAMISON, --- 693
  ---, Col. 87
  Alexander 802
  Andrew 489
  C. C. 439, 455, 470, 480, 802
  Jane C. 898
  Joseph 84, 187, 188, 233, 267, 269,
    418, 421
  Raphael 898
  Sandy 695
  T. W. 237, 830
  William 120
Jamison, C. C. & Co. 438
JANES, ---, Bishop 578
  Henry 464
  Henry, Mrs. 605
JANNEY, E. W. 927
  Henry, Mrs. 604
  R. M. 155, 602

JANNEY, Richard M. 746, 747, 801
Jansentown 937
Japett, John & Co. 100
JARBOE, ---, Mr. 152
JARRETT, Anna 582
  Henry C. 689, 693
  Lefevre 200, 801
  M. L. 755
  Samuel 582
  Thomas 582
Jarrettsville Turnpike 907, 909, 915
JARVIS, Leonard 262, 471, 802
  Nathan S. 152, 802
Jarvis Building 640
Jarvis Hospital 152
JAUBERT, Hector 802
JAY, T. H. 874
  Thomas W. 240, 255
JEAN, Alice A. 830
  George B. 495
  Ichabod 178
JEFFERIS, Gravenor M. 244
JEFFERS, Franklin 159
JEFFERSON, --- 684, 686, 693, 694
  ---, Mr. 685
  ---, Mrs. 684
  Cornelia 691
  Joe 689
  John B. H. 740
  Joseph 694, 695, 802
  Young F. 686
Jefferson Medical School 748
Jefferson Reformer 616
Jefferson Street 769
Jefferson Street M.E. Church 578
JEFFRIES, James 127
  W. 244
JEGGLE, Meinard 543
JELLY, Alexander M. 549
JENDALL, James 849
JENIFER, Daniel 741, 802, 813, 817,
    818, 903
  Eliza 802
  Walter H. 801, 847
Jenifer Family 886
JENKINS, ---, Mr. 343
  A. H. 462
  Albert 365
  Alfred 472, 801, 938
  Alphonsus L. 382
  Ap 382
  Augustus L. 483
  Austin 367, 471, 501
  C. Taylor 640
  Charity 802
  Charity Ann (WHEELER) 382
  Charles H. 159
  E. Austin 472, 938
  E., Mrs. 595
  Edward 188, 246, 595, 802
  Elizabeth (GOLD) 382

JENKINS, F. X. 441
  Felix 457
  Francis X. 382
  Frederick 252
  G. 95, 269
  George 447
  George C. 485
  Henry W. 847
  Hugh 409, 439, 440, 471, 801, 802
  Ignatius 382
  J. Stricker 245, 801
  J. W. 365
  J., Mrs. 595
  Jason, Mrs. 595
  John H. 159
  John W. 351, 447, 472, 847
  Joseph 840
  Joseph W. 410, 484, 880
  Louis W. 194
  Louis William 188, 382, 802
  M. C. 627
  M. Courtenay 801
  Martha A. 382
  Mary (COURTNEY) 382
  Matthew 301
  Michael 382, 472, 484, 802
  Michael Courtney 382
  Michaella, Sister 598
  Oliver 235, 236
  Oliver L. 382
  Oswald 802
  Rebecca A. (HUNTER) 382
  T. C. 440, 458
  T. Robert 382, 459, 483, 698
  Theodore 382
  Thomas 382
  Thomas C. 188, 298, 440, 470, 471
  Thomas H. 302
  Thomas Robert 382
  William 246, 382, 404, 470, 483, 532, 593, 802
  William Edward 382
  William H. 190, 205
Jenkins, T. Robert & Sons 382
Jenkins' Lane 896
JENKS, William R.C. 159
JENNEP, William C. 485
JENNER, ---, Dr. 734
JENNINGS, --- 698, 703
  ---, Mrs. 582
  ---, Rev. Dr. 582
  Edmund 704
  Gibbons 65
  Hannah 582
  N. H. 740
  S. K. 581, 675, 802
  Samuel K. 582, 616, 737, 786
  Thomas 709, 802
Jennings Filter Manufacturing Co. 511
JEPHSON, J. 95, 269

JEPHSON, John 95
Jericho 924, 925
Jericho Mills 836, 892
JERNINGHAM, ---, Mrs. 641
  Elizabeth (CATON) 802
JEROME, John H. T. 123, 802, 820, 876
  John Hauson Thomas 187
Jerusalem Baptist, Southampton Co., Va. 556
Jerusalem Encampment No. 1 894
Jerusalem Plank-Road 897
Jerusalem Royal Arch Chapter 878
Jervis Hospital 132
JESSON, ---, Capt. 83
  Robert 65
JESSOP, ---, Mr. 217
  Abraham 247
  Abram 814, 815
  Amanda C. 925
  Ann C. (PRICE) 925
  Cecelia P. 925
  Charles 116, 239, 310, 812, 925
  Charles M. 925
  Edwin 917, 925
  Elizabeth (HAILE) 925
  Emma M. (BOOTH) 925
  George 879
  George W. 925
  Joshua 813, 921, 925
  Mary (GORSUCH) 925
  Susan (HAILE) 925
  William 170, 187, 197, 207, 214, 238, 247, 261, 310, 456, 457, 483, 592, 727, 867, 879
Jessop Family 907
JESSOPS, William 89
JESSUP, ---, Capt. 668
Jessup's 342
JEWELL, ---, Postmaster-General 494
  Lewis 592
JEWETT, Isaac W. 488
  John 488
JEWITT, John 244
JILLARD, John 251
  William H. 137, 801, 847
JOB, Morris 780
JOHANNES, Henry C. 159
  J. G. 130
  John G. 159
JOHN, ---, Rev. 773
John Wesley M.E. Church 580
JOHNS, ---, Bishop 908
  ---, Dr. 557
  ---, Mrs., Dr. 595
  ---, Rev. Dr. 521, 660, 840, 933
  Abraham 45
  Ann (WORTHINGTON) 864
  Aquila 76, 101
  Auquila 921
  H. V. D. 524, 525, 643, 802, 826

JOHNS, Hannah (BOND) 921
  Henry 884
  Jacob 921
  John 521, 524, 801, 865, 866, 867, 884, 902
  John T. 802
  John Tolly 866
  Kensey 463, 861
  Kinsey 865
  Richard 38, 74, 116, 801, 802, 812, 864, 865, 866
  Ruth 102
  Sarah 801, 802
  Sarah (WEEMS) 864
  Sarah C. (WEEMS) 865
  Susan 864
  William J. 840
Johns Family 884
JOHNSON, --- 698
  ---, Chancellor 714
  ---, Col. 850
  ---, Dr. 732, 741
  ---, Gov. 709, 779
  ---, Mayor 783
  ---, Mr. 408
  ---, Mrs. 264, 596
  ---, President 138, 152, 163
  ---, Rev. Dr. 828
  ---, Rev. Mr. 920
  A. 362
  Alex B. 820
  Alexander 889
  Andrew 142
  B. R. 846
  B. T. 723
  Benjamin 903
  Bowie F. 159
  Bradley T. 138, 720
  Cecelia P. (JESSOP) 925
  Charles 159
  Charles W. 925
  Chris. 298
  Christopher 207, 214, 407, 432, 433, 452, 545, 743, 802, 826
  E. 733
  Edward 77, 84, 86, 89, 118, 173, 187, 192, 197, 214, 249, 268, 433, 592, 699, 732, 733, 801, 802, 826
  Edwin 552
  Elijah H. 159
  Elisha S. 812, 865
  Elizabeth 863
  Elizabeth (CRADOCK) 861
  F. 828
  Fayette 861, 865
  Francis 864
  George B. 526
  George W. 159, 352
  George William 864
  Gershon 311, 312
  Greenleaf 281

JOHNSON, H. E. 585, 600, 602, 838
  Harvey E. 568
  Henry 37, 247, 525, 802
  Henry E. 584, 698, 851
  Henry Elliott 851
  Hickman 865
  Horatio 74
  J. Lee 602
  J. R. 590, 675
  J. S. 525
  James 613, 820, 866
  Jane (LOWE) 866
  Jeremiah 38, 70, 728, 863, 910
  John 101, 452, 555, 802
  Joseph E. 352
  Joseph G. 191
  L. Lee 602
  Louis E. 159
  Luke 911
  Macok W. 500
  Margaret A. 398
  Margaret Ann 839
  Mary M. 801
  Matthew 911, 920
  Maurice 298
  O. R. 342
  Oscar 908
  Reverdy 113, 122, 126, 127, 128, 195, 198, 232, 499, 508, 521, 526, 713, 714, 737, 784, 785, 786, 801, 820
  Rinaldo 74
  Robert 191, 433, 741
  Samuel 839
  Sarah 884
  Stephen T. 742
  Stephen Theodore 741
  T. 102, 103
  Thomas 38, 70, 73, 74, 75, 76, 77, 79, 101, 118, 169, 193, 195, 706, 707, 732, 733, 816, 819, 899
  Thomas M. 596
  Thomas W. 448, 468
  Upshur 508
  Victoria 877
  W. 102
  W. H. 636
  W. R. 849
  William 149, 205, 680
  William F. 355, 816, 819, 888
  William Fell 802, 818, 876
  William J. 840, 886
  Wilmot 440
Johnson, Sutton & Co. 410
Johnson & Company 261
Johnson Building 142, 489
Johnson Family 858, 927
Johnson Square 280
JOHNSTON, ---, Gen. 147
  ---, Mr. 481, 694
  C. 547

JOHNSTON, Christopher 70, 454,
  455, 545, 546, 745, 802
 Edward 136
 Finley 802
 G. 547
 George W. 253
 Henry 33, 818
 Henry E. 851
 Jeremiah 72
 Joe 865
 John 101
 Julius A. 743
 L. 363
 Malcolm H. 820
 R. M. 657
 Robert 734
 Samuel 801
 Thomas 120
 Thomas D. 802, 931
 William 801
 William T. 866
 William Tilghman 801
 Zachary F. 802
Johnston Bros. & Co. 481
Johnston Line 306
JOHONNOT, George 194
JOICE, S. J. 191
JOLLIFFE, Amos 866
JOLLY, William 522
JONES, ---, Dr. 505, 741
 ---, Maj. 90
 A. F. 472
 Alexander 288, 463, 471, 472, 473,
  484, 577
 Alexander Franklin 473
 Andrew D. 412
 Ann 459
 Ann (SHAW) 473
 Anthony 911
 Benetta Eugenia 473
 Benjamin 45, 920
 C. H. 604, 743
 Caleb 472
 Carleton S. 159
 Carrie 889
 Charles 159, 935
 Charles H. 468, 469, 745, 746
 Charlotte 889
 Clara 886
 Custis P. 526
 Daniel 656
 David 49, 54, 208
 E. L. 149, 253
 E. T. 136
 Edward 706
 Edward F. 791
 Edwin L. 242, 484
 Eliza 889
 Elizabeth 889
 Elizabeth (DORSEY) 889
 Elizabeth Ellen 473

JONES, Emily E. 227
 Emma Virginia 473
 Eugenia L. 855
 Fannie 889
 Frances 213
 Frank F. 222
 George E. 548
 H. C. 194
 H. P. 670
 Henry 471
 Hugh B. 250, 256, 483
 Inigo 459
 Isaac D. 128, 440, 601
 Isabella C. 473
 Isabella C. (SHAW) 473
 J. 102
 J. H. 516
 J. W. 874, 905
 James 889
 James D. 251
 James H. 241
 Jane 460
 Jane (THOMPSON) 459
 Jemima 582
 Jenkins 553
 John 889
 John B. 617
 John F. 836
 John M. 190, 191, 576, 761
 John S. 551
 Joseph 746, 801, 802, 861, 889
 Joseph H. 553
 Josephine 821
 Joshua 120, 194, 205, 558, 612, 801
 Josiah N. 659
 L. R. 855
 Maggie 889
 Mary 889
 Mary (BENNETT) 472
 Mary Ann 473
 Mathias 741
 Nicholas 70, 205, 244, 484, 728
 Nora 886
 Philip 51, 52, 53, 55, 58
 Quartley 662
 R. E. 813, 888
 R. H. 393
 Randolph 889
 Reuben 889
 Reuben E. 813
 Reuben Elsrood 889
 Richard 459, 911
 Richard H. 89, 244, 459
 Robert 889
 S. 439
 Samuel 192, 463, 464, 515, 675, 801,
  854, 911
 Samuel G. 244
 Sarah 889
 Stephen W. 159
 Susannah 473

JONES, Susannah (ELSROOD) 889
  Talbot 188, 316, 317, 318, 461, 470, 577, 802
  Talbot Dixon 412
  Talbott 854
  Thomas 70, 73, 459, 490, 707, 709, 729, 814, 889
  Thomas Bennett 473
  Tiberius G. 563
  W. 102
  W. H. 149, 846
  W. T. 247
  Walter R. 254
  William 89, 101, 244, 246, 247, 252, 393, 407, 889
  William B. 472
  William Caleb 472
  William D. 256
  William F. 761
  William Gwinn 244
  William Gwynn 188, 189, 609
  William H. 159, 489
  William J. 729
  William P. 141
  William R. 483, 802
Jones, Samuel 313
Jones & Woodward 412
Jones' Addition to Baltimore Town 554
Jones' Falls 50, 57, 214, 217, 218, 518, 697, 726, 727, 768, 811, 836, 838, 839, 842, 877, 886, 887
Jones' Falls:
  Bridges & Floods 208
Jones' Town 47, 54, 62
Jones' Town:
  List of Lot Owners 55, 56
  Plat 52
  Survey 55
Joppa 40, 42, 43, 44, 46, 47, 60, 77, 224, 311, 496, 519, 707, 726, 757, 778, 815, 816, 857, 864, 909, 910, 918, 920, 921, 922, 923, 924
Joppa Cemetery Inscriptions 923
Joppa Iron-Works 925
Joppa Mills 220
Joppa Road 894, 922
Joppa: 1725 Plat 45
JORDAN, Amanda 871
  Ann (STEELE) 871
  Archibald Steele 871
  B. F. 872
  Benjamin 871
  Benjamin F. 813, 871
  Benjamin Franklin 871
  Dominic 801
  E. C. 187
  Edward C. 871
  George 694
  Hanson P. 161
  Harriet 871

JORDAN, Harriet R. 871
  James 871
  James P. 871
  John 871
  John Lawrence 871
  John S. 871
  Joseph 871
  Juliet E. (ANDERSON) 871
  Mary J. 871
  Mary Sophronia 871
  Otho 871
  Rachel 871
  Rachel A. 871
  Rebecca 871
  Rebecca (TURNER) 871
  Samuel 871
  Samuel M. 871
  Thomas 871
  Thomas R. 871
  Thomas Ross 871
  William 694, 928
  William L. 540
Jordan & Rose 149
JOSEPH, Alexis 801
  William 195
Josephs' Lottery-office 262
JOUBERT, James H. N. 235
  James Neator 534, 598
  Nicholas 236
Journal of Commerce 630, 648
Journal of the American Silk Society 624
Journal of the Times 614
JOYCE, Eugene T. 194
  John 836
  Stephen 145, 146
  Stephen J. 615
JOYNER, Robert 732
JOYNES, Thomas R. 556
JUCE, Emma 694
  Fanny 694
JUDD, Mary 43
  Michael 43
JUDEN, John 558
Judges of City Courts 729
Judges of the Orphans' Court 1855-81 728
JUDICK, J. H. 465
  J. Henry 472
  Joseph 472
JUDSON, Jonathan 70
JUKE, ---, Col. 849
JULOCE, James 911
JUNGER, Sigmund 642
JUNGERNICKEL, Henry M. 673
Junior Artillerists 669
Juvenile Amicable Society 678
Juvenile Mirror 625
KAHLER, Charles P. 534
  John J. 191
Kahler & Smith 263

KAIN, J. J. 538
KAINE, Hugh 65
  James 65
  John 65
KAISER, Charles 605
  William 935
KALB, David 820
KALBFUS, Lewis, Mrs. 596
Kaleidoscope 386
KALKMAN, Von Hollen 802
Kaminskey's Tavern 58
Kanawha Valley 335
KANBE, Ernest 605
KANE, ---, Col. 130, 137, 198
  ---, Dr. 802
  ---, Mayor 184, 494, 755
  Elisha K. 839
  G. P. 302
  George P. 133, 141, 166, 181, 187, 199, 200, 210, 222, 242, 249, 271, 438, 439, 440, 441, 497, 498, 694, 695, 728, 788, 802, 931
  Henry 911
  Marshal 128, 133, 789, 790, 791
  Michael 264
  William E. 241
Kane Artic Expedition 663
KARNS, Robert 159
KARTHAUS, C. W. 439
  Charles W. 372
  Peter A. 461
Karthaus, C. W. & Co. 438
KARTHAWS, Charles W. 246
KATZENBERGER, J. H. 487
KAUFFELT, John B. 802
KAUFFMAN, Abraham 312
  Hiram 380
  J. H. 550
KAUFMAN, --- 358
  Angelica 676
  Conrad 264
  John T. 813
KAUFMANN, L. 446
KAUPP, Charles L. 159
KAWFFELT, James B. 441
KEACH, Charles W. 465
  Lawson P. 465
KEALE, Richard 39
KEAN, Charles 687, 689
  Edmund 686, 694
  Sarah 212
  William 95
KEARNEY, Nicholas 535
Kearneysville Depot 146
KEATING, Thomas 877
KECK, Josiah L. 446
KEECH, John R. 920
  John Ryder 911
  W. S. 886
  William H. 911
  William S. 813, 814, 820, 902, 903

KEECHY, W. T. 874
KEEGER, ---, Mr. 628
KEEKE, Nicholas 744
KEELY, Thomas 836
KEEN, George V. 367, 368
  Richard 38
KEENAN, ---, Dr. 262
  Peter 262
KEENE, ---, Dr. 741
  ---, Mr. 686
  Eleonora (MARTIN) 802
  George V. 579
  John 192
  Joseph R. 159
  Laura 695
  Richard Raynall 802
  William B. 741
KEENER, A. D. 551
  Chris. 439
  Christian 63, 172, 362, 393, 402, 594, 771, 802, 827
  David 159, 464, 740, 824
  Melcher 402
  Melchior 205, 515
  Melchoir 244
  William H. 842
KEEPORTS, ---, Capt. 78, 482
  George 117
  George P. 72, 187, 216, 520
  George Peter 70
  Jacob 802
  Jake 58
KEER, J. W. 548
KEERL, Ellen (DOUGLASS) 774
  Eversfield Fraser 773
  George 402
  George H. 740, 774
  George Henry 773
  George I. 252
  Henry 252, 432, 734, 750, 773, 774, 802
  John C. 470, 773
  John Hubert Donnell 773
  Richard Dobbs Spaight 773
  S. 241
  Samuel 241, 252, 773
  Susan (MUNDELL) 773
  Thomas M. 773, 774
  William 774
KEERSTED, Luke 461
KEHLENBECK, John H. 250
KEICH, W. S. 813
KEIGHLER, ---, Mr. 217
  W. H. 345, 471
  William H. 469, 596
KEILHOLTZ, George 255
  Otis 191, 202, 495
KEIM, Charles W. 390
  Susan Douglas 389
KEISER, M. F. 471
KEITH, ---, Gov. 65

KEITH, James 464
Naomi 464
KELL, ---, Judge 139, 849
  Elizabeth 139
  Thomas 101, 119, 120, 173, 187, 188, 194, 802, 814, 850, 934
KELLER, Christian 89
  John 570, 802
  Josiah 380
  May 596
Keller & Forman 438
Keller & Grenough 506
KELLEY, A. D. 302
  Alexander D. 471
  Eli S. 834
  James J. 886
  John D. 487
  Thomas 877
KELLOGG, O. 577
KELLUM, Edward M. 255
KELLY, ---, Gen. 652
---, Miss 687
---, Mr. 682
  Alexander 770
  Alford 552
  Caleb 465
  Charles F. 538
  Cornelius A. 802
  Edward 727, 870
  F. H. 247
  Hannah (WILSON) 770
  Hosea 872
  James 193
  Joseph 193
  M. 303
  M. J. 629
  Martha (WILSON) 770
  Math. 393
  Matthew 463
  Michael J. 145
  Nicholas 355
  P. 236
  Stephen A. 538
  Thomas 191, 193
  Timothy 462, 802
  Washington 472
  William J. 191
KELSAY, R. B. 562
KELSEY, William 582
KELSO, ---, Mr. 343
  J. 86
  J. R. 192
  James 74
  John 84, 89, 234, 343, 393, 826
  John R. 190, 193, 199, 222, 827
  John T. 153
  Thomas 77, 192, 199, 233, 234, 249, 452, 466, 478, 582, 604, 667, 802, 890
  William 159, 911
Kelso & Ferguson 439

Kelso M.E. Home for Orphan Children 604
KEMBLE, James 38
  Roger 682
  Thomas 688
Kemble Co. of Baltimore 695
KEMER, Joseph 102
Kemer, J. & Co. 102
KEMP, ---, Bishop 267, 522, 865, 911, 921
---, Rt. Rev. Bishop 469
  Alfred 869
  Charles O. 869
  E. L. 523
  Edward D. 189, 728, 802, 814
  Elizabeth 802
  Ella 855
  Howard 869
  J. McK. 161
  James 205, 520, 521, 802
  Richard 523
  Simon J. 472
  Simon T. 935
  Thomas E. 159, 908
Kemp Hall 914
Kemp's Addition 61
KEMPER, Jackson 879
Kemper's Battery 897
KENDALL, A. C. 255
  Amos 506, 508
  John E. 506
Kendall & Kerr 423
Kendall Race-course 501
KENDIG, ---, Mr. 861
KENLY, ---, Capt. 352
---, Col. 139, 199
---, Gen. 140, 148
---, Provost-Marshal 133, 136
  Daniel 816
  Edward 133, 252
  George T. 441, 442
  J. R. 354
  John R. 113, 114, 133, 134, 135, 136, 147, 149, 159, 199, 200
  Marshal 199
  W. W. 222
  William L. 159, 222
KENNARD, Agnes Maria (ONION) 922
  Alexander Anderson 922
  Baltis H. 579
  Baltus H. 194, 195
  G. J. 366
  George I. 193, 488
  George J. 466
  John 582
  Louis E. 159
  Mary 582
  Samuel 261
  Thomas A. 159
Kennard's Ship Yard 293

KENNEDY, --- 54
---, Mr. 346, 653, 654, 664
---, Mrs. 889
Andrew 821, 822
Ann Clayton (PENDLETON) 821
Anthony 130, 194, 195, 498, 652,
  816, 820, 821, 822
Edward 802
H. H. 587
Henry 782
Herbert M. 813
Howard 507
J. 70
J. F. 77
J. P. 680
J. P., Mrs. 802
John 77, 92, 207, 209, 434, 821
John A. 802
John H. 189
John P. 61, 120, 122, 123, 127, 128,
  140, 194, 195, 345, 393, 498, 502,
  643, 646, 652, 658, 660, 663, 679,
  682, 822, 890
John Pendleton 642, 802, 816
Joseph 432
Murdock 779
N. R. 189
Patrick 76, 730, 740
Philip Clayton 802
Philip P. 822
S. 614
Thomas 194
William 100, 288, 302, 466, 488,
  652, 802, 838, 887, 889, 938
KENNER, William 802
KENNEY, David 927
  Thomas M. 202
KENNY, Francis 927
KENRICK, ---, Archbishop 236,
  529, 530, 533, 536, 537, 538, 539,
  540, 599, 629, 822, 892, 917, 933
---, Right Rev. Bishop 537
Francis P. 541
Francis Patrick 528, 802
Patrick 647
Kenrick Building Association No. 4
  & 5 511
KENSETT, Thomas 281, 292, 466,
  777, 802
KENT, --- 715, 726
  Archibald 251
  Emanuel 172, 187, 244, 250, 455,
    802
  James 757
  Joseph 195, 729
  Thomas H. 729, 742
Kent Island 39, 40, 927
Kent Isle 373
Kent Point 309
KEPLER, Samuel 813, 902
KERCHNER, Frederick A. 469

KERFOOT, F. H. 566
  John B. 914
KERFORTS, George F. 592
KERK, Samuel 191
KERN, John A. 586
KERNAN, Charles 245
  Eugene 191
  James 802
  John 224
  Thomas P. 191, 194, 802
  William C. 935
Kernan Brothers 696
KERNEY, M. J. 629
  Martin J. 194, 648
Kerneysville 342
Kernstown 342
KERR, ---, Mr. 271, 632
  A. S. 551
  Andrew S. 230
  Arch. 577
  Archibald 438, 461
  Charles G. 191, 193, 195, 624, 631
  John 561
  R. J. 508, 729
Kerr's Wharf 292
KERSHAW, ---, Gen. 923
KESLEY, William 582
Kesley's School-house 225
KESMODEL, Martin 488
KESTLER, Peter B. 202
KETTLEWELL, Charles 400
  John 400, 463, 497, 498, 601, 802,
    814
  Johna 397
  Rebecca 400
KEUHN, Adolph 159
KEY, --- 707, 769, 907
---, Mr. 493
  Abner 189
  Francis 802
  Francis S. 616, 802
  Francis Scott 97, 642, 685
  Gabriel P. 253
  H. G. S. 845
  Henry G. S. 128
  Mary Taylor 802
  Philip 118
  Philip B. 802, 816
  Philip Barton 802
KEYL, G. W. 570
KEYS, J. R. 873, 874
  J. W. 873
  T. W. 873
Keyser 342
KEYSER, ---, Mr. 357
  C. C. 190, 191
  Charles M. 123, 189, 193, 240, 241,
    462, 770, 802, 827, 937
  Derick 802
  Elizabeth 802

KEYSER, George 188, 190, 241, 254, 381, 760, 802
Mary E. (WILSON) 770
Michael F. 471
P. L. 597
W. W. 240
William 339, 381, 446, 494, 817
William W. 241
Keyser Bros. & Co. 426
Keyser Family 852
KIBLIN, R. S. 802
KIDD, Milton Y. 162
Kidder, Peabody & Co. 350
KIDWELL, S. B. 231
KIEFFER, G. S. 936
KIEL, August 597
KIERL, John 467
KIERSTEAD, Luke 92
KIERSTED, J. 102
L. 102
KILBOURN, E. G. 127, 802
KILGOUR, ---, Mr. 128, 783
Robert 782
KILLGOUR, ---, Mr. 681
KILLMEYER, Max 159
KILTY, ---, Rear-Admiral 802
John 712
KIMBALL, Hiram 927
Leonard 439
W. P. 193
KIMBERLY, Charles W. 610, 636, 802
Edward 489
H. 380
Henry 262
J. M. 190
Samuel 380
KIMMEL, --- 166
Anthony 802
Michael 250, 251
William 162, 722
KIMMELL, Anthony 253, 254
Solomon 414
William 193, 721
KING, --- 791
---, Dr. 741
---, Miss 595
---, Mr. 217, 295, 340
A. T., Miss 605
Adam E. 151, 152, 497, 498
Benjamin 101
Charles F. 538
David 195, 813, 820
Francis T. 222, 232, 252, 466, 469, 478, 483, 488, 596, 600, 601, 604, 746, 747
George W. 191, 802
J. 102
Jacob 802
John 189, 338, 339, 341, 446, 471, 509, 573, 574, 741, 802

KING, John C 720
John C. 466, 723, 729
Joseph 252, 438, 483, 595, 802, 937
Joseph, Mrs. 594
Laura A. 917
Mary 596
Preston 147
Richard 153
Robert G. 159
Samuel R. 449
Solomon 488
Thomas 65, 802
Thomas A. 588
W. R. 123
Wallace 368
William 202
William J. 193, 466
King & Sutton's Lumber Yard 262
King Charles I 705
King Charles II 705
King David Lodge 903
King George's Street 680
King William's Free School 223
King's Arms 680
KINGDON, John 874
KINGSBURY, --- 55
Kingsbury Furnace 424
Kingsbury Lands 424
Kingsley & Co. 359
Kingsville 910, 918, 921
Kingwood 330
KINNEMON, P. S. 751, 802
KINSEY, ---, Mr. 434
Edward 579, 867
Margaret 50
KINSOLVING, George H. 523
KINZER, J. D. 584
KIPP, ---, Bishop 674
John 244, 393, 802
KIPPS, Francis 54
KIRBY, Ann 795
James T. 191
John 249
Joshua 77
Rebecca 395
Samuel 462, 466, 470
Thomas E. 740
KIRD, John M. 407
KIRK, ---, Mr. 257
Bennet 250
George A. 178, 193, 194
Samuel 190, 193, 222, 242, 249, 462, 802
Thomas 246
William J. 446
KIRKLAND, ---, Mrs. 595
Alexander 463, 471, 802
John W. 177
Ogden A. 178
R. R. 288, 488
Robert R. 155

114

Kirkland, ---, Messrs. & Co. 516
KIRKLE, James C. 465
KIRKPATRICK, James 773
KIRKUS, William 524, 802
KIRKWOOD, Edwin C. 159
 Philip 190
 R. J. 828
 William 814
KIRTZ, R. A. 929
KIRWIN, ---, Capt. 135
 William B. 802
KIRZINSKY, Henry 159
KITSEN, John E. 149
 Samuel 149
 William 149
Kittochtinny Hills 66
KITTS, John 190, 193, 802
 Thomas 560
Kizer, David & Co. 438
KLASEY, George 255
KLASSSEN, J. 247
KLECKNER, Joseph 490
 Louisa 490
KLEES, ---, Mr. 405
 Elizabeth (FETT) 405
 Henry 404, 405
 John 404, 405
Klees, Henry & Son 404
KLEIBACKER, C. B. 604
KLEIN, ---, Miss 411
 George 605
KLEINEIDAM, Robert 541
KLEINFELTER, V. V. 472
KLEPSTEIN, ---, Dr. 701
KLINE, Henry H. 875
KLINEFELTER, ---, Mr. 264
 Michael 188, 192
 V. V. 579
 Van Vert 446
KNABE, Ernest 487
 William 403, 802
Knabe & Gahle 263
Knabe Gahle & Co. 262
Knabe's Hal 674
Knable & Co. 403
Knaff Building 488
KNAPP, Jacob 555, 563
 Samuel 592
KNAUSS, --- 676
KNEASS, Strickland 210
KNELL, Henry 280, 802
 J. Henry 280
KNEW, Harvey 367
KNIGHT, ---, Mr. 320, 322, 323, 324
 A. S. 303
 E. 627
 Edward 236
 Nathaniel 89, 593
 Robert 246
 Samuel T. 802
 W. M. 847

KNIGHTON, Nicholas 358
Knights of Honor 762, 889
Knights of Pythias 762, 840
Knights of St. Venceslaus 543
Knights of Templar 903
Knights of the Golden Eagle 762
KNIPP, Frederick 261
KNOBELOCK, Simon 159
KNOEFF, C. 597
Knolls 288
KNOPPEL, John 159
KNORR, William 262, 288
KNOTT, ---, Mr. 721
 A. Leo 194, 236, 721, 722
 Aloysius Leo 720
 Edward 720
 Elizabeth Sprigg (SWEENEY) 720
 John 720
 Zachary 720
KNOTTS, George 189
KNOWDEN, Samuel 722
Knowles' 342
KNOX, F. 102
 James 442
 Mary 770
 Reynolds 247
 Samuel 770
 William 482
Knox, Usher & McCulloh 432
Knox Presbyterian Church 552
Knox's Cotton Factory 262
KNYPHAUSEN, --- 852
KOECHLING, Henry M. 802
KOEHL, John 571, 590
KOENIG, C. S. 439
 Frederick 433
 Henry 433
 Leonard 929
 Michael 543
KOGELSHATZ, Adolph 159
KOHL, D. F. 597
KOHLER, William H. 813
KOLLER, William H. 814
 William K. 813
KOLMAN, George 929
KOLP, John 830
KONCZ, A. 543
 P. 543
KONECKE, Nicholas 569
KONIG, Augustus 225
 Frederick 298, 389
 Henry 298
KOONS, C. H. 488
 Joseph 139
KOONSMARY, William 256
KOONTZ, ---, Col. 264
 George S. 342
KOPPELMAN, J. H. 929
KOPPELMANN, J. G. 468
KOSSUTH, --- 626
KRABER, Daniel 207

115

KRACK, John 573
KRAFFT, Charles L. 126
  J. P. 372, 439
KRAFT, --- 274
  Charles L. 190, 194
  Frederick A. 194
  J. C. 190, 191
  John W. 159
KRAGER, John H. 191
  Joseph H. 191
  T. 889
KRAMER, John W. 159
  Samuel 159
KRANCH, ---, Rev. Mr. 569
  Charles P. 569
  Kranich & Bach 674
KRAPP, ---, Prof. 597
KRATT, Martin 597
KRAUS, ---, Rev. Dr. 588
  A. 573
KRAUSE, John 929
KREAGER, J. 241
  Joseph 241
KREBBS, W. H. H. 159
KREBS, G. W. 252
  George W. 192
  J. Wesley 579
  Jacob 802
  John Wesley 802
  Samuel 582
  W. 579
  W. G. 729
  William 98, 120, 188, 192, 250, 313, 456, 470, 667, 785
  William George 802
KREIN, John 159
KREMELBERG, J. D. 195, 372
KREMMELBURG, J. D. 851
KREUTZER, Christopher 495
KREUZER, Christopher 468
  Joseph 468, 641
  Kreuzer Bros. 641
KRIES, George J. 938
KROES, Peter 538
KROESEN, Isaac 523
KROFT, J. G. 379
  Kroft, J. G. & Co. 379
KROH, George L. 802
KROHN, ---, Capt. 298
KROUT, A. H. 873
  Michael 873
KRUDENER, ---, Baron 321
KUEST, Catherine A. 930
KUGLER, Benjamin 500, 501
  George W. 159
KUHBORD, Jacob 571
KUHN, ---, Lt. 91
  John J. 159
KUHNS, Joseph H. 202
KUMMER, John 241
  S. Agnes 802

KUNITZ, Henry 159
KUNKER, J. H. 237, 821
KUNKLE, ---, Mr. 688
  George 693, 696
  Kunkle's Ethiopian Opera-House 693
KURTZ, ---, Mr. 568
  ---, Rev. Dr. 870
  B. 840, 877
  Benjamin 631, 802, 929
  Christian 927
  Daniel 568
  Edward 470
  T. Daniel 594
  T. Newton 631, 802
KUSICK, John W. 136
KYLE, Adam B. 802
  Adam Barclay 415
  George B. 788
  George H. 440, 802
L'HOMME, ---, Father 534
  Francis 236, 803
  La Plata 354
LA ROCHE, G. 102
LA VALETTE, ---, Gen. 80
LABES, James 252
LABESIUS, ---, Dr. 740
  John 730
  Lacaze & Mallett 102
LACHEY, ---, Rev. Mr. 571
LADD, Luther C. 790
  Ladies' Altar Society 543
  Ladies' Companion 613
  Ladies' Depository 156
  Ladies' Hebrew Hospital Association 747
  Ladies' Newspaper 628
  Ladies' Relief Association 593, 599
  Lafayette 78, 354
LAFAYETTE, --- 79, 924, 925, 937
  ---, Gen. 80, 854, 885
  Lafayette Fire Company 242
  Lafayette Guards 669
  Lafayette Hose Company 255
  Lafayette Light Dragoons 744
  Lafayette Market 593
  Lafayette Market-House 208
  Lafayette Road 925
  Lafayette Square 280
  Lafayette Square Presbyterian Church 550, 551
  Lafayette Station 353
LAFETRA, Jacob 248, 249
LAFEYETTE, --- 679
LAFFAN, William M. 624
  Laffan, William M. & Co. 624
LAFFERTY, William 248, 249
LAFFITTE, John 372
  John S. 890
  LaGrange Works 872
LAHAVAN, John 70

Lake 347
Lake Chapman 219
Lake Clifton 220, 221, 886, 890, 926
Lake Montebello 220, 221, 886
Lake Roland 218, 220, 221, 274, 344, 355, 356, 886
Lake Roland Road 817
Lake Superior Copper-Mines 843
LAMAR, Eugene 146
  Louisa 726
  William 726
LAMARDE, Jean 202
LAMB, John 95
LAMBDIN, Edward S. 177
  John 803
LAMBERT, S. A. 359
LAMDEN, Edward S. 190
LAMDIN, Edward S. 190
LAMLE, John 929
LAMMOT, Daniel 207, 250
Lamokin 351
Lamokin Junction 350
LAMOTTE, L. A. J. 855
LAMPLEY, John, Mrs. 202
LANAGAN, M. 688
  Michael J. 802
LANAHAN, ---, Rev. Dr. 837
  John 323, 577, 599
  Thomas M. 723
Lancashire Forge 816
Lancashire Furnace 424
LANCASTER, Joseph 742
Lancaster Furnace 425
LANCE, Bob 58
Land We Love, The 637
LANDER, ---, Gen. 335
  D. C. 307
LANDERMAN, Henry R. 241
LANDIS, David C. 803
  H. C. 485
  Henry C. 485
LANDS, Samuel 64
LANDSTREET, Anna V. 852
  John 471, 852, 855
  Samuel, Mrs. 596
  W. 640
  William T. 159
LANE, ---, Maj. 91
  ---, Rev. Mr. 838
  John 251
  John F. 581
  Joseph 127
  Thomas 246
  W. H. 838
Lane Roland 839
LANG, Charles 826
  F. O. 821
  George E. 927
LANGE, Mary, Sister 598
LANGFORD, Henry S. 194

LANGHERTY, David 479
LANGTON, Thomas 392
LANGWORTHY, Edward 224, 608, 803, 861
LANIER, Jacob 253
  Mary (DAY) 655
  Sidney 233, 655, 803
LANKFORD, Henry S. 191
LANMAN, Charles R. 233
LANNAY, Peter L. 434
LANSDALE, Thomas 70, 73, 813
  William 740
Lanvale Cotton-factory 217
Lanvale Factory 838
Lanvale Street 937
LANVILLE, John T. 191
Lapourelle & Maughlin 262
LARCH, Valentine 803
LAREW, Abraham 247
  M. 261
LARKAIN, William 759
Larkington 639
LARKINS, E. 350
Larned's University School 233
LAROQUE, Emile 740
  Francis Edward 803
  J. M. 802
Laroque's Drug-Store 213
LARRABEE, Daniel 433
  Henry C. 190
  William F. 159
LARSH, Silas 195
  Valentine 514
LATANE, James A. 525
LATBOT, William A. 659
LATHAM, A. H. 558
LATIMER, ---, Bishop 346
  Randolph B. 814
  Sarah 346
  T. S. 604, 637, 743
  Thomas 598
  Thomas S. 738, 745, 746
  William 346
  William R. 802
  William W. 659
LATOUCHE, James W. 592
LATREYTE, J. 103
LATROBE, ---, Mayor 185, 220, 394, 417, 626, 728, 755
  ---, Mr. 181, 184
  ---, Rev. Mr. 526
  B. H. 180, 210, 434, 532, 802
  Benjamin F. 210
  Benjamin H. 288, 324, 337, 348, 350, 438, 936
  Charles H. 211
  F. C. 260, 288, 447, 494, 495, 509, 698
  Ferdinand C. 166, 180, 187, 194, 222, 276, 446, 508

LATROBE, J. H. B. 207, 271, 274,
  434, 499, 657, 667, 826, 928
 J. H. B., Mrs. 155, 156, 595
 John H. B. 178, 180, 273, 276, 358,
  488, 646, 658, 659, 667, 688, 691,
  715, 716, 719, 803, 827, 890
 John H. B., Mrs. 156
 Margaret C. 803
Lattel, J. & Co. 102
LATY, Ann Owens 429
LAUDERMAN, Henry L. 192
 Henry R. 188, 189
LAUER, Ignatius 747
 S. 237
LAUGHLIN, David 552
LAUMASTER, Jacob 343
Lauraville 886, 929, 930
Laurel 342, 407
Laurel Cemetery 933
Laurel Factory 409
Laurel Mill 409, 836
LAURENSON, Philip 189, 192, 194,
  235
 S. B. 812
LAUTENBACH, Robert 740
LAVELY, William 75
LAVENDER, Benjamin A. 932
Lavender Hill 886, 931
LAW, Anthony 247
 George 803
 James 433, 461, 803
 James O. 187, 803
Law Building(s) 126, 137, 592
Law Grays, The 668
Law Library 652
Law Reporter, The 637
LAWFORD, T. W. 195
 Thomas W. 603
LAWRASON, Louisa S.
  (LEVERING) 771
 W. W. 563
 William W. 771
Lawrason & Smith 481
LAWRENCE, ---, Col. 633
 Amos 317
 Benjamin 71
 Daniel 779
 F. L. 586
 Lewis 310
 Richard 592
 Thomas 188
 Thomas L. 92
Lawrence Street 769
LAWRENSON, Philip 532, 593, 595
LAWSEN, Alex. 205
LAWSON, --- 54
 ---, Mr. 816
 ---, Mrs. 261
 A. 814
 Alexander 54, 56, 58, 59, 433, 545,
  803, 921

LAWSON, Diana 803
 Ephraim 803
 George 803
 John 344
 R. 465
 Richard 175, 192, 238, 239, 483,
  803, 823
 Richard T. H. 449
 Robert 92, 485
Lawson, Richard & Co. 432
LAWTON, John 487
LAYPOLE, Andrew (Isadore) 146,
  202
Lazaretto 91, 95, 291
Lazaretto Lot 62
Lazaretto Point 90, 926, 929
Lazaretto Warehouse, Quarantine
  261
LAZARUS, Ferdinand 149
LAZEAR, J. 369
 Jesse 370, 802, 829
 William L. 828
LEACH, Benjamin 911
 John 911
LEADBETTER, John 386
Leadenhall Street 769
Leadenhall Street Baptist Church
  567
Leadenhall Street Colored Baptist
  Church 568
Leader, The 636
LEAF, Henry 877
LEAGUE, Luke 307
LEAKIN, ---, Mr. 343, 612
 ---, Rev. Mr. 521, 822
 G. A. 159
 George A. 153
 George Armistead 522
 S. C. 122, 615, 785, 786, 850
 Sheppard A. 802
 Sheppard C. 187, 393, 771, 802, 814,
  928
 Shepperd C. 343
LEAKY, M. 149
LEAMAN, Thomas 870
LEAMY, J. C. 740
LEAR, William 114
LEARY, Augustus M. 159
 C. L. L. 195
 Cornelius L. L. 194
 J. 489
 John 488
 Peter 159, 252, 394, 463, 667, 814
Lebasse & Sautin 687
LEBESIUS, ---, Dr. 731
LECKER, ---, Archbishop 858
LEE, --- 223, 859
 ---, Bishop 581
 ---, Col. 132
 ---, Gen. 135, 335, 780, 865
 ---, Gov. 79, 80

LEE, ---, Mr. 545
  Charles 73, 607, 608, 779, 781
  Charles C. 159
  Corbin 816, 819
  E., Miss 802
  Elizabeth (GORSUCH) 922
  Evelyn (PAGE) 774
  George 298
  George W. 922
  Gideon 928
  Hanson 783
  Harry 782
  Isaac C. 462
  J. Harry 604
  James 38, 189
  James F. 194
  Jesse 575
  Jesse W. 159
  John 170, 246, 461
  John W. 593
  John W. M. 659, 660
  Joshua 671
  Josiah 440, 480, 507, 693, 803
  Light Horse Harry 702
  Martha A. (JENKINS) 382
  Mary C. 671
  R. E. 670
  Richard 600, 803
  Richard Henry 72, 774
  Robert E. 292, 702, 782
  Thomas J. 817
  Thomas S. 534, 845, 938
  Thomas Sim 79
  Thomas Sinn 195
  William 231, 745, 916
  Z. Collins 382, 485, 729, 803, 876
  Zadoc Collins 717
  Zed. Collins 485
  Lee, Josiah & Co. 481
  Lee Mob 779
  Lee Street Baptist Church 556, 564, 567
Lee's Legion 783
LEEDS, ---, Rev. Dr. 891, 931
  George 523
  John V. 873
  Mary L. (RUTLEDGE) 873
  Sarah J. (RUTLEDGE) 873
  T. J. 873
  Leeds, ---, Dutchess of 796, 821
LEEKE, James 744
  Mary 744
  William H. 747
LEET, Edward 65
LEFARER, Nicholas 803
LEFEBORE, Edmund C. 159
LEFEVRE, Abraham 610, 803
  J. 151
  J. A. 548
LEFFEL, --- 838
LEFTWICH, J. T. 547

LEGARE, Hugh Swinton 713
LEGG, Clarissa 183
  John C. 442
LEGGETT, George 310
  John 77
LEGGETT, William 688
Lego's Point 309
LEGRAND, ---, Judge 138, 699
  Eleanor 803
  John C. 127, 194, 267, 717, 718
  John Carroll 803
  Samuel D. 189, 803
LEGROS, John F. 433
LEHMAN, Abraham 446
Lehmann's Hall 550
LEHR, H. 597
  Robert 195, 458, 478, 485
LEIB, Georgia 872
  John S. 345, 346
  S. Allen 871
LEIBFRITZ, ---, Rev. Father 928
Leibrandt & McDowell Stove Co. 427
Leiderkrantz, The 672
LEIFIELD, Bernard 468
LEIGHTNER, George 569
  William P. 466
LEILICH, Emma 877
LEIMGRUBER, Max 542
  Maxim 541
LEIONEER, Paul 103
LEISTER, ---, Mr. 866
LEITCH, Emily (SEIDENSTRICKER) 485
  W. A. 485
LELAND, William W. 516
LELOUP, Charles 190
LEMAN, Walter M. 693
LEMMEUS, I. 674
LEMMON, --- 727
  ---, Miss 594
  Alexis 819
  H. M. 580
  Jacob 374
  Joshua 187
  Richard 76, 224, 554, 803, 827, 937
  Robert 298, 728
  W. P. 438
  William P. 440, 802
  Lemmon, Richard's Wharf 311
  Lemmon, Robert & Co. 438
LENCHAN, Peter 236
LENDRUM, Andrew 815, 919
Lennox & Singer 694
Lenschow Musical Association 673
LEON, Christopher 70
LEONARD, B. E. 739
  Joseph 803
  W. T. 189
  William H. 159
  William J. 163

Leonardstown 634
Leopold & Co. 446
LEPLY, Christian 855
LEPSON, Daniel 190
LERAY, F. X. 236
LESLIE, ---, Capt. 293
---, Gen. 773
Mrs., Capt. 595
Robert 234, 273, 288, 440, 601, 802, 803
Leslie, Robert & Co. 433
LESTER, ---, Mr. 217, 261
J. M. 194
James M. 194, 465, 802, 820
Lester, John & Co. 298
LETCHER, ---, Gov. 138, 147, 669
LETHERBURY, Peregine 757
LETTIG, George 433
LETTY, George 379
LETZINGER, George 820
LEVADOUN, ---, Rev. Mr. 234
LEVELY, --- 104
---, Capt. 106
---, Mr. 568
George 238, 423, 727
William 803
LEVERING, --- 93, 828
---, Capt. 267
A. J. 254
A. R. 84, 189, 252
Aaron 187, 188, 393, 727, 803
Aaron R. 92, 123, 194, 771
E. 487
E. J. 813
E., Mrs. 604
Eugene 441, 448, 465, 598, 602
Eugene, Mrs. 596
F. A. 802
George A. 192, 380
Hannah (WILSON) 771
John 245, 299, 803
Joshua 600, 828
Louisa S. 771
Nathan 84, 254, 393, 803
Peter 84, 188, 458, 470
Peter, Mrs. 556
Samuel S. 441, 802
T. W. 302, 484
Thomas U. 242
Thomas W. 245, 440, 771
William T. 502
Levering, Aaron R. 803
Levering, E. & Co. 383
LEVINGTON, William 526
LEVY, Benjamin 74
David 803
Jacob F. 592
Nathan 482
Thomas P. 249
LEWIN, ---, Rev. Dr. 931
LEWIS, ---, Gen. 88

LEWIS, ---, Mr. 494, 614
A. 439
Abraham J. 802
Allen T. 465
C. W. 191, 194
Columbus W. 178, 187
Edward 802
Eli 345
Eugene 380
Francis 264
J. E. 439
J. Frank 191, 193
John W. 159
Joseph 73, 252, 921
Martin 675, 802
R. 241
Richard 53, 241
T. H. 585
William 519
William Charles 803
William Penn 416
Lewis & Pocomoke Canal Company 313
LEWYN, Gabriel 432
Lexington Market 501, 575, 844, 849
Lexington Monumental Building Association 511
Lexington Street 769
Lexington Street M.P. Mission 583
LEYBURN, John 551
LEYH, ---, Mr. 655
Edward 654
LEYPOLD, Frederick 89, 188, 246, 803
Libby Prison 800
Liberal Building Association 511
Liberia, Africa 567
Liberia Herald 567
Liberty 26
Liberty Engine-House 127
Liberty Fire Company 240, 241, 242, 247, 261, 483
Liberty Road 868
Liberty Street 769
Liberty Street Fire Company 240
Library Association of the Mechanical Fire Company 245
Library Company of Baltimore 658
LICHY, E. G. 149
S. L. 149
LIDDLE, ---, Mrs. 595
LIEB, Daniel 872
Thomas 159
LIEBER, F. 648
Francis 896
LIEMON, P. 102
LIGHT, George 889
Job 573
Light Street Building Association 511

Light Street City Station 579
Light Street Fire Company 240
Light Street German M.E. Church 577
Light Street M.E. Church 576, 826
Light Street Meeting-House 608
Light Street Methodist Church 148, 233, 574, 575, 679
Light Street Presbyterian Church 550
Light Street Wharf 262
Light-Ship, The 627
LIGHTBOURNE, A. W. 890
LIGHTNER, ---, Mr. 207
 George 572
 Isaac F. 189
 Nathaniel 189
 W. P. 365
 William H. 903
LIGON, ---, Gov. 361, 744, 787
 T. Watkins 600
LIGOU, Thomas Watkins 195
LIKE, William 50
LILIENTHAL, M. 589
Lilliandale 890
LILLY, A. W. 569
 Charles L. 159
 Richard 191, 394, 802
 Solomon H. 159
Lily of the Valley, The 635
LINASS, John 65
 Thomas 65
 William 65
LINCH, John 803
LINCOLN, ---, Mrs. 128
 ---, President 133, 135, 137, 139, 142, 145, 146, 147, 150, 151, 695, 805
 Abraham 127, 128, 691
Lincoln's Inn 703
LIND, E. G. 272, 675, 934
 Jenny 673, 690
Lind & Murdoch 664
Lindan & Moore 614
Linden 354
LINDEN, E. C. 597
Linden Hope 916
LINDENBERGER, --- 521
 ---, Mr. 568
 Frederick 773
 George 70, 75, 196, 244, 545, 728, 780, 803
 Jacob 803
Lindenberger, G. & C. 433
LINDENBURGER, George 167
LINDENFELTER, John 927
LINDENSTRUTH, Aug. W. 159
Lindlay's Coffee-House 681
LINDSAY, ---, Mr. 681
 Charlotte Elizabeth (GITTINGS) 917

LINDSAY, Elizabeth (AULL) 762
 George W. 256, 728, 762
 James E. 917
 Robert 575
Lindsay, George W. & Son 762
LINDSEY, James 505
Lindsey's Coffee-House 80
LINEBERGER, William 192
LINGAN, ---, Gen. 783
 James M. 782
 Thomas 73
Linganore 313
LINGENFELTER, John 189, 190
LINHARD, George 803
 John 534, 803
 William 803
LINK, Peter 820
LINN, ---, Rev. Dr. 830
 ---, Rev. Mr. 842
 John H. 636
LINNEY, J. H. 814
LINTHICUM, J. G. 828
 James G. 191
 John Lewis 498
 Joshua 358
Linthicum Estate 848
LINTON, William 190
Linville 342
LINVILLE, J. H. 359
Linwood 357
Lipp, F. X. & Co. 629
LIPPINCOTT, John 913
 Sarah A. 421
Lippincott & Co. 650
LIPSCOMB, ---, Dr. 636
 A. A. 616
 Andrew Adgate 649
 Philip 802
LIPSEY, William 592
LISSON, Hugh 419
LIST, F. 605
Literary & Commercial Seminary 233
Literary Bulletin 630
Literary Journal, The 630
Literary Society 543
LITSINGER, Amanda M. 902
 Henry 902
LITTIG, Frederick S. 240, 241, 251, 320
 George 246
 J. M. 462
 John 472
 Margaret E. 386
 Peter 423
 Philip 58, 244, 457, 592
LITTLE, Charles 253
 Edward 250
 George 872
 Henry 114
 John 547

LITTLE, Mary (CALDER) 873
  Peter 250, 251, 456, 457, 803, 814, 819
  Thomas 438
  William 253
  William E. 872
  William H. 872
Little Cacapon 342
Little Falls of the Gunpowder 874
Little Gunpowder 916, 922
Little Gunpowder Falls 811, 907, 915, 920, 924, 925
Little Gunpowder River 922, 925
Little Sisters of the Poor 597
Little Washington 879
LITTLEJOHN, ---, Dr. 732
  M. 735
  Miles 733, 734, 803, 824
Littleton 342
LITTLETON, Charles 902
LITZENGER, Joseph 263
Liverpool Line 306
LIVERS, Arnold 532
LIVEZEY, Elias 826
Llowbarrer's Inspection 49
LLOYD, --- 921
  ---, Col. 851
  Anne Steele 718
  Daniel 718
  Edward 35, 195, 718, 845, 847, 848, 850, 851
  John H. 140
  John W. 889
  Thomas 70, 497, 498, 802
  Virginia (UPSHUR) 719
Lloyd Street Mutual Building Association 511
Lloyd's Hotel 264
LOADES, James D. 159
LOANE, Henry E. 194
  John W. 258
LOBDELL, ---, Special Agent 500
LOBE, Maurice I. 638
Loch Raven 359, 886, 905
Loch Raven Dam 220, 221
LOCKARD, Edward 836
LOCKE, George R. 720
  Milo W. 526
  Thomas M. 240, 241, 242, 244, 245
  Thomas M., Mrs. 556
LOCKWOOD, ---, Gen. 147, 148
  Ellison J. 159
  H. A. 498
  Henry H. 146
  R. M. 576, 596
  William F. 738, 861
Locust Grove Iron-Furnace 931
Locust Point 14, 29, 56, 131, 142, 277, 278, 284, 290, 292, 303, 336, 340, 342, 350, 391, 400, 434, 539, 669, 772, 793, 849, 879, 928

Locust Point Ferry Co. 292
Locust Point Union Mission Chapel 583
LODGE, ---, Dr. 757
  E. A. 756
LOEBER, John 820
LOERSH, Valentine 571
Log Cabin 616
Log Cabin Permanent Building Association 511
LOGAN, ---, Mr. 494
  Cecilia 654
  Cornelius A. 654
  David 469
  Eliza 654
  J. D. 698
  James 191, 495
  John A. 496
  Joseph T. 256
  Olive 654
LOGSDON, John T. 855
LOGUE, John C. 803
Lombard Street 769
Lombard Street Infirmary 800
London Inns of Court 703
London Magazine 764
LONEY, Amos 62, 432
  F. B. 851
  Francis B. 155, 210
  H. D. 178
  Henry D. 191, 193
  John 370
  Thomas D. 441
  William 463, 934
  William H. 579
Loney, B. S. & W. A. 263
Loney's Lane 934
LONG, ---, Col. 318
  Abraham 244
  Ann S. 803
  E. B. 302
  Ellis B. 412
  Harriet R. (JORDAN) 871
  Henry 249
  Henry K. 802
  James 74, 173, 174, 803, 849
  John M. 159
  Kennedy 92, 547, 803
  R. 76
  R. C. 201, 520, 675
  R. Carey 537, 660, 674, 694
  Reuben 252
  Robert 76, 310, 803, 816
  Robert C. 202, 667
  Robert Carey 320, 456, 457, 483, 500, 610, 659, 685, 692, 803
  Stephen H. 318
  Thomas 814
  William 871
Long & Powell 600
Long Branch 354

Long Bridge 139, 144, 354
Long Calm 894
Long Green 800, 802, 908, 914, 916, 917
Long Green Catholic Church 917
Long Green Land 382
Long Green Road 918
Long Green Valley 18, 917
Long Wharf, Canton 250
LONGACRE, ---, Rev. Dr. 837
 ---, Rev. Mr. 601
 Andrew 576
Longchamps 925
Longchamps Road 924
LONGFELLOW 78
LONGNECKER, C. 900
 David 905
 H. C. 749, 899
 J. B. 900
 John B. 899
 John H. 802, 814, 898, 903
LONGSTON, ---, Miss 576
 James A. 576
Lonsdale Manufacturing Co. 408
LONYI, Albert 159
LOOMIS, George F. 829
 George T. 820
 William 433
LOPER, J. M. 803
LORAN, Charles 651
LORBACHER, Catharine 423
LORD, Grenville 577
 Joseph L. 643
Lord Proprietary 704
LORING, ---, Admiral 293
LORMAN, --- 521
 'A. 466
 Alexander 470, 802, 803
 Gustav W. 440
 Henry 470
 Mary 803
 William 89, 187, 216, 235, 252, 298, 316, 317, 318, 324, 393, 439, 440, 452, 455, 470, 483, 500, 501, 520, 569, 734, 751, 770, 803, 824
Lorman, William & Son 438
LOTZ, C. 597
LOUDENSLAGER, ---, Mr. 291
Loudenslager Hill 90
Loudenslager's Tavern 276
LOUDERMAN, H. R. 934
Loudon Park Cemetery 820, 825, 826
LOUDOUN, ---, Earl of 115
Louisville Gazette 619
LOUT, John 252
LOVE, ---, Dr. 741
 Albert T. 879
 Alfred 817
 James 65
 John 38

LOVE, Joseph K. 594
 Thomas 734, 741, 803, 819, 877, 879, 911
Love Point Light-house 309
LOVEALL, Henry 552, 553, 554
LOVEGROVE, James 241, 803
 Thomas J. 245
LOVEJOY, Perley R. 159, 834
Lovely Lane 658, 678
Lovely Lane Methodist Chapel 574
LOVERING, G. A. 190
 George H. 381
LOVETT, M. S. 625
Lovington 877
LOW, Henderson P. 188
 Joshua 874
 Lewis 264
 Nancy 58
 Sarah A. 874
 Susannah (FREDERICK) 874
LOWDER, Richard 65
LOWE, ---, Ex-Gov. 128, 130
 ---, Gov. 876
 Alfred 866, 867
 Amos 866
 Asenath 866
 Charles E. 159
 Cornelius 803
 E. L. 128
 Elizabeth (WELLER) 866
 Enoch Louis 123, 195
 Flora (DORSEY) 866
 J. M. 817
 James 264
 Jane 866
 Jeremiah 866
 John 64, 866
 Merab 866
 N. 102
 Nicholas 866
 Ralph 866
 Thomas 585
 Thomas W. 802
 Titura (BAKER) 866
 William 45
Lowe Family 717
LOWELL, James Russell 233, 653
LOWER, Brook W. 615
 Lower, Samuel & Co. 615
Lower Broadway Market-house 262
Lower Island Point 309
LOWNDS, James 487
LOWRY, ---, Maj. 83, 668
 James D. 279
 L. D. 802
 Lowry D. 245
 Philip W. 245
 William 497, 498
LOXLEY, Benjamin 101
Loy's 357

Loyola College 536, 538, 544, 702, 882
Loyola College Library 667
Loyola Perpetual Building Association 511
LUBKERT, ---, Rev. Mr. 570
LUCAS, ---, Capt. 58
 Alexander 612
 C. Z. 190
 Charles L. 593
 Edmund 761
 F. 439, 486
 Fielder 471
 Fielding 63, 192, 205, 225, 265, 266, 470, 471, 659, 667, 672, 803, 890
 Henry A. 802
 James 189, 191, 466, 802
 John A. 250
 Margaret 896
 R. J. 886
 Samuel 189, 760
 T., Mrs. 594
 Thomas 803
 W. F. 458
 William F. 698
LUCCA, --- 673
LUCCHESI, Frederick 673
LUCKET, James H. 254
LUCKETT, J. H. 288, 903
 James H. 190
LUCKEY, Joseph 253
Lucky Mistake 386
LUCY, Thomas 802
LUDDINGTON, William J. C. 803
LUDLOW, ---, Mr. 694
 A. C. 189
Ludlow & Gould 402
LUDLUM, F. R. 638
LUDWIG, ---, Dr. 731
LUEHRMANN, William 542
LUKE, Francis 255
LUKENS, Benjamin 926
 Hannah (COOPER) 926
 Julia A. 926
LULL, ---, Mrs. 212
Lumber Exchange 449
Lumber Exchange Building 277
LUMPKIN, Tony 688
LUNDY, Benjamin 803
 Esther 803
LUNEBURG, John 252
Lunn's Lot 50, 59, 61
Luns Lot 49
LUPTON, William 758
 William B. 250
LUPUS, ---, Mr. 841
 Edward 802
LURMAN, ---, Mrs. 155
 Gustav W. 802
 Gustavus 365

LUSBY, David K. 820
 Edward R. 802
 Lusby Estate 826
LUSHUER, Christopher 592
LUTHER, Martin 605
Lutheran Chapel at Canton 571
Lutheran Chapel Monument Street 569
Lutheran Church 556
Lutheran Observer 631, 655, 877
Lutheran Orphan Asylum 597
Lutheran Theological Seminary Gettysburg 570
Lutherville 28, 30, 347, 655, 876, 877, 902, 906
Lutherville Female Seminary 877
LUTTGERDING, Henry C. 830
LUTZ, C. N. 252
 Charles A. 159
 Tobias 927, 929
 Valentine 929
 William 929
LUX, ---, Capt. 403
 Agnes (WALKER) 803
 Catherine (BIDDLE) 803
 Darby 37, 56, 57, 58, 70, 71, 73, 74, 519, 803, 819, 844
 Darley 815
 George 70, 803
 William 57, 67, 69, 71, 72, 75, 100, 205, 244, 728, 768, 803, 819, 934, 935
Lux & Bowley 432
Lux & Smith 432
LYCETT, George 526, 886
Lyceum Observer, The 636
LYETH, John 247
 Samuel 247
LYFORD, ---, Mr. 630
 W. G. 615
 William G. 629, 659
Lyken's Valley Railroad 345
LYLE, D. C. 831
 Hugh 101
LYLES, H. 103
 W. 103
LYMAN, ---, Rev. 892
 D. E. 236, 538
LYNCH, ---, Bishop 529, 599, 802
 ---, Commander 802
 ---, Mr. 822
 A. A. 137, 820
 Andrew A. 820
 Anitonia, Mother 802
 Deborah 862
 Edward 252
 J. H. 600, 604
 J. H., Mrs. 600
 John 76, 188
 John S. 194, 738
 Joshua 159, 190, 191

LYNCH, Luke 159
  Nicholas 246, 251
  William F. 802
LYNES, William 557
LYNN, ---, Dr. 741
  Adam 519
  George 741
  John 99
LYON, ---, Dr. 868
  Braxton 148
  F. D. 128
  John C. 822
  Josiah 38
  Lemuel Z. 159
  Mary 723, 834
  Robert 723, 834, 845
  Samuel H. 136
  Susan 834
  Thomas C. 723
  Truxton 361
  William 37, 54, 58, 205, 252, 544, 545, 547, 730, 834
LYONS, J. M. 870
  William 374
  William B. 200
LYTLE, James 817
  Thomas 872
LYTTLETON, Thomas 224
M'KIM - See MC KIM
M.E. Church South 794
MAAS, Charles L. 237
MAC CREERY - See MC CREERY
MAC FARLAND - See MC FARLAND
MAC GILL - See MC GILL
MAC KRILL, Joseph 734
MAC LEOD, --- 619
MAC TAVISH - See MC TAVISH
MACARTNEY - See MC CARTNEY
MACATNEY, Francis 577
MACAULEY - See MC CAULEY
MACCOMAR, Daniel 921
MACCUBBIN - See MC CUBBIN
MACCUBBINS - See MC CUBBINS
MACDONALD - See MC DONALD
Macdonald & Ridgely 438
MACE, ---, Dr. 741
  Alford 190, 354, 803
  Alfred 729
  John 742
  Oscar A. 159
  William H. 195, 927
MACEY, William 298
MACGILL - See MC GILL
MacGregor Clan 923
MACHEN, ---, Mr. 897
  A. W. 723
  Arthur W. 129
  Arthur Webster 720
MACHENHEIMER, John 433

MACHENHEIMER, Peter 804
MACHIN, ---, Mr. 694
MACHLIN, William 261
MACILROY, Thomas 372
MACKALL, Benjamin 709
  Leonard 745
  Leonard Covington 383
  Richard 84
MACKAY, John 439
MACKENHEIMER, ---, Capt. 83, 668
  Catherine 804
  John 170, 187, 188, 197, 238, 239, 246, 569, 803, 804
MACKENZIE - See MC KENZIE
MACKEY, ---, Miss 874
  Richard 874
  Richard G. 870
MACKIE, ---, Mr. 60
  Ebenezer 76, 452
MACKIN, James F. 539
MACKINTOSH, James 212
MACNAMAR, H. 579
MACOMAR, Daniel 921
MACOMERS, Daniel 921
MACREADY, --- 691, 694
MACTIER, Alexander 804
  Samuel 547
MADDOX, Charles T. 493
  William J. 190
MADDUX, James 190, 191
MADISON, ---, Gen. 751
---, Mr. 296
---, President 98, 782
Madison Avenue Land & Building Association 511
Madison Avenue M.E. Church 577
Madison Square 281
Madison Square Baptist Church 567
Madison Square Building Association No. 1 511
Madison Square M.E. Church 575
Madison Street 769
Madison Street Baptist Chruch 560
Madison Street Presbyterian Church 552
MAENGER, George 820
MAFFIT, S. S. 137
MAFFITT, Samuel S. 146
MAGEE, C. F. 298
  Thomas 522
Magee, J.'s Academy 233
MAGGS, Jane 432
Magician, The 624
MAGILL, O. P. 905
  P. H. 441, 448
Magnetic Telegraph Co. 505, 506, 507, 508
MAGNIEN, A. 236, 544
Magnolia 351, 922, 924
MAGOFFIN, J. 70
Magothy River 309, 843

MAGRAW, James C. 162, 803
  R. M. 288, 345
  Robert M. 190, 355, 357, 804
MAGRUDER, ---, Capt. 88
  ---, Dr. 741
  Alexander C. 715
  Allen B. 637
  C. C. 600
  D. F. 372
  D. R. 358
  Dennis P. 804
  Eleanora 862
  Enoch 223
  F. W. 253
  Gustavus 372
  R. B. 680
  Rebecca R. 804
  Richard B. 91, 188, 804
  S. S. 101
  T. J. 447, 448, 587
  Thomas J. 155
  Zadock 741
Magruder, William B. & Co. 298
MAGUIRE, ---, Capt. 361
  ---, Mr. 672
  ---, Rev. Father 932
  Bernard A. 536
  Charles 189
  Hugh 233, 671
  J. L. 804
  John T. 246
  Joseph 236
MAHAN, ---, Mr. 628
  Milo 521, 803
MAHEW, William E. 440
MAHON, John J. 191, 193
  Joseph 159
MAHOOD, James 804
MAHOOL, Thomas 592
Maiden Choice Road 937, 938
MAIER, L. D. 570, 929
MAIGERS, Peter 519
MAITLAND, B. 288
MAKALL, Edward 244
MALCOLM, James 804, 903
MALCOM, J. 362
Male Central High School 226, 227
Male Free School 233
Male Free School of St. Peter's
  Church 237
Male Grammar & Primary School
  No. 1 228
MALLERY, Garrick 391
MALLET, ---, Mr. 736
  John W. 233
Mallet's Ball-Room 680
MALLETT, Michael 103
MALLILUN, Richard 153
MALLONEE, Josiah 869
MALLORY, D. D. 448, 487, 600
  John 188

MALLOY, Charles 439
  J. 837
  John 472
  L. S. 538
  Lawrence 540
MALONEY, Francis 790
  William 790
MALSTER, ---, Mr. 305
  William T. 304, 307, 314
  Malster & Reaney 304, 305
MALTBY, C. S. 516
  Maltby House 53, 516
Man-of-War Shoals 312
Manassas 897
Manchester 867, 873
Manchester Academy 889
Manchester Road 869
MANDE, William 89
MANECKE, Otto 793
MANKIN, H. 370
  Henry 263, 288, 838, 896
  Isaiah 372, 438, 577
  Josiah 804
MANKINS, Henry 838
MANKO, R. H. 447
MANLEY, J. H. 903
  Stephen H. 804
MANLY, ---, Dr. 567
  Dominic 889
  Gaston, Mrs. 604
  John S. 200
MANN, ---, Col. 626
  Anthony 740
  Camill M. 612
  Charles H. 898
  Elizabeth A. 467
  John G. 468
Mann's Hotel 517
MANNAGHAN, Alexander 911
MANNING, C. P. 211, 354
  Charles P. 218, 222
  Charles T. 222
  George O. 466, 473
  H. E. 641
  Peter 536
  William T. 222
Manning & Hope 261
Mannington 342
Manor Episcopal Church 880
Manor Grange, No. 163 P. of H. 909
Manor Point 905
Manor Road 922
MANRO, Jonathan 458
MANSE, Peter 777
MANSELL, ---, Mr. 678
MANSFIELD, --- 703
  J. B. 636
  James T. 159
Mansfield, Hobbs & Co. 636
Mansion House 311
Mantua 876

Mantua Grange 855, 883
Mantua Grange of the Patrons of Husbandry 864
Mantua Mills 854, 855, 883
MANTZ, A. K. 365
 D. Allen 256
 Francis 804
 Menry 240
Manual Labor School 231
Manual Labor School for Indigent Boys 937
Maple Hill 838
MARBLE, Manton 640
Marble Lodge No. 123, I.O.O.F. 877
MARBURG, William A. 803
Marburg Bros. 372
MARCH, ---, Gov. 814
 Mary Ann 526
MARCHER, G. H. 555
MARCOU, Philippe B. 233
Marcus Hook 311
MARDEN, Jesse 140, 193, 434
MAREAN, Silas 803
MARECHAL, ---, Archbishop 237, 528, 532, 595, 804
 ---, Dr. 533
 Ambrose 234, 235, 527, 594
Marian Brothers 542
MARIE, Bettie Bose (GITTINGS) 917
 William Wilson 917
Marietta & Cincinnati Co. 338
Marine Bank 451, 795
Marine Hospital 182, 187, 277, 733, 747, 749
Marine Insurance Co. 298
Marine Observatory 805
Marion Hall 524
Marion Rifle Corps 669
MARIONO, J. B. 735
MARIS, George 247
 Mathias 555
MARK, William T. 813
MARKEL, Charles 488
MARKELL, Charles 471
Market Street 251, 608, 658, 692, 744, 852
Market Street on the Point 557
Market-house 680
MARKLAND, Charles E. 869
 Edward 205
 James H. 193
 William T. 194, 303, 467
MARKLEY, Albert W. 366
MARKOE, Frank 637
Marlboro' 354
MARLEY, Richard 189, 803
Marley Creek 358
MARMAYONE, A. 101
MARMION, --- 686
MARQUIS, D. C. 549, 551

MARRIOTT, ---, Lt. 114
 E. 95, 269
 J. H. 95, 269
 J. McKine 770
 James E. 114
 James N. 95
 John 95, 269
 Margaret M. 770
 Mary Cruse (WILSON) 770
 Telfair 191, 599
 William H. 497, 498, 805
Marriottsville 15, 342
MARSDEN, Frederick 264
Marsden & Brother 263
MARSH, Dennis 120, 906
 Elijah 906
 Ellen 906, 911
 Grafton 737
 John 247, 905
 Joseph 902
 Joshua 804, 904, 906, 911
 Josiah 902, 906
 Rebecca 906
 Salome 159, 191
 Stephen 906
 Thomas 35
Marsh (Centre) Market 206
Marsh Family 717
Marsh Family Burying Ground 895
Marsh Market 129, 501
Marsh Run 347
MARSHALL, --- 682, 709, 715
 ---, Chief Justice 753, 804
 ---, Dr. 741
 ---, Mr. 296
 ---, Mrs. 682
 Agnes H. 753
 Amanda C. (JESSOP) 925
 Charles 130, 195, 600, 723, 817
 E. A. 688
 H. Dora 886
 Henry 925
 John 194, 212, 256
 John E. 444, 445, 747
 John H. 193, 194
 John T. 855
 R. A. 600
 Sally 449
 Thomas 212, 728, 804
 Thomas J. 351
 Thomas John 449
 W. L. 159
 William 741
 William F. 935
 William L. 127, 129, 717, 729
 William R. 549
 William T. 159, 177
Marshall & Fisher 702
Marshall Family 870
MARSHEK, Jacob 263
MARSTERS, J. 555

MARSTON, H. W. 447
MARTELL, Justus 927
MARTIN, --- 698, 712, 723, 726
---, Dr. 741, 750
---, Judge 150, 165, 198
---, Mr. 360
A. 241
Alexander 609, 804
Andrew 241
Anthony B. 740
Catharine (WHITE) 749
Daniel 195
David 240, 462, 803
Eleonora 802
Ennalls 736, 741, 742
Eudora (HIGGINS) 749
Florence 927
George 380, 592
George H. 442
H. Newell 233
Hannah 583
Hy. T. 526
Isaac 749
J. Everett 636
Jacob 855
James 84, 194, 253
James A. 159
Jesse 803
John 100, 101, 102, 738
John S. 576
John T. 869
Joseph J. 446, 840
Joseph Lloyd 745, 749
Joseph P. 446
Julia 808
Jus. 100
L., Miss 582
Letitia M. 583
Lorana D. (CHEERU) 749
Luther 76, 375, 521, 708, 709, 710, 711, 716, 728, 781, 802, 804, 808
Maria 804
Maria M. 583
Nicholas 100, 101
R. N. 803
Robert K. 220, 222
Robert M. 717
S. H. 187
Samuel 737
Samuel B. 738
T. T. 140
Thomas 431
Thomas E. 200
William 252, 766, 803, 820
William E. 803
Martin, ---, Messrs. & Co. 628
MARTINET, Simon J. 495
MARTING, James 551
Martingham & Williton 477
Martinsburg 342, 791
Martinsburg Station 361

MARTLER, Alexander 298
MARYE, George T. 190
Maryland & Virginia Steam Navigation Co. 480
Maryland Academy of Art 261, 674, 675
Maryland Academy of Fine Arts 675
Maryland Academy of Music 511
Maryland Academy of Science 668, 739
Maryland Academy of Sciences Library 667
Maryland Agricultural & Mechanical Association 845, 847, 851
Maryland Agricultural College 750, 885
Maryland Agricultural Society 845
Maryland Art Association 674
Maryland Artillery 671
Maryland Association for the Improvement of the Breed of Horses 850
Maryland Avenue Fire Company 818
Maryland Baptist Association 628
Maryland Baptist Union Association 555, 557, 559, 561
Maryland Battalion 731
Maryland Beneficial Association 511
Maryland Bible Society 668, 708
Maryland Blind Asylum 253
Maryland Cadets 668
Maryland Calico Print-Works 842
Maryland Canal 313, 314
Maryland Censor 614
Maryland Club 668
Maryland Club House 137, 150
Maryland College of Pharmacy 700, 740
Maryland Colonization Journal 613
Maryland Colonization Society 668
Maryland Committee of the US Christian Church 153
Maryland Company 682
Maryland Democrat, The 628
Maryland Educational Journal 636
Maryland Eye & Ear Infirmary 747
Maryland Farmer 640, 642
Maryland Farmers' Club 845
Maryland Fertilizing & Manufacturing Co. 460, 511
Maryland Fire Insurance Co. 171, 477, 487, 491, 852
Maryland Floating Elevator Co. 380, 511
Maryland Gazette 605, 606, 816
Maryland Gazette & Baltimore General Advertiser 608
Maryland Glass-Works 402

Maryland Guards 669
Maryland Historical Society 648,
  651, 654, 655, 658, 659, 663, 675,
  775, 807
Maryland Horticultural Society
  398
Maryland Hospital 751, 824
Maryland Hospital for the Insane
  620, 752
Maryland Hospital for the Insane
  Library 667
Maryland House of Correction 602
Maryland Hussars 928
Maryland Industrial Chemical Co.
  511
Maryland Industrial School for
  Girls 820
Maryland Inebriate Asylum 600,
  641
Maryland Infantry 800
Maryland Institute 123, 124, 127,
  128, 139, 141, 142, 146, 152, 155,
  166, 206, 214, 231, 267, 651, 668,
  722, 845
Maryland Institute Building
  Association No. 3 511
Maryland Institute for the
  Promotion of Mechanic Arts 667
Maryland Institute Library 667
Maryland Institute School of
  Design 667, 668
Maryland Institution for Education
  of Deaf & Dumb 601
Maryland Institution for
  Instruction of the Blind 479,
  601, 702, 890
Maryland Insurance 480
Maryland Insurance Company 175,
  214, 298, 771
Maryland Insurance Fire Company
  239
Maryland Jockey Club 352, 834,
  848, 850, 851
Maryland Journal 492, 493, 609,
  800, 815, 898, 900, 901
*Maryland Journal & Baltimore
  Advertiser* 606, 607, 608
*Maryland Journal & Baltimore
  Universal Daily Advertiser* 608
Maryland Law Record 641, 642
Maryland Life Insurance Co. 489,
  491
Maryland Line 798, 805, 806, 871,
  872, 873
Maryland Line Circle N.E.C. 873
Maryland Line in the Confederate
  States 668
Maryland Line Railroad Co. 344
Maryland Lying-in Asylum 738
*Maryland Medical & Surgical
  Journal* 624

Maryland Medical Institute 700
Maryland Medical Journal, The 641
Maryland Militia 801, 803, 807
Maryland Mounted Guard 821
Maryland Music Festival 673
Maryland Mutual Permanent
  Building & Loan Co. 511
Maryland National Guard 671, 792,
  898
Maryland News-Sheet 633
Maryland Penitentiary 202, 602,
  697, 700, 809
Maryland Penitentiary: Wardens
  1811-1881 205
Maryland Pilgrims' Association 668
Maryland Prisoners' Aid Association
  154, 602, 603
Maryland Reformer, The 628
Maryland Republican 634, 639, 801
Maryland Savings Institution 473
Maryland Savings-Bank of Baltimore
  473
Maryland School Journal, The 641
Maryland Society for the Prevention
  of Cruelty to Animals 668
Maryland State Agricultural Society
  885
Maryland State Asylum for the
  Insane 823
Maryland State Board of Health
  752, 753
Maryland State Fair 146, 635
Maryland State Grange 835
Maryland State Insane Asylum 820
Maryland Statesman, The 628
Maryland Steamboat Co. 302, 511
Maryland Sugar Refinery 418, 795
Maryland Sunday-School Union
  154, 557, 668
Maryland Tavern 845
Maryland Telephone Co. 509, 511
Maryland Temperance Herald 625
Maryland Times 632, 633
Maryland Tract Society 154, 557
Maryland Tubing Transportation Co.
  856
Maryland Union Coal Co. of
  Maryland 390
Maryland Union Commission 155
Maryland University 613, 644, 751,
  753
Maryland University of Medicine
  917
Maryland White Lead Co. 460, 511
Maryland White Lead Works 402
Maryland Woman's Hospital 738,
  739, 748
Marylander 615, 645
MASEY, J. 261
MASON, ---, Mr. 408
  ---, Mrs. 684

MASON, Benjamin 173, 192
  Charles 66
  Esther 396
  Francis 112
  Hugh 396
  J. T. 498
  J. Thomson 195
  James D. 441, 466, 488, 489
  John 845
  John S. 845
  John Thompson 129, 497, 717, 803
  John Thomson 600
  Mary (COOKE) 397
  Mary (DENT) 397
  Nehemiah 396
  Peter 245
  R. C. 396
  R. R. 908, 911
  Richard 246, 484, 804
  Richard C. 262, 345, 396, 803
  William 803
Mason, James D. & Sons 349
Mason & Johnson 839
Masonic Fraternity 744
Masonic Hall 559, 586, 590, 672, 728, 729, 740, 757
Masonic Order 757, 640
Masonic Temple 691, 750
Masonic Temple at Towson 878
MASS, Samuel 192
Massachusetts Historical Society 653
MASSEY, Samuel 766
MASSIE, Jennie 834
MASSIOTT, William A. 191
MASTER, L. 433
MATCHETT, R. J. 616
  Richard 614
  Richard J. 805
Maternite Lying-in Hospital 747
MATHER, Nicholas 814
  Ralph 804
MATHEWMAN, L. 101
MATHEWS, D. M. 820
  George 425, 587
  L. 393
  Mary Juliana, Sister 598
  Roger 728
  Thomas 374
  Thomas R. 464
  Wilber F. 159
  William 455, 560
Mathey, Riddle & Co. 102
MATHIAS, Jacob 355
MATHICK, Samuel T. 252
MATHIOT, --- 166
  August 803
  Augustus 759
MATHIOTT, Augustus 189
MATHOIT, Augustus 760
MATIAN, Nicholas, Capt. 40

MATLACK, Samuel T. 484
MATTERSON, H. B. 691
MATTESE, ---, Mr. 262
Matthew, Ridley & Co. 101
MATTHEWS, -- 195
  ---, Father 599
  ---, Gen. 78
  ---, Gov. 791
  ---, Mr. 815, 912
  A. C. N. 246
  Aldridge 912
  Alfred 880
  Aloysius 599
  Amos 369, 906, 911
  Ann 884
  Ann (GRIFFITH) 884
  Aquilla 912
  Benjamin 379
  Benjamin F. 161
  Bernadine, Mother 599
  Caleb Bentley 884
  Charles 687, 884
  Clyde 912
  D. M. 906, 910
  Daniel 884
  Dennis M. 917
  Dennis Marsh 911
  Edward H. 912
  Eleanor 599
  Eli A. 912
  Elizabeth 884
  Elizabeth (HANWAY) 884
  Ellen 912
  Ellen (MARSH) 906, 911
  Evan 883
  Ezekiel 872
  Francis 884
  George 70, 73, 804, 884
  George H. 579
  Gideon 884
  Granville 818
  Hannah 884
  Hattie W. (ALDRIDGE) 912
  Henry 830
  Isaac 579
  J. D. 548
  James 465
  James P. 611, 638
  John 40, 351, 778, 884
  John D. 912
  John L. 194
  Joseph 241, 487, 884
  Joshua 249
  L. 470
  L. H. 256
  Mahlon 884
  Mary 883, 884
  Miriam 884
  Mordica 911
  Oliver 884
  R. Stocket 576

MATTHEWS, R. Stockett 149, 194, 195, 762
Rachel 884
Rachel (PRICE) 883
Rachel A. 379
Rebecca 884
Rebecca (PRICE) 883
Roger 45, 819, 919
Ruth 884
Samuel 247, 249, 884
Samuel H. 256, 884
Sarah 884
Sarah (BROWN) 884
Sarah (JOHNSON) 884
Sarah (THOMAS) 884
Stanley 884
Susannah 884
Thomas 56, 248, 803, 804, 883, 884
Thomas A. 488
Thomas H. 488, 912
Thomas L. 161
Thomas R. 441, 803
W. W. 912
William 423, 592, 804, 876, 883, 884
Matthews Family 883
MATTHIOT, George 249
MATTINGLY, Elizabeth 803
George 303
John F. 804
MATTISON, J. B. 365
MAUDSLEY, James 759
MAUGHLIN, Hugh A. 159
MAUKIN, Henry 364
MAULSBY, David L. 467
Mary Ellen (GEORGE) 467
William P. 722
MAUMBERG, Segus 149
MAUND, ---, Miss 595
George C. 193
MAUPIN, Chapman 229
MAURER, Peter 245
Mauretown 342
MAXWELL, Asaell 44
David 38
F. G. 586, 587
James 814, 818, 819, 919, 921
James M. 549
James, Col. 44, 45
John W. 201
Maxwell, John W. & Co. 219
MAY, Benjamin 727
Charles 816
Dominic 673
Henry 133, 136, 137, 199, 719, 729, 804, 816
James 673
James A. 241
S. Henry 804
May & Payson 432
May-Pole 513

MAYBERRY, John 803
Lawrence 202
MAYBURY, Thomas 556
MAYDWELL, John 246
MAYER, --- 270
---, Capt. 804
---, Mr. 389, 651
Anne (SCHLEY) 395
Brantz 159, 388, 617, 650, 658, 659, 803, 877
C. F. 298, 596, 659
Charles 313
Charles F. 193, 387, 388, 463, 658, 692, 714, 725, 737, 803, 804, 817, 826, 827
Charles F., Mrs. 596
Christian 388, 439, 456, 457, 470, 650, 805
Christopher 388
Henry 804
Henry C. 665
J. J. 395
Jacob 433
John Jeremiah 395
Lewis 252, 388, 572
Melchior 388
Susan Douglas (KEIM) 389
Susan O. 388
Susan O. (MAYER) 388
Mayer, Carroll & Co. 389
Mayer & Brantz 439
Mayer & Bro. 263
MAYHEW, W. E. 345, 471
William E. 464, 484, 596, 663, 804
Mayhew & Hobby 439
MAYNARD, Horace 142
MAYNARDIER, ---, Miss 905
George 814
Henry 845
MAYRE, George T. 251
MC ABEE, W. 873
MC ALEER, Mary Ann, Sister 937
MC ALEESE, Charles J. 194
MC ALLESE, H. Clay 159
MC ALLISTER, ---, Capt. 817
A. 76
John 76
R. A. 126
Robert A. 194
William H. 585
MC ATEE, W. B. 442
Walter B. 444
William B. 445
MC BEE, M. A. 820
MC BLAIR, ---, Mr. 925
Charles 534
M. 439
Michael 804
William M. 498
MC BOYCE, James 911
MC BRIDE, --- 693

MC BRIDE, Hugh 101
  Louisa 908
  William 101
MC CABE, Edward 312
  James D. 523
  John 779
  John C. 617
MC CAFFRAY, Henry 472
MC CAHAN, J. E. 870
  John C. 272
  Susanna 935
MC CAINE, Alexander 251, 595
MC CALL, G. 70
MC CANDLESS, George 61, 298, 727, 803, 804
  Ignatius P. 253
  Robert 298
MC CANN, James 534
  John 790
  William 488, 818
MC CANNON, James 173, 175, 187, 225, 238, 572, 804, 935
MC CART, John 191
MC CARTHY, David 106
MC CARTIE, William 432
MC CARTNEY (MACARTNEY), Francis 803
  John 936
MC CARTY, J. B. 103
MC CASTLE, Murdock 74
MC CAUGHAN, Davis 251
MC CAULEY (MACAULEY, MACCAULEY), Daniel J. 812, 813, 820
  I. A. 579
  J. A. 840
  John W. 815
  Lawrence 538
  Patrick 188, 192, 318, 615
MC CAUSLAND, Marcus 298, 470, 644, 804
MC CAWLEY, Joseph 191
MC CLAIN, Charles B. 814
MC CLANAGAN, Blair 101
MC CLEARY, William 89
MC CLELLAN, --- 135, 150
  ---, Gen. 611
  Arthur R. 870
  D. W. B. 254
  George 748
  George B. 149, 722
  Kate 598, 602
  S. 241
  Samuel 192, 241, 254
  W. 269
  W. W. 444, 445, 695
  William 191
  William R. 444
Mc Clellan's Alley Fire Company 240
MC CLELLAND, Carey 370, 468

MC CLELLAND, John 77
MC CLENAM, James 311
MC CLEOD, Alexander 74
  Daniel 74
MC CLINTOCK, John 443
  John M. 729
  M. 255
MC CLOSKEY, David 212
MC CLURE, ---, Mrs. 594
  J. 101, 102
  James 922
  James A. L. 194
  John 68, 89, 100, 101, 102, 439, 779, 804
  William 38
Mc Clure, John & Co. 100, 101
MC CLYMONT, William 190, 193, 803
MC COLGAN, ---, Father 538
  ---, Rev. Father 544
  Edward 236, 534, 537, 539, 543, 805, 938
  James 194
MC COLLOCH, James 77
  James H. 77, 95
MC COMAS, --- 933
  ---, Sergt. 129
  Amos 190, 193, 260
  Charles A. 245
  Gabriel A. 871
  H. G. 95, 269
  Henry 94
  Henry G. 267
  J. Glenn 917
  J. M. 820, 872, 876, 908
  J. Marche 161
  James B. 814, 815
  John M. 817
  John W. 159
  Rachel A. (JORDAN) 871
MC COMBS, --- 166
MC CONKEY, Elizabeth 576
  James 92
  John W. 842
  Rebecca 596
  William 149, 249, 576, 582, 803
Mc Conkey & Parr 828
MC CONNELL, Charles 70
  John C. 159
MC CORMICK, J. 624
  James O. 189
  Thomas 582
MC COSH, ---, Dr. 550
MC COSKER, Thomas 194
MC COY, ---, Mr. 434, 661
  C. W. C. 155
  Charles Seward 406
  Charles W.C. 406
  D. P. 667
  Duncan 662
  George Bartlett 406

MC COY, Gowan 662
  Harry 193, 441
  Henry B. 159
  James 102
  John 548, 592
  John W. 288, 365, 446, 484, 609, 660, 662, 666, 825
  Lewis Macatee 406
  Lucretia (BARTLETT) 406
  M. S. 255
  Maury 406
  P. 538
  Peter 539
  Sarah (WILLIAMSON) 660
  Stephen 255, 660, 662, 803
  Thomas 662
MC CREA, S. 614
  Thomas 834
MC CREARY, ---, Sec. of War 793
MC CREERY (MACCREERY), W. 214
  William 70, 117, 173, 192, 193, 197, 239, 482, 483, 520, 545, 679
MC CREEY, William 804
MC CRON, J. 569
  John 267, 804
MC CRONE, Alexander F. 161
MC CUBBIN (MACCUBBIN, MACCUBINS, MC KUBBIN), George 452
  John C. 804
  John D. 872
  Mary Clare (CARROLL) 706
  Nicholas 706
  Samuel 45, 466, 803
  Samuel J. 219
  William 71, 174
  William F. 872
  Zach. 73
  Zachariah 70, 72, 73, 74, 116, 174, 310, 521, 812
MC CULLOCH, D. G. 191
  David 46, 545, 923
  J. H. 84
  J. W. 84
  James 83
  James H. 194, 407, 497, 498, 805, 819
  James W. 85, 120, 313, 819
  John S. 133
  May 46
MC CULLOGH, James W. 188
MC CULLOH, ---, Mr. 699
  ---, Mrs. 594
  C. F. 509
  David 432
  Isabella 804
  James H. 393, 470, 577, 826
  James W. 394
  Joseph H. 455
  M., Mrs. 604

MC CULLOH, Samuel 804
MC CULLOUGH, ---, Mr. 225
  Benjamin 871
  David 814, 921
  George 559
  James H. 870
  James W. 804
  John G. 465
  Lysander 813
  Mc Culough Iron Co. 424
MC CURDY, Hugh 77, 433, 455, 547
MC CURE, John 392
MC CURLEY, Felix 189, 191, 468, 805
MC CURRY, Henry 202, 505
MC DANIEL, J. E. 740
  James L. 369
MC DERMOTT, Francis 776
  Jane Monica 776
MC DEVITT, J. 538
  James 538, 539
MC DONALD (MACDONALD), --- 804
  ---, Mr. 441
  A. 470, 874
  Alex. 252
  Alexander 89, 316, 393, 453, 455, 534, 547, 804, 805, 902
  David H. 189
  Elizabeth 804
  George 202, 793, 886
  George W. 149
  J. 873
  James 938
  James H. 159
  Mary 804
  Samuel 92, 249, 720, 805
  Sarah 595, 804
  Thomas 159
  Thomas M. 814
  William 84, 92, 98, 120, 192, 205, 300, 393, 456, 457, 470, 484, 804, 805, 824, 887, 929, 933
  William A. 855
  Mc Donald, William & Co. 311
  Mc Donald, William & Son 439
  Mc Donald & Son 300
MC DONNELL, A. 236
  John 826
MC DONOGH, John 651, 804, 831
  William 804
  Mc Donogh 357
  Mc Donogh Farm School & Fund 724
  Mc Donogh Institute 829, 830
  Mc Donogh Institute & Farm-School 831
  Mc Donogh Monument 270
  Mc Donoghville 831
MC DONOUGH, Elizabeth 804
  John 270, 804, 805

Mc Donough Educational Fund
  176, 177
Mc Donough Fund 697
MC DOWELL, Edward G. 449
  Edward G., Mrs. 605
  George H. 245, 854
  M. 547
  Max. 547
  Maxwell 470, 545, 742
  O. M. 155
  Robert 804
MC ELDERRY, ---, Mr. 785
  H. 784
  Hugh 188, 288, 805, 824
  John 804
  Thomas 82, 83, 84, 197, 202, 214,
    215, 238, 249, 432, 456, 483, 545,
    547, 727, 804
Mc Elderry & Floyd's Lumber-yard
  262
Mc Elderry Street 769
Mc Elderry Wharf 215
Mc Elderry's Wharf 240, 261, 386
MC ELDERY, Hugh 120
  Thomas 77, 170
Mc Eldery's Dock 174
MC ELDOWNEY, J. 549
MC ELFRESH, C. 577
MC ELHING, George 911
MC ELMOYLE, A. 550
MC ELROY, G. 583
  James 241, 871
  James W. 194
  John 380, 721, 803
MC EVOY, James 488
MC FADDEN, John 261
Mc Fadden, John & Co. 298
Mc Faden & Harris 439
MC FADON, John 77, 483
MC FAREN, William 850
MC FARLAND (MACFARLAND),
  ---, Rev. Mr. 521, 804
  C. Dodd 761
  Malcolm 523
  Marcus 77
MC GARIGLE, John 611
MC GAW, George K. 449
MC GEE, J. 902
  James 65
  Lydia 821
MC GEOCH, John 245
MC GIBBON, James 674
MC GILL (MACGILL), ---, Bishop
  539
  ---, Right Rev. 529
  Charles 804
  O. P. 813, 814
  Oliver P. 820
  P. 263
  P. H. 442, 484
  Patrick 882

MC GILL (MACGILL) Patrick H.
  449, 473
  Richard G. 882
  Samuel Ford 803
Mc Gill's Run 854
MC GINN, R. C. 902
MC GINNIS, ---, Dr. 745
  Francis J. 489
MC GINNISS, Francis J. 484
MC GIRR, J. S. 871
MC GLENNAN, Thomas 263
MC GLONE, John T. 194
MC GOWAN, Henry 242
  John 804
Mc Gowan, J. & Son 263
MC GRATH, ---, Mr. 682
MC GRAU, James C. 814
Mc Guan & Bouldin 481
MC GUIRE, Thomas C. 191, 193
MC GURK, E. A. 538
MC HENRY, ---, Mr. 172
  Daniel 432, 804
  Dennis 188
  Francis D. 299
  J. H. 890
  J. Howard 356, 495
  James 79, 82, 116, 117, 187, 193,
    194, 195, 214, 235, 291, 547, 679,
    736, 804, 814, 826
  James Howard 836
  John 62, 727, 804, 845
  Julia Elizabeth (HOWARD) 804
  Ramsey 847
  Thomas 728
  Thomas D. 244
Mc Henry, F. D.'s Wharf 299
Mc Henry & Shaw 439
Mc Henry Street 769
MC ILHANEY, ---, Miss 595
MC ILVAINE, ---, Bishop 524, 702
  J. W. 829
MC INTIRE, ---, Prof. 754, 771
  George M. 754
  James 751, 753
MC INTOSH, ---, Capt. 897
  D. G. 814
  David G. 903
  David Gregg 896
  James 896
  James H. 896
  John 515, 803
  Margaret (LUCAS) 896
  Martha (GREGG) 896
  Virginia J. (PEGRAM) 897
Mc Intosh's Battery 897
MC INTYRE, James 846
MC IVAIN, John 159
MC JILTON, ---, Mr. 498
  ---, Rev. Dr. 525
  Daniel 432, 805

MC JILTON, J. N. 153, 362, 364, 479, 523, 601, 649, 675, 890
John F. 190, 469, 612, 803
John N. 497, 526, 616, 625, 630, 650, 803, 933
John S. 498
MC KAIG, ---, Mr. 725, 726
Frisby Tilghman 726
Margaret Ann (TILGHMAN) 726
Nina Lamar 726
Patrick 724
Rachel (STAR) 724
Thomas I. 498
Thomas J. 507, 600, 723
Thomas Jefferson 724
MC KANE, John 92
MC KEAN, Ann 795
John 241, 245, 470, 547
John A. 555, 561
Laetitia 732
Thomas 732, 795
MC KECHNIE, Lundin 735
MC KEE, C. B. 549
MC KEEN, John 252
MC KENNA, Francis 77
Thomas 77
MC KENNEY, James A. 879
MC KENZIE (MACKENZIE), --- 684
---, Dr. 74, 733
---, Mrs. 684
Colin 734, 735, 742, 750, 751, 803, 804, 823, 824
E. 538
John P. 738, 750, 754, 804
Thomas 364
Thomas G. 740, 750
Thomas S. 803
MC KEW, D. L. 745
MC KEWEN, William 136, 199
William F. 200, 729
MC KIM (M'KIM, MC KIMM), --- 521
--- (HASLETT) 476
A. 70, 100, 195, 392
Alex. 935
Alexander 83, 120, 128, 169, 170, 172, 194, 197, 215, 235, 239, 298, 393, 407, 432, 452, 476, 482, 483, 554, 555, 572, 595, 727, 733, 769, 804, 814, 816, 823
H. 507
Hastell 476
Hollins 471, 478, 482
Isaac 89, 192, 193, 265, 266, 313, 316, 317, 318, 437, 438, 470, 476, 769, 804, 805
Jane 769

MC KIM (M'KIM, MC KIMM), John 77, 89, 98, 120, 176, 203, 215, 216, 298, 316, 375, 393, 438, 461, 464, 470, 476, 547, 554, 692, 727, 804, 805
John S. 506, 804
Margaret (DUNCAN) 476
R. 100, 392
Robert 70, 393, 407, 432, 470, 476
Samuel 89, 246, 458, 484, 824
Susan 601
Thomas 476
William 128, 139, 244, 440, 471, 476, 507, 601, 659, 803
William D. 298, 458, 476, 805
Mc Kim, A. & Co. 102
Mc Kim, John & Co. 476
Mc Kim, John, Jr. & Co. 433
Mc Kim & Co. 476, 477, 481
Mc Kim Estate 138
Mc Kim House 132
Mc Kim Mansion 152
Mc Kim Street 769
MC KINLEY, William 255
MC KINNEL, Henry 194
MC KINNELL, Henry 189
John 247
MC KIRDY, John 101
MC KNIGHT, John 313
MC KOSKEY, Alexander 804
MC LAMBAN, James 902
MC LANAHAN, Richard 262
Samuel 551
MC LANE, --- 166
---, Mr. 328, 329, 369
Charles M. 880
H. B. 222
J. L. 851
James L. 187, 194, 210, 222, 357, 368, 723, 851
Lewis 851
Louis 327, 675, 804
R. M. 128, 195
Robert 194
Robert M. 113, 130, 194, 227
MC LAUGHLIN, Andrew 516, 804
Augustus, Mrs. 133
John Fairfax 637
Mathew 251, 252
Patrick 288, 803
William 159, 374, 814
MC LEAN, Charles 878
Charles B. 903
Charles G. 551
Cornelius 194, 804
John 932
Thomas B. 159
W. W. 803
William 550
MC LEOUD, Robert 920
MC LOUGHLIN, James E. 506

MC LOUGHLIN, Matthew 459
W. 935
William 545, 572
MC LURE, A. 70
John 70, 76, 79, 206, 727
Mc Lure's Wharf 287
MC MACHEN, David 70
MC MAHON, ---, 115, 116, 122, 698, 704, 723
John 790
John V. L. 120, 122, 126, 193, 194, 315, 499, 713, 725
John Van Lear 658, 712, 804
V. L. 738
MC MANUS, ---, Father 597
---, Rev. 892
B. F. 937
B. J. 822
Bernard J. 236, 538, 539, 938
J. B. 539
MC MECHAN, David 779
MC MECHEN, David 70, 116, 173, 187, 194, 196, 592, 707, 708
William 62, 470
Mc Mechen's 342
MC MECHIN, ---, Mr. 172
William 804
MC MEYERS, John 592
MC MILLAN, James 600
MC MULLEN, John 149, 409
MC MULLIN, N. 902
MC MURRAY, ---, Mr. 777, 778
Ann 775
Ann S. 776
Anne 776
Caroline 776
Catharine 776
Jane Monica (MC DERMOTT) 776
John 775
Louis 775, 776
Samuel 775, 776
Sarah 775
Sarah (SELLMAN) 776
MC NABB, James 255
John 65, 530
MC NALLY, Henry R. 472, 935
John 236, 534
Michael 719
Michael S. 805
MC NEAL, Daniel 251
Hugh 255
James 846
John 103
Joseph W. 161
MC NEILL, William G. 318
MC NELLY, William 261
William J. 159
MC NERHANY, Francis 628
MC NIEL, James 466
MC NULTY, John 804
John R. 195

MC PHAIE, D. H. 159
MC PHAIL, Daniel 804
Daniel H. 114, 241
J. L. 242
James 199
James L. 193, 242, 253, 803
William 193, 345, 803, 804
MC PHERSON (MACPHERSON), ---, Dr. 851
---, Mr. 517
---, Mrs. 595
Isaac 89, 247, 253, 470, 593, 826, 827
James 465
John 192, 850
John H. T. 194
R. A., Mrs. 605
Samuel 245
William 742, 803
Mc Pherson's Gardens 761
MC PHIAL, James L. 260
MC QUIGGIN, Giles 650
MC QUILLON, Rowland 432
MC REILLY, J. 576
MC ROBERTS, Archibald 463
MC SHANE, Henry 281, 459, 495
James F. 187, 733
Mc Shane, Henry & Co. 420
MC SHERRY, ---, Mrs. 156
James 628, 825
Richard 743, 745
MC TAVISH (MACTAVISH), Charles Carroll 803
Emily 596, 938
Emily (CATON) 803
Francis O. 222
John 803
MC VEIGH, Kathleen 830
MC VEY, Samuel 578
MC WILLIAMS, J. J. 194
John 191, 193
John J. 194, 803
MEAD, P. N. 936
MEADE, ---, Gen. 135
George 102
P. N. 524
Meade, George & Co. 101
Meadow Farm 828
Meadow Mill 837
Meadows 694, 829
MEADS, Mary 583
Robert B. 159
MEAHER, Abby 628
MEAKIN, Samuel 191
MEANLEY, J. P. 448
Meanley & Gray 446
MEARIS, Malcolm W. 190, 250
Mechanic's Press 613
Mechanical Fire Company 238, 240, 241, 242, 244, 245, 253, 258, 484
Mechanical Institute 261

Mechanics' 473
Mechanics' Bank 315, 404, 450, 451, 457, 805, 810, 935
Mechanics' Gazette & Merchants' Daily Advertiser 614
Mechanics' Hall 605
Mechanics' Hall Perpetual Loan & Savings Society 511
Mechanics' Lexington Permanent Building & Loan Association No. 6 511
Mechanics' Lodge of Odd-Fellows 775
Mechanics' Savings Fund Society of Baltimore 462
Mechanics' Savings Institution 473
Mechanics' Western Permanent Building Society 511
Mechanicstown 318, 355, 357
Mechanicsville 817
Mechanicsville on the Chickahominy 897
Mechanicsville Riflemen 817
MEDCALF, William M. 893
Medfield 838
Medical & Chirurgical Faculty of Maryland 739, 742, 744, 746, 750, 751
Medical & Chirurgical Society 735, 840
Medical & Chirurgical Society of Baltimore 739, 740
Medical & Chirurgical Society of Maryland 734, 743
Medical & Surgical Journal 743
Medical & Surgical Reporter 739
Medical Board of Examiners, State of Maryland 734
Medical Society of Baltimore 732, 735
MEDINGER, John G. 449
MEDTART, ---, Gen. 263
  Jacob 569
  Joshua 569, 805
Medway Manufacturing Co. 408
MEEKING, Samuel 762
MEERS, John 191
MEETEER, William 120, 176, 188, 192, 246
MEETER, William 393, 667
MEGARY, Alexander 834
MEINEKE, Charles 673
MEIR, L. D. 830
MEISTER, Charles 571
MEIXSEL, Joseph H. 441
MEIXSELL, Howard 762
MELCHIOR, Nathan 803
MELIRON, Merab (LOWE) 866
  Samuel 866
MELLOR, Mark 813, 820
MELLS, Richard 757

Melvale 130, 347
MELVERN, ---, Rev. Mr. 880
MELVIN, A. T. 902
Members of the House of Delegates 819
Members of the Provincial Conventions 819
MEMMERT, Frederick 159
Memorial Church 524
Memorial M.E. Chapel 584
Memorial P.E. Church 524
Memorial Protestant Episcopal Church 402
MENARD, J. Willis 636
MENGER, H. 597
MENGERT, T. H. 571
MENGST, J. H. 929
MENNICK, George W. 673
MENSCHING, Caroline 373
Mercantile Library Association 253, 417, 651, 659, 660, 661, 795
MERCER, Andrew 153
  Charles H. 276, 466, 493, 577, 600, 603, 831
  J. 70
  John 38, 73
  John F. 845
  John Francis 195
MERCERON, Mollie 886
MERCHANT, Ephraim 592
  W. T. 855
Merchant, The 616
Merchants Club 449
Merchants' & Manufacturers' Association 402
Merchants' & Mechanics' Permanent Building & Loan Co. 511
Merchants' & Miners' Transportation Co. 302, 307, 404, 511
Merchants' & Traders' Banking Association 762
Merchants' Bank 231, 451, 700, 799, 807
Merchants' Coffee-House 407
Merchants' Exchange 481, 495, 497, 630
Merchants' Fire Insurance 480
Merchants' Mutual Insurance Co. 484, 491
Merchants' National Bank 451, 463, 464, 469
Merchants' Shot-Tower Co. 265, 421, 511
Merchants' Sugar Refinery 418
MEREDITH, ---, Miss 595
  Gilmor 466, 494
  Hannah 803
  J. 547, 680, 840
  John F. 129, 498
  Jonathan 298, 452, 457, 679, 712, 803, 804

MEREDITH, Joseph H. 675
  Joseph H., Mrs. 596
  Joshua 911
  Micajah 813
  Philip 264
  Richard 880
  Thomas 461, 471, 805, 921
  Thomas T. 188, 804
  William 250
Meredith's Bridge 220
Meredith's Ford 220, 905, 907
Meredith's Ford & Sweet Air Line 913
Meredith's Ford Turnpike 908, 909, 915
MERICHE, A. 213
MERILLET, J. C. M. 637
MERLE, --- 676
MEROLLA, E. D. 600
MERREFIELD, Joseph 746, 747
MERRETT, Caleb 246
  W. H. 917
  W. H., Mrs. 917
MERRICK, William H., Mrs. 156
MERRIFIELD, Joseph 598, 600, 602
MERRIKEN, Charles 173
  J. 95, 269
  William 191
MERRILAT, J. C. 804
MERRILL, Peter 365
  Stephen 225
Merrill & Thomas 132
MERRIMAN, John 850
MERRITT, Caleb 246
  Joseph B. 159
  N. S. 855
  William 927
  William K. 803
MERRY, ---, Mrs. 683
Merry's Tavern 733
Merryfield & Stinchcomb 263
MERRYMAN, --- 521
  ---, Messrs. 896
  Ann Louisa (GITTINGS) 885
  Anna 864
  Anna Maria (GOTT) 885
  Benjamin 71, 804, 911
  Charles 885
  Elijah 804, 819, 911
  Elizabeth 881
  George 219, 222, 359, 365, 817, 904
  George H. 877
  Henry 877
  Job 804
  Job M. 804
  John 68, 69, 74, 75, 76, 132, 170, 172, 173, 192, 200, 239, 352, 364, 365, 470, 520, 680, 728, 804, 814, 820, 847, 851, 864, 876, 877, 879, 880, 884, 885, 903, 909, 911, 921
  John of Hayfields 817

MERRYMAN, Joseph 578, 814, 892
  Joseph P. 195
  Joshua 77, 814, 864
  Margaret 804
  N. 255
  Nicholas 70, 116, 728, 812, 911
  Nicholas R. 120, 879
  Nicholas Rogers 885
  Rebecca 883
  Samuel 804
  Sarah 804, 864
  William 814, 869
Merryman Family 885
MERRYWEATHER, O. P. 205
MERSER, Jacob 804
MERVIC, John 566
MESHAW, Thomas 256
MESICK, B. 209
MESSENOCOI, --- 102
MESSER, William 361
MESSERSMITH, Samuel 569
MESSICK, Baptist 251
MESSIMER, J. E. 873
MESSONNIER, Elizabeth 804
  Henry 458, 804
Metamora Hall 762
METCALF, --- 122
  Lorana D. (CHEERU) 749
METCALFE, William M. 804
METEER, William 252
Methodism 573
Methodist Book Concern 746
Methodist Church 151
Methodist Episcopal Church South 585, 586
Methodist Meeting-house 238
Methodist Protestant 651
Methodist Protestant Church 583
Methodist Protestant Church Book Committee 616
Methodist Protestant, The 617
Methodist Protestants 581
Metropolitan 613, 629
Metropolitan Hall 680
Metropolitan Junction 342
Metropolitan M.E. Church Washington 604
Metropolitan Magazine 648
Metropolitan Savings-Bank 472, 473
METTAM, Joseph 836
  Samuel B. 814, 834
METTE, J. M. 252
METTEE, Joseph S. 159
METZ, Augustus 673
  Ferdinand 159
METZEL, George V. 254
METZGER, D. 252
  Daniel 189
  F. 740
  Frederick 92
Mexican Volunteers 801

Mexican War 887, 892, 895
MEYD, Francis 468
MEYER, Charles 805
  Charles J. 600, 603
  Christian 569
  Conrad 804
  F. 597
  Ferdinand 488
  Frederick 571
  Frederick C. 190
  George 241
  Godfrey 189
  Harman F. 159
  Herman F. 509
  Jacob 571, 572, 841
  Thomas 189
MEYERS, ---, Mrs. 595
  ---, Rev. Father 835
  B. F. 830
  Charles H. 137, 804
  Daniel E. 202
  Godfried 246
  Henry 188, 189, 192, 255, 938
  Jacob 298, 592
  Lewis 468
MEZICK, Baptist 188, 438, 461
  J. 303
MICHAEL, H. J. 602
  J. E. 604
  J. Edwin 743
Michael & Bros. 154
Michaelsville 918
MICKLE, John 118, 169, 170, 239, 804
  Robert 77, 433, 456
MIDDING, James 911
Middle Branch 48
Middle Police Station House 261
Middle River 517, 811, 918, 926
Middle River Lower Hundred 70, 812
Middle River North Upper Hundred 812
Middle River Upper Hundred 70, 71, 812, 910
Middleburg 357
Middlesex Hundred 70, 71, 812, 859
MIDDLETON, ---, Mrs. 569
  C. F. 365
  Gilbert 804
  J. I. 442, 444, 495
  J. Izard 502
  J. T. 442, 462
  James 804
  John A. 803
  John H. 362
  John I. 449
  John T. 445
  Joseph 99, 311
  Richard H. 255

MIDDLETON, William 99
  William G. 245
Middletown 342, 870, 889
Middletown Ferry 347
Middletown Lodge No. 92, I.O.O.F. 870, 874
Midway & Forks of Elkhorn Baptist Church 566
MILEMON, George 805
MILES, Aquila 187
  Dixon H. 804
  F. T. 743, 745, 937
  George H. 657, 803
  Hezekiah 84
  J. 241
  Joseph M. 241
  Joshua 911
  N. R. 912
  Philip S. 790
  Richard 581
  Richard H. 351
  S. G. 365
  Samuel G. 149, 155
  William 65, 657
Miles River 309
Miles' Ship Yard 293
MILHAUT, P. 102
MILHOLLAND, Edward F. 937
  James 667, 803
  Robert D. 804
MILHUEN, John 254
MILKE, John 917
Mill Creek Landing 310
Mill Creek Particular Baptist CHurch 553
MILLANDER, John H. 813
MILLARD, Pauline, Sister 598
MILLEMAN, George 84, 727
MILLENDER, Henry 869
  J. H. 869
  John H. 161, 869
MILLER, ---, Brig. Gen. 87
  ---, Dr. 741
  ---, Rev. Father 544
  A. 576
  A. A. 822, 916
  A. D. 194
  A. R. 516
  Abijah 855
  Adam 405
  Alfred A. 523
  August 886
  D. H. 302, 484
  Daniel 155, 410, 411, 412, 466, 803
  Decatur H. 140, 193, 303, 304, 373, 390, 415, 440, 494, 495, 509, 698
  E. A. 871
  Edgar G. 473, 502
  Elizabeth (PRICE) 883
  Elizabeth L. (WHELEN) 412
  Francis A. 242, 250, 255

MILLER, George 870
　George C. 465, 804
　George H. 489
　H. 636
　H. Clay 413
　H., Jr. 372
　Henry Clay 411, 412
　Horace 872
　Horatio 189
　J. F. 917
　J. H. 786
　J. S. 525
　Jacob 89, 187, 192, 459, 572, 804, 824
　Jacob W. 159
　James H. 624, 646, 675
　Joaquin 655
　Joel 593, 637, 638
　John 187, 298, 573
　John D. 92
　John M. 491
　John P. 241
　John S. 526
　John W. 159
　Joseph 873
　L. V. 372
　Lewis 247
　Lewis C. 579
　Luke H. 468
　M. A. 191
　M. Alexander 191
　Michael 541
　Milyor 592
　Nicholas 193
　Oliver 721
　Peter L. 538, 544
　Philip 571
　Richard 246
　Robert 120, 192, 252, 265, 266, 470, 804
　Stephen 813
　Theodore K. 411, 412, 550
　Theodore R. 281
　W. D. 365
　Warrick 883
　William 550, 741, 804
　William D. 302, 468, 469
　William E. 872
　William H. 202
　William L. 903
　William R. 412
Miller, Daniel & Co. 410, 411
Miller Family 869
Miller's 342
Miller's Hotel 139
Millersville 342
MILLES, A. L. 229
MILLESE, William 246
MILLESS, L. O. 159
MILLET, --- 675
MILLHOLLAND, A. V. 191

MILLHOLLAND, R. D. 463, 548
　Robert 188
　Robert E. 189
MILLIAN, Patrick 261
MILLIGAN, --- 166
MILLIKEN, B. H. 266
　Benjamin H. 265
　R. H. 550
　William H. 488
MILLIKIN, Robert 805
MILLIMAN, John 213
Millington 909
Millington Lodge No. 166, A. F. & A. M. 909
MILLS, ---, Mr. 567
　Charles H. 370
　Ezekiel 246
　John 139
　John S. 593
　R. 266
　Robert 209, 210, 265
　S. S. 191, 193
　S. Sands 191, 635
　Samuel J. 601
　Samuel S. 139, 246, 728
　Sands S. 194
　Thomas A. 159
Mills, John M. & Co. 635
Mills, S. S. & Bro. 635
Mills, Troxall & Co. 629
Mills & Bro. 263
Mills & Murray 263
MILNOR, Joseph K. 487
MILROY, ---, Gen. 671
　John 137, 191, 193, 200
MILTENBERGER, Anthony 189, 253
　Anthony F. W. 803
　George W. 701
MILTENBURGER, Anthony 786
Milton Academy 883
MILWATERS, Thomas 252
MINDE, J. C. 192
Mine Bank Lane 934
Mine Bank Run Road 886
Mine River Hundred 910
Mine Run Hundred 70, 71, 910
Minerva 613, 646
Minerva & Emerald 617
Minerva & Saturday Post 613
MINGE, ---, Dr. 850
MINIFE, J. Woodfin 159
MINIFIE, William 667, 690, 695
MINOR, Addison L. 830
Minors' Savings Association of East Baltimore 473
MINSHALL, Joshua 64
MINTONYE, W. L. 304
Mirror, New York 649
MISSION, Henry 298
MITCHELL, ---, Mr. 902
　Abraham 741

MITCHELL, Amanda M.
  (LITSINGER) 902
  Arthur 89, 188, 247, 248, 249
  Cahas 149
  Cassandra W. (DANIELS) 902
  Edgar C. 902
  Edward 242, 250
  Francis I. 532
  George E. 804
  George T. 159
  J. Winfield 902
  James 465
  James M. 188
  John 100, 191, 252, 362, 803, 892
  John G. 194
  Joseph B. 814, 902
  Joseph Burden 901
  Joshua 901
  Lawrence 803
  M. P. 438
  Maggie 689, 695
  Mary 689
  Mary (SANDERS) 901
  May Amanda 902
  Monroe 936
  Perry G. 813
  Peter 515
  Robert 469
  Thomas 380, 901
  Virginia B. 902
  Walter 128, 351
  William 159
  William Francis 902
  William K. 193, 813
  William P. 804
MITCHNER, William Allen 641, 642
MITLAN, William H. 153
MITLER, Daniel 803
MITTENBERGER, ---, Mr. 207
MITTNACHT, Henry 740
MOALE, --- 521
  ---, Mr. 50, 58
  Anna 804
  Eleanor (OWINGS) 862
  Elizabeth 864
  Frances 804
  Frances (OWINGS) 862
  Frederick L. 509
  George N. 370
  Helen (NORTH) 55
  Henry 472
  J. C. 680
  John 38, 40, 48, 50, 55, 57, 60, 61, 69, 71, 72, 73, 80, 205, 244, 424, 514, 518, 520, 521, 726, 727, 728, 768, 804, 814, 819, 864, 934
  L. H. 173
  R. H. 192
  Rachel 864
  Rachel (HAMMOND) 864

MOALE, Randal H. 864
  Randall H. 593, 804
  Richard 69, 71, 574, 804, 864
  Richard H. 173
  Robert 77
  Robert M. 804
  Robert N. 861
  Robert North 862
  Samuel 91, 188, 804, 864
  Thomas 862
Moale's Point 816, 864
Mobtown 778
MODINA, ---, Miss 651
MODNA, ---, Miss 617
MOEL, P. E. 742
MOFFETT, Edwin W. 159
  Noah 244
MOHLER, J. 365
MOHLMANN, ---, Prof. 625
MOHR, John 159
MOLLOY, Mary L. 927
MOLTHE, Magnus 159
MOMFORD, Thomas 39
MONCREIF, Archibald 482
MONCREIFT, Archibald 77
MONCRIEF, Archibald 804
MONCRIEFF, Archibald 452
MONDEL, William 461
Monitor 627, 630, 647
Monitor & Sentinel, The 637
Monkton 20, 21, 347, 864, 907, 908, 909, 913, 916
MONKUR, J. C. 739
  J. C. S. 755, 786, 803
Monkur's Institute 522
MONMONIER, J. F. 189, 469
  John F. 137, 189
  John T. 746
Monocacy 332, 899
Monocacy Junction 335
Monocacy Monthly Meeting 884
Monocacy Viaduct 323
MONROE, --- 112
  ---, Miss 595
  ---, Mr. 295, 296
  D. S. 839
  Edmund 928
  Isaac 612
  Thomas H. W. 804
  W. R. 359
  William A. 578
  William R. 739
Monroe M.E. Church 579
Monroe Street 769
Monrovia 342, 567
MONSARAT, D. S. 246
  N. 595
  Oscar 246
MONSARRAT, Oscar 740
MONSONAT, Nicholas 803
Mont Alto 830

Mont Alto Presbyterian Church 828, 829
MONTAGUE, Charles P. 129, 820
William L. 155, 190
Montebello 31, 887, 889, 890
MONTGOMERY, ---, Capt. 92
John 61, 84, 91, 187, 194, 804
R. 102
William 592
William T. 804
Montgomery County 50
Montgomery Guards 669
Montgomery Street 769
Monthly Argus, The 637
Monthly Chronicle of Religion & Learning, The 641
Monthly Visitor 625
Montmorency 862
Montrose P.E. Church 866
Montvieu 873
Montview 880
Monument 616, 649, 650
Monument Square 113, 120, 123, 124, 125, 130, 138, 140, 142, 145, 149, 163, 267, 497, 513, 785, 787, 876
Monument Street M.E. Church 578
Monumental Fire Insurance Co. 511
Monumental Fountain 628
Monumental Gasoline Street Lamp Manufacturing Co. 511
Monumental Hose Company 255
Monumental Hose Fire Company 242
Monumental Journal, The 640
Monumental Literary Gazette 630
Monumental Lodge of Free & Accepted Masons 775
Monumental Lyceum 609
Monumental Perpetual Building & Savings Society No. 5 511
Monumental Railway 370
Monumental Rifles 669
Monumental Steamboat Co. 511
Monumental Theatre 695, 696
MOODY, Converse 159
David 317
William 193
MOON, Edward 125, 380
Richard 105
MOONEY, --- 202
M. E. 191
Robert S. 159
MOORE, --- 85
---, Capt. 88, 112, 116
---, Dr. 741
---, Lt. Col. 87
---, Mr. 376, 614, 759
Ann 883
Athanasius 246

MOORE, Daniel 737
David 804
Edward 381
Elder 558
Elizabeth 634, 804
Ely 928
George 65
George W. 159
J. D. 579
J. Faris 193, 740
J. R. 241
James 203
James T. 872
John 58, 380, 488
John R. 241, 244, 252, 253, 271, 484
Joseph 355
Malvina 839
Mordecai 587
N. Ruxton 70
Nicholas 117, 201
Nicholas B. 195
Nicholas R. 804, 819
Nicholas Ruxton 80, 83, 519, 804
Philip 187, 192, 450, 459, 729, 805
Rachel 883
Robert 61, 65, 251, 734, 817, 832, 845, 891
S. 850
Samuel 188, 192, 234, 393, 402, 486, 680, 805
Stephen 187
Stephen H. 84, 87, 189, 805, 814, 816
T. 102
Thomas 65, 101, 804
Thomas H. 193, 815, 905
Walter 883
William 373, 574
William S. 159, 470
Moore, Robert & Co. 899
Moore Family 588, 893
Moore Family of Moore Orchard 839
Moore's Bridge 432
MOORES, Daniel 734, 741, 804
David 742
Mollie 877
MOOYER, H. 597
MORAN, J. J. 367, 840
Michael 261
MORANVILLE, J. F. 535
John Francis 804
MORDECAI, J. R. 442, 905
Randolph 445
MORE, --- 924
MOREAU, Moses 77
MOREHEAD, --- 122
---, Col. 132, 136, 199
MORETON, --- 682
MORFETT, J. 602
MORFIT, Henry M. 194, 804

MORFIT, James 153
MORFITT, H. M. 130
 Henry M. 137
MORFOOT, William 814
MORGAN, ---, Ex.-Gov. 147
---, Gen. 80
---, Mr. 365
---, Senator 147
G. E. 746
Gerald E. 746
Gerard E. 745
J. 734
J. Asbury 139
James A. 803
John 386
L. A. 538
Littleton J. 576
N. J. B. 601
Thomas 432, 779
Wilbur P. 159
Morgan & Co. 476
MORIARTY, ---, Rev. Father 933
MORISON, ---, Dr. 666
 Earnest Nathaniel 665
 George Brown 665
 George Burnap 666
 John Holmes 666
 Mary Ann (HOPKINS) 665
 N. H. 661, 667
 Nathaniel 665
 Nathaniel Holmes 665
 Robert Brown 665
 Sidney Buchanan (BROWN) 665
 William George 666
MORLING, F. L. 837, 838
Morning Chronicle 614, 615
Morning Post 613
Morning Star, The 628
MORNINGSTAR, Addie 834
MORONG, Edwin P. 159
MORRELL, Peter 128
MORRIS, --- 521
---, Dr. 556, 665
---, Gen. 140, 141, 144, 150
---, Gov. 804
---, Maj. 131
---, Mr. 295, 682, 881
---, Mrs. 682
---, Rev. Dr. 659, 877
Alice 873
Andrew J. 202
Benjamin 921
Caspar 746
Catharine C. 756
Charles D. 233
Charles T. 263
Eliza Hay 803
George 343, 545, 547
George P. 870
George S. 233
Gouverneur 398

MORRIS, Hannah (TYSON) 772
 Henry D. 880
 Isabella 605
 J. B. 393
 J. G. 569
 John 194, 600, 602, 721, 745, 938
 John B. 128, 188, 225, 316, 317, 318, 324, 458, 784, 785, 786, 803
 John B., Mrs. 604
 John G. 493, 569, 649, 655, 656, 664, 745, 774, 803, 847, 877, 929
 John S. 487
 John T. 190, 231, 242, 258, 272, 601, 828, 890
 Joseph 920
 Keziah 595
 Levin H. 194
 Mark 225
 Pochon William 252
 Robert 101, 102, 690
 Robert A. 159
 Samuel 189
 T. H. 851
 T. J., Mrs. 604
 Thomas C. 188, 246
 Thomas H. 472, 697, 803
 Thomas J. 729, 790
 W. W. 151, 804
 William 201, 202, 252, 756
 William B. 193
 William E. 484
 William H. 908
 William W. 141
 Wistsar 346
Morris' Island 897
MORRISON, --- 910
 E. 465
 Elisha S. 159
 F. D. 601, 890
 George 226
 George F. 524
 J. F. 202, 260
 J. Frank 202, 502
 James 261
 James H. 522
 John W. 159
 Robert B. 162
 William D. 161
MORROW, Isaac H. 114
 James S. 187
 John 65
 Robert 73
MORRY, ---, Misses 569
MORSE, ---, Mr. 652
---, Prof. 620
---, Professor 503, 504, 505, 507, 508
Harmon N. 233
S. F. B. 506
Samuel F. B. 502
Thomas W. 194, 200
Morse Building 508

143

Morse Memorial Association 508
MORSEL, Benjamin 247
MORSELL, Eleanor 413
MORSS, Jacob B. 861
MORTON, ---, Mr. 493
  Albert 159
  Dudley T. 488
  George 351
  Henry E. 358
  John A. 470
  Moore 872
  Nathaniel 804
  Ralfe 39
MOSER, Andreas 159
Moses, J. & Co. 101
MOSHER, George R. 462
  James 62, 84, 86, 89, 175, 187, 188, 192, 205, 215, 216, 244, 393, 437, 450, 456, 457, 458, 470, 498, 500, 545, 547, 592, 593, 667, 685, 692, 727, 804, 805, 824
MOSS, John A. 579
  Samuel 803
Moss Neck 670
MOST, Henry 189
Mother Theresa 807
Mothers' Meeting 552
MOTT, A. G. 887
  John 249, 470
  Joshua 89, 192, 248, 249, 463
  Mott & Co. 281
MOTTER, Isaac 355
  Joshua 355
MOTTU, Theodore 356, 579
Moundsville 342
Mount Airy 342
Mount Airy Farm 893
Mount Ararat 924
Mount Ararat Mason Lodge, No. 44 915
Mount Calvary Chapel of St. Mary 525
Mount Calvary Church 934
Mount Calvary Episcopal Church 601, 703
Mount Calvary P.E. Church 523, 806
Mount Carmel 869, 875
Mount Carmel Cemetery 890, 933, 934
Mount Carmel Episcopal CHurch 875
Mount Carmel P.E. Church 869
Mount Carroll 834
Mount Carroll Land Co. 511
Mount Clare 261, 321, 380, 418, 563, 705, 707, 796, 797, 846, 936
Mount Clare Depot 319, 323, 502, 517, 788
Mount Clare Hotel 517
Mount Clare Permanent Loan & Building Association 511
Mount Clare Shops 331
Mount de Sales Academy of the Visitation 820, 822
Mount DeSales 896
Mount Dougherty 937
Mount Gillian P.M. Church 866
Mount Hope 357
Mount Hope Asylum for the Insane 834
Mount Hope Catholic Chapel 544
Mount Hope College 853
Mount Hope Insane Asylum 720
Mount Hope Institution 841
Mount Hope Literary Gazette 613
Mount Hope Retreat 748, 834, 853
Mount Jackson 342
Mount Lebanon Church 890
Mount Lebanon M.P. Church 526
Mount Moriah Lodge 903, 902
Mount Moriah Lodge A. F. & A. M. 871
Mount Moriah Lodge of Masons 878
Mount Moriah Lodge of Towsontown 894
Mount Olivet Baptist Church, Va. 564
Mount Olivet Cemetery 820, 826
Mount Olivet M.E. Church 831
Mount Olivet Methodist Cemetery 575
Mount Olivet Mission M.E. Chapel 826
Mount Orange Cemetery 934
Mount Paran Lodge No. 162, A.F. & A.M. 832
Mount Paran Sunday-School 830
Mount Peru 923, 924, 925
Mount Pisgah M.E. Mission 580
Mount Pleasant 88, 354, 816, 825, 896
Mount Royal 49
Mount Royal Forge 425
Mount Royal Mill 218, 219
Mount Royal Reservoir 132, 147, 219, 221, 274
Mount St. Agnes Academy 834, 839, 840
Mount St. Joseph's College 820, 826
Mount St. Mary's College 234, 235, 532, 657, 852
Mount St. Vincent 853
Mount Tabor M.E. Church 870
Mount Vernon 224, 836, 839, 875
Mount Vernon Building Association No. 2 & No. 3 511
Mount Vernon Cemetery 274, 839
Mount Vernon Company 409, 511
Mount Vernon Company Cotton Mill 264

Mount Vernon Factory 507
Mount Vernon Fire Company 242
Mount Vernon Guards 668
Mount Vernon Hook & Ladder Company 251, 256
Mount Vernon Hotel 516, 697
Mount Vernon Lodge 640, 874
Mount Vernon M.E. Church 266, 280, 576, 723, 839, 882
Mount Vernon Manufacturing Co. 404, 838
Mount Vernon Mills 817, 838, 839
Mount Vernon Place 128, 265, 266, 347, 664, 666, 675
Mount Vernon Place M.E. Church 567
Mount Vernon Square 280
Mount Washington 15, 17, 18, 22, 347, 407, 409, 834, 839, 880, 886
Mount Washington Female College 840
Mount Washington Presbyterian Church 840
Mount Washington Station 842
Mount Welcome 723
Mount Winans 936
Mount Wolf 347
Mount Zepher 603
Mount Zion Baptist Church 559, 560
Mount Zion Church of the U.B. 869
Mount Zion Colored Methodist Church 581
Mount Zion Lodge No. 87, I.O.O.F. 834, 836
Mount Zion Lutheran Church 931
Mount Zion M.E. Church 871
Mountain Pass 275
MOUNTENAY, Alexander 49, 50
Mountenay's Neck 49, 50, 59
Mountview 878
MOWBRAY, G. W. 874
MOWEL, Joseph 908
 Joseph W. 916
MOWELL, ---, Mr. 880
 Amanda 878
 Anna Catherine (HELVINA) 879
 Elizabeth F. (ABEY) 880
 Ella V. 880
 Joseph W. 880, 916
 Peter 365, 488, 803, 878, 879
MOWERS, S. A. 573
MOWTON, John 667
MOXLEY, ---, Mr. 688
 B. G. Douglass 383
 Sophia M. P. 383
 Thomas 696
MOZIER, James 497
MUCHNEW, Christopher 911
Mud Theatre 501, 689, 694

MUDD, Angela, Mother 599
MUDGE, Abner R. 803
MUELLER, Joseph 803
MUHLEY, Charles W. 202
MUIR, John 102
MUIRHEAD, William 761
MULES, Isaac 189, 190, 465, 577
 T. H. 366
 Thomas 193
 Thomas H. 190, 194
MULLALY, John B. 538
MULLAN, John P. 534
 Jonathan 534
MULLEDY, Samuel 538
MULLEN, James 190, 804, 817
 John George 131
 Jonathan 803
 O. 190
 Patrick 247
 Robert 431
MULLER, ---, Mr. 217
 J. 570
 Julius E. 673
 Louis 125, 442
 M. 642
 Peter L. 803
 Philip H. 190, 303
 William R. 803
MULLIGAN, John 236
Mulligan's Wagon Train 147
Mulliken 354
MULLIKIN, B. D. 821, 850
 B. H. 470
MULLIN, Laura M. 229
 M. A. 191
 Michael A. 194
MULLOOLEY, Thomas 149
MUMMA, --- 783
MUMMEY, Catherine 582
 Guinilda 582
 Thomas 187, 188, 247
MUNDAY, Henry 65
MUNDELL, Alexander 773
 Susan 773
 Thomas 773
 William 187
MUNDLE, William 246
MUNNICKHUYSEN, John 520
MUNROE, Charles 506
 Isaac 188, 462, 805
 W. R. 813
MUNSEY, ---, Rev. Dr. 636
 William E. 803
MUNSON, ---, Mr. 774
 Israel 879
 John W. 367
MURDOCH, ---, Mr. 637
 A. F. 600, 604
 Alexander 547, 549, 846
 Alexander F. 603
 C. B., Mrs. 598

MURDOCH, E. B. 602
  E. B., Mrs. 597
  F., Mrs. 156
  Thomas, Mrs. 155, 156
  W. F. 365, 471
  William 298
  William F. 364
Murdoch, William & Co. 439
MURDOCK, Alexander 463, 464, 803
  Harry C. 696
  James E. 693, 694
  Thomas 804
  Thomas F. 745
MURKLAND, W. U. 549, 840
MURPHY, --- 104, 299
  ---, Capt. 108, 296
  ---, Rev. Mr. 929
  Cornelius 793
  George 609
  J. W. 506
  James 105
  James E. 136
  John 89, 472, 592, 624, 627, 932
  Michael 790
  Patrick 262
  R. R. 579, 889
  Thomas 253, 610, 804
  Thomas J. 690
  Thomas W. 260
  William 295, 519, 658, 866, 920
Murphy, John & Co. 629, 762
Murphy & Spaulding 649
MURRAY, ---, Mr. 296, 784, 924
  A. 102
  Alexander 100, 101, 103, 159, 293
  Daniel 194, 782
  H. C. 153, 194, 281
  Henry M. 301, 804
  Heron 688
  J. J. 830
  J. T. 838
  James 288, 709, 741, 804, 923
  John 120
  Joseph 519
  Matthew 814
  Robert 149
  Thomas 233
  Thomas J. 202
  Washington 880
  William 741
  William H. 458, 672
  William J. 193
  William W. 738
  Zipporah 71
Murray & Hazelhurst, Vulcan Iron-Works 254
Murray & Hazlehurst 258
Murray Institute 369, 468
Murray's Tavern 312
MURROW, ---, Dr. 741

MURROW, Benjamin 741
MUSCHETT, Walter 372
MUSE, J. E. 846
MUSGRAVE, ---, Maj. 783
  G. W. 839, 902
  James 125
MUSGROVE, James 466
Musical Association 672
Musical Olio, The 617
MUSKETT, Walter 95
MUSSELMAN, George R. 487
  John 193
MUTH, Louis 929
  Philip 241
Mutual Benefit Life Co. of New Jersey 643
Mutual Fire Insurance Co. 488
Mutual Life 490
Mutual Life Insurance Co. of N.Y. 489, 490
Mutual Rights & Christian Intelligencer 616
Mutual Rights & Methodist Protestant 616
Mutual Rights, The 616
My Lady's Manor 526, 907, 913
MYER, ---, Father 237
  Albert T. 395
  Anna 395
  Anna (RINGGOLD) 395
  Constance 395
  Elizabaeth 395
  Jacob 395
  James 484
  Mary (WELSH) 395
  Mary J. 395
  Mary J. (FOLEY) 395
  Robert J. 395
  T. J. 441
  Thomas 395
  Thomas J. 395, 472
  Thomas R. 395
  William S. 395
Myer Garden 89
MYERLY, Frederick S. 869
MYERS, ---, Capt. 88
  A. J. 600
  A. Joseph 484
  Andrew J. 367
  Belinda M. (SLAGLE) 379
  Charles 380, 804
  Christian 172
  E. S. 162
  Edward 887
  Edward S. 820, 876, 896
  Emanuel 159
  George 250, 804
  Harriet 774
  Henry 92, 189, 236, 250, 537, 786, 803
  Henry J. 379

MYERS, Henry, Mrs. 594
 Hugh 264
 J. T. 356
 Jacob 71, 75, 170, 188, 190, 192,
  245, 246, 250, 514, 773, 804, 907
 Johnzey 869
 Joseph 91
 Lewis 468, 840
 Margaret 804
 Maria 804
 Philip 525
 Samuel 805, 907
 Sophia 907
 Thomas 153
 William 534
Myers Family 774
Myers' Tanyard 200
Naaman's Creek 311
NABB, James 845
NACE, George 812
 William 855
NACHMAN, Abraham 841
 Adolph 202
 George W. 237
NADAL, B. H. 839
NAFF, Franklin H. 805
NAGOT, ---, Father 235
 ---, Rev. Mr. 531
 Francis Charles 234, 805
NAILER, George 759
NAILL, David W. 846
NALLEY, Uzial 351
NALLS, B. F. 193
 Benjamin F. 190
NAMUTH, E. F. 191
Nancarrow Survey 932
NANCE, George 116
Nanticoke Indians 724
Nanticoke River 313
NAPEAR, James H. 625
Natatorium & Physical Culture
 Association 511
National Agricultural Association
 885
National Bank of Baltimore 451,
 455, 469
National Board of Health 753
National Cemetery at Gettysburg
 146
National Chemical Fertilizer
 Association 398
National Exchange Bank 451, 466,
 469, 800
National Farmers & Planters' Bank
 451, 464, 469, 478
National Fire Insurance Co. 406,
 484, 487, 491
National Gazette 611, 648
National Intelligencer 648, 653
National Line 306
National Magazine 613

National Marine Bank 451, 461, 469
National Mechanics' Bank 451, 456,
 458, 469, 482
National Medical Society 750
National Museum & Weekly Gazette
 612
National Protective Union 489
National Theatre 683, 694
National Union Bank 451, 456, 469
Navassa Phosphate Co. 398
Navy-Yard Baptist Church D.C. 560
Navy-Yard Station 354
NAYLOR, Amos 855
 H. R. 577
 Robert F. 363
NEAL, ---, Mr. 612
 Abner 187, 233, 470
 F. 365
 John 642, 643, 644
 John M. 253
 William 672
Neal, W. & J. 262
NEALE, Abner 593, 826, 827
 Annie 527
 Bennett 526
 Charles 599
 F. C. 472
 Francis 351, 472, 805
 Isabella 786
 J. G. 268
 Leonard 235, 527, 531, 805
 Mary Leonard, Sister 598
 R. 95, 269
Neale, McKim & Co. 433
NEALS, James, Capt. 36
Neck Road 934
Necrology 794
NEDLES, Charles E. 219
NEEDHAM, --- 499
 Asa 368
 George F. 441
 S. H. 805
 Sumner H. 790
NEEDLES, Charles 275
 Edward 240, 241
 J. 241
 John 241, 262, 602, 675
 John A. 153, 242, 245
Needles Family 588
NEEL, A. A. P. 587
NEER, J. P. 447
 J. Potts 489
NEFF, John 745, 746
 Peter 254, 348, 484
NEIBLING, Frederick 381
NEIDHEIMER, John 250
NEIDIG, ---, Rev. Mr. 573
NEIGHBORS, Henry 246
NEIL, William 392, 547
NEILL, A. 364
 W. 102

147

NEILL, William 79, 101, 727
Neill, William & Co. 102
NEILLE, John 741
NEILSON, ---, Mr. 331, 613
  Ann (VANBIBBER) 866
  Charles F. M. 159
  George 218
  Hugh 866
  J. Crawford 675, 697
  John 246
  Joseph 189
  O. H. 439
  Oliver H. 470
  Robert 188, 470, 760
  Thomas 262
  Thomas N. 805
  W. H. 145
  William H. 146, 162, 194, 633, 635
NELKER, John F. 488
NELMS, N., Mrs. 594
NELSON, --- 698
  ---, Gov. 80
  ---, Miss 693
  ---, Mr. 783
  ---, Secretary 774
  Benjamin 60
  Edward C. 877
  Henry 782
  Jarrett 872
  John 126, 499, 713, 715, 725, 805, 872, 876
  Nathan 813, 875, 908
  Thomas M. 774
  Thomas T. 813
  Wakeman 149
  William 526
NENINGER, --- 673
  ---, Prof. 267
  J. 672
NENNINGER, J. 694
NENO, Hervio 694
Neptune Insurance Co. 480, 805
Nervous Diseases Dispensary 748
NESBET, Alexander 712
Nesbit 79
NESBIT, Alexander 805
  John 102
NEUMANN, ---, Rev. Father 541
  ---, Right Rev. Bishop 542
  John N. 540
NEVETT, Mary 715
NEVIN, Thomas 877
NEVINS, ---, Mrs. 594
  William 546, 547, 805
NEW, J. P. 466
New Albion 373
New American Theatre 265, 693
New Amstel 36, 40
New Assembly Rooms 141, 522, 586, 664, 679, 680, 738

New Castle & French-town Turnpike & Railroad Co. 314
New Central Theatre 696
New Chestnut Street Theatre, Philadelphia 688
New Church Street 519
New Correspondent 655
New Cumberland 347
New Eclectic, The 637, 657
New England Coffee-House 740
New Era 617
New Freedom 347, 870
New Holliday Theatre 685
New Jersey Central 350
New Jerusalem Church 588, 804
New Jerusalem Society 560
New Line Expedition 311
New Market 342, 720, 873, 874, 915
New Market Fire Company 240, 241, 242, 250, 251, 256, 258, 483
New Market-house 433
New Michael's Building Association 511
New Orleans Morse Telegraph Line 507
New Orleans Crescent 610
New Point Comfort 310
New Sweden 33
New Texas Greens 817
New Theatre 681, 682, 684
New Theatre & Circus 690
New Windsor 357
New York & Baltimore Transportation Line Co. 511
New York & Maryland Line Co. 344
New York Central 347
New York Gazette & Post-Boy 605
New York Herald 621
New York Iron & Coal Co. 328
New York Medical Journal 739
New York World & Express 633
New Yorker 651
NEWBELLE, Frank T. 854
NEWBOLD, James F. 191
Newbold & Sons 446
Newburg 342
NEWCOMB, ---, Lt. 91
  Simon 233
NEWCOMER, Amelia (EHLEN) 479
  B. F. 346, 444, 445, 471, 477, 483, 676, 728, 890
  Benjamin F. 440, 479
  Benjamin Franklin 478
  Catharine 479
  Catharine (NEWCOMER) 479
  Christian 479
  Henry 479
  John 479
  Peter 479
Newcomer & Co. 479

Newcomer & Stonebraker 479
NEWELL, ---, Rev. Dr. 625
  M. A. 231, 641
  William 519
NEWHAN, S. 597
Newington Building Association of Baltimore 775
Newington Land & Loan Co. 511, 775
Newington Park 603, 834
NEWKIRK, Mathew 348, 349
NEWMAN, G. A. 515
  G. H. 439
  L. P. D. 190, 263, 637, 838
  Louis 149
  William 522
Newman, Ross Campbell & Co. 410
Newport 351
NEWPORT, R. N. 624
News-Sheet 633
Newsham & Co. 263
NEWTON, William 101
  Willoughby 846
Newton, J. & Co. 629
Newton Academy Library 667
Newton Theological Seminary 556
Newton University Hospital 152
Newtown 342
NICE, George P. 562
  Henry 577
NICHOLAI, Laura 886
NICHOLAS, --- 88
  ---, Col. 817
  J. A. 850
  J. Spear 932
  John Spear 190, 194, 896
  William J. 256
Nicholas & Co. 265
NICHOLL, David 241
  John D. 817
NICHOLLS, J. R. 902
  W. I. 191
  W. J. 242
  William I. 190
  William J. 272
NICHOLS, Charles 452
  H. 101
  Henry 452, 455
  J. 678
  J. R. 584
  John 101
  John F. 640
  John R. 583
  John S. 864
  Joseph 738
  W. C. 862
  William I. 498
NICHOLSON, ---, Capt. 95
  ---, Col. 146
  ---, Gov. 919
  ---, Mr. 781

NICHOLSON, Benj. 71
  Benjamin 69, 70, 71, 72, 73, 707, 779, 805, 819, 845, 860, 863
  Christopher 475
  Columbus 475
  Edward E. 159
  Francis 195
  Gustavus 475, 484
  Isaac L. 475, 526
  Jacob C. 805
  James 72, 79, 99, 779, 805
  James B. 270
  John 244, 409, 439, 732
  John F. 637
  John J. 475
  John Joseph 861
  John S. 475, 805
  John, Mrs. 605
  Joseph H. 84, 98, 203, 205, 450, 461, 729
  Joseph Hopper 712, 805
  Joshua 202
  Joshua H. 91
  Nathan 921
  Samuel F. 805
  William 805
  William R. 525
Nicholson, Isaac L. & Co. 475
Nicholson, J. J. & Sons 475
Nicholson Family 862
NICKERSON, C. V. 613
  Thomas 805
NICKILSON, John 380
NICKLESON, James 65
NICODEMUS, Josiah 805
Nicodemus Road 854
NICOLAI, Charles H. 820
  Eliza E. 229
NICOLLS, Henry 172, 173
  James 77
NICOLS, Henry 192, 658
  Jeremiah 452
NIERNSEE, ---, Mr. 331
  John E. 444
  John R. 445, 747
Niernsee & Neilson 669
Night Day 263
NIGHTINGALE, Samuel 254
NILE, Henry 902
NILES, ---, Mr. 84, 86
  Anna 805
  Hezekiah 188, 244, 393, 484, 614, 667, 760, 805
  Sally Ann 614
  William Ogden 614, 615, 625, 805
Niles' National Register 614
Niles' Register 614
NILSSON, --- 673
NIMOCKS, Franklin B. 114
NIND, William 233, 805
NINDE, ---, Mrs. 595

NINDE, J. C. 192
  James C. 805
Ninth District School Teachers 886
Ninth District School Trustees 886
Ninth District Teachers of Colored Schools 886
Ninth West Columbia Building Association 511
NISBET, Alexander 547
NISS, George W. 488
Nitre Mining Bureau 915
NITZE, C. 195
NIXAN, William 224
NIXON, William 520
NIZER, Thomas A. 892
No. 6 Engine-House 524
NOAH, --- 687
NOAL, Perry E. 741
NOBLE, Denis 231
NOBLITT, Dell 346
NOCK, N. N. 855
NOCOLAI, Charles H. 195
NOEDEL, G. W. 695
NOEL, ---, Dr. 741
  Basil 311
  P. E. 742
  Perry E. 741
  Septimus 292
  William A. 159
NOLAN, Michael 264
NOLEN, Elizabeth (BARTLETT) 406
NOLI, ---, Rev. Father 534
NOLTE, John Martin 805
NOONAN, J. 544
NORDEN, John 35
Norfolk 816
NORFOLK, Joseph 358
Norfolk Line 262, 350
Normal Classes 227
Normal School Library 667
NORMAN, Thomas 592
  William B. 159
NORRIS, Alexander 846
  Aquilla 74
  Benjamin 921
  C. Sidney 190, 193, 366
  C. Sydney 177
  Charles H. 805
  Edward 253, 805, 921
  Edward T. 412
  Ephialet 923
  G. Somerville 867
  G. W. 814
  George 937
  George R. 923
  George S. 937
  George W. 937
  Isaac 805
  J. C. 855
  J. Cloud 630, 635

NORRIS, J. Olney 444, 445, 449
  J. S. 596
  J. Saurin 466, 604, 649
  J. Saurin, Mrs. 596
  Jacob 159, 244
  John 757, 805
  John B. 869
  John C. 253
  Luther A. 95
  R. S. 583, 832
  R. Scott 584
  R., Mrs. 156
  Richard 575, 805, 855, 867, 885
  Richard, Mrs. 155
  Robert 253
  Silas 253
  Stephen F. 229
  Thomas 155
  W. B. 302
  W. M. 872
  William 439, 470, 483, 593, 827
  William E. 805
  William H. 159, 198, 463, 785
  William Henry 126, 128
Norris & Bro. 263
Norris Caldwell & Co. 263
NORTH, ---, Capt. 53
  Frances 864
  Helen 55
  Robert 37, 53, 54, 55, 56, 521, 864
  Thomas 864
North American 612
North American & Mercantile Daily Advertiser 613
North American Review 589, 644
North American Telegraph Line 504
North Avenue Prestyberian Church 551
North Baltimore, The 641
North Baltimore M.E. Church 586
North Baltimore M.E. Church South 586
North Baltimore Mutual Loan Association No. 2 512
North Baltimore Passenger Railway Co. 512
North Bond Street Building Association No. 7 & No. 8 511
North Branch 830
North Branch of the Patapsco 868
North Broadway Building Association No. 4 512
North Central Co. 353
North Central Railroad 346, 347
North East 351
North East Forge 424
North German Lloyd Line 303, 306, 336, 379
North Howard Building Association Nos. 3 & 4 511

North Hundred 70, 71, 910
North Mountain 342
North Point 17, 28, 86, 87, 90, 92, 137, 155, 278, 289, 609, 610, 656, 744, 749, 872, 926, 927, 933
North Point House 933
North Point Road 518, 926
Northampton Furnace 425
Northeastern Dispensary 748
NORTHERMAN, George 582
　Isabella 582
Northern Central Co. 346
Northern Central Railroad 18, 55, 130, 147, 178, 275, 283, 305, 314, 342, 344, 345, 353, 354, 355, 356, 359, 380, 385, 410, 517, 677, 703, 789, 790, 815, 818, 834, 836, 839, 841, 869, 870, 871, 872, 873, 874, 876, 877, 879, 880, 882, 883, 885, 886, 891, 905, 907, 908, 914, 915, 916, 926, 928
Northern Central Railroad Station 218, 694
Northern Fountain 213
Northwest Mission Church 572
NORTON, John W. 506
NORVELL, ---, Mr. 613
NORWOOD, --- 895
　Charles C. 190
　Edward 71
　Lamford 729
　Randolph 159
NOSS, H. 597
NOTLEY, Thomas 195
Notre Dame Academy 891
Nottingham 88
Nottingham Forges 816
Nottingham Iron-Furnace 425
Novelleu Zeitung, The 629
NOWLAN, Francis 805
NOWLAND, --- 514
NOYER, Levi 225
NOYES, Enoch 745
　S. D. 549, 550, 551
NOYLE, Jacob 95
NULLER, J. N. 303
NUMSEN, John W. 484, 489
　William 469
NURSER, Jacob 805
Nursery & Child's Hospital 379, 602
NUSSBAUM, H. 589
NUTWELL, George W. 358
NYSSEN, Gerald H. 538
O'BRIEN, --- 166
---, Rev. Father 933
　M. 256, 302
　Mathew 805
　Matthew 222
　Owen 629
　Patrick 358, 936

O'BRIEN, William J. 190, 193
O'CALLAGHAN, H. H. 506
　Joseph 538
O'CARROLL, Joanna 71, 862
O'CATARACT, Jehu 644
O'CONNER, Hugh 815
　James 468
O'CONNOR, Charles 166, 641
　John 751, 805
　Michael 538, 544, 805
O'DELL, J. D. 814
　J. Dixon 815
　W. C. 832
　Walter I. 813
O'DONNEL, John 592
O'DONNELL, ---, Mr. 781
　C. O. 191, 785, 786
　C. Oliver 368, 472, 501, 540, 842, 938
　Charles Oliver 805
　Columbus 128, 188, 199, 218, 222, 273, 393, 466, 501, 805, 881, 928
　John 82, 194, 214, 215, 264, 452, 679, 805, 928
O'Donnell's Wharf 215, 418
O'DONOVAN, C. 487
　Charles 745
　John H. 755, 805
O'HARA, ---, Bishop 539
　Michael 886
　Thomas 877
O'HERN, Michael P. 368
O'KEEFE, David 249
O'LAUGHLIN, Michael 805
O'LAW, James 249
O'LEARY, John 189
O'MAHONEY, Edward 194
O'NEAL, John 898
O'Neal, Deakins & Co. 101
O'NEALE, J. St. C. 577
O'NEILL, Charles Z. 159
　Henry E. 159
O'REILLY, Henry 506
　Michael 540
　Philip 882
　Robert 254
O'TOOL, ---, Rev. Mr. 538
Oak Grove 896
Oak Hall 689
Oak Hill Cemetery, Georgetown 896
Oakland 342, 357, 871
Oakley 877, 878
OAKLEY, Jacob 212
Oakley Nail & Anchor Manufactory 425
OBER, Catharine 401
　Catharine (TENNEY) 400
　Ella B. 401
　G. 191
　Gustavus 400, 401, 477
　John K. 400, 401

OBER, Kate 477
  Mary E. 401
  Matilda G. 401
  Rebecca (KETTLEWELL) 400
  Robert 397, 400, 401
  Virginia R. 401
Ober, Gustavus & Sons 400
OBERMYER, Leonard 537
Oblate Sisters of Providence 235, 598
Observatory 292
Ocean 624
Ocean Mutual Insurance Co. 801
OCKERMAN, J. F. 579
Octorara 350
Odd-Fellow's Hall 760, 821, 855, 899, 902
Odd-Fellow's Hall, Cockeysville 878
Odd-Fellow's Hall, Pikesville 836
Odd-Fellow's Library 667
Odd-Fellow's Magazine 616
Odd-Fellow's Mirror, The 627
ODELL, William C. 830
ODEN, Benjamin 351
  Eliza 351
Odenton 342, 354
Odorless Excavating Apparatus Co. 512
OELRICHS, Henry 805
OETTINGER, Moses 250
OFFUTT, Denton 847
OGDEN, ---, Maj. 291, 292
  Amos 819
OGG, George 519
OGLE, ---, Gov. 65, 851
  B. 850
  Benjamin 195, 848
  Henry 920
  Jesse R. 193
  Samuel 195, 848, 849
  William 64
OGLEBY, James 73, 215, 805
OGSDEN, John 89
OGSTON, John 251, 470
Ohio Central Co. 334
OHLL, Augustus 929
OKELY, John 459
Okisko Manufacturing Co. 833
Old American Company 682
Old Assembly-Rooms 679
Old Baltimore 40, 42, 43
Old Baltimore Town 496
Old Battery 765
Old Christ Church 572
Old City Hall 692
Old City Mills 345
Old Congress Hall 263, 663
Old Defender, The 629
Old Drury 688, 689
Old Feast Nursery 878

Old Field Point 398
Old Frame House 584
Old House Point 43
Old Manor Road 910
Old Mud Theatre 137, 265
Old Museum 626
Old Philadelphia Road 812
Old Point Comfort 137, 310
Old Saratoga Brewery 263
Old Theatre 588
Old Town 54, 59, 61, 62, 138, 554, 784
Old Town Bank 400, 451, 466, 469
Old Town Savings Institution of Baltimore 466
Old Trap Road 926
Old Whitehall Flouring-Mill 409
Old York Road 518, 909, 916
OLDFIELD, ---, Miss 682
  ---, Mrs. 684
  Granville Sharp 805
OLDHAM, Edward 73
OLDMIXON, ---, Mrs. 682
OLER, William H. 385
Olio, The 637
OLIVANE, Augustus 255
Olive Branch Independent Methodist Church 585
OLIVER, --- 466
  ---, Mr. 781
  Charles A. 256
  Elizabeth 805
  John 233, 298, 437, 438, 454, 470, 805, 826, 827
  Robert 83, 291, 293, 298, 316, 317, 318, 324, 438, 452, 592, 780, 805, 890, 931
  Thomas Fitch 861
  William B. 482
Oliver & Thompson 433
Oliver Hibernian Free School 233
Olympic Theatre 689, 690, 696
Onanock Landing 310
ONDERDONK, ---, Rt. Rev. Dr. 236
  D. W. 159
ONDESLUYS, Adrian 805
ONION, ---, Mr. 816
  Agnes Maria 922
  Ann Olevia 392
  Beale Howard 922
  Edward Day 391, 392
  Edward M. 559
  Elizabeth (DAY) 922
  Elizabeth (ROUSE) 391, 922
  Elizabeth A. 392
  Elizabeth A. (ONION) 392
  Elizabeth Ann (BUCKMILLER) 392
  Hannah Juliet 922
  James E. 392
  James H. 814, 815
  John W. 922

ONION, Julia Ann (RAWLINGS) 392
　Lloyd 922
　Lloyd Day 391
　Louis G. 392
　May (BAKER) 922
　Rebecca 922
　Robert S. 392
　Stephen 424, 805, 922, 923
　Thomas A. 191
　Virginia C. 392
　William 391
　William Francis Heath 922
　Zaccheus 425, 922
　Zaccheus Barrett 71
　Zachariah 921
　Zacheus 921
Onion Iron-Works 424
Onion's Inheritance 922, 923
Opequon 342
OPIE, Thomas 602, 738
OPPENHEIMER, H. 589
Orange Grove 24, 25
Orange Grove Mills 15, 882
Orangeville 927, 928
Orangeville Horse Guards 817
Orchard Street M.E. Church 580
ORD, Edward O. C. 148
Order of Harugari 928
Order of St. Lawrence 640
Ore-Knob Copper Co. of N.C. 512, 771
Oregon 30, 876
OREM, Cooper 838
　D. W. 127
　J. Bailey 159
　John M. 468, 469, 805
　Josiah 256
　Mary (PEAKE) 838
　William Morris 397
Orem Chapel 931
Orleans Building Association B 512
Orleans Road 342
ORMOND, ---, Duke of 753
---, Earl of 705
ORMSBY, James 432
ORNDORFF, F. H. 488
　John H. 439
　W. W. 191
　William H. 368
　William W. 191
Orphaline Charity School 594
Orphan Asylum Society 841
Orphans Home 154
Orphean Family 693
ORR, David F. 449
　William C. 472
ORRICK, ---, Capt. 915
　Edward 819
　John 805

ORRICK, John C. 819, 820, 889
　Mary 869
Orthodox Friends Meeting House 588
ORTWINE, William 487
OSBORN, James 555
　John 406
　Joseph 343
　Lucretia (BARTLETT) 406
　William M. 580
　William S. 444
OSBORNE, Cyrus P. 552
　Samuel G. 921
　William 43
　William H. 740
OSBOURNE, James 559
　N. 729
　William 38
OSGOOD, R. H. 303
　Robert H. 589
Osgood, H. & R. H. 438
OSLER, E. P. 263
OSNABURGS, Thomas Fulton 408
OSSWALD, Ernest 159
OSTENDORF, Clemens 468, 488
OSWALD, Eleazer 608, 780
OTT, George L. 159
　James Creamer 628
Otter Point 370
OTTERBEIN, William 573
Otterbein Chapel 573
Otterbein Church 573
OTTERBINE, William 805
OTTERMAN, Joseph 690
OTTO, John 929
　P. 597
OUDESLUYS, Charles 600
　Charles L. 602, 828
OUDISLUYS, Charles L. 487
OULD, Isabella (WILSON) 770
　Lancaster 546, 547, 770
Our American Youth 637
Our National Pulpit 641
Our Newspaper 635
Our Opinion 631
OVERTON, Thomas 35
OWEN, ---, Dr. 742
　Catharine 556
　E. D. 578
　J. M. 365
　John 188, 734, 735, 741, 805
　Kennedy, Mrs. 594
　Richard 931
OWENS, --- 693
---, Rev. Dr. 144
　Benjamin B. 159
　Benjamin Ferguson 113
　Clara 820
　E. B. 442
　Edward T. 471, 576
　George D. 870

153

OWENS, Imogine 927
J. L. 364
James 395, 488, 576
James S. 351, 640, 805
John 98, 742, 877
John Cockey 805
John E. 369, 645, 693, 694, 695, 887
Jonas 300, 797
Joseph 188, 205
M. J. 191
Mary E. 797
Mary M. J. 395
Owen Griffith 805
Rebecca (WORTHINGTON) 640
Samuel 482
Samuel W. 820, 821
Stephen 911
W. H. 365
William H. 193, 805
Owensville 358
OWICKS, ---, Mrs. 680
OWINGS, ---, Mrs. 582
Ann 862
Ann (HALDERMAN) 862
Bale 862
Beal 116
Beale 38, 812, 862
Beall 862
C. Howard 814
Caleb 805
Christopher 71, 116, 728, 812, 862
Deborah 862
Deborah (LYNCH) 862
Edward 862
Eleanor 862
Eleanora (MAGRUDER) 862
Frances 862
Hannah 862
Helen 862
Henry 358
Henry W. 159
J. L. 365
J. W. 515
James W. 902
John C. 805
John Cockey 860, 862
Joshua 519, 832, 857, 862, 867
Marcella 832, 862
Mary 582, 832, 862
Michael 862
Nathaniel 253
Rachel 862
Rebecca 862
Richard 117, 574, 575, 819, 862, 867
Ruth (COCKEY) 862
Samuel 38, 40, 71, 73, 118, 172, 173, 187, 200, 358, 374, 519, 805, 814, 819, 843, 845, 857, 861, 862
Sarah 862

OWINGS, Stephen 814
Stephen Hart 519
Thomas 862
Urath 843, 862
Urath (RANDALL) 862
Urith C. 843
William 816, 862
Owings Family 843, 858, 862
Owings' Mills 18, 21, 355, 356, 357, 854, 855, 857, 862
Owl, The 641
Owl Branch 870
Oxford 309, 886, 888, 890
Oxford & York Narrow-Gauge Railroad 357
OYSTON, John 439
P.E. Brotherhood of Baltimore 598
PABISCH, Francis Joseph 805
PACA, --- 703
---, Gov. 81
Aquila 45, 818, 819
John 40, 778, 819, 920, 921
William 195, 706, 707, 729
Paca Street 769
Paca Street Christian Church 591
PACKER, W. F. 345
PADIAN, Richard 877
Padner Park 803
PAGE, ---, Mr. 515
Charles G. 506
Evelyn 774
George 805
Henry 488
I. R. 187
James 742
W. J. 192
William J. 189, 193
PAGELS, George H. 191, 488
PAGET, James 748
PAGON, William H. 415
Paid Fire Department 242, 249, 255, 256, 257, 258, 486, 697
PAILLOTTEL, Joseph 225
PAILY, Donal 149
PAINE, ---, Bishop 822
---, Mr. 58, 905
A. W. 506
Clinton P. 484
D. 507
Robert H. 523
Thomas 433
Paint Branch 342
PAINTER, Charles 355
David 869
Painter's Traveling Ice-Cream Saloon 147
PALMER, --- 654
---, Dr. 637
Edward 593
John M. 160
Paul 552, 554

PALMER, Thomas 254
 V. B. 628
 W. C. 599
 W. C., Mrs. 599
 W. S. 826
 William C. 600
Palmer's Island 35, 39, 40
PAMER, Abraham 37
PANCOAST, J. C. 153
PANNEL, John 592
PANNETTI, John M. P. 160
Pantheon 261
Paper Mills 870
PAPPLER, Jacob 365
PAQUINET, I. B. 235
Pardoner's Discovery 923
PAREPA, --- 673
PARESCO, Angelo M. 833
PARISH, Edward 38
 Thomas 836
 William 249
Parish Library 654
Parish of Gunpowder 919
Parish Record, The 637
Park 851
Park Estate 872
Park Mill 409, 836, 837
Park Passenger Railway 366
Park Place Squares 280
Park Railway Co. 368
PARKE, ---, Maj. Gen. 289
 Eleanor 82
 Henry F. 236
 Lloyd B. 805
PARKER, ---, Chief Justice 702
 Charles 555
 Charles D. 566
 E. L. 466, 806
 Edwin L. 195
 Foxhall Alexander 805
 Francis 592
 George 407
 George A. 350
 James 592
 Jane 662
 John 919
 Joseph 805
 L. L. 576
 N. H. 908
 Nathan 615
 Nicholas 812
 Nicholas H. 820
 O. A. 368, 456, 489
 Oliver A. 367, 485, 488
 Peter, Sir 88
 Robert 48
 Thomas 99, 217
 William 669, 821
Parker, E. L. & Co. 263
Parker Vein Coal Co. 302
Parker's Haven 61, 168

Parkhill, William & Co. 630
PARKHURST, Jared 805
PARKIN, Richard W. 76
 Thomas 77
PARKINSON, Ed. 103
 Elder 558
 M. 101
PARKISON, Ida R. 877
 Mary Y. 855
PARKS, Abraham 252
 Caleb 484
 Elisha 879
 John 261, 727
 Joseph 879
 Margaret (CALDER) 873
 Mayberry 249
 William 89, 249, 605
Parkton 13, 347, 871, 872, 873, 875
Parkton & Manchester Railroad 873
Parkton Presbyterian Church 873
Parkton Station 869
Parkville 931
PARLETT, B. F. 466, 576
 Benjamin F. 489, 577
 J. B. 895
 Martin 53, 54
Parlett, B. F. & Co. 372
Parlett Family 927
Parlor Gazette 628
Parlor Journal 628
PARNHAM, John 741
PARR, ---, Mr. 441
 D. Preston 155, 637, 638
 D. Preston, Mrs. 155
 David 122, 249, 255
 H. A. 442
 I. M. 307, 365, 494
 Israel M. 155, 440, 441, 442, 444, 494
 James L. 191
Parr's Ridge 15, 20, 318, 323, 811
PARRAN, C. S. 358
 John 99, 358
 Thomas 741
PARRISH, ---, Capt. 805
 Edward 871, 872
 Mary 883
 Samuel H. 586
Parrish's Fear 49
Parrott's Creek Landing 310
Parrsville 322
PARRY, Cyrus B. 805
PARSONS, ---, Prof. 702
 ---, Rev. Mr. 534
 Alice A. 855
 E. 876, 883
 John 237
 Jonathan 100
 Joshua 834
 S. 149
 Thomas 582

PARSONS, William 236
　William D. 538
Parsons' Ship Yard 293
Parthenian, The 629
Particular Baptist Church 554
Particular Baptists 553
PARTRIDGE, ---, Mr. 300
　Buckler 56
　James R. 194
　Joseph G. 343
PASCAULT, Lewis 188, 207, 250, 261, 298, 455, 806
PASQUIET, John 805
Passanger Railway Association 365
PASSANO, Leonard 155
　Louis 490, 806
　Mary E. 490
PASSAVANT, W. A. 569
Passionist Fathers 825
PASSMORE, J. C. 914
Pastor's Aid Society 552
Patapsco 357, 473, 841, 862, 935
Patapsco Bank of Ellicott City 474
Patapsco Baptists 554
Patapsco Bridge & Iron-Works 425
Patapsco Building 480
Patapsco Building Association No. 2 512
Patapsco Canal Company 313
Patapsco Company 240, 292, 512
Patapsco Cotton-Factory 816
Patapsco Falls 517, 519, 830, 854, 857, 861
Patapsco Fire Company 241, 242, 254, 369, 484
Patapsco Flour-Mills 882
Patapsco Guano Co. 512
Patapsco Hundred 517, 518, 918
Patapsco Improvement Co. 937
Patapsco Iron-Works 424, 815
Patapsco Land Co. 358
Patapsco Lodge No. 5, U.O.G.B. 605
Patapsco Lower Hundred 70, 71, 812
Patapsco Mission of the M.P. Church 832
Patapsco Neck 695, 881
Patapsco Neck M.E. Church 933
Patapsco River 811, 812, 816, 820, 821, 823, 862, 926, 929, 937
Patapsco River Improvement Board 289, 290
Patapsco Station Society of Friends 587
Patapsco Upper Hundred 70, 71, 812
Patapsco Valley 321
Patent Safety Extinguisher Lamp Co. 512
Patmos Masonic Lodge 894

PATRICK, W. H. 237
PATRIDGE, James 265, 266
Patriot 612, 644, 650, 795, 799, 802, 803
PATTEN, T. 102
　Thomas 102
PATTERSON, --- 466
　---, Gen. 335
　---, Miss 574
　---, Mr. 60, 346, 441
　---, Mrs. 595
　A. B. 187, 194, 817
　Abraham 194
　Andrew 889
　Arch. 100
　Archibald 101
　D. 103
　E. 438
　Edward 806, 826, 851, 890
　Elizabeth 786, 925
　Emma 490
　George 74, 806, 816, 846
　Granville Sharp 748
　H. Lenore 916
　Henry 770
　Henry, Mrs. 595
　J. W. 438, 680
　John 253, 343, 806
　John H. 745
　John J. 368
　John S. 222
　Joseph 806
　Joseph W. 192, 316, 327, 393, 464, 680
　Margaret 582
　Mary L. (WILSON) 770
　Nora 834
　P. W. 370
　Robert 461
　S. N. 490
　Thomas 582
　Thomas N. 447
　W. H. 368
　W. L. 909
　William 76, 79, 84, 86, 89, 100, 101, 168, 188, 192, 206, 214, 224, 261, 276, 291, 298, 316, 317, 318, 324, 327, 343, 361, 393, 402, 407, 437, 439, 452, 454, 470, 545, 547, 549, 577, 592, 770, 805, 806, 845, 928
　William A. 934
　William R. 160
Patterson, William & Bro. 102, 432
Patterson, William & Sons 438
Patterson & Druid Hill Parks City Passenger Railway 370
Patterson Chapel 577
Patterson Nail Factory 220
Patterson Park 87, 90, 132, 147, 152, 273, 276, 277, 750

Patterson Park Building Union No.
  2 512
Patterson Ramsay & Co. 307
Patterson's Creek 342
Patterson's Wharf 262, 287
PATTI, Adelina 673
PATTISON, Granville Sharp 755
  J. 836
PATTON, ---, Capt. 574
  George 60
  Matthew 70, 727
  Robert 74
  W. 608
Patuxent 342, 354, 918
Patuxent Cotton-Factory 408
Patuxent Iron-Works Co. 669
Patuxent Manufacturing Co. 408
Patuxent River 669
PAUL, ---, Mr. 910
  August 279
  John 924
  John P. 582
  Maria 582
  Peter 292
  W. Edward 160
Paul Bertalou's Legion 382
Paul Pry 628
PAULEY, James 250
PAULL, H. E. 870
Pavilion Hotel 515
Paw Paw 342
PAWLEY, Finley 446
  James 806
Pawley's Museum 806
PAXTON, --- 37
PAYNE, --- 686
  Allen 484
  Augusta M. 916
  B. M. 820
  B. N. 369
  Benjamin 128, 814
  Benjamin M. 806
  Benjamin N. 902
  Benjamin W. 898
  D. A. 581
  James 263
  John 898
  John Howard 642, 680, 684
  M. C. 850
Payne's 514
Payne's Tavern 57
PAYSON, Henry 77, 84, 86, 89, 192,
  216, 267, 298, 433, 437, 439, 450,
  455, 456, 470, 483, 589, 667, 727,
  806, 814, 824, 828
Payson, Henry & Co. 372, 439
Payson Street Building Association
  No. 3 512
PEABODY, --- 654
  ---, Mr. 653, 659, 664, 665, 666, 667
  George 231, 663, 806, 890

Peabody, George & Co. 476, 663
Peabody, Riggs & Co. 663
Peabody Conservatory of Music 666
Peabody Fire Insurance Co. 488,
  491, 880
Peabody Heights 886, 888, 890
Peabody Heights Co. 512, 890
Peabody Heights Railroad 368, 815
Peabody Institute 266, 280, 421,
  475, 569, 653, 662, 665, 666, 675,
  676, 770
Peabody Institute Conservatory of
  Music 673
Peabody Institute Library 655
Peabody Library 656
Peabody Orchestra 232, 655
Peabody Savings Institution of
  Baltimore City 473
Peach Bottom 344
Peach Bottom Narrow-Gague
  Railway 359
PEACHEY, William T. 592
  William Travers 433
PEACHY, Fanny H. 806
  Thomas G. 806
PEACOCK, Daniel 911
  Jesse 911
  John 38, 251
PEAKE, Mary 838
  Robert 838
Peake, Walker & Co. 629
Peake & Co. 630
PEALE, Charles W. 691
  Charles Wilson 431, 639, 674, 691,
    806
  Edmund 693, 695
  Rachel (BREWER) 639
  Raphael 691
  Rembrandt 267, 500, 501, 639, 642,
    674, 691, 692, 806
  Reuben 176
  Rubens 691, 692
  Saint George 74
Peale's Museum 176, 692
PEARCE, ---, Gen. 908
  C. R. 298
  David 298
  Edward 904
  Edward S. 907
  Elizabeth (BACON) 907
  George 817
  J. M. 908
  Jacob M. 908
  James Alford 846
  John B. 120, 820, 876, 907
  John Bacon 907
  Josiah 817
  Laura J. (HOLMES) 908
  Luke J. 745
  Mary 913
  N. 439

PEARCE, Nathaniel 372, 806
  Rose B. 821
  Sarah (BOSLEY) 913
  Sophia (MYERS) 907
  Thomas 907, 917
  Thomas G. 875
  William 907, 913
PEARRE, J. A. 128
PEARSON, Aubry 473
  Roger B. 508
  William H. 160
PECHIN, Catherine 806
  William 84, 194, 609, 610, 615, 806
PECK, E. W. S. 841
  Francis 581
  Nathaniel 584
  Thomas E. 548, 550
PECKIN, William 246
PECKWORTH, John P. 559
PEDDICORD, Nicholas 816
Peddicord's Hope 816
PEDUZI, Peter 246
Peedee Light Artillery 897
PEELE, Samuel 53
PEERCE, ---, Mr. 912
  Anne (FERGUSON) 912
  Edward 912
  Edward S. 913
  George 913
  Louisa (SMITH) 913
  Thomas 913
  William F. 913
  William Ferguson 912
Peggy Stewart 640
PEGRAM, John 897
  Virginia J. 897
  William I. 897
PEIRCE, ---, Gen. 493
  Charles S. 233
PEKIN, William 246
PELBY, --- 687
PELLICOT, Julius 160
PEMBERTON, Samuel 759
Pembroke School for Boys Library 667
PENCHEY, William T. 77
PENDER, ---, Gen. 670
PENDERGAST, Charles A. 189
  William 806
Pendleman & Bro. 896
PENDLETON, Ann Clayton 821
  Boyd 652
  Edmund 72
  George H. 722
  Nathaniel 652
  P. P. 193, 210, 365, 442, 805
  Philip 652, 821
  Robert W. 806
  W. N. 879
  William Nelson 865
Pendleton, Riley & Co. 373

PENINGTON, William 299
Penmar 356
PENN, --- 37
  Alexander 190
  Hanson 324
  Richard 66
  Thomas 66
PENNIMAN, E. J. 466
  Elisha 406
  George C. 506, 507
  John R. 406
  Juliette 748
  N. G. 448
  Nicholas G. 817
  Susan (BARTLETT) 406
  W. R. 880
PENNINGTON, --- 521
  ---, Mr. 376
  A. H. 192
  Charles 91, 806
  Charles J. 190
  H. 481
  Henry 89, 161, 249, 806
  J. 481, 672
  James 805
  Josiah 407, 812
  Josias 116, 202, 215, 522, 592, 680, 805
  Timothy Hanson 806
  William 462
  William C. 483
Pennsylvania Avenue German M.E. Church 578
Pennsylvania Canal 325, 343, 344
Pennsylvania Central Railroad 283
Pennsylvania Chronicle & Universal Advertiser 605, 606
Pennsylvania Co. 346, 350, 353
Pennsylvania Railroad 284, 345, 353, 677
Pennsylvanian 615
PENNY, Elizabeth 864
  Henry 864
Penny Magazine 616
PENTLAND, James 194, 604, 889, 892
PENTZ, Charles A. 380
  Daniel 380
  Henry 380
  J. W. 380
  James L. 276
  John J. 380
  John W. 276
  Samuel S. 380
  William J. 380
People's Appeal, The 641
People's Friend, The 616
People's Gift & Temperance Advertiser, The 628
People's Mutual Land Co. 762

People's Passenger Railway Co. 368, 512
People's Permanent Land & Loan Co. 512
People's Voice 815, 855
People's Weekly, The 637
Peoples' Bank 451
Peoples' Bank of Baltimore 465, 469
Peoples' Gas Co. 472
PEPIN, ---, Mr. 689
PEPPER, Jacob 253
PERCIVAL, C. S. 673
 Joseph F. 77
Perdue Family 907
Perdue Ford 905
PEREGOY, ---, Mr. 505, 888
 Annie Bates 887
 Charles 189, 194, 887
 Hannah Wall (TIMANUS) 887
 Henry 869
 J. F. 190
 James 189, 192, 577, 578
 Joseph M. 615, 806
 Joseph W. (M.) 190
 Nicholas 887
 Ruth 887
Peregoy Family 927
PERIGO, Daniel 252
 Joseph 252
 Nathan 931
PERINE, D. M. 784, 903
 David M. 127, 128, 814, 893
 E. G. 440
 E. Glenn 481
 Maulden 806
 T. P. 604
 Thomas P. 604
PERITANY, Edward 38
PERKEN, ---, Dr. 741
PERKINS, ---, Capt. 99
 ---, Dr. 255
 B. B. 441
 E. 595
 E. H. 487, 740
 Elijah H. 549
 James 37
 John D. 742
 Richard 168
 Thomas 249
 Thomas H. 317
 W. H. 488
 William H. 155, 489, 600
Perkins & Saltonstall 439
Perkins' Spring 214
Perkins' Spring Square 281
Permanent Land Co. 512
PERMYLIA, Rebecca 584
PEROT, W. H. 887
 William H. 441, 484
Perpetual Building Association 512

PERRIGO, --- 895
 Daniel 188
PERRINE, D. M. 891
 David M. 887
PERRON, Joseph 833
PERRY, ---, Commodore 89, 477, 895
 A. A. 489
 Allen A. 488
 Benjamin 149
 Edmund 351
 Elmira 925
 Galbraith 523, 525
 Galbraith B. 525, 641
 Herman H. 440
 J. St. L. 191
 M. N., Mrs. 604
 W. C. 431
 W. J. 586
 William 757
Perry Hall 800, 916, 918
Perry Hall M.E. Church South 918
Perry Street 769
PERRYMAN, Samuel 38
Perrymansville 42, 43, 351
Perryville 36, 131, 349, 351
Perseverance Permanent Building & Loan Co. 512
PERSON, ---, Mr. 362
Peru Mills 923
PETER, George 663
PETERKIN, ---, Mrs. 595
 ---, Rev. Mr. 902
 George W. 439
 Joshua 526
 William 592
PETERS, C. G. 252
 Catharine 419
 Christian G. 160
 Clarence 792
 Ed. 103
 Elizabeth 689
 George 247
 George A. 761
 J. Montgomery 195
 Jesse T. 189, 480
 Joseph J. 202
 Michel 92
 Peter F. 488
 Richard 66
 Thomas 261
 William 190
 William C. 628
Peters, I. & Co. 361
Peters & Co. 423
Petersburg 897
PETERSON, Frank H. 886
PETHERBRIDGE, E. R. 132, 140, 250
 Edward R. 160
PETIT, Isaac 762
PETRI, John F. 673

159

Petrus Building Association No. 6
  512
PETSCH, Leopold 541
Pettets Mills 375
PETTIBONE, Julia E. 426
PETTICOART, Dorsey 519
  William 519
PHEARSON, Jesse 592
PHELAN, ---, Rev. Father 530
PHELPS, Charles 723
  Charles E. 160, 164, 190, 722
  Francis P. 738
  Greenberry 249
  J. W. 805
  Laura R. E. 927
PHELTZ, Gustavus A. 817
PHENIX, Thomas 188, 189, 248,
  249
Philadelphia, Wilmington &
  Baltimore Railroad 284, 348, 353,
  354, 355, 815, 916, 923, 926, 931
Philadelphia & Baltimore Central
  Railroad 350
Philadelphia & Delaware County
  Railroad 348
Philadelphia & Erie Railroad 345
Philadelphia & Reading Railroad
  345
Philadelphia & Wilmington
  Railroad 558
Philadelphia Academy of Natural
  Sciences 656
Philadelphia Baptist Association
  553
Philadelphia Broad Street Baptist
  Church 564
Philadelphia Guano Co. 398
Philadelphia Ledger 622
Philadelphia Presbytery 551
Philadelphia Railroad Depot 789
Philadelphia Road 130, 934
Philadelphia Turnpike 916, 922,
  924, 925, 926, 927, 928, 931, 934
PHILIP, Thomas 728
PHILIPS, Brian 805
  Isaac 89, 293
  J., Jr. 515
  James 592
  Philip 43
  Solomon H. 465
  William 252
Philips Exeter Academy 665
PHILLIP, Samuel 466
PHILLIPS, ---, Capt. 311
  ---, Mr. 598
  Amy 893
  B. F. 441
  Ellen Penny 893
  Isaac 188, 250, 438, 470, 589
  J. B. 695
  J. H. 555, 565, 889

PHILLIPS, James 818, 819
  John B. 442
  John H. 564
  John L. 927
  Sallie O. 821
  Samuel 806
  Thomas 893
  Thomas P. 815
  W. 524
  William 806
  William J. 260
Phillips, Samuel & Co. 380
Phillips & Co. 260
Philopolis 876, 877, 883
Philosopher's Walk 275
Philosophical Society 648
PHILPOT, ---, Mr. 59, 60
  Brian 37, 59, 70, 72, 205, 244, 768
  Bryan 58, 806, 861
  Edward 817
  Edward P. 820, 866
  Elizabeth 865
  John 74, 120, 128, 806, 814
  Thomas 814
Philpot Family 862
Philpot Street 577
Philpot's Bridge 174
Philpot's Hill 116, 682, 689
PHILPOTT, Anna (MERRYMAN)
  864
  Bryan 863
  Clarissa 863
  Edward Pickering 863
  Elizabeth 863
  Elizabeth (JOHNSON) 863
  John 863
  Mary 863
  Sarah (MERRYMAN) 864
Phoenix 21, 347, 881, 908, 909
Phoenix & Budget 650
Phoenix Factory 408, 840
Phoenix Iron-Works 420
Phoenix M.P. Church 880
Phoenix Mills 410
Phoenix Station 880, 914
Photographic Rays of Light, The 641
Physician & Surgeon 637, 739
Piankatank River 303
PIATT, ---, Don 144
PICCOLOMINI, --- 673
PICKELL, John F. 507
  John P. 485
PICKENS, ---, Gov. 897
PICKERALL, Thomas 48
PICKERING, Samuel 813
  Timothy 78
Pickering Lodge 837
PICKERSGILL, ---, Mrs. 595
PICKET, Heathcoat 921
PICKETT, --- 924
  ---, Capt. 294

PICKETT, George E. 751
PICKMAN, W. R. 523
PICKNELL, John 484
PIDGEON, John 95
Pidgeon Hills 235
Piedmont 342
Piedmont Air-Line Railroads 302
Piedmont Guano & Manufacturing Co. 399, 512
Piedmont Railroad 357
PIEL, Herman F. 820
PIERCE, Franklin 123, 846
  H. Lindsley 160
  Humphrey 483
  John 253
  Thomas 466
  William 255, 911
  William F. 911
  William H. 160
PIERPONT, --- 375
  John 642, 643, 644
PIERSOL, John 908
PIERSON, Hannah A. 852
PIET, John 805
  John B. 145, 629
PIGGOT, ---, Rev. Mr. 521
Piggot, T. S. & Co. 635
PIGGOTT, A. S. 874
  A. Snowden 651, 806
  Augustine 822
  Austin 896
  Robert 576
  Thomas 806
  Thomas S. 139
PIGOTT, Robert 526
PIKE, ---, Capt. 663
Pikesville 357, 518, 834, 835, 837, 844, 846, 862
Pikesville Arsenal 896
Pikesville Baptist Church 836
Pikesville Catholic Church 835
PILCH, James 246
PILERT, John B. 605
  John J. 814
Pilgrim's Rest 842
PILKINGTON, J. F. (E.) 194
  T. 252
Pilot Line 312
Pilot Stages 311
Pilot, The 624
PILSON, Anna 834
  George 903
Pimlico 352, 369, 370, 829, 844, 848, 851, 854, 923
Pimlico Fair Grounds 834
PINCKNEY, --- 805
PINDELL, ---, Dr. 741
  A. T. 879
  Addi 189
  Richard 741
Pindell Family 862

PINDLE, Addi 189
Pine Grove U.B. Church 871
Pine Street Loan & Building Association 512
Piney Hill 876
Piney Run 517, 857, 869, 876
PINKNEY, --- 698, 703, 704, 712, 723, 726
---, Bishop 866, 908, 931
---, Maj. 98
---, Mr. 296
  Ann 806
  Ann Maria (RODGERS) 806
  Campbell W. 729
  Campbell Whyte 717
  Charles 645, 806
  Edward C. 615, 616, 806
  Edward Coate(s) 643, 644, 645
  Frederick 190, 643, 645, 805
  H. 850
  Jonathan 456
  Margaret Hile 806
  Ninian 114
  Robert 432
  Robert F. 805
  William 88, 91, 118, 189, 195, 375, 461, 497, 498, 521, 615, 643, 645, 648, 679, 708, 709, 711, 806
Pinkney, Wirt & Taney 652
PINNEY, Peter 92
Pioneer Hook & Ladder Company 242, 256, 257, 258
Pipe Creek 573, 643
Pipe Creek Hundred 70, 71, 812, 859
PIPER, Adeline 899
  Jackson 814, 898, 899, 902
  James 91, 114, 261, 593, 899
  James S. 113
  John R. 254
PIQUETT, Daniel 191
  John 472
  John T. 805
Piscataway 312
PISE, M. Louis A. 805
PISTER, ---, Rev. 605
  J. 570
PITCHER, G. H. 149
  T., Mrs. 917
  Thomas J. 927
PITT, --- 704
  Faris C. 484
  John C. 241
  Thomas J. 234
  William 674, 816
  William T. 441
Pitt Street 551, 559
PITTMAN, Joseph K. 160
Pittman, Edward & Son 481
PITTS, ---, Rev. Mr. 902

PITTS, Charles H. 130, 137, 194, 633, 718, 806
Pittsburgh & Connellsville Railroad Co. 339
Pittsburgh Saturday Evening Visitor 617
Pius Memorial Catholic Church 540
PIZARRO, Jose Antonio, Don 805
 Joseph A. 236
PLACIDE, Paul D. 160
Plaines, The 847
Plains, The 705, 852
Plantagenet 423
PLASKITT, Joshua 231
PLATER, ---, Col. 849
 George 195, 848
PLATT, Betsy Ward (BEACH) 394
 Elanson 394
 H. S. 395
 Harriet (HEMMINGWAY) 394
 Harriet M. 395
 Isaac 394
 James B. 395
 Jennie E. 395
 L. B. 395
 Mary E. 821
 Sandy Beach 394, 395
 William S. 395
Platt & Co. 394, 395
PLATTE, Henry 264
Pleasant Hill M.E. Church 857
Pleasant Valley 21, 26, 31, 342
Pleasant Valley Baptist Church 558
PLEASANTS, E. B. 359
 J. H. 494
 J. Hall 178, 195, 439, 440, 697, 698, 842, 887
 John 239
 John H. 505
 John P. 172, 238, 482, 483
Pleasants, J. P. & Son 439
Pleasants, John P. & Sons 373
PLETCH, James 252
PLITZ, F. 597
PLOTTNER, ---, Rev. Mr. 902
Plough, Loom & Anvil 616, 628
PLOWDEN, Edmund J. 351
PLOWMAN, ---, Mr. 60
 George H. 160
 John 244
 Jonathan 38, 59, 69, 205, 519, 544, 545, 547, 805
Plug-Uglies 631, 787
Plum Point Landing 309
PLUMER, Wiliam Swann 805
PLUMMER, ---, Mrs., Dr. 595
 John F. 139, 234, 761
 William S. 548, 839
PLUMSTEAD, Thomas 66

PLUNKET, ---, Capt. 116
 David 118, 169
PLUNKETT, ---, Rev. Father 933
 David 82, 545, 779
PLUNKTET, David 70
Pocahontas 915
Pocahontas Lodge No. 103 931
Pocahontas Mill 408, 832
Pocahontas Tribe No. 3, Improved Order of Red Men 888
POCOCK, Daniel 911
 David 911
Pocomoke Company 312
POE, David 76, 78, 80, 170, 187, 238, 239, 569, 646, 779, 806
 Eager Allan 271
 Edgar A. 617, 645, 646, 649, 650, 651, 806
 Edgar Allan 270
 Edgar Allen 796, 805
 Elizabeth 806
 Elizabeth (ARNOLD) 645
 George 805
 Jacob 806
 John P. 137, 231, 359
 Michael 425
 Neilson 126, 137, 270
 Nelson 615, 728
 Thomas 806
 Virginia E. 806
 William 617
 William Henry 646
Poe Memorial Celebration 640
Poe Monument 270, 271
Point Breeze Hotel 927
Point Lookout 135, 154, 310, 358, 359
Point Market 173, 174
Point of Rocks 318, 324, 325, 335, 337, 342
POISAL, ---, Rev. Dr. 830
 Francis A. 160
 John 586, 636
 W. M. 584
Poland, Jenkins & Co. 404
POLE, Sadie M. 820
 William 814
Police Gazette 645
Polish Synagogue 589
Political Examiner 613, 615
POLK, ---, Dr. 805
 Charles Peale 691
 Ernest 160
 James 497, 498, 805
 James K. 122, 753
 Lucius C. 362
 Robert 100
POLLARD, John 565
 Peter 250
POLLOCK, Henry 190
 M. H. 190

POLLOCK, Oliver 250
POLMYER, W. 627
Pomona 836
POMP, ---, Mr. 572
  Nicholas 571
POMPLITZ, August 805
Pongoteague Landing 310
PONTIER, ---, Detective 141
POOL, ---, Mr. 425
Pool & Hunt 258
Pool's Island 42, 312
POOLE, ---, Mr. 219, 837
  Robert 834, 838
Poole & Ferguson 838
Poole & Hunt 245, 838, 839, 888
Poole & Hunt's Foundry 275
Poole's Island 87
Poole's Island Light-house 309
POOR, Charles M. 251
  John F. 252
  William A. 805
Poor Association 469, 661, 754, 794
Poor Society 539
POPE, Abner 253
  Daniel, Mrs. 604
  Folger 245
  Franklin F. 441
  George A. 147, 603
  Joseph 128
  Joseph D. 896
  Richard 65
Pope's Creek 353, 354
Poplar Hill 311
Poplar Island 87, 717
Poplars Meeting-House 882
POPLEIN, N. 365
  Nicholas 222, 364, 806
Poplein Silicated Phosphate
  Fertilizer Co. 512
POPPLEIN, N. 470
  Nicholas 281
POPPLER, George A. 276
POPPLETON, Thomas H. 62
Porcupine 614
PORINE, T. P. 761
Port Deposit 39, 342, 349
Port Herman 41
Port Republic 358
Port Royal 312
Port Tobacco 34, 312
Port Tobacco Parish 877
Port-Folio 644, 648
PORTER, ---, Lt. 298
  ---, Mr. 367
  B. Buck 467
  Daniel 292
  David 100, 103, 592, 805
  G. Ellis 743
  George N. 630
  George U. 222, 440, 441, 640
  George W. 191

PORTER, Gertrude 886
  Henry O. 805
  John 919
  John E. 898
  John Mercer 61
  Lawrence 49
  Nathaniel D. 160
  Rebecca 805
  William 927
Porter Street 769
Portico, The 612, 616, 643
Portland 816
Portland Street Perpetual Building
  Association Nos. 2 & 3 512
Portland Street Perpetual Savings &
  Building Association 512
PORTTENS, Robert 70, 727
POSEY, John 763
  John P. 254
POSINGTON, Thomas 252
POST, Eugene 806
  Priscilla Ridgely 806
  Richard B. 488
POSTLETHWAITE, William M. 525
POTEET, Zeph. 817
  Zephaniah 820
Potomac Building Association 512
Potomac Canal Company 313
Potomac Company 312, 325
Potomac Depot 354
Potomac Fire Insurance Co. 488,
  491
Potomac Line 301
Potomac River 812
Potomac Steamboat Co. 303, 512
POTTENGER, Thomas B. 729
POTTER, ---, Dr. 755
  ---, Supervising Architect 494
  John Brown 118
  Martin 849
  N. 806
  Nathaniel 120, 624, 734, 735, 736,
    737, 741, 742, 755
Potter's Course 849
Potter's Field 934
POTTINGER, Robert 741
POTTS, Richard 313, 424, 600, 709,
  824
Potupaco (Port Tobacco) 34
POUDER, ---, Mrs. 595
  George 483
  James M. 487
  W. P. 241
  William P. 241, 498, 617
POULSON, T. L. 579
  Thomas L. 580
POULTNEY, Ann 806
  Evan 252, 784, 806
  Evan T. 252
  Philip 253, 498, 805, 817, 820
  Samuel 252

163

POULTNEY, Thomas 433, 441, 455, 483, 658, 806, 893
POULTON, R. A. 193
 Robert A. 191
POUMAIRAT, Charles H. 806
POUND, Fannie L. 751
POUNDER, James M. 487
POWELL, A. H. 604, 745
 Edward B. 401
 George W. 590
 H. F. 640
 Henry 189
 J. H. 845
 James 53
 John 39
 Lily B. (SMITH) 402
 Mary 47, 202
 Thomas 806
 W. H. 415
 W. S. 397
 William H. 249
 William S. 449
 William Sutheron 401, 402
 Powell's Prepared Chemicals 402
POWER, Edward 149, 805
 John 253
 William 700
POWERS, James 253
 Thomas H., Mrs. 525
Powhatan 369, 407, 815, 821, 829, 830, 832, 915
Powhatan Cotton-Works 408
Powhatan Dam 828
Powhatan Hall 570
Powhatan Lake 370
Powhatan Lodge No. 23, Independent Order of Mechanics 832
Powhatan Mill 408, 832
Powhatan Tribe No. 30, U.O.R.M. 605
POWNALL, Levi 875
PRACHT, A. C. 362
Practice Hall 737
Praeger Family 688
PRATT, --- 104
 ---, Gov. 138
 ---, Governor 114
 ---, Mr. 441, 465
 David Guerney 806
 E. 426
 Enoch 139, 367, 417, 440, 464, 471, 478, 487, 488, 494, 600, 667, 887
 Enoch, Mrs. 596
 Enogh 603
 Horace 806
 Isaac 464
 J. D. 302, 596
 Joseph Long 615
 Maria Louisa (HYDZ) 465
 Naomi (KEITH) 464

PRATT, Phineas 464
 R. Horace 615, 617, 651
 Thomas G. 146, 162, 195, 351, 504, 721, 806, 822
 Trueman 580, 805
 Pratt, Cloud & Bro. 627
 Pratt, Cloud & Brother 615
 Pratt, E. & Bro. 464
 Pratt, Middleton 262
 Pratt Street 769
 Pratt Street Dock 768
 Pratt Street Wharf 321
 Pratt's Tavern 312
PRECHTEL, George 854, 855
PREECE, Richard W. 229
PRENIER, Henry L. E. 160
PRENTISS, Clifton K. 160
 John 838
 Prentiss & Cole 612
 Prepratory College 541
PRESBURY, Elizabeth 805, 806
 George 172, 920, 921
 George G. 728, 805, 806, 921
 George Goldsmith 71, 806, 814
 May Bedel 425
 Robertson 921
 W. R. 921
 Presbyterian Church 146, 212, 420
 Presbyterian Church in the United States 551
 Presbyterian Critic & Monthly Review, The 631
 Presbyterian Eye & Ear Hospital 747
 Presbytery of Baltimore 548, 549, 550, 551
 Presbytery of New Castle 544
 Presbytery of Philadelphia 544, 551
 Presbytery of the Cheaspeake 549
 Presbytery of the Patapsco 549
 Presbytery of the Rappahannock 549
 Presiding Justices 728
PRESSMAN, George 75
PRESSTMAN, Benjamin C. 194, 195, 717
 George 82, 170, 206, 727, 887
 Thomas 252
 William 298
PRESTBURY, George Goldsmith 728
PRESTMAN, Amanda (MOWELL) 878
 Emma Mowell 879
 Frances 805
 Francis 554
 George 61, 187, 192, 483, 554, 555, 805, 935
 William R. 878
PRESTON, J. 921
 Thomas 919, 920
 W. P. 369

PRESTON, William 130
  William C. 122, 714
PREVOST, F. H. 729
PREY, A. 597
PRICE, ---, Dr. 757
  Abraham H. 819
  Amos 254
  Ann 883
  Ann (GRIFFITH) 884
  Ann (MOORE) 883
  Ann C. 925
  Ann S. 756
  Aquilla 38, 884
  Augustus M. 190, 805
  Beale 883
  Benjamin 191, 487, 883
  Bettie 869
  C. Wesley 877
  Catherine 883
  Catherine (PRICE) 883
  Charles H. 883
  Daniel 880, 883
  Edward 883
  Edward H. 190, 191
  Eldridge C. 757
  Elias C. 755, 756
  Elizabeth 883
  Elizabeth (COLE) 883
  Elizabeth Ann 883
  Ezra 883
  Francis 928
  Frederick 569, 806
  George W. 880
  Hezekiah 84, 459
  Isaac 869
  Isaac M. 912
  Isabella 883
  Israel 249, 883
  J. F. 814
  J. S. 873
  Jacob 805, 806
  James 298, 805
  James B. 814
  Jane Watermon 883
  Jennie 872
  Jennie R. 821
  Job A. 575
  John 883
  John H. 600, 717, 814
  John L. 883
  John M. 872
  Joseph 741
  Keturah 883
  Mahlon C. 756
  Mark M. 688
  Martha A. (COWMAN) 757
  Mary 883
  Mary (ISGRIG) 883
  Mary (MATTHEWS) 883
  Mary (PARRISH) 883
  Mary Ann (TURNER) 872

PRICE, Mary Roberts 883
  Miriam 883
  Mordecai 53, 756, 883
  Oliver 883
  Oliver M. 883
  Rachel 883
  Rachel (MOORE) 883
  Rebecca 883
  Rebecca (MERRYMAN) 883
  Richard 190, 883
  Richard J. 628
  Richard, Mrs. 600
  Ruth Ann (ROBERTS) 883
  S. M. 912
  Samuel 756, 883
  Samuel M. 818, 882, 883, 912
  Sarah 883
  Sophia 883
  Susan 883
  Thomas 72, 883
  Thomas J. 819
  Thomas R. 817
  Walter 463
  Warrick 883
  William 194, 251, 299, 456, 459, 729, 805, 828, 883
  Zachariah 883
Price Family 883, 907
Price's Chance 883
Price's Ship-yard 293
Price-Current 629
Priceville 876, 877, 883, 886
PRIDHAM, N. C. 524
  Nicholas H. 523
PRIESTLEY, James 658
PRIESTLY, Edward 246
  James 225
PRILL, Frederick 246
  Rachel E. 834
Primitive Baptists 566
PRIMROSE, James S. 826
  William F. 826
PRINCE, William H. 160
Prince Frederick 358
Principico Forge 424
Principio & Kingsbury Iron-Works 425
Principio Company 76, 290, 424
Principio Furnace Co. 50
Principio Iron Co. 391, 922
PRINDELL, Eleanor (BOND) 863
  John 863
PRINDLE, F. C. 304
PRINGEY, Frederick 160
PRINGLE, --- 103
  M. 678
  Mark 83, 192, 291, 392, 454, 520, 679, 806
  Mark U. 782
Printing-House Square 626
Prisoners' Aid Association 602

PRITCHARD, Thomas H. 152, 563
PROCTER, William 89
  Wilson 604
PROCTOR, John 433, 922
  William 251
  Wilson 191
Produce & Fish Exchange Co. 445
PROEBSTING, T. C. 439
PROFIT, Jonas 39
Progressive World, The 642
Proprietors of the Susquehanna
  Canal 312
Prospect 843
Prospect Hill 275
Prospect Lodge No. 110, I.O.O.F.
  880
PROSSER, U. 95, 269
PROST, Joseph 540
Protestant Episcopal Church of
  Maryland 860
Protestant Epsicopal Sunday-School
  Society 724
Protestant Infant Asylum 598, 601
Protestant Methodist Ridge
  Meeting-House 866
PROUD, John G. 245, 462, 806
  Robert M. 190, 598
PROUDFIT, John 902
Providence Baptist Association 568
Providence Lodge No. 116,
  Independent Order of
  Odd-Fellows 821
Providence Patriot 622
Providential of Baltimore 512
PRUNNETT, T. W. 822
PRYOR, George W. 246
  Richard W. 160
Public Ledger 617, 629
Public School Library 667
Public School Teachers' Association
  754
PUE, ---, Dr. 730
  Arthur 734, 741
PUGH, Arthur 805
  David 690
PULASKI, ---, Count 77, 78
  Pulaski Legion 795
  Pulaski Street 769
  Pulaski's Legion 77, 668
PULLMAN, R. H. 590
Pulpit of Baltimore, The 641
PUNETT, T. W. 820
PURCELL, John 191
  John J. 178, 179
PURDUE, Walter 911
PURDY, ---, Mrs. 595
PURNELL, Charles B. 806
  George Washington 741
  Isaac 461
  John 741
  Littleton B. 449

PURNELL, Lizzie 886
  W. H. 140
  William H. 129, 493, 847
PURTGAN, Thomas 929
PURVES, George T. 551
PURVIANCE, ---, Com., Mrs. 595
  ---, Commodore, Mrs. 604
  ---, Judge 138, 476, 699, 770
  ---, Mr. 60
  Eliza 806
  Fanny 806
  Frances 806
  Frank 934
  G. D. 546, 601
  George D. 805
  J. H. 77
  James 77, 194, 548, 806, 826, 827
  John 192, 470, 547, 712, 805, 806
  Margaret 595, 601, 805
  Margaret S. 595
  R. 79, 100, 101, 102, 189, 392
  Robert 79, 189, 194, 343, 463, 497,
    498, 544, 545, 546, 547, 806, 931
  S. 100, 101, 102, 392
  Samuel 59, 69, 70, 71, 73, 78, 79, 80,
    100, 168, 806, 819, 845
PURVIS, James F. 578, 805
  James F., Mrs. 155
  Purvis & Co. 481
PUSEY, Caleb 399
  Nathan 466
PUTNAM, H. 101
PUTNEY, T. 24
PYKE, Abraham 91, 250
PYLE, William 190
Pylesville 359
Pyne & Harrison 673
QUAIL, G. Q. 365
  George K. 152, 190, 806
  George R. 465
Quaker Bottom 30, 877, 883, 884
Quaker Neck 303
Quantico 354
Quantico Creek 313
QUANTRILL, Thomas 92
Quarles & Co. 446
Queen's Insurance Co. of England
  489
Queenstown 309, 342, 710, 717
QUICK, George 929
QUIGLEY, --- 166
  ---, Rev. Father 933
QUINAN, Thomas 526
QUINCY, W. H. 258
Quincy Granite Railway Company
  317
QUINLAN, Leonard G. 137, 806, 820
  Maggie E. 922
QUINLIN, L. G. 190
QUINN, John 368
QUISICK, John 252

QUITMAN, ---, Gen. 134
RABB, Dietrich 246
RABILLON, Leonance 233
  Leonce 675
RABORG, ---, Mr. 780
  Christian 394
  Christopher 187, 456, 569, 572, 807
  Goddard 241, 806
  Samuel 252
  William 569
  Raborg & Doudle 433
RABURG, Christopher 246
  Franklin 254
RADCLIFFE, Samuel J. 160
RADDATZ, Charles F. 229
RAGAN, John 312
RAIBER, Joseph 605
Railroad Permanent Building
  Association 512
Railway Dining Hotel 515
RAINE, ---, Col. 626, 627
  Edward 627
  F. 508, 851
  Frederick 155, 191, 195, 624, 625,
    654, 698
  James 625
  Pamelia (BULL) 627
  William 625, 627, 806
  Raine's Hall 841
RAISIN, I. Freeman 729
  Robert Wilson 806
RAITHBURN, D. L. 908
RALPH, ---, Mr. 861
---, Rev. Mr. 520
  George 757, 806, 836
RAMAGE, ---, Sailing Master 91
RAMAN, Daniel 343
RAMIE, Mary, Sister 802
RAMSAY, ---, Capt. 432
---, Mr. 207
  J. A. 194
  James 439
  James S. 549
  Joseph 189
  Nathaniel 497, 498
  Ramsay, H. A. & Co. 425
  Ramsay's Sulphur Springs 312
RAMSBURG, ---, Mr. 494
  N. A. 191
RAMSDELL, ---, Capt. 780
RAMSEY, J. B., Mrs. 605
  James G. 242, 251
  John 252
  N. 72
  Nathaniel 76, 77, 779, 807
  Robert 818
  Ramsey's Wharf 303
RANDALL, ---, Maj. 96
  A. 95, 269
  Alexander 149, 165, 600, 825
  Aquilla 933

RANDALL, Beal 120, 188, 814
  Beale 192, 816, 819, 820
  Christopher 71, 519, 857
  George Hubner 807
  James C. 191
  Joseph C. 191
  Joseph K. 695
  Thomas 813
  Thomas B. W. 820
  Urath 862
  William 70, 72, 241
  William T. 815
  Randallstown 370, 830
RANDAUNE, John 236
  John B. 236
RANDLE, William T. 936
RANDOLPH, --- 270
---, Dr. 232
---, Mr. 217, 781
  A. M. 524
  Eaton 101
  Harriet D. 226
  Innes 611, 641
  J. L. 342
  James T. 132, 191
  John 251, 351, 643, 781
  John W. 189, 190, 199, 219, 222,
    303, 354, 366, 463, 580, 806
  Peyton 72
  Thompson 226
  Randolph & Brother 263
  Randolph Chapel 264
RANKARD, John 261
  Rankatank Creek 310
RANKIN, ---, Rev. Dr. 236, 828
---, Rev. Mr. 521
  Charles W. 523
  Robert 77, 807
  Samuel 463, 807
  Samuel M. 820, 916
  Samuel N. 818
RANSON, A. H. 270
RAPP, ---, Mr. 630
Rappahannock Navigation Co. 480
Rappahannock Steam Packet Co.
  360
RAPSON, J. F. 566
RASBE, H. 874
RASIN, Bessie 398
  Grace 398
  Isaac Freeman 398
  Margaret A. (JOHNSON) 398
  Mary Rebecca (RINGGOLD) 398
  Mary Ringgold 398
  Phoebe (WILSON) 398
  R. W. L. 397, 398, 446, 502, 938
  Robert Cooper 398
  Viola 398
  William 398
  William Blackiston 398
  William Wilson 398

Rasin, R. W. L. & Co. 398
RATCLIFF, L. Sue (RUTLEDGE) 873
W. W. 873
RATHBONE, William 806
RATHEL, Joseph 658
Ratien & Koneche 433
RATTOONE, Elijah 520
RAU, E. W. 821
  John C. 255
  Philip B. 487
RAUB, George 927
  John 928
RAUTH, G. 597
Raven's Rock 220
RAW, John C. 807
Rawling's 342
RAWLINGS, Benjamin 188
  Daniel 741
  Eliza A. 639
  Joshua 392
  Julia Ann 392
  Richard 38
RAWSON, Matthew 592
RAY, John B. 190
  Richard M. 160
  W. G. 191
Ray, The 627
RAYBOLD, Thomas J. 160
RAYHICE, D. 190
RAYMO, Lewis 153
RAYMOND, ---, Mrs. 594
  Daniel 120
  G. V. 254
  Gilbert 236
  John D. 160
RAYNER, Isador 194, 723
  William S. 152, 281, 466, 502, 817, 828, 841
RAYNOR, George W. 637
Rayville 871
REA, Henry S. 740
  John H. 262
READ, --- 375
  ---, Dr. 742
  ---, Mrs. 156, 835
  ---, Rev. Mr. 521
  Calvin H. 556
  Charles A. 821
  Corinthia V. J. 556
  D. D. 641
  George 438, 806
  James 39
  John 911
  John D. 250
  Kate C. 935
  Larkin 249
  Robert 246, 604
  Sophia Catherine 807
  William 438
  William G. 785

READ, William George 627, 806, 807, 835
READEL, John D. 758, 807, 814
READELL, John 246
READY, John 244, 470
  Samuel 189, 192, 806
Ready, Samuel, Asylum 806
REAFFLER, Henry 380
Real Estate & Savings-Bank of Baltimore 512
Real Estate Register, The 635
Real Estate Savings Institution 473
Reamer, A. C. & Co. 515
REANEY, John G. 484
  Thomas 305
  W. B. 305
  W. L. 526
Reaney, Neafe & Co. 252
Reaney, Neafie & Co. 250, 258, 305
REANY, William 176, 192, 241, 463
REARDON, Henry 538
Reason & Wetheall 249
REAVEN, Elizabeth 921
Rechabite Hall 126
RECKORD, David Burnett 926
  Edward L. 926
  Elmira 926
  Elmira (PERRY) 925
  Hannah 926
  Henry 916, 925, 926
  Henry Herman 926
  John 925
  John Henry 926
  Julia A. 926
  Julia A. (LUKENS) 926
  Lydia A. (ZIMMERMAN) 926
  Milton Atchison 926
  Milton H. 926
  Walter P. 926
  William H. 926
Reckordville 916, 925, 926
Red Book 613, 642, 652
Red C Oil Manufacturing Co. 512
Red Cleft 370
Red Hill 33
Red Lion, Sign of 312
Red Lion Tavern 924
Red Men of Baltimore 762
Red Men's Hall 151, 231, 552
REDDEHASE, Charles 160
REDDING, William 614
  William F. 254
Redeemer, P.E. Church of 525
Redemptorist Fathers 598, 890, 929
Redemptorists 540, 541, 928
REDWOOD, Allan H. 675
REED, Anna 605
  B. C. 886
  Elias H. 834
  Enoch 523
  George A. 761, 932, 933

REED, James 592
  John 160
  Nelson 225, 807
  Seth G. 160
  W. Hirst 579, 580
  William 255, 790
REEDER, Alice 427
  Andrew J. 427
  Charles 307, 320, 323, 394, 466, 807
  Charles M. 427
  Frances 427
  Frances Ann (SHERLOCK) 427
  Leonard 427
  Oliver 427
  Teresa 427
Reeder, C. & Co. 427
Reeder, Charles 427
Reeder, Charles & Co. 303
Reeder, Charles & Sons 426
Reeder's, Charles, Marine-Engine Works 426
REEKERS, J. J. 427, 439
REESE, --- 133, 467
---, Rev. Dr. 816
A. A., Rev. 580
A. D., Rev. 931
Andrew 226, 261, 487
Anna Maria 656
Aquilla A. 160
Charles, Mrs. 604
D. 102
D. M. 191
Daniel E. 582
Daniel M., Rev. 806
David 806
E. Yates 190, 616, 617, 625, 649
Edward Yates, Rev. 651
Frederick 569
Frederick F., Rev. 524
G. H. 489
George L. 806
Gerard H. 466, 488
H. D. 934
J. 825
J. L. 192
Jacob 355, 592, 600
John 160, 176, 188, 192, 209, 225, 250, 484, 569, 807
John C. 240
John E. 241, 253
John L. 192
John L., Jr. 487
John S. 582
John S., Jr. 253
John S., Rev. Dr. 807
John, Capt. 656
Levi R. 582
Louis 446
Margaret 582
Mary 582

REESE, P. B. 577
  Rebecca R. 582
  Ruth 582
  Samuel 255
  Thomas L. 449
  Thomas M. 578
  William 465
  William D. 160
  William S. 194, 195, 497
  William Smith 498
  Yates 616
Reese, John S. & Co. 397
REESIDE, ---, Commodore 517
  J. F. 517
REESO, D. 103
REEVE, Tappin 806
REEVES, William 780
Reformed Magistrate System 602
Reformed Presbyterian Church 551, 797
Regents of the College of Medicine of Maryland 736
REGESTER, J. A. 586
  R. W. 190
  R. Wilson 160
  S. 586
  S. W. 447
  Samuel W. 446
  W. G. 745
  Wilson G. 743
REGISTER, Samuel 807
  Samuel W. 260
Register, Joshua & Sons 178, 420
Registers of Wills 1851-81 728
Regulators 631
Rehoboth 743
REIBER, Adam 840
REICHE, P. H. 745
REID, ---, Rev. Mr. 238
  Andrew 547, 600
  B. G. W. 578, 579
  J. D. 505
  James 431
  Jesse 192
  John L. 155
  John O. 576
  William George 486
REIGART, Philip 246
REIL, J. B. 902
REILLY, Edward 902
  George 189, 190, 806
  J. McKendree 578
  Patrick 246
REIMAN, Alexander 440
  Daniel 806
  William J. 162, 365
REINAGLE, ---, Mr. 682
  Alexander 683, 806
REINECKER, Conrad 806
  George 173, 187, 807
  John 807

REINHARD, H. E. 202
REINHART, Charles C. 807
Reinhart, E. W. & Co. 615
REINICKER, Charles H. C. 160
  Conrad 458
  George 247, 514
  John F. 160
REIP, A. H. 263
  Alfred 472
  E. H. 762
REIS, Edmund J. 556, 559
  Edward J. 554
REISCHE, P. H. 889
REISS, Alfred H. 938
REISTER, ---, Mr. 855
  J. A. 855
  Peter 807
Reisterstown 13, 15, 19, 20, 26, 42, 357, 807, 815, 816, 817, 830, 854, 855, 856, 857, 861, 865, 866, 867, 868
Reisterstown M.E. Chapel 866
Reisterstown Riflemen 855
Reisterstown Turnpike 310, 865
REITER, Philip R. 251
Relay 342
Relay House 130, 131, 132, 136, 320, 324, 361, 502, 935, 937
Relay Station 344
Relief Association of the Maryland Penitentiary 602
Relief Building Association 512
Religious Cabinet, The 627
Remington 64
REMINGTON, Edward 355
  William 896
Remington Estate 64
REMSEN, Ira 233
RENCH, Andrew 128
RENDELL, Jno. 205
RENNERT, Robert 468, 495, 517
Rennert House 517
RENNOLDS, Lindsay H. 189
RENSHAW, James 247
  Jane 744
  Thomas W. 820
  William 807
RENTZEL, George 95
RENWICK, Robert 806
REPER, Joseph 311
REPOLD, George 298, 433, 458
Republican 612, 761, 801
Republican & Argus 615
REPUT, George 95
Rescue, The 927
Reservoir Hill 276
RESH, Jacob 869
RESINGER, Sarah 485
Retreat Street Fire Company 818
Retrospect, The 635
REUTER, ---, President 700

REUTER, F. 540
REVERE, William H. 160
REVILLA, ---, Capt. 112
REYBURN, James 252
  Thomas G. 439
REYNELL, Richard 484
REYNOLDS, --- 122
  Alfred D. 161
  B. 95, 269
  Edward 351
  F. H. 525
  George 250
  George B. 935
  H. R. 201
  Henry R. 806
  J. 201
  J. Edward 600
  Jesse A. 161
  John 919
  Joseph 891
  Josiah 807
  Lindsay H. 195
  R. 246
  Robert W. 161
  W. 471
  William 462, 471, 550, 828
Reynolds, Smith & Co. 402
RHEIM, Josiah 806
RHETT, Thomas Grimke 806
RHOADES, George R. 149
Rialto Building 397, 421
RIAN, John 103
RICARD, Benjamin 807
RICARDS, John R. 806
RICAUD, Benjamin 461
Riccard's Cliftes 39
RICE, --- 723
  Annie L. (SEIDENSTRICKER) 485
  F. 280
  Frederick 368, 381
  George W. 191
  Jacob 367, 806
  John 807
  Joseph 77, 238
  M. F. B. 485
  Patrick 806
  S. A. 271
  Sara A. 272
  Sara S. 230
  T. D. (Daddy) 693
  Thomas H. 191
Rice, Hayden & Co. 641
Rice & Co. 432
RICH, ---, Rev. Dr. 931
  Arthur 879
  Arthur A. 856
  Arthur J. 866, 867
  Edward W. 856
  Thomas R. 141
Rich Neck 49
RICHARD, G. 455

RICHARDS, ---, Mr. 558
---, Rev. Mr. 557
 Elder 558
 George 782
 John C. 470
 Lewis 554, 556
 Richard 70
 Timothy 249
 William 561
Richards, Leftwich & Co. 373
Richards, T. A. & Bro. 617
Richards & Winter 637
RICHARDSON, ---, Mr. 43, 645
 A. L. 638
 B. H. 192, 394
 Beale H. 145, 194, 205, 498, 615, 616, 806
 C. Herbert 902
 Charles 749
 Charles H. 160
 E. 874, 909
 Edward J. 806
 Emma 917
 Francis 146
 Francis A. 145, 615
 George R. 714, 715, 807
 George W. 484
 J. 95, 269
 J. W. 193, 902
 John 367
 John B. 160
 Joshua 311
 Joshua N. 160
 Lawrence 919, 920
 Mary 722
 S. McLee 470
 Samuel 911
 Samuel McD. 522, 600
 Thomas 908
 William 298, 587
 William M. 249
Richardson's Oil-Cloth Mill 931
Richardson's Reserve 923
RICHEY, Joseph 806
 Thomas 888
RICHINGS, Caroline 693
Richmond 897
Richmond & York River Line 302
Richmond African Baptist
 Missionary Society 567
Richmond College 567
Richmond Eclectic 637
Richmond Market 207
Richmond Seminary 556
RICKETTS, ---, Mr. 312
 Benjamin 921
 John 640
 Wesley 281, 367
RICKS, Samuel 264
RICKSTINE, John 241
RIDDELL, Alexander 433

RIDDELL, Robert 433
RIDDICK, J. H. 580
RIDDLE, ---, Capt. 299
 Beal D. 160
 George B. 627
 H. R. 466
 J. 70
 John 922
 K., Miss 605
 Sarah (GORSUCH) 922
RIDDLEMOSER, Michael 532
RIDER, Edward 813, 887, 898, 903
 Edward S. 807
 George W. 256
Rider's 347
Rider's Grove 344
Rider's Station 21
Rider's Switch, N.C.R.R. 807
RIDGAWAY, H. B. 896
Ridge's Straits 310
RIDGELY, --- 521, 761, 851, 925
 ---, Capt. 885
 ---, Com. 807
 ---, Dr. 731
 ---, Gen. 845, 907
 ---, Mrs. 595
 ---, Mrs. of Hampton 902, 906
 Andrew S. 190
 Andrew Sterett 729, 806
 Ann 669, 806
 B. Rush 877
 C. 678
 C. G. 189, 850
 C. of Hampton 680
 Charles 37, 53, 60, 61, 69, 70, 71, 72, 75, 76, 100, 117, 193, 194, 195, 267, 316, 343, 374, 386, 393, 425, 455, 456, 518, 519, 545, 594, 728, 778, 806, 814, 816, 819, 844, 857, 934
 Charles G. 189
 Charles of Hampton 679, 736, 817, 819, 848, 906
 Charles W. 154
 Daniel B. 806
 David 703
 Deborah 719
 Elizabeth 862
 F. 730
 Fred. 76
 H. 128, 456
 H. Clay 820, 830
 Henry 639, 728, 806, 807
 James L. 63, 189, 194, 195, 269, 270, 370, 488, 760, 814, 815, 934
 John 60, 61, 69, 71, 128, 205, 222, 244, 425, 719, 726, 741, 768, 807, 814, 819, 850
 John of Hampton 816, 818, 849, 902, 903
 Mary B. 703

RIDGELY, N. G. 680
  Nicholas 252, 806, 814, 817
  Nicholas G. 77, 265, 266, 806
  Nicholas O. 807
  Nicholas Orrich 250
  Noah 188, 189
  Randolph 114
  Richard 168, 193, 375, 452, 521, 845
  Sarah 639
  William 70, 71, 117, 195, 728, 806, 814
Ridgely & Edgar 438
Ridgely & Pringle 79
Ridgely Encampment No. 15, I.O.O.F. 874
Ridgely Estate at Hampton 771
Ridgely Family of Hampton 904
Ridgely's Delight 49, 50
RIDGEWAY, Thomas G. 465
  William 463
RIDGLEY, Nicholas 454
Ridgley Building Association 512
Ridgley Family of Hampton 886
RIDLEY, -- 346
  Matthew 76, 79, 392, 806
Ridley & Pringle 102
RIDOUT, Daniel A. 886
RIEFLE, Henry 381
RIELLY, John 202
RIEMAN, A. 484
  Alexander 357, 420, 462
  Catharine (PETERS) 419
  Daniel 419
  Henry 419, 420, 463, 471, 807
  Joseph H. 125, 420, 441, 461, 494, 640, 698, 847, 887, 892
  Robert G. 806
  Samuel 419
  William J. 487
  William Jones 420
Rieman, Henry & Sons 420, 892
RIESE, John 269
RIESER, August 840
RIFFLEMEYER, Charles H. 155
RIGBY, J. J. 252
  James H. 160
RIGDON, ---, Policeman 720
  Robert M. 202
RIGGS, ---, Dr. 899
  Elisha 807
  George S. 362
  Richard 855
RIGUEUR, Victor 231
RILEY, A. R. 928
  Bennett 114
  George H. 917
  J. McKendree 139
  John T. 877
  Lewis 106
  Samuel S. 241

RILEY, William 73, 89, 244, 893
RIMBY, Jacob 160
RINCE, L. L. 534
RIND, William 657
RINEHARDT, John 793
RINEHART, --- 666, 676
  David 355
  E. Thomas 442
  George 193, 194
  Henry C. 502
  Nathan H. 662
  W. P. 237
  William 272
RINGGOLD, Anna 395
  Benjamin 92
  French 311
  J. 678
  J. T. 635
  Jacob 295
  James 398, 851
  John 398
  Mary Hanson 416
  Mary Rebecca 398
  Rebecca (KIRBY) 395
  S. 113
  Samuel 114
  Thomas 398, 416
RINGROSE, John W. 189
Rip-Raps 631, 787
RIPLEY, ---, Gen. 895
  Boswell S. 629
RIPPARD, William H. 160
RIPPLE, Lewis 469
RISEL, Henry 253
Rising Sun 513
RISTEAU, Abraham 70, 921
  Benjamin Denny 863
  Catharine 858, 921
  Catherine 842
  Charles Walker 863
  David 921
  Eleanor 863
  Elizabeth (DENNY) 863
  Elizabeth (REAVEN) 921
  Frances 863
  Francis (TODD) 863
  George 40, 69, 70, 71, 72, 807, 819, 863
  Isaac 47, 921
  John 53, 518, 519, 814, 842, 858, 863
  John Talbot 863, 921
  Joseph 921
  Katharine 863
  Katherine 863
  Mary 921
  Mary (STOKES) 921
  Rebecca 863
  Robert Carman 863
  Sarah 921
  Talbot 921

RISTEAU, Talbott 814
 Thomas 863
 Thomas C. 819, 820
 Thomas Cradock 863
 Thomas E. 745
 William McLaughlin 863
Risteau Family 862
RISTON, John A. 807
RISTOU, James 921
RITCHIE, Albert 195
 Thomas 505
RITER, S. S. 241
RITNEY, John 254
Rittenhouse Family 852
RIUFES, Fau 372
Riversdale 353
Riverside Park 90, 278
RIZER, Eugene J. 160
ROACH, ---, Dr. 741
 John 246
 Michael 213, 254
 William H. 740
ROACHE, Charles M. 408, 832
ROBB, Charles G. 253
 E. T. 472
 John 592
 John A. 187, 194, 241, 548, 807, 847
 Joseph 140, 193
 William 83, 298, 433, 545, 547, 679
 Robb, J. A., Ship Yard 293
 Robb, John A. & Co. 145
 Robb & Donaldson's Ship Yard 293
 Robb Ship Yard 302
ROBBINS, Ernest 551
 Horace W. 806
 Horace W., Mrs. 596
 James J. 691
 Robert Emmett Perpetual Building Association 512
ROBERTS, --- 166, 350
 ---, Mr. 224
 ---, Rev. Dr. 600
 A. A. 525
 B. Rush 740
 E. P. 614
 E. W. 576
 Edward 448, 469, 576
 Edward P. 246, 615, 807
 G. C. 600
 G. C. M. 624
 George 233, 470, 575, 806, 826, 827
 George B. 346
 George C. M. 745, 754
 Henry 160
 Isaac G. 438
 Jane (WATERMON) 883
 John 45, 247, 584, 910
 John, Mrs. 604
 Joseph 190, 199, 740

ROBERTS, L. B. 641
 Lewis J. 813, 887
 Lovell 766
 M. 441
 Matthias 441
 Philip 877
 Rebecca Jane 582
 Ruth Ann 883
 Thomas 173, 187
 Thomas A. 600
 W. H. 365
 William 357
 William D. 189, 255
 William H. 883
ROBERTSON, ---, Mr. 494
 Agnes 693
 Alvin 191
 J. J. 879
 N. C. 729
 Richard 920
 Thomas 732
 William 178, 362
Robin Hood's Forest 669
ROBINS, --- 684
ROBINSON, ---, Dr. 550
 A. 595
 A. C. 125, 128
 Alex. H. 751
 Alexander 576, 727
 Alexander C. 126, 130, 137
 Aley 406
 Andrew 727
 Archibald 592
 Benjamin 149
 Charles 406
 David 53
 E. B. 253
 E. U. 463
 E. W. 487, 488
 Edward W. 125, 463, 472
 Edwin 351
 Ephraim 173, 187, 206, 239, 247
 George 251, 574, 597, 729, 806
 George L. 751, 806
 George N. 806
 Henry 692
 J. H. 696
 J. J. 463
 J. S. 263
 James 61, 917
 James B. 917
 John 95, 149, 194, 261
 John P. 865, 879
 Jonas 518
 Joseph 314, 608, 613, 627, 630, 690, 807
 Joseph J. 190, 191, 193
 Lewis H. 597
 Mary Leeke (DASHIELL) 744
 Matthew 744
 Richard 921

ROBINSON, Roland 292
  Samuel J. 814
  Solomon 77
  Stuart 227, 549, 551, 846, 896
  Thomas 100
  Vashtie 406
  William 152, 153, 201, 202, 249, 465, 592
  William C. 139
  Robinson & Clap 438
  Robinson & Lord 281
  Robinson's Library 672
ROBSON, Stuart 688
ROBUCK, Louis 673
ROBY, ---, Mr. 841
  George W. 160
ROCHAMBEAU, --- 769
  ---, Count 530
ROCHBRUNE, Lewis 293
ROCHE, G. J. 247
  John A. 190
  Michael 488
ROCHESTER, J. S. Earl 625
  William R. 189
ROCK, ---, Mr. 568
Rock Creek 527
Rock Mills 218
Rock Run 370
Rock Spring Episcopal Church 911
Rockaway Beach 109
Rockdale 830, 832, 870
Rockdale Baptist Chapel 567
Rockdale Cotton-Factory 408
Rockdale Paper-Mills 870
ROCKHOLD, Charles 911
  Edward 871
Rockland 842
Rockland Cotton-Factory 408
Rockland Farm 726
Rocks of Deer Creek 359
Rockville 342
Rocky Ridge 356, 357
RODDER, Martin 575
Rodemer's 342
RODEWALD, Henry 372
RODGERS, Alexander 806
  Ann Maria 806
  Charles 836
  G. H. 604
  Henry T. 659
  John 241, 546, 806, 807, 836
  John A. 667
  John H. 470
  Micajah 813
  Nicholas 521
  R. S. 600
  William 741
RODLEY, Samuel 100
  Thomas 380
RODMAN, ---, Lt. 91
  ---, Sailing Master 91

RODNEY, ---, Mr. 781
ROE, Hannah 911
  Moll 924
  Thomas Lee 806
  Walter 70, 433, 519
  William 911
ROEDER, A. 588
  George 917
ROELKEY, Edward 442
ROEMER, H. B. 231
ROESCH, George 541
ROFF, James 160
ROGERS, --- 521
  ---, Capt. 104
  ---, Commodore 91, 276
  ---, Mr. 274, 275, 504, 507, 835
  A. J. 927
  Ann R. (HALL) 723
  Benjamin 61, 71, 73, 205, 244, 374, 728, 814, 909, 910
  C. B. 834
  C. Howard 487
  C. Lyon 818, 833, 835, 836
  Charles 71
  Charles L. 834
  Charles Lyon 834
  E. Law 190, 256, 851
  Edmund Law 194, 665, 847, 851
  Eleanor 719, 806
  Evans 488
  George 244, 393, 394
  Guy 592
  H. W. 370
  Henry J. 260, 503, 504, 505, 506, 507, 806
  Henry W. 598, 806
  Hortensia M. 806
  Jacob 244, 452, 470
  James 112
  James B. 737
  James Lyon 835
  John 100, 101, 103, 241, 249, 253, 254, 293, 547
  John H. 92, 188
  John J. 487
  Joseph 247, 460, 484, 927
  Kennedy Grogan 835
  Lloyd 806
  Lloyd N. 273, 345, 807
  M. W. 302
  Mary (LYON) 723, 834
  Micajah 723, 834
  Moses 301
  Nathan 440, 484, 807
  Nicholas 37, 58, 79, 82, 173, 174, 175, 192, 200, 274, 449, 455, 482, 658, 679, 699, 748, 768, 806, 807, 814, 885
  Philip 70, 82, 118, 169, 172, 173, 225, 298, 457, 483, 574, 728, 806, 807, 816

ROGERS, Rebecca 806
  Rebecca (GROGAN) 835
  Robert Lyon 723
  Samuel 103, 586, 918
  Sarah A. 909
  Seth 807
  T. 252
  William 37, 54, 57, 58, 103, 205,
    466, 768, 807
  William F. 160
  William H. 148
Rogers, John & Son 247, 253
Rogers & Owens 261
Rogers & Owings 298
Rogers & Son 256
Rogers Family 885
Rogers' 514
Rogers' Bastion 90
Rogers' Inspection 203
ROGGE, Charles 246
ROHN, ---, Mrs. 806
ROHRER, J. Q. A. 555
Roland 347
Roland Run 220
ROLANDO, Henry 806
ROLFE, John 915
  Pocahontas 915
Rollin's Ferry Road 936
ROLLINS, William Thomas 927
ROLLO, Archibald 920
Roloson & Co. 263
Rolph's Neck 303
Roman Amphitheatre 694
RONEY, William 92, 188, 667
ROOP, David 355
ROPER, David 567, 568
ROPES, Archer 807
ROSE, A. A. 194
  Isaac 149
  J. B. 153
  Jacob 598
  John 488, 526
  Solomon 149
  Thomas 525
  W. P. 149
Rose, J. B. & Co. 637
Rose Hill 490
Rose Street 251
Rosebank 891
Roseby's Rock 342
Rosedale 931
ROSEMAN, W. V. 832
ROSENBERGER, J. A. 688
ROSENBURG, Lewis 841
ROSENFELD, Goody 841
  Goody, Mrs. 603
  Jacob 642
Rosenswig, E. & Co. 263
ROSENTHAL, Alfred S. 840
ROSEVILLE, Emily 669
ROSEWALD, J. 589

Roslin 719
ROSS, --- 90, 93, 94
  ---, Gen. 89, 96, 267, 269, 277, 609,
    771, 832, 881, 933
  ---, Miss 916
  Anna H. 258
  Benjamin C. 188, 189, 192, 807
  David 545, 916
  David J. 807
  John 77, 298, 733
  John W. 485, 539
  Reuben 258
  Robert 88
  Robert F. 191, 806
  Theodore 270
  W. E. W. 495
  William 89, 187, 188, 209, 461, 824
  William E. W. 160
Ross, Charles A. & Co. 263
ROSSELL, S. A. 467
ROSSI, A. 539
ROSSITER, Joel T. 572
Rossville 916, 927, 931
ROST, George 806
ROSZEL, ---, Rev. Mr. 933
  Roszel's (S.A.) School 233
ROSZELL, S. S. 586
ROTBROCK, Jacob 572
ROTHBORNE, ---, Rev. Dr. 806
ROTHROCK, Jacob 807
  Joseph M. 160
Rothrock & Peacock 263
Rothschild Building Association Nos.
  10 11 & 12 512
ROUEY, William 667
Rough & Ready Rifle Corps 817
Rough-Skins 631, 787
Round Top Church 555, 556
ROUS, Charles 442
ROUSBY, ---, Mrs. 905
  Rousby Hall 99, 905
ROUSE, Elizabeth 391, 922
  John 471
ROUSEY, William 814
ROUSSEAU, --- 147
Roussel & Hicks 390
ROUX, Paul 202, 505
ROW, Joshua 911
Rowbotham & Maywood 688
ROWE, James M. 253
  John K. 877
  Joseph A. 806
  R. S. 584
ROWLAND, Henry A. 233
  Robert 65
  Thomas 734
ROWLES, Joshua 253
Rowlesburg 342
Royal Arcanum 762
Royal Spanish Academy of History
  648

ROYALL, Ann 630
ROYSTON, Abraham 871
  Georgia 870
  John 806
  Joshua 576
ROZZELL, S. S. 617, 636
RUBENS, ---, 702
RUBY, ---, Mr. 901
  Anne E. (WHITTER) 901
  Joseph 900
  Sarah (BARNHART) 900
  W. H. 903
  William 899
  William H. 817, 870, 886, 898, 902
  William Henry 900
RUCKLE, Samuel 253
RUDDACH, D. J. 463
  Joseph 472
  Mary E. 472
  Rebecca 472
RUDISELL, ---, Rev. Mr. 874
  A. W. 889
RUDOLPH, H. 192
RUELBERG, Charles 160
Rugby's Institute 357
RUHL, W. 873
RULAND, George 541
RULE, Henry 160
RULON, Samuel 241
RUMEY, --- 102
RUMPLER, Gabriel 540
RUMSEY, Benjamin 46, 707, 709, 729, 921
  Elinor 46
  James 374, 431, 928
  John B. 917
  John Beall 923
  William 65
  Rumsey Mansion 46
RUPPERT, Joseph 190
RUPPRECHT, Andreas 931
Rural Register 614, 635
Rural Retreat 871
RUSE, John 807
RUSHWORTH, Richard 758
RUSK, David 61
  George 845
  George A. 276
  H. Welles 194
  Robert 380
  T. J. 380
  Thomas J. 276, 380
  William 249, 255, 380, 463, 806
  William L. 380
RUSSEL, James 253
  John 573
  Thomas 102
RUSSELL, ---, Miss 694
  A. H. 281, 444
  A. W. 550
  Alexander 89, 125, 188, 189, 582

RUSSELL, Charlotte 694
  E. J. F. 740
  E. Walton 740
  G. 850
  G. W. 806
  George 255
  George W. 362
  J. 77, 152
  James 253
  M. L., Miss 605
  Mary B. 604
  Ormon 924
  Samuel 249
  Stephen 924
  T. 680
  Thomas 61, 70, 79, 100, 103, 168, 392, 424, 728
  Thomason, Mrs. 806
  Walter 39
  William 76, 424, 519, 592, 728, 814
  William A. 855
RUST, George 807
RUTH, Francis J. 231
RUTHERFORD, Alexander 160
RUTHS, George 160
RUTLAND, T. 102
RUTLEDGE, Abraham 911
  Benjamin 817
  C. A. 911
  E. Hall 187
  Elizabeth 873
  Elizabeth (HOWARD) 873
  Ephraim 911
  Jacob 911
  John 911
  John F. 873
  John R. 911
  Joshua 873, 911
  L. Sue 873
  Mary L. 873
  Nathan 872
  R. F. 872
  Rebecca J. (FYFFE) 873
  Rufus F. 873
  Sarah J. 873
  Shadrach 911
  Thomas 813, 814, 873
  Thomas G. 873
  William 815, 873
RUTNER, M. R. 886
RUTTER, ---, Lt. 91
  Hanson P. 814
  John 77
  Jonathan 187
  Thomas 71, 73, 75, 353, 592, 727, 729, 814
  Thomas B. 464
  Thomas G. 484
RYAN, D. 681
  Edward 212
  J. J. 250

RYAN, John 855
P. 538
Richard 65
W. M. 826
William H. 806
RYDER, ---, Father 536
RYLAND, Robert 567
William 261
RYLY, Edward 65
SABEL, John 246
Sabillasville 357
SACHS, John 160
SACHSE, Edward 807
Sacred Heart Catholic Church 928, 929
Sacred Heart of Jesus Catholic Church 839
Sacred Musical Society 646
SADLER, ---, Mr. 691
Warren H. 237
Sadler's Property 896
SADSBURY, Joseph 542
SADTLER, B. 929
George T. 487
Philip B. 91, 808
William H. 820
Safe Deposit & Trust Co. 478, 479, 512
Safe Deposit Building 445, 478, 485
Safety Axle & Top Standard Co. 512
SAGER, William 263
Sagouan Manufacturing Co. 408
Sailors' City Bethel 577
SALE, ---, Rev. Dr. 589
Salem M.E. Church 922
Salem United Brethren Mission 573
Salisbury Mill 217
Salisbury Plains 49, 203
SALMON, Edward W. 808
George 103, 118, 169, 172, 174, 214, 455, 546, 547, 727, 728, 733, 808, 814
George, Mrs. 808
SALTER, ---, Midshipman 91
Theodore E. 253
Saltpetre Creek 811
SALZBACHER, ---, Rev. Dr. 540
Sam's Creek 573
Sam's Creek Railroad Company 314
SAMPSON, David 911
Isaac 911
Richard 518, 911
SAMS, J. J. 524
SAND, John A. 573
SANDERS, Anna K. 868
B. C. 394
B. J. 463
Benedict I. 189

SANDERS, George 459, 469, 485, 577
Henry 191, 194
Humphrey 250
Jacob 868
L. A. 256
Mary 901
Samuel F. 579
Thomas 102
SANDERSON, ---, Mrs. 224
F. 834
Francis 70, 432, 852
Frank 834
Hannah A. (PIERSON) 852
Henry 253
Henry S. 808, 814
Thomas 847, 852
Thomas Nelson 807
Washington 149
SANDFORD, ---, Mr. 770
Jane (WILSON) 770
W. 920
SANDS, ---, Mr. 613, 615
B. N. 470
Benjamin 244
Samuel 559, 609, 614, 615, 616, 625, 635, 845, 846
William B. 818, 886
Sands, Lent & Co. 694
Sands & Lents' Amphitheatre 345
Sandy Bottom 895
Sandy Hook 324, 342
Sandy Point 147, 309
Sandy Point Light 289
Sandy Spring(s) 723, 834
SANFORD, E. S. 359, 360
SANGSTON, George E. 485, 729
L. 365
Lawrence 130, 137, 155, 194, 201, 633, 807
Sangston, James A. & Co. 413
Sanitary & Christian Commissions 144
Sanitary Messenger 752
SANNER, James B. 194, 202
Santa Clara Mining Association 512
SANTMYER, Charles A. 160
John M. 160
SAPP, Benjamin F. 935
J. Wesley 935
Joseph 191
SAPPINGTON, Francis Brown 741
Richard 740
Thomas 462
Sarah Ann Street Methodist Church 580
Saratoga Street 769
SARBAUGH, Jacob 160
SARDO, N. 628
SARGANT, J. 579
SARGEANT, Thomas Bartow 807

SARGENT, ---, Rev. Dr. 144
  Achsah 701
  Thomas B. 576, 701, 929
Sassafras River Steamboat Co. 512
SATER, Henry 552, 553, 554
Sater Hill(s) 64, 843, 905
Sater's Baptist Church 553, 554, 905
SATOR, Henry 552
Satter Ridge 895
Saturday Bulletin, The 637
Saturday Evening Express 624
Saturday Evening Herald 615
Saturday Herald 614
Saturday Morning Visitor 617
Saturday Night, The 637, 641
Saturday Post, The 641
Saturday Visitor 615, 625, 627, 645, 651
Satyr Ridge 221
SAUER, C. 597
  William 929
SAUERBERG, J. D. 637
SAUERWEIN, George 241, 254, 487, 807
  P. G. 140
  P. G. (B.) 365
  Peter 199, 254, 441, 808
  Peter G. 190
SAULSBURY, A. J. 210
  Andrew J. 193, 807
SAUMENIG, Charles 160
  Louisa C. 230
SAUNDERS, ---, Mr. 759
  Thomas 101
SAURWEIN, P. G. 139
Savage 342
SAVAGE, George 200
  Margaret (TEACKLE) 743
  Patrick 65
  Susan E. 743
  Thomas Littleton 743
Savage Creek 313, 314
Savage Factory 838
Savage Manufacturing Co. 408, 836
Savage Mill 412
Savage Mountain 388
Savannah Daily News 628
SAVILLE, A. M. O. 362
  Thomas 160
SAVIN, F. A. 638
Savings 473
Savings-Bank of Baltimore 469, 470, 473
SAVORY, William 920, 921
SAXTON, A. H. 187
SAY, Henri 927
SAYE, James 920
SAYLOR, Daniel P. 355
Scales Town 311
SCALLY, S. L. 814

Scarborough, ---, Earl of 744
SCARBURGH, Edmund 556
SCARF, Isaac T. 896
SCARFF, Henry 755
  J. H. 754
  John Henry 755
  Joshua Hardesty 755
SCARLET, Thomas 65
SCATTAGLIA, --- 536
SCHAD, Charles M. 160
SCHAEFFER, ---, Mr. 441
  ---, Rev. Mr. 573
  Albert 542
  Baltzell 582
  Baltzer 170, 176, 187, 197, 246, 545, 808
  C. A. 547
  Eleanora 808
  F. Littig 219, 222, 354, 580
  Francis B. 114
  Fred. 89
  Frederick 173, 187, 188, 249, 461, 734
  George 551
  George B. 253
  George E. 808
  John 808
  Lewis B. 597
Schaeffer & Maund 614, 615
Schafer, D. B. & Co. 636
SCHAFFER, Daniel 917
  Fred. G. 808
  Frederick 433
SCHALITZKY, Anthony 160
SCHALL, ---, Rev. Mr. 587
SCHALTZ, John 569
SCHARF, George 808
  J. T. 657
  J. Thomas 194, 635, 638
  Thomas G. 191, 515, 817, 927
  William 808
Scharf's Hall 586
SCHARTZOUR (SCHWARTZAUER), Daniel 188
SCHARZ, John 597
SCHATT, J. J. 825
SCHAUB, Augustus 821
  Jacob 808
SCHAUER, Elias F. 541
SCHAUMBERG, Atkinson 641
SCHEFFER, Ary 676
  William J. 808
SCHEIB, ---, Mr. 570
  Henry 568
SCHENCK, ---, Gen. 139, 142, 143, 144, 145, 146, 615, 633, 897
  Noah Hunt 524
  Robert E. 141
SCHENKEL, Jacob 191
SCHENKLE, Jacob 191
SCHERER, Joseph 446

SCHERZER, Louis 160
Scheutzen Park 277
SCHIETH, ---, Rev. Mr. 571
SCHILLER, --- 647
  E. 825
SCHLENNIG, Fritz 160
SCHLEY, --- 698
  Anne 395
  Catharine 808
  Frederick 129
  George 162
  Jacob 782
  William 499, 645, 702, 716, 717, 721, 725, 807
  William Louis 160
SCHLINGLOF, Luther 852
SCHLOEGEL, C. H. A. 830
SCHLOEGLE, C. A. 570
SCHLOSS, F., Mrs. 603
  William 487, 841
SCHLUTENBERGER, W. 927
SCHLUTER, Helen 423
Schlutter & Bro. 446
SCHMIDT, Christian 740
  John 641
  Michael 160
  Vincent 673
  W. L. 438
SCHMITT, William L. 808
SCHMITZ, Hy. 605
SCHMUCK, Jacob 807
SCHMUCKER, Samuel D. 600
SCHNAUFFER, Charles Henry 630, 808
  William 508, 630
SCHNEBEL, Daniel 571, 590
SCHNEEBERGER, Henry W. 589
SCHNEIDER, Casp. 605
SCHNIVELY, Jacob 741
SCHOBBAN, Edward A. 488
SCHOCK, George 255
SCHOFIELD, A. N., Miss 605
  Lizzie 821
  Tilghman 818
SCHOLL, George 569
SCHONE, J. Harman 927
SCHONTZ, J. B. 600
SCHREIBER, Peter S. 236
SCHREINER, Carl 605
SCHRIVER, Augustus 487
  John 207
  John S. 808
  Peter S. 534
SCHROB, Henry 573
Schroder, Henry & Son 438
SCHROEDER, ---, Mr. 494
  ---, Rev. Mr. 521
  A. F. 193
  Andrew F. 488, 495
  H. B. 855
  H., Mrs. 594

SCHROEDER, Henry 89, 197, 239, 456, 470, 483, 545, 569, 572, 826, 827
  John 467
  John Frederick 654
  W. F. 299
  William 245, 485, 782
SCHRYVER, E. M. 442
SCHUCHTZ, John H. 808
SCHUCKHARDT, H. 597
Schuetzen Ges. von Baltimore County 605
SCHULTZ, A. H. 468
  Arnold 247
  Bolster 160
  Charles 254
  Elizabeth 395
  Henry A. 191
Schultz, Konig & Co. 346
SCHULTZE, John 246, 572
SCHUMACHER, A. 307
  Albert 306, 365
  C. 191
SCHUMACKER, A. 697
  Albert 440, 807
SCHUMAKER, Frederick 465
SCHUNCK, John 593
SCHWAB, John C. 160
SCHWARTZ, A. 366
  A. J. 393, 407
  Andrew 190, 193
  J. 569
  John 740
  John A. 160
Schwartz Estate 825
SCHWARTZAUER, Daniel 189
SCHWARTZE, A. J. 470
  A. T. 461
SCHWARZ, William 468
SCHWARZAUER, Daniel 92, 189
SCHWARZHAUPT, Charles 597
SCHWATKA, Charles A. 241
  T. A. 836
SCHWEAR, F. 597
SCHWEITZER, John S. 247
  Joseph F. 247
SCHWERDER, G. 597
SCHWING, Henry 673
SCLICHTER, H. 573
SCOFIELD, James 808
SCOTCHBURN, Thomas 759
SCOTT, ---, Dr. 741
  ---, Gen. 130, 131, 136, 887
  ---, Judge 200
  ---, Mr. 915
  ---, Rev. Dr. 674
  A. C. 912
  Alexander 311
  Austin 233
  B. H. 855
  Daniel 44, 45, 819, 919, 920

SCOTT, E. H. 855
　Ed. 912
　Edward 735, 740
　Edwin 877
　Eliza M. 594
　Francis P. 740
　Frank 884
　George 515, 834
　Gustavus 733
　H. 880
　Harrison 880
　Hugh Roy 524
　J. 678
　J. R. 693
　J., Mrs. 595
　James 509, 921
　James H. 834
　John 189, 194, 522, 554, 576, 594, 595, 728, 808, 813, 824
　John H. 915
　John R. 694
　Julia (MARTIN) 808
　Maggie A. 915
　Martha Rebecca (BOSLEY) 884
　Matthew 70
　Mollie E. 886
　Otho 898, 923
　P., Mrs. 595
　Robert 251
　Rossiter 247, 248, 249, 484
　T. P. 729
　T. Parkin 113, 129, 130, 137, 141, 194, 195, 723, 807, 896, 934
　T. Parkin, Mrs. 155, 156
　Thomas A. 346, 677
　Thomas M. 814, 815, 877
　Thomas Parken 189
　Thomas Parkin 717, 718
　Townsend 463, 480, 807
　Upton 741
　Walter 773
　William 921
　Winfield 84, 123, 895
Scott, T. & Son 481
Scott Street Permanent Building Association 512
SCREIBER, Peter 537
Screw-Dock Co. 480
SCRIBNER, Samuel 463, 559
Sea Girt House 927
Seaboard & Roanoke Railroad 284, 302
Seabrook 354
SEABROOK, Richard 250
　Thomas 353
Seamans' Floating Bethel 577
Seamen's Union Bethel 577
Seamen's Union Bethel Church 803
Searles, J. H. & Edward 262
SEARLY, Elizabeth 522
SEARS, Annie 605

SEARS, George 77, 83, 291, 293, 298
　Isaac 909
　Rebecca 909
SEATER, Henry 519
SEAVER, J. O. 870
Second Baptist Church 557, 559, 560, 564, 801
Second Baptist Church of Atlanta, Ga. 562
Second District School Trustees 830
Second District Teachers 830
Second District Teachers of Colored Schools 830
Second English Lutheran Church 569
Second Evangelical Church 590
Second Evangelical Lutheran Church 571
Second German Evangelical Lutheran Church 570
Second Lutheran Church 801
Second Lutheran Congregation 587
Second Manassas 897
Second Maryland Confederate Cavalry 906
Second Maryland Regiment of Veteran Volunteers 922
Second Mine Run 871
Second National Bank 451, 463, 469, 806
Second Presbyterian Church 546, 547, 548, 549, 588
Second Presbytery of Philadelphia 551
Second Regiment Baltimore County 863
Second Southwark Baptist Church of Philadelphia 561
Second Street German Reformed Church 573
Security Fire 490
SEDGWICK, --- 671
　Richard 65
　William T. 233
SEEGER, Barbara (BECK) 423
　Bena (STECKINFINGER) 423
　Jacob 423
　John Jacob 423
　Paul August 423
　W. F. 570
SEEKAMP, Albert 298, 433, 808
SEELEY, Matilda L. 498
SEELOS, Francis X. 541
SEELY, L. W. 562
SEEMULLER, August 807
　John R. 222, 441
　William 222
Seemuller, A. & Sons 373
SEFER, Daniel 246
SEFTON, John 693
SEGLER, Frederick 569

SEHRT, John C. 160
SEIBOLD, Lewis P. 160
SEIDENSTRICKER, ---, Mr. 486
  Albert B. 485
  Ann 485
  Annie L. 485
  Charles 485
  Daniel F. 485
  Elizabeth (BARNHART) 485
  Emily 485
  Frederick 485
  Henry 485
  J. B. 365
  John B. 189, 193, 199, 219, 222, 233, 365, 469, 484, 786
  John Barnhart 485
  John R. 193, 194
  Lizzie 485
  Mary 485
  Mary H. 485
  Mary H. (CRAGG) 485
  Sarah (RESINGER) 485
  Sophia 485
SEIM, Henry 191, 193, 205
SEIN, Thomas 433
SEIPP, Charles 597, 807
  G. W. 814
SEITZ, Noah 877
Seitzland 347
SELBY, John S. 807
SELDENER, Louis 807
SELDNER, Lewis 466
SELIGMAN, Abraham 281
Selinger & Newman's Dry-Goods House 413
SELLERS, M. B. 698
  Mathew B. 367
  Mulberry 776
  S. H. Lee 831
SELLMAN, ---, Mr. 494
  Alfred 720
  Eleanor 776
  Eleanor (GILL) 776
  J. J. H. 468
  J. J. M. 193
  James C. 439
  John 127, 776
  John J. M. 362
  John S. 351
  John Stephen 351
  Johnzee 776
  Jonathan 776
  Sarah 776
  Vachel 776
  Victoria 720
  W. A. B. 746
  William 776
SELTZER, Sebastian 246
Seminaire de St. Sulpice 236
Seminole War 887
SEMMES, Charles W. 818, 855, 866

SEMMES, Matilda 808
  Raphael 114
SEMPLE, Robert 567
Seneca 313
SENEY, Joseph 118
  Joshua 728
SENTORN, --- 780
SEQUIN, John 809
SERGEANT, Epes 651
  John 120, 122
  Samuel R. 807
  Thomas B. 578
Session of the Central Church 754
SETH, Robert L. 126, 194, 807
SETON, Eliza Ann 235
Seven Mountains 41
Seven Stars 758
Seven-Foot Knoll 309
Seven-Foot Knoll Light 289
Seventh Baptist Church 556, 561, 562, 563, 565, 567
Seventh District School Teachers 871
Seventh District School Trustees 872
Seventh District Teachers of Colored Schools 872
Seventh German American Building Association 512
Severn 354
Severn River 862, 864, 882
SEWAL, Reuben 577
SEWALL, Frances 424
  Frank, Mrs. 262
  Henry 233
  Joshua 519
SEWARD, ---, Mr. 653
SEWELL, ---, Mr. 208
  ---, Rev. Dr. 775
  Charles 530
  Christopher 519
  Henry 233
  J. J. 102
  James 671
  John 921
  John M. 252
  Mary A. 807
  N. P. 517
  R. 902
  Thomas 141, 160, 190, 192, 193, 394, 471, 576, 578, 808, 830
Sewell Lot 208
SEXTON, N. G. 936
  Richard 523
  S. B. 936
SEYLER, F. 484
SEYLN, Frederick 188
SEYLOR, Frederick 241
SEYMOUR, --- 165
  ---, Mrs. 684
  George 160

SEYMOUR, John 195
  Lucy 650
  Nelson 807
SHAAFF, John Thomas 741, 742
SHADE, George S. 253
SHADFORD, George 575
SHADWELL, D., Mrs. 202
SHAEFFER, Baltzer 89, 192, 827
  E. K. 484
  William 487
SHAFFER, Calvin 927
  F. L. 192
  Frederick Littig 807
  George 808
  Roger 205
SHAFFIELD, William 191
SHAFFNER, G. 190
SHAKESPEARE, ---, Mr. 681
  Shakespeare Hotel 311, 492
SHALL, James 343
SHAMBERG, Henry 247
SHAMBERGER, Jacob 818
SHAMBURG, Francis 160
Shamokin Valley & Pottsville
  Railroad Co. 345
Shane 871
SHANE, J. 902
  John H. 160
SHANEY, John 299
SHANKLIN, John W. 917
  W. J. 886
SHANKS, Daniel 256
SHANLEY, Thomas 241
SHANNON, ---, Miss 899
  J. P. 362
  Samuel 576
SHANON, J. P. 201
SHAPPERLE, C. 446
SHARE, Joseph 252
  Richard 808
Share, Joseph & Son 252
SHARETTS, William L. 222
SHARKEY, John 471
SHARP, A. P. 740
  Benjamin 911
  Horatio 911
  Peter 592
Sharp's Island 87, 309
SHARPE, ---, Gov. 37, 38, 66, 704,
  768, 848
  Horatio 67, 115, 195
  P. 102
  Peter 174
Sharpe Street M.E. Church 580
SHARPLEY, John 808, 881
SHAUCH, Jacob N. 870
SHAUL, Joseph 870
Shaum & Reitz 460
SHAVE, Richard 870
SHAVER, Abraham 870
  Isaac 870

SHAW, --- 252
  ---, Miss 596
  ---, Mr. 261
  Alexander 467
  Amos B. 465
  Ann 473
  Archibald 187
  Daniel 71, 910, 911
  Elias 465
  George M. 817
  Isabella C. 473
  James Wesley 258
  Jane Maxwell 867
  John 249, 644, 648, 735, 736, 808
  Joseph 248, 867
  Nancy 867
  Nathan 252, 456
  Rual 673
  Samuel 253
  Samuel H. 807
  W. C. 439
Shaw Family 927
Shawan 876, 877
Shawan Road 866
SHEA, John Augustus 628
  John Gilmary 33
  Thomas 526
SHEAFE, Henry 75
SHEAFF, Henry 70
SHEALEY, George W. 161
SHEALY, E. Addie 886
SHEARER, ---, Dr. 751
  Harriet (FOX) 751
  Thomas 750
Shearith Israel Synagogue 589
SHEEKELLS, John O. 579
SHEEKEY, Roger 48
SHEELER, John 427
Sheep Butchers' & Wool-Pulling
  Association No. 2 512
SHEFFIELD, ---, Lord 292
SHELBY, F. 380
SHELDON, A. W. 638
Shell Road 926
Shellpot Creek 311
SHELLY, William H. 190, 246
Shelter for Aged & Infirm Colored
  Persons 604
Shenandoah & Cumberland Valley
  Railroad 284
SHEPHARD, John 37
SHEPHERD, H. E. 271
  Henry E. 231, 272
  Moses 924
  Peter 728, 808
  Sarah 880
  Shepherd Asylum 924
  Shepherd Family 880
SHEPPARD, ---, Mr. 58
  Caroline M. (HOLMES) 428
  Ephraim 428

SHEPPARD, Franklin L. 428
  Isaac 428
  Isaac A. 428
  Mary (WESTCOTT) 428
  Moses 89, 458, 470, 808, 892, 893
  Peter 75, 76, 194, 819
  Thomas 84, 92, 187, 188, 192, 251, 299, 437, 438, 456, 457, 470, 808, 892
  Thomas L. 299
  Thomas S. 189, 192, 244, 252, 484
  Washington 202
  William 911
Sheppard, Isaac A. & Co. 427, 428
Sheppard Asylum 892
SHEREDIN, Thomas 814
SHEREDINE, ---, Col. 424
  ---, Maj. 55
  Daniel 424
  Murray 118
  T. 205, 857
  Thomas 45, 50, 53, 54, 55, 56, 57, 223, 518, 728, 808, 814, 815, 819
  Upton 118
SHERER, George E. 146
SHERIDAN, --- 149, 704
  Charles 903
  Philip, Gen. 336
  Rebecca 834
Sheriffs:
  1687-1851 814
  1851-1881 728
SHERLEY, M. E. 899
SHERLOCK, Frances 427
  Frances Ann 427
  John 679
  Peter 427
SHERMAN, ---, Gen. 897
  ---, Secretary 495
  Frederick Henry 742
  Washington 917
SHERMER, D. A. 584, 617
SHERRADINE, Stephen 780
SHERRERD, William D. 490
SHERROD, Ann 596
SHERWIN, Henry 557
SHERWOOD, G. W. 729
  George W. 195, 808
  James H. 160
  Philip 251
  Richard P. 807
  William S. 807
Sherwood & Co. 625, 630
Sherwood Chapel 865
Sherwood Churchyard Interments 879
Sherwood M.E. Chapel 891
Sherwood P.E. Church 879
SHIELDS, Caleb 70
  David 244, 554, 555, 769
  Jane (MC KIM) 769

SHIELDS, Jean 554
  Mary 769
  Richard D. 487
  Thomas 488
Shields Guards 668
Shiloh Baptist Church 562, 566
Shiloh Colored Baptist Church 568
Shiloh Lodge No. 111, I.O.O.F. 832
SHINN, Asa 616
SHINNICK, James 251
SHIPLEY, Alanson F. 855
  Benjamin 808
  Benjamin R. 908
  C. Howard 818
  Charles 365, 370, 587, 813
  Columbus 813
  Columbus J. 815
  Columbus T. 820
  J. S. 190
  Jesse 254
  Lester 586
  Nicholas H. 351
  Richard A. 244
  Samuel T. 820
  Sellman 776
  W. 515
  W. H. 818
  William H. 814
SHIPPARD, John 519
SHIPPEN, Henry 97
Shippensburg 356
SHIRK, Henry 578, 887
Shirley 702
SHOBER, Frederick 605
SHOCK, Thomas A. 807
Shoe & Leather Board of Trade 405, 417
SHOEBELS, Richard 312
SHOEMAKER, ---, Mr. 360
  Augusta C. (ECCLESTON) 360
  S. M. 346, 466, 478
  Samuel 144, 354, 364, 415, 516
  Samuel M. 155, 359, 466, 484, 494, 818
  William 899
  William S. 193, 363
Shoemaker, William & Son 303
Shoir Lane 935
SHOLL, John 443
  Susan 443
SHONE, James H. 440
SHONTZ, J. B. 600, 602
  T. B. 603
SHOOK, D. G. 855
SHORB, ---, Mr. 866
SHORT, Charles H. 255
  John H. 254
SHOWACRE, John 465
  M. S. 194, 495
SHOWER, Jacob 819
SHOWERS, Adam 819

SHOWERS, John 71
Shrewsbury 347
SHRIGLEY, ---, Dr. 467
 James 467
SHRIGLY, J. 831
SHRIM, John 187, 246, 569
SHRIVER, Andrew 395
 Annie M. 878
 Augustus 357, 882
 C. C. 472
 C. S. 447
 Calvin S. 473
 Daniel C. 160
 David H. 355
 Edward 493, 847
 Elizabeth (SCHULTZ) 395
 Francis 488
 George W. 161
 H. 367
 Henry 368, 467
 J. Alexander 303, 464, 478, 484
 John S. 320
 Mary M. J. (OWENS) 395
 S. S. 829, 878
 Thomas B. 446
 William 395
 Shriver Line 303
SHROEDER, Andrew F. 191
SHRYOCK, Henry S. 467
 William H. 466
SHUDENBURG, William 927
SHULE, John 38
SHULT, Charles H. 250
SHULTZ, Arnold 247
 John 407
SHUMACKER, Jonathan 127
Shurtzs, W. S. & Co. 263
SHUTER, James 484
SHUTT, ---, Col. 126
 A. P. 124, 202, 808
 Augustus P. 249
SHYROCK, H. S. 466
 Henry S. 478
 Thomas J. 449
SHYTE, Archibald 549
SIBIRT, E. 597
SICKEL, B. 570
 J. L. 448
SICKELS, ---, Mr. 218
Sickle Singleton & Co. 265
SICKLEMORE, Michell 39
 Samuel 818, 919
 Sicklemore Dock 923
SICKLES, ---, Gen. 897
SICLEMORE, Samuel 920
SIDES, Benjamin 839
SIEFORTH, John 160
SIGEL, Francis 630
Sigel's Wagon Train 147
SIGELEN, C. G. W. 929
Sign of St. Luke 433

Sign of the Golden Swan 432
Sign of the Spinning-Wheel 432
Sign of the Sun 432
Signal Service Observatory 278
SIHLER, Christian 233
SILBERZAHN, Adam 605
SILSBEE, Josh 693
Silver Spring 275, 342
SILVERWOOD, William 194
SIMKINS, Eli 864
 Maria North (CARNAN) 864
SIMMONDS, --- 506
SIMMONS, Azariah H. 622
 Cephas 808
 George 921
 John A. 253
 William C. 254
SIMMONT, P. 586
SIMMS, Hugh 917, 925
 Joseph 189, 190, 193, 465, 807, 932
 W. C. 242
 William C. 808
 William L. 254
Simms' Choice 923
SIMON, Edmund 160
 Frederick W. 160
 William 738
SIMONS, Robert 149
SIMPKINS, Eli 265, 266
SIMPSON, ---, Bishop 577, 578, 599
 ---, Mr. 312
 Benjamin L. 160
 Edmund 690
 George B. 508
 I. H. 289
 James 434, 592
 James Alexander 807
 John 250
 Josiah 147
 Maggie 886
 R. B. 254
 R. P. 253
 Resin B. 462
 T. W. 160, 830
 Thomas 35
 Walker 197
 Walter 187, 214, 245, 575
Simpson, J. E. & Co. 304
Simpson, James E. & Co. 303
Simpson's Improved Dry-Dock 303
SIMS, ---, Rev. Dr. 889
SINCLAIR, ---, Mrs. 693
 Deborah S. 930
 John 244, 264, 470
 Robert 807, 930
 Robert H. 231
 William 501, 698, 808
 William H. 252
Sinclair's Nursery 896
SINGLETON, Charles 246
 H. L. 548, 637

184

SINN, William E. 691
SINNERS, Elijah R. 192, 193
SINNOTT, John 237
  John D. 737
SINSHEIMER, L. 487
  Lewis 841
SINSZ, Philip 488
SIPPINCOTT, Samuel 421
Sir John's Run 342, 431
SISSON, H. 365
  Hugh 205, 271, 272, 303, 421, 459, 485, 489, 879
  John B. 421
  Martin 421
  Mary (BEARD) 421
  Richard 592
  Sarah A. (LIPPINCOTT) 421
Sisson, Hugh & Sons 542
Sister Anacaria 595
Sister Euphemia 595
Sister Felicita 595
Sister Gertrude 595
Sister Julia 595
Sister Louise 595
Sister Marcellina 595
Sister Mary Aloysia 595
Sister Mary Frances 595
Sister Mary Joseph 597
Sister Mary Rose 595
Sister Mary Stella 595
Sister Mary Ursula 803
Sister Matilda 595
Sister Maurice 595
Sister Valentine 595
Sisters of Charity 144, 235, 535, 537, 538, 595, 598, 600, 802, 803, 834, 853, 889, 937
Sisters of Mercy 538, 810, 840
Sisters of Notre Dame 541, 542, 598, 891, 928, 929
Sisters of Providence 534, 544
Sisters of St. Francis 917
Sisters of the Good Shepherd 597
Sisters of the Holy Cross 237, 536
Sisters of the Visitation 822
SITER, E. A. 301
SITLER, Abraham 432, 591
SITTLE, Isaiah 470
SIVEL, Henry 160
Sixth Baptist Church 561
Sixth District School Teachers 870
Sixth District School Trustees 870
Sixth German American Building Association 512
Sixth German Reformed Church 573
Sixth Maryland Regiment 793, 794
Sixth Presbyterian Church 548
Sixth Regiment 792
Sixth Regiment Armory 568
Sixth Synagogue 589

SKILLMAN, Charles 761
  George R. 600
  Harry 889
SKILLOM, William 100
SKINNER, ---, Mr. 492
  Henry 808
  J. J. 440
  James 99, 809
  Jeremiah 808
  John S. 493, 614, 616, 628, 761, 808, 850, 890
  S. P. 616
  Sallie 770
  William H. 281, 288
Skinner's Ship Yard 293
SKRIM, John 91
SLADE, Abraham 871
  Chris. 872
  Chris. C. 908
  Christopher 872
  Christopher C. 820
  Elizabeth 843
  Franklin 836
  James 218
  John B. 855
  Jonas 910
  Josiah 910
  Josias 70, 910, 911, 921
  Levi A. 820
  Nelson W. 808
  Silas 872
  W. M. A. 855
  William 71, 910, 911
  William A. 813, 814, 815
  William M. 813
Slade Family 907
Slader's Tavern 876
SLAGLE, Belinda M. 379
  C. W. 441, 442
  Charles 598
  Charles F. 602
  Charles N. 379
  Charles W. 378, 379, 487
  Charles William 379
  D. Clinton 379
  D. W. 442
  David 379
  David N. 379
  Hannah (WINEBRENNER) 379
  Henry P. 379
  Jacob W. 379
  Katie S. 379
  Lillie A. 379
  Mary H. 379
  Rachel A. (MATTHEWS) 379
  Ross 379
Slagle, C. W. & Co. 379
SLATER, James 548
  John Y. 646
  William 77, 896, 931, 932
Slater, John Y. & Co. 636

SLATTERY, J. 544
  Michael 236, 536, 807, 932, 938
SLAUGHTER, Albert G. 724
  Emily Gallatin 724
  Sleepy Creek 342
SLEIGER, Peter 808
SLEIGH, ---, Mr. 59
  Thomas 57, 205
SLEMMER, Christian 188
  Ghriste 393
SLICER, ---, Rev. Dr. 144, 837
  Abraham 578
  Andrew 807
  H. 577
  Henry 575, 577, 578, 599, 807, 882, 892, 928
  Henry W. 155
  Thomas R. 877
SLIGH, John 203
  Thomas 203
  Thomms 50
SLINGLUFF, ---, Miss 770
  Anna V. (LANDSTREET) 852
  C. B. 369
  C. Bohn 820, 852
  C. D. 471, 807
  Charles B. 260, 852
  Charles Bohn 852
  Charles D. 222, 462, 852
  Charles Deardorff 852
  Eliza M. (HAINES) 852
  Elizabeth (DEARDORFF) 852
  Fielder 370, 723
  Fielder C. 222, 852
  Frances E. (CROSS) 852
  Frank 852
  Horace 852
  Jesse 370, 461, 477, 808, 852, 905
  Luther 852
  Mary F. (COCKEY) 852
  Sarah A. 477, 852
  Upton 414, 852
Slingluff Family 852
Slingluff, C. D. & Son 852
Slingluff, Devries & Co. 414, 868
Slingluff & Co. 852
Slingluff & Stevenson 852
SLOAN, Charles 808
  George F. 463, 487
  George L. 487
  James 77, 89, 187, 459, 509, 547, 569, 699, 808, 938
  Mary 699
SLOTHOWER, George 356, 807, 820
SLUBEY, Nicholas 483
SLUBY, Nicholas 452
  Nicolas 453
SMALL, ---, Mr. 347
  George 339, 343, 346, 441, 444, 466, 485, 688, 689, 851
  Jacob 187, 192, 225, 276, 438, 470

SMALL, John 807
  Josiah 471
  Josias 253
  Lawrence 346
  Mary Grant (JACKSON) 347
  Moses 612
  P. B. 551
  Philip A. 346
  Philip Albright 807
  Robert 39
  Samuel 253, 346
  Sarah (LATIMER) 346
  William F. 343, 667
Small, George & Co. 346
Small, George & Son 346
Small, P. A. & S. 346
SMALLWOOD, ---, Col. 73
  ---, Gen. 77
  William 72, 74, 118, 195, 246, 730
Smallwood Street 769
SMARDEN, Elias 813
SMART, John G. 549
SMEATON, James 816
SMEDLEY, Enos 369
  Nathan 369
SMILEY, John 160
SMITH, --- 60, 102, 238, 310, 398, 424, 516
  ---, Capt. 931
  ---, Col. 780
  ---, Dr. 547, 742
  ---, Gen. 55, 86, 91, 96, 97, 117, 118, 267, 786, 924
  ---, Maj. Gen. 933
  A. Thomas 506
  Abijah 391
  Abraham 592
  Abram G. 160
  Alan P. 509
  Albert 821
  Alexander 189, 241
  Alexander H. 809
  Allan P. 742, 745, 746
  Allan P., Mrs. 675
  Andrew 92, 642, 776
  Andrew C. 160
  Arthur 592
  Asa H. 194, 250, 255, 368, 828
  B. F. 489
  B. C. 932
  Bartholomew E. 260
  Bayard, Mrs. 156
  C. H. 577
  C. T. 505
  Charles 919
  Charles R. 256
  Charles T. 689
  Christian H. 254
  Conrad 58, 571
  Cornelius J. 916
  Daniel, Col. 82

SMITH, David 244
David C. 808
Demarest J. 160
Dennis A. 437, 456, 457, 935
E. H. 580, 877
Edmund 346
Elizabeth 808
Ephriam 249
F. O. J. 506, 508
F. T. 442
Francis F. J. 506
George 160, 252, 919
George A. 887
George M. 194, 465
George O. 194
Gideon B. 434, 614, 624, 751, 807
H. C. 415, 466
H. H. 877
H. Tillard 194
Henry 468, 487, 808
Henry C. 160, 441, 446, 447, 448, 469, 484, 488, 489, 494, 576
Henry Clay 448, 449
Isaac 77
Isaac H. 160
J. 82, 365
J. Brown 402
J. Dean 599
J. J. 583, 740
J. P. 573
J. S. 680
J. Spear 547, 728
J. T. 550
J. Thomas 455, 456
J. T. 840
Jacob 192
Jacob G. 816
James 177, 343, 735, 742, 779, 808
James P. 252
Jas. 103
Jasper 264
Job 170, 173, 187, 189, 192, 194, 239, 246, 348, 458, 461, 485, 576, 807, 816, 913
John 59, 65, 69, 70, 72, 73, 75, 76, 79, 193, 194, 205, 241, 244, 248, 251, 343, 355, 357, 432, 468, 544, 545, 547, 577, 592, 776, 780, 807, 840, 908, 923
John C. 465, 807
John D. 734
John L. 162, 194
John M. 249
John M., Mrs. 596
John S. 437
John Spear 651, 658, 659, 807
John Thomas 576
John, Capt. 32, 34, 39, 40, 294
John, Col. 56
Joseph 84, 244, 592, 757, 853, 908
Joseph Sim 741

SMITH, Joseph T. 548, 550, 551, 600, 746
Joshua 355
Juliette (PENNIMAN) 748
Lambert 77
Lily B. 402
Louisa 913
Louisa (SMITH) 913
M. H. 342
Margaret 808
Mary B. 808
Mary O. 936
Matthews 807
Mildmay 592
Milton E. 871
N. 291
N. R. 137, 807
Nathan R. 357, 720, 744, 748, 756, 899, 915
Nathaniel 72, 79, 547, 727, 779
Nicholas 249
Nicholas M. 468
Peter 263, 809
Philip 248
R. 82, 103, 262, 925
R. B. 448
R. Henry 166
Ralph 372
Rebecca (HERRING) 853
Richard 592
Robert 82, 95, 172, 187, 193, 194, 195, 214, 238, 239, 253, 298, 437, 470, 547, 699, 707, 807, 845
Robert S. 161, 820
Roger 534, 808
S. 73, 102, 298, 674
S. B. 302
S. J. 584
S. P. 412, 847
S. R. 225, 365
S. W. 680, 850
Samuel 70, 72, 75, 76, 78, 83, 85, 89, 92, 98, 101, 118, 168, 187, 194, 195, 206, 215, 268, 392, 432, 452, 476, 486, 545, 547, 667, 780, 785, 808, 828, 921
Samuel D. 187
Samuel P. 846
Samuel R. 188, 487
Samuel W. 125, 193
Samuel W., Mrs. 155
Sarah Jane (BOGGS) 854
Socrates A. 160
Stephen 746
T. L. 506
Thomas 298, 776, 932
Thomas H. 777
Thomas M. 126, 139, 194, 232, 746, 747

SMITH, Thorogood 76, 82, 102, 172, 187, 293, 452, 453, 455, 592, 679, 682, 728, 808
Tom Walsh 641
W. 102, 707
W. C. 608
W. Hamilton 820
W. P. 697
W. Prescott, Mrs. 155, 156
Walter E. 178
William 60, 69, 70, 72, 74, 76, 77, 79, 80, 101, 102, 103, 116, 117, 195, 214, 246, 298, 392, 452, 544, 545, 547, 549, 726, 727, 778, 807, 808, 814, 815, 892, 921, 934
William B. 592, 845
William C. 592
William H. 817
William H. V. 472
William Kilty 808
William M. 160
William Prescott 272, 336, 628, 674, 675, 807
William R. 77, 247, 808
Winston D. 249
Smith, Johnson & Co. 102
Smith, Matthews & Co. 101
Smith, R. & Co. 103
Smith, S. & Co. 101
Smith, T. N. & Co. 212
Smith, William Prescott Monument 272
Smith & Buchanan 298
Smith & Curlett 262
Smith's Dock 174
Smith's Point 310
Smith's Shop 311
Smith's Wharf 261, 287, 433
Smithfield Baptist, Isle of Wight Co., Va. 556
Smithsburg 357
SMITHURST, Tabitha 386
SMOOT, John 102
SMUCKER, Samuel S. 807
SMULL, G. W. 746
W. G. 745
SMYRK, A. E. 191
Alfred E. 728
SMYSER, Henry C. 161
M. L. 928
William H. 160
Smyser's 347
SMYTH, ---, Dr. 733, 751
James 742, 823, 824
SMYTHE, Herbert B. 523
SNETHEN, Nicholas 583, 616
SNIDER, Nicholas 729
Snike's Temperance House 761
SNODGRASS, ---, Dr. 617, 627
Catherine (HART) 774
J. E. 651

SNODGRASS, J. Evans 625
Mary Ann 774
Sarah M. 808
William 774, 808
SNOW, E. J. 442
Snow, John N. & Co. 439
SNOWDEN, Ann (RIDGELY) 669
DeWilton 669
Eleanor 808
Eliza (WARFIELD) 669
Emily Roseville 669
Francis 116, 174, 808, 812
H. 841
Henry 593, 807
John B. 819
Lawrence 66
Mary (RICHARDSON) 722
Patience (HOPKINS) 722
Philip 722, 728
Richard 669, 722, 828
Richard H. 807
S. Emma (HOFF) 722
Samuel 367, 488, 719, 722, 723
Thomas 324, 669
Snowden Family 588
Snowy Creek 342
Snuggrass Family 774
SNYDER, ---, Rev. Mr. 573
A. G. 523
Charles 573
George W. 191
Henry 189, 193, 210, 211, 343, 364, 807
John 76, 187, 197, 246, 592
John C. 734
Richard 249
William L. 160
Sociable Society 678
Social Democratic Turners' Union Library 667
Society for Organizing Charities of Baltimore City 702
Society for Protection of Children from Cruelty & Immorality 154
Society for Relief of Widows & Orphans 577
Society for the Education of Hebrew Poor & Orphan Children 598
Society for the Protection of Children 600, 602
Society Hill 896
Society of Baptists 591
Society of Friends 133, 587, 588, 883, 884, 886
Society of Jesus 833
Society of St. Sulpice 234
Society of St. Vincent de Paul 539
Society of the Army & Navy of the Confederate States 668

Society of the Children of Mary 539
Society of the Cincinnati 668
Society of the Covenanters of Baltimore 551
Society of the Rosary 538
Society of the Sacred Heart of Jesus 539
Society of the Sanctuary 539
Sodality of the Blessed Virgin 538, 539
Sodality of the Immaculate Conception 543
Sodality of the Sacred Heart 537
SOHL, John 740
SOHN, John 929
Soldiers' Delight 15, 26, 30, 31, 709, 730, 866
Soldiers' Delight Hundred 70, 71, 519, 812, 857, 859
Soldiers' Home 154
Soldiers' Rest Rooms 149
SOLLER, John 571
Soller's Flats 292
SOLLERS, --- 808
  Basil 246
  George L. 160
  Thomas 69, 70, 71, 73, 189, 728, 808, 814
  Thomas O. 808
  Thomas P. O. 202
Sollers Point Road 518
SOLOMON, Isaac 358, 569, 808
  Levi 808
SOLOMON, Martin 380
Solomon's Lamp Lighthouse 310
Sombrero Guano Co. 398
SOMERLOCK, John F. 193
SOMERS, ---, Rev. Mr. 902
Somerset & Cambria Railroad 340
SOMERVILL, James 808
SOMERVILLE, ---, Mr. 822
  Charles S. 358
  H. V. 850
  Henry V. 120
  James 239
  John N. 845
SOMMER, John 161
SOMMERLOCK, J. F. 191, 193
SOMMERS, John 817
SOMMERVILLE, H. V. 816
  James 76
SONNEBORN, Henry 448, 841
Sons of Liberty 668, 761
Sontag, William L. & Co. 298
SOPER, Samuel J. 194
  W. Horace 813
SOPPING, W. 759
SORAN, Charles 189, 190, 808
SORRELL, Francis 253
SORTER, G. A. 688

SOUJEAU, J. 102
SOULE, Joshua 576
Soup-Houses 592
SOURIN, E. 627
  Edward J. 538
South, The 632, 635
South Baltimore Free Methodist Society 585
South Baltimore Land Co. 358
South Baltimore M.P. Church 584
South Baltimore Mutual Permanent Loan & Savings Association 512
South Church 550
South Fremont Street Building Association No. 7 512
South Fremont Street Loan & Savings Co. 512
South Liberty Street Permanent Building Association 512
South Mountain 318
South Paca Street Building Association 512
South Riber 358
South River 88, 639, 669
South Sharp Street Workingmen's Savings Association Nos. 1 & 2 512
South Wolfe Street Building Association 512
SOUTHARD, L. H. 666
  W. H. 688
SOUTHCOMB, --- 104
  Carey 189
  John 106
SOUTHERLAND, S. B. 583, 838
Southern & Atlantic Telegraph Line 504
Southern Baptist Convention 564
Southern Baptist Theological Seminary 566
Southern Daily Pony Express 620
Southern Dispensary 748
Southern Educational Monthly, The 637
Southern Educational Society 674
Southern Herald 635, 639
Southern Home Journal 636, 646
Southern Literary Messenger 646
Southern Magazine 637, 657
Southern Maryland Commission Agency 512
Southern Maryland Railroad 358, 359
Southern Metropolis & Catholic Miscellany, The 637
Southern Relief Association 155
Southern Review 636, 637, 657
Southern Society 636
Southern Star, The 641
Souvenir 644
SOWER, Christopher 605

SOWER, Samuel 807
SOWERVELL, James 70
SPAIGHT, Richard Dobbs 773
SPALDING, ---, Archbishop 151, 530, 533, 537, 539, 540, 543, 598, 826, 837, 892, 937
---, Dr. 544
---, Miss 595
B. R., Mrs. 156
M. J. 627
Martin J. 542, 938
Martin John 529, 647, 807
Richard 529
SPANGLER, Baltzer 312
J. A. 918
J. N. 586
James D. 160
Michael H. 92
Spark's Station 883
Sparks 347
SPARKS, ---, Master 915
---, Mr. 590
Aaron 915
Alfred 872
Edward R. 728
Elijah 915, 916
Elizabeth 915
Elizabeth (SPARKS) 915
Elizabeth (WIER) 915
Francis E. 915
Jared 589, 642, 643, 644, 647, 651, 723
Josiah 911, 915
Josias 911
Maggie A. (SCOTT) 915
Marcelena A. 915
Matthew 916
Sparks Family 907, 916
Sparks' American Biography 589
Sparrow's Point 292, 301
SPEAKE, George 250
SPEAR, A. L. 761
John 70
Joseph 77
Otis 487
William 59, 69, 70, 74, 100, 167, 547, 728, 780, 808, 814
William, Mrs. 808
Spear, William & Co. 103
Spear's Wharf 59, 195, 287, 307
SPEARS, William 189
SPECK, Henry 727
Spectator, The 641
SPEDDEN, Edward 189, 190, 462
John 808
Levin 99
SPEDDIN, Levin 103
SPEED, ---, Attorney-General 151
J. J. 808
Joseph J. 485
SPENCE, ---, Capt. 89

SPENCE, Aza 600
Carroll 194, 195, 705
Charles S. 194, 896
Robert T. 807, 813
Robert Trail 807
W. W. 441, 494, 549, 817, 828
W. W., Mrs. 156, 595
William W. 501, 546, 547
SPENCER, ---, Miss 156
C. Jervis 126
Edward 186, 611, 624, 656, 903
J. 695
J. H. 365
J. R. 365
Jervis 355, 814, 820
Samuel 342
W. P. 365
William H. 149
SPERRY, J. Austin 624, 625
William 695
Spesutia Island 35, 41, 42, 924
Spesutia Lower Hundred 812
Spesutia Upper Hundred 812
Spesutiae Hundred 918
SPICER, Ishmael 672
Samuel 190, 253
Samuel G. 728
Thomas 729, 807
Spicer's Inheritance 49
SPIES, J. Godfrey 191
SPILKER, Charles 807
SPILLER, Robert M. 489, 807
SPILLMAN, Henry 915
SPILMAN, --- 39
Henry 245, 257, 264
Henry C. 487
James 189
T. J. 190
Spiritualists 592
SPOON, ---, Rev. Mr. 521
SPOONER, John A. 160
S. 102
Sportsman's Hall 816
SPOTTSWOOD, T. B. 830
SPRAGUE, Augustus 144
Volney 915
SPRAIGHT, Jeremiah 587
SPRECHER, ---, Rev. 569
SPRECKELSON, G. A. B. 485
George A. B. 485
SPRECKLSEN, George V. 463
SPRIGG, Daniel 464, 807
Joseph A. 481, 482
Otho 782
Samuel 195, 850
SPRIGGS, --- 223, 859
SPRING, Robert 693
Spring Garden 50, 56
Spring Gardens 16, 17, 29, 48, 91, 144, 278, 288, 402, 501

Spring Grange No. 153, Patrons of Husbandry 870
Spring Grove 824, 825
Spring Grove State Insane Asylum 662, 823
Spring Hill 64, 413
Spring Lake 274
SPRINGER, David C. 194, 498
Springfield 904, 912, 913
Springfield Copper Mine 772
SPROSTON, ---, Lieut. 807
 John Glendy 808
SPRUGT, F. 938
SPRY, Francis 808
SPURNE, John 36
Spurrier's Town 311
SPURRIRER, W. 189
Spy, The 624
ST. CLAIR, ---, Mr. 694
 Robert 934
 William 871
St. Agnes Catholic Church 796, 822, 826
St. Agnes Catholic Hospital Chapel 544
St. Agnes Hospital 744, 748, 937
St. Alphonsus' Catholic Church 264, 540, 541, 543, 544, 598, 673, 917
St. Alphonsus' Hall 541, 673
St. Andrew's Catholic Church 539
St. Andrew's Infirmary 601
St. Andrew's P.E. Church 258, 522, 525, 891
St. Andrew's Society 668, 754
St. Ann's Academy 889
St. Ann's Catholic Church 539, 889
St. Ann's Church, Annapolis 671
St. Ann's Episcopal Church 911
St. Ann's Ladies' Beneficial Society 543
St. Ann's P.E. Church 863
St. Ann's Parish 704, 904
St. Anthony's Orphan Asylum 598
St. Anthony's Orphan Asylum Library 667
St. Asaph Junction 354
St. Augustine's Catholic Church 937
St. Augustine's Church 795
St. Barnabas' P.E. Church 525
St. Bartholomew's Church 526
St. Bartholomew's P.E. Church 637
St. Bernard's Catholic Church 539, 891
St. Bridget Catholic Church, Canton 536
St. Bridget's Catholic Church 529, 539, 540, 928
St. Catharine's Normal Institute Library 667

St. Catharine's Normal School 237
St. Charles College 382, 235, 236, 529
St. Charles Hotel 539
St. Clair Hotel 142, 516
St. Clement's P.E. Church 931
St. Cyril & Method Beneficial Society 543
St. Denis 936
St. Edward's Catholic Church 840
St. Francis Xavier Catholic Church 538, 543
St. Francis' Catholic Chapel 544
St. Francis' Convent & Academy 598
St. George's Mission Chapel 526
St. George's Parish 812, 815, 918, 919, 920
St. George's Society 668
St. Henry's Society 543
St. Ignatius' Catholic Church 538, 543, 544
St. James 908, 909
St. James' Academy 874, 915
St. James' Catholic Church 541, 542, 544
St. James' College 702
St. James' Episcopal Church 907, 911
St. James' Episcopal College 888
St. James' First African Church 525
St. James' Graveyard 911
St. James' Hall Building Association Nos. 4, 5, 6, 7, & 8 512
St. James' Home for Boys 938
St. James' P.E. Church 909, 915, 916
St. James' P.E. College 914
St. James' Parish 857, 859, 860, 861, 910, 920
St. James' Savings Institution 512
St. James' School 916
St. Johannes' German Reformed Church 572
St. John Baptist P.E. Church 524
St. John the Evangelist Catholic Church 540
St. John's Catholic Church 532, 538, 539, 597, 917
St. John's Church 523, 825, 912
St. John's College 639, 643, 666, 714, 715, 716, 722, 749, 863
St. John's Dutch Reformed Church 561
St. John's English Evangelical Lutheran Church 584
St. John's Episcopal Church 840, 918
St. John's German Evangelical Lutheran Church 570
St. John's German Reformed Church 840

St. John's in the Valley 862, 879
St. John's Independent Methodist Church 585
St. John's Literary Institute 539, 721
St. John's Lodge of Freemasons 184
St. John's M.E. Chapel 585
St. John's M.E. Church 801, 877
St. John's Methodist Church 580, 583
St. John's Mission of the M.E. Church 883
St. John's P.E. Church 524, 839, 861, 866, 888, 909, 910, 921, 923
St. John's P.E. Church in the Valley 865
St. John's Parish 517, 518, 812, 857, 865, 910, 911, 918, 919, 920
St. John's Reformed Church 830
St. John's School 223
St. John's Society 543
St. Joseph Passionist Monastery 534
St. Joseph's 916, 933
St. Joseph's Academy Library 667
St. Joseph's Beneficial Society 543
St. Joseph's Catholic Church 536, 537, 538, 807, 833, 890, 917, 932
St. Joseph's Cemetery 542
St. Joseph's College 529
St. Joseph's Convent, Emmitsburg 235
St. Joseph's Female Orphan Asylum 529
St. Joseph's Hospital 747
St. Joseph's House of Industry 597
St. Joseph's Passionist Monastery 820, 825
St. Joseph's Seminary 529
St. Joseph's Society 543
St. Josephs' Catholic Church 882
St. Lawrence's Catholic Chapel 539
St. Leo's Italian Catholic Church 543
St. Leonard's 358
St. Leonard's Creek 88
St. Luke's Academy 865
St. Luke's German Evangelical Church 570
St. Luke's Mission Chapel 526
St. Luke's P.E. Church 236, 523, 828
St. Marcus' German Evangelical Lutheran 570
St. Mark's English Lutheran Church 548, 569
St. Mark's on the Hill 836
St. Mark's P.E. Church 523, 835
St. Martin's Canal & Navigation Company 314

St. Martin's Catholic Church 537, 539, 597
St. Martin's German Evangelical Lutheran Church 570
St. Martin's Perpetual Building Association 512
St. Mary's 704, 856
St. Mary's Asylum 595
St. Mary's Catholic Chapel 539, 544
St. Mary's Catholic Church 536, 892
St. Mary's Chapel 235, 236
St. Mary's City 359
St. Mary's College 138, 234, 235, 236, 528, 644, 648, 650, 654, 698, 701, 702, 716, 718, 721, 726, 744, 750, 799, 801, 805, 909
St. Mary's Female Orphan Asylum 594, 889
St. Mary's Female Orphan Asylum Library 667
St. Mary's Industrial School for Boys 826, 937, 938
St. Mary's Orphaline Female School 594
St. Mary's P.E. Church 828, 837
St. Mary's Seminary 234, 236, 527, 529, 531, 533, 535, 536, 797, 803, 805
St. Mary's Seminary Library 667
St. Mary's Social & Literary Association 641
St. Mary's Star of the Sea Cathedral 537, 539
St. Mary's Theological Seminary 534
St. Mary's, Baltimore 532
St. Matthew's 522
St. Matthew's Evangelical Lutheran Church 543
St. Matthew's German Evangelical Church 811
St. Matthew's German Evangelical Lutheran Church 570
St. Matthew's P.E. Chapel 524
St. Matthew's P.E. Mission Chapel 525
St. Michael's 293, 309
St. Michael's & All Angels' P.E. 524
St. Michael's Catholic Church 542
St. Michael's German Catholic Hall 543
St. Michael's German Catholic Parish 929
St. Michael's P.E. Church 867
St. Michael's Society 543
St. Nicholas 515
St. Nicholas Hotel 265, 517
St. Patrick's Beneficial Society 882
St. Patrick's Benevolent Society 535
St. Patrick's Catholic Cemetery 535
St. Patrick's Catholic Church 529, 532, 534, 536, 540, 601, 796, 932

St. Patrick's Catholic Church Cemetery 933
St. Patrick's Church 797
St. Patrick's Free School 535
St. Patrick's Hall 536
St. Paul's (School) 224
St. Paul's Cemetery 649
St. Paul's Church 518, 521
St. Paul's E.P. Church 672
St. Paul's English Lutheran Church 570
St. Paul's English Reformed Church 572
St. Paul's Episcopal Church 389, 571, 572, 573, 574, 589, 709, 720, 795
St. Paul's German Evangelical Church 570
St. Paul's German United Evangelical Church 890
St. Paul's Lutheran Church 868
St. Paul's M.E. Church 803
St. Paul's M.E. Church, South 586
St. Paul's P.E. Church 262, 574, 809, 879, 888, 920
St. Paul's Parish 517, 526, 557, 812, 857, 858, 860, 862, 863, 919
St. Peter's 234, 519
St. Peter's Cathedral Male Academy 529
St. Peter's Catholic Church 527, 528, 530, 532, 535, 537, 539
St. Peter's Cemetery 538, 826
St. Peter's English Evangelical Lutheran Church 570
St. Peter's German Evangelical Lutheran Church 570, 933
St. Peter's Lutheran Church 870
St. Peter's Lutheran Mission 571
St. Peter's P.E. Church 274, 522, 523, 576
St. Peter's P.E. Church Home 593
St. Peter's Protestant Episcopal Church 154
St. Peter's School & Orphan Asylum 592
St. Peter's Society 538
St. Philip's Catholic CHurch 909
St. Philip's Church 525
St. Stanislaus' Koska Polish Catholic Church 543
St. Stephen's German Evangelical Lutheran Church 570, 571
St. Stephen's P.E. Church 523, 564
St. Stephen's Parish 805
St. Tammany Society 761
St. Thomas Aquinas Catholic Church 837
St. Thomas P.E. Church 836, 868
St. Thomas Parish 796
St. Thomas' Churchyard 861, 863
St. Thomas' Colored M.P. Church 584
St. Thomas' Graveyard Epitaphs 864
St. Thomas' P.E. Church 574, 798, 815, 861, 863, 864, 865
St. Thomas' Parish 223, 519, 812, 841, 854, 857, 858, 859, 860, 861, 862, 863, 867, 911
St. Timothy's Church 821
St. Timothy's Hall 821, 922
St. Timothy's P.E. Church 822
St. Venceslaus' Beneficial Society 543
St. Venceslaus' Bohemian Catholic Church 543
St. Vincent de Paul Catholic Church 537
St. Vincent de Paul's Beneficial Society 882
St. Vincent's Catholic Church 534, 536, 541
St. Vincent's Church 799
St. Vincent's Conference 542
St. Vincent's Hospital 744, 748
St. Vincent's Infant Asylum 600
St. Vincent's Male Orphan Asylum Library 667
St. Vincent's Temperance Society 537
STABLER, A. G. 872
A. G., Mrs. 600
A. J. 872
Daniel 815
E. H. 362
Edward 603
Jordan 449
Stabler Family 588
Stablersville 875
STACEY, William 861
STACY, William 864
STAFFORD, --- 104
---, Dr. 132
---, Lady 808, 821, 937
Joseph 112
W. S. 105, 108
William J. 807
Stafford, ---, Baron of 802
STAHLER, Henry 817
STALEY, George L. 840
Thomas 818, 919, 920
Stamford Farm 863
Stanard's Mill 357
Standard 638
Standard Oil Co. 385
STANDIFORD, Adolphus M. 874
Benjamin 874
Daniel 874
Edward 911
Emma 874
Hannah 874

STANDIFORD, Irving 874
  J. 873, 874
  James 874
  James A. 814, 874
  James R. 807
  John 73
  Molly Jane 874
  Rachel (AMOS) 874
  Rosa 874
  Sarah 874
  Sarah A. (LOW) 874
  Thomas 874
  William 911, 921
STANLEY, Charles 688
  J. W. 103
  John P., Mrs. 596
  Robert 592
  Stanley & Co. 399
  Stanleys & Baker 399
STANSBURY, --- 809
  ---, Col. 913
  ---, Gen. 868
  Ann S. 808
  Arabella 477
  Carville 903
  Carville S. 931
  Corville 137
  Daniel 808
  Dixon 70, 202, 477, 820, 910, 921
  Edward 71, 910, 911
  Elijah 187, 188, 192, 194, 432, 593, 690, 758, 807, 808, 886, 934
  Eliza 807
  J. B. 252
  J. E. 190, 808
  J. J. 112
  Jacob 247, 808
  James B. 343, 484, 808
  John 463
  John E. 188, 189, 192
  John L. 813
  John S. 834
  Nicholas 251, 461
  S. 807
  T. 103
  Thomas 894, 908
  Tobias 88, 518, 809
  Tobias A. 807
  Tobias E. 84, 92, 195, 205, 457, 592, 808, 819, 934
  William 188, 248, 249, 593, 911
STANSEY, Lewis 840
STANSFIELD, Thomas B. 830
STANTON, ---, Secretary 163
  Benjamin 256
  David L. 160
  Edwin M. 164
  James 191, 193
STANWITCH, Hilt 58
STAPLES, ---, Capt. 109
  S. W. 303

STAPLETON, J. K. 241
  James K. 402
  Joseph K. 92, 176, 188, 240, 244, 393, 470, 808
  Joseph R. 241
  P. K. 667
STAR, Rachel 724
Star Spangled Banner 609, 685, 686
Star Tavern 361
STARCK, ---, Mr. 732
  Jacob 514
  John 77, 311, 672, 808
STARK, ---, Mr. 407
  John 244, 809
STARKEY, John 920, 921
STARKWEATHER, Norris G. 160
STARR, Edward W. 245
  J. J. 871
  John 807
  Phillippa 582
  Robert 484
  S. W. 855
  Samuel 195
  Samuel W. 866
  Wesley 471, 582, 583, 807
  William 89, 241, 807
  William H. (M.) 194
  William M. 189, 253, 256
Starr M.P. Church 583
Starr, R. & Co. 372
STARRS, William 236
State Agricultural Association 829, 835, 846
State Agricultural Fair 846
State Attorneys 814
State Grange 917
State Mutual Fire Insurance Co. 490
State Normal School 231
State Prison Library 667
State Senators from Baltimore County, 1811-1882 820
Statesman 637
Statesman & Maryland Advertiser 613
STAUFFER, Jacob 247
Staunton 342
STAUNTON, James 191
  M. 538
Stauropolis, ---, Bishop of 527
STAYLOR, H. 190
  Henry 189, 808
  Henry M. 193
  John 194
  John J. 190
  William 808
STECKHEIM, ---, Mr. 422
STECKINFINGER, Bena 423
STEDMAN, J. F. 889
STEEL, John 238, 780
STEELE, --- 698, 723
  ---, Mr. 716

STEELE, Ann 871
  I. Nevett 195, 725
  I. Nevitt 126, 137, 887
  Isaac Nevett 715
  J. Nevett 707
  James 715
  John 170, 239, 483, 544, 871
  Mary (NEVETT) 715
  Robert 580
  T. 102
  Thomas 100, 101, 102
STEER, William 380
STEEVER, George 92
STEIFF, C. M. 263
  Charles M. 808
STEIGELMAN, J. A. 249
STEIGER, --- 54
  ---, Mr. 60
  Andrew 61, 208, 571, 730, 808
  Jacob 807
  Mary 808
Steiger's Meadow 52, 54, 60, 61
STEIN, Edward 160
  Myer 155
STEINER, ---, Capt. 113
  David C. 160
  Henry 91
  L. H. 840
STELLMAN, Francis G. 417
  J. W. 417
  John 417, 418, 487
  Sarah Ann (CAPPEAU) 418
Stellman, Henricks & Co. 264, 417
Stellman, John & Sons 417
Stellman & Henricks 417
STELLWAGEN, Daniel S. 472
Stemmer's Run 351
Stemmer's Run Station 931
STENGEL, Gottlieb 818
STENHOUSE, ---, Dr. 730
  Alexander 547, 740
STENSON, --- 514
  William 77, 432, 526
STEPHEN, J. W. 112
  John 83, 194
STEPHENS, Albert 807
  Alexander 808
  Alexander H. 657
  Daniel 919
  George G. 194
  James M. 160
  John 202, 729
  Joseph R. 255
STEPHENSON, --- 344
  Henry 814
  James 524
  John 547
  Josiah 249
  Sater 931
Stephenson's 342
Stepney Parish, Somerset Co. 521

STERET, James 261, 545
STERETT, --- 103
  ---, Lt. 84
  ---, Lt. Col. 88
  Clement 808
  David 679
  Deborah 719
  Deborah (RIDGELY) 719
  Isaac S. 114
  J. 101, 102, 678
  James 71, 92, 98, 167, 205, 244, 461, 544, 547, 807, 808, 845
  John 79, 100, 101, 102, 168, 292, 452, 547, 719, 727, 808
  Joseph 77, 91, 298, 455, 679, 807
  Polly 719, 917
  Samuel 82, 83, 86, 89, 92, 117, 118, 202, 235, 298, 545, 679, 680, 808
  William 70, 808
Sterett, John & Co. 101, 102
STERITT, Samuel 203, 807
STERLING, A. 140, 152, 547, 717
  Arch. 593
  Archibald 139, 195, 199, 369, 466, 893
  James 239
  R. H. 746
  Thomas J. 160
  William 808
Sterling, Ahrens & Co. 418
Sterling Manufacturing Co. 512
STERN, B. 149
  Simon 468
STERNHEIMER, Nathan 149
STERRET, John 808
STERRETT, ---, Capt. 77
  ---, Gen. 808
  ---, Miss 71
  John 61, 194, 392, 808
  M., Mrs. 808
  Mary B. 909
  Rebecca (SEARS) 909
  Samuel 77, 194, 909
STEUART, ---, Dr. 730
  ---, Maj. Gen. 130
  G. H. 361
  George 704
  George H. 92, 132, 152, 194, 680
  J. J. 192
  James 734, 735
  James A. 187
  John M. 189
  Robert 194
  W. H. 190
  William 187, 188, 265, 267
  William H. 189
STEUBEN, --- 769
Steuben Lodge No. 41, U.O.G.B. 821
STEVENS, ---, Mr. 136, 494
  C. P. 576
  F. P. 194, 495

STEVENS, F. P., Mrs. 600
　F. Putnam 193, 194
　Francis P. 153, 193
　J. 846
　J. C. 850
　J. M. 272
　John 592
　John O. 506
　Joseph 246
　Nicholas B. 160
　Richard 89, 188, 808
　Robertson 101
　S. S. 153
　Samuel 195
　Samuel S. 807
　William 193
Stevens' Ship Yard 293
STEVENSON, ---, Mr. 60
　Ann 808, 809
　Cosmo G. 192
　Edward 38, 728, 818
　George 545
　George P. 437, 733
　Henry 38, 76, 203, 544, 728, 730,
　　733, 734, 741, 771, 808, 809, 816,
　　842, 862
　Henry S. 808
　J. M. 550
　J. S. 740
　John 38, 71, 72, 73, 75, 76, 194,
　　223, 369, 432, 544, 545, 730, 765,
　　768, 808, 814, 816, 819, 887, 910
　John M. 142, 160
　John W. 166
　Joshua 71, 809, 902
　Julia Ann 842
　Sater 265, 808
　W. 222
　Wesley 218
　William 523
Stevenson, Steward & Co. 101
Stevenson & Slingluff 852
Stevenson's Folly 730
Stevenson's Station 834, 841
STEVER, George 189, 249
STEWARD, S. 101, 102
Steward, S. & Co. 102
Steward, S. & Son 103
STEWART, ---, Lt. Col. 91
　---, Mr. 692, 759
　---, Mrs. 595
　A. 641
　A. S. 190, 191
　Adam 403
　Ann 808
　Archibald 455, 569
　C. M. 456
　C. Morton 195, 232, 304, 483, 484,
　　489, 577
　C. R. 516
　Charles 78

STEWART, Charles Morton 303, 494
　Charles R. 351
　D. 101, 102, 103, 365
　D. & Co. 101
　David 75, 83, 173, 192, 193, 195,
　　291, 293, 392, 452, 454, 455, 463,
　　486, 545, 546, 547, 660, 740, 779,
　　808, 809
　Dugald 773
　Edward 253
　Emily Gallatin (SLAUGHTER) 724
　Emily Slaughter 724
　George H. 807, 933
　George H., Mrs. 808
　H. H. 304
　Henry C. 160
　J. D. 191
　James 380, 403, 592, 629, 734, 735,
　　742, 845, 911
　James A. 733, 745, 746
　James A., Mrs. 156
　James E. 113, 114, 134, 807
　James L. 258
　John 71, 92, 102, 191, 193, 467, 809,
　　910, 911, 921
　John D. 245, 264, 807
　Joseph J. 164
　Lafayette 641
　Mary Ellen 467
　Nancy (GLASGO) 467
　R. 595
　R. S. 358, 745, 824, 825, 847
　R. St. John 241
　Richardson 187, 592, 808
　Robert 89, 170, 187, 214, 249, 456,
　　727, 808
　Robert St. John 241, 242, 249
　Sarah 808
　Stephen 79, 392
　T. R. 846
　Thomas 745
　Thomas H. 160
　W. A. 723
　W. E. 938
　W. H. 409
　W. R. 845
　William 120, 187, 194, 241, 249, 250,
　　316, 317, 318, 393, 457, 470, 667,
　　727, 738, 758, 808
　William A. 190, 194, 721, 723, 724,
　　831
　William B. 840
　William E. 178, 191, 194
　William H. 160
　William R. 737
　William S. 808
Stewart, Charles J. & Co. 636
Stewart, D. & Co. 101
Stewart, David & Co. 100
Stewart, David & Sons 298, 433
Stewart, John & Co. 101

Stewart, William & Co. 439, 854
Stewart & Plunket 433, 766
Stewart & Salmon 79, 102
Stewart Bros. 641
STICHER, John 250
STICKNEY, H. F. 365, 466
  J. Henry 484
Stickney Iron Co. 426, 512
Stickney's Iron-Furnace 926
STIDHAM, J. F. 555
STIEFEL, Dora 821
  Edward W. 820
  Edwin V. 813
  Julius 934
STIER, Henry J. d'Aertzlaer 702
  Rosalie Eugenia 702
STIFFLER, John N. 161
STIGELLI, --- 673
STILES, ---, Lt. 93
  F. 100
  George 84, 87, 98, 187, 254, 305, 592, 807
  Henry S. 348
Still House Lane 759
STILLE, ---, Dr. 700
STILLMAN, John 456
STILLSON, J. B. 153
STILTZ, Lizzie E. 872
STINCHCOMB, George W. 178
  J. 189
  John 519
  John D. 160
  Joshua 189
  N. P. 820
  Nathaniel 38, 519, 857
STINECKE, Henry A. 808
STINGER, ---, Mr. 493
STINGLE, Christian 380
STIRLING, ---, Brig. Gen., Lord 73
  ---, Mr. 273, 719
  A. 253, 470
  Anne Steele (LLOYD) 718
  Archibald 128, 149, 193, 194, 281, 440, 470, 549, 718, 723, 729
  D. 193
  James 718
  John 872
  Joseph 215
STITT, Adam 902
  J. B. 575, 837, 839, 902
STOCK, T. 154
Stock Exchange 927
Stock Exchange Improvement Co. 482
STOCKBRIDGE, George H. 233
  Henry 140, 194, 195, 814
  Henry, Mrs. 596, 605
  Jason 902
  Louisa 426
STOCKDALE, George L. 814
  George W. 855

STOCKDALE, James 194
STOCKETT, Francis 818
  J. Shaff 190
  Lewis 818
  Thomas 818
  Thomas Noble 741
STOCKSDALE, Silas H. 886
STOCKTON, ---, Mr. 311
  Aaron 251
  E. H., Miss 650
  R. 849
  Richard C. 311, 808
  T. H. 616
  Thomas H. 551
  William F. 311
  William S. 583, 616
Stockton, Falls & Co. 849
Stockton & Stokes 311, 319, 492
Stockton & Stokes Coach Factory 212
STODDARD, Benjamin 808, 809
  Isaac T. 537
  J. T. 673
  Rebecca 809
STODDER, David 168, 293, 780
  James 172
STODDERT, David 809
STOGSTILL, Eli 867
Stokely Manor 918
STOKES, ---, Dr. 834
  ---, Mr. 924
  George C. 838, 840, 866
  I. Wells 814
  James 462
  John 44, 45, 223, 814, 920
  John W. 270
  Mary 921
  William A. 627
  William B. 311
Stokes & Lowndes 481
STOLL, Rosa 231
STOLT, B. 597
STONE, --- 707
  ---, Bishop 154, 879
  James A. 252
  James H. 137, 249, 368, 807
  John H. 76, 195
  Llewellyn P. 160
  Michael Jenifer 118
  Murray 521
  Thomas 193, 707
  W. B. 600
  William 70, 99, 195, 639
  William B. 351
  William Murry 808
Stone Chapel Baptist 868
Stone Owl, The 641
STONEBRAKER, George 569
  Joseph H. 161
  Samuel 479, 807
  Washington 161

STONEBURNER, Jacob G. 473
STONEBURY, Jane 769
Stony Creek 88
Stony Run 354
Stony Works 836
STORCH, Emma 927
STORK, C. A. 830
  Charles A. 569
  T. 569
STORM, Jeremiah 368
  S. P. 817
  Samuel 814
  Samuel W. 814
STORY, ---, Judge 861
  Enoch 605, 606
  George L. 592
  Robert F. 592
  William E. 233
STOUFFER, ---, Mr. 343, 629
  Ann Clair 807
  Barbara 808
  Charles F. 591, 628
  George Close 807
  George T. 591
  Henry 89, 187, 192, 206, 239, 298, 312, 461, 808
  Jacob 807
  John 250, 591
  Stouffer, J. & J. 439
  Stouffer & Closs 298
  Stouffer Family 852
STOURTON, ---, Lord 527
STOUT, Henry 675
  John 101
STOVER, Jacob 922
STRAHAN, Ebenezer 582
STRAKOSCH, --- 673
STRAN, Frank 889
  Thomas D. 240
  Thomas P. 189, 240, 241, 484, 808
  William 246
  William H. 258, 484
Strasburg 342
Strasburg Academy 839
Strasburg Junction 342
STRASSBURGER, L. 597
STRAUS, Henry 468, 841
  Levi 468
Strawberry Alley 574
Strawberry Alley M.E. Church 580
STRAWBRIDGE, Robert 573, 575, 931
Strawbridge M.E. Church 578
Strawbridge's Log Meeting-House 573
STRAYER, W. M. 583
STREBECK, George 58
  William 247
STREEPER, Charles 178, 191, 193
STREET, Charles 911
  Samuel 572

STREET, Thomas 365
  William 253
STREETER, S. F. 153, 807
  Sebastian F. 190, 659, 807
STRICKER, ---, Brig. Gen. 89
---, Capt. 83, 668, 733
---, Col. 83, 547
---, Gen. 93, 94, 95, 96, 97, 98, 267, 783, 808
  Charlotte 808
  John 77, 83, 84, 92, 118, 172, 187, 194, 197, 238, 239, 261, 268, 293, 298, 310, 438, 455, 470, 545, 569, 733, 808, 820
  Martha 808
STRICKLAND, William 348
STRINGER, Richard 74
  Thomas C. 886
STRINGFELLOW, ---, Rev. Mr. 521
  J. S. 524
STROBEL, John 500
STROBLE, John P. 252
STROHMEYER, George 597
STRONG, Leonard 35
STROWD, Jacob 911
STRUDDEHOFF, Barney 246
STRYKER, Augustus P. 525
Sts. Peter & Paul's Society 543
STUART, --- 143
  David 101, 288
  George 160
  George H. 254
  James 920
  James A. 743
  Robert 724
  William 452, 484
Stuart's Nail-Factory 425
STUBBS, Francis 888
Stueben Lodge No. 41 U.O.G.B. 605
STUERKEN, Claus 570
STUMP, ---, Miss 913
---, Mr. 376
  A. H. 471
  Alexander H. 464
  Douglass H. 464
  Henry 717, 807
  Herman 808
  John 77, 170, 238, 455
  Samuel 189, 241, 458
  William 834
STUYVESANT, --- 40
STYER, George 452
STYLES, ---, Capt. 99
  Hester 596
Sudbrook 836
SUDSBURG, Joseph M. 160
Suffolk, Va. 896
Sugar Loaf 342
SULLIVAN, Frank 440
  George M. 254
  James M. 187

SULLIVAN, John 160
  John C. 820
  John H. 160
  John McKew 808
  P. H. 481
  P. H., Mrs. 596
  Patrick H. 440
  Paul James 608
  Robert 193, 276
  Thomas H. 250
  William 190, 317
SULLIVANE, James 741
Sulphur Spring 30
Sulphur Spring Road 820, 936
SULTZER, Thomas D. 140, 190
  W. H. H. 495
SUMMER, John S. 659
Summerfield 843
Summers & Bryan 396
Summers & Townsend 263
SUMMERVILLE, Richard 249
Summerville German Lutheran Church 904
Summit Grange No. 164, Patrons of Husbandry 870
SUMNER, Henry P. 470
  John S. 538
  John Steel 659
SUMWAIT, Frederick 247
SUMWALT, David 385
  George 245
  George W. 153
  J. B. 830
  Joshua B. 363, 364, 366
  Samuel 578
  Thomas S. 254
Sun Building 286
Sun Iron Building 493, 507, 606, 618, 621
Sun, The 610, 614, 617, 618, 619, 620, 621, 622, 623, 624, 628, 630, 645, 650, 656, 675, 688, 709, 796, 801, 807, 816, 887, 934
Sunday Bulletin 624, 641
Sunday Dispatch, The 630
Sunday Herald, The 641
Sunday Messenger 613
Sunday Morning Atlas, The 629
Sunday Morning Dispatch, The 629
Sunday Morning Times, The 635
Sunday Telegram 635, 640
Sunday Times, The 641
Sunday-School & Family Gazette 616
Sunday-School Friend 617
Sunday-School Society 801
Sunday-School Society of Central M.E. Church South 586
Sunday-School Society of Fayette Street 580
SUNDERLAND, G. W. 889

SUNDERLIN, G. W. 838
  George W. 563
Sunny Brook 908, 909
Sunnyside 870
SUPER, Daniel 258, 484
SUPPLEE, Franklin 728
  J. Frank 412, 448
Susquehanna & Potomac Canal Company 313
Susquehanna Canal Co. 342
Susquehanna Ferry 920
Susquehanna Hundred 812
Susquehanna Point 36
Susquehanna Railroad 345, 694, 896
Susquehanna River 918
Susquehanna Steamboat Co. 512
SUTER, George 189
  J. S. 190
  James S. 193, 218, 219, 222, 469, 807
  John 250
  John H. 160
  Martin 160
SUTHENLING, A. 252
SUTHERLAND, Jane 808
  Sinclair 808
SUTRO, Emanuel 674
  Otto 272, 446, 447, 633, 669, 673, 674
  Rosa (WARENDORF) 674
SUTTON, Isaac 187
  James L. 359, 818
  Jeremiah 45
  Joseph 71, 910, 911
  Lewis 498
SWAIN, William M. 506, 622, 807
Swain, Abell & Simmons 617
SWAN, Ann Elizabeth 700
  Elizabeth 808
  James 547, 700
  John 76, 82, 172, 432, 452, 454, 547, 700, 807, 808
  John E. 252
  Joseph 77, 432, 809
  Mathew 252
  Robert 114
  William 462, 807
Swan Creek 370
Swan Point 42
SWANN, --- 142, 166, 273, 330, 331
  ---, Gov. 163, 164, 200, 352, 486, 601
  ---, Mayor 125, 126, 176, 198, 267, 273, 274, 363, 787
  C. O. 222
  Eliz. Gilmor 807
  James 464
  John 197, 545, 808, 903
  Joseph 455
  T. 595
  Thomas 124, 128, 149, 164, 180, 187, 195, 197, 222, 272, 276, 302, 329, 404, 466, 494, 664, 771, 807

SWANN, Thomas, Mrs. 595
Swann Creek 77
Swann Lake 218
SWANSON, Edward 35, 922
Swanton 342
SWARTZ, A. J. 298
  Charles 572
  Peter 249
SWAYNE, B. B. 155
  Benjamin F. 488
Swedenborgian Society 525, 560
SWEENEY, Allen 720
  D. 873, 874
  Elizabeth Sprigg 720
  John 160
  M. B. 892
SWEENY, ---, Mr. 225
Sweet Air 720, 836, 837, 908, 910, 916, 917
Sweet Air & Dulany's Valley Turnpike 916
Sweet Air Road 907, 909
Sweet Air U.B. Mission Chapel 837
Sweetair 410
SWEETING, Edward T. 160
Sweeting & Sterrett 439
SWIFT, ---, Col. 86
  Ebenezer 406
  J. G. 85
  John E. 813
  Joseph G. 343
  Susan 406
  W. R. 439, 470
  William H. 349
  William R. 470
SWINDELL, William 125, 140, 193
SWITZER, D. H. 577
SWOPE, ---, Rev. Mr. 521, 571, 573
  C. E. 914
SWYNN, William 644
Sycamore Permanent Building & Savings Association No. 1 512
SYDNER, Richard 433
SYESTER, A. K. 165
SYKES, James 667, 808
Sykesville 342
SYLVESTER, J. J. 233
SYMINGTON, James 253, 808
  James F. 317
  Thomas 253, 391
  W. A. 441
Syracuse Lodge No. 55, Knights of Pythias 855
SZEMELENYI, ---, Mr. 666
SZOLD, Benjamin 589, 934
SZEMELENGI, Ernest 673
Tabernacle Baptist Church of Philadelphia 562
TAGART, Samuel H. 189, 191, 698, 831
TAGERT, ---, Mr. 279

TAGGART, Samuel H. 876, 896
  William 876
TAGGERT, Samuel H. 494
TALBOT, --- 166
---, Mr. 362
  A. D. 902
  C. A. 190
  Edward 71, 877
  George 64
  J. F. C. 906
  Mary 881
  Thomas 910, 921
TALBOTT, --- 431
---, Mr. 637
  Charles A. 160, 190
  Charles Augustus 809
  Edward C. 903
  John 911
  Nicholas B. 160
  William 818
  William A. 809
Talbott & Wood 637
TALIAFERRO, A. G. 753
  Agnes H. (MARSHALL) 753
  Mary Archer 753
TALL, Bruff W. 160
Tammany Street 551
TANEY, ---, Chief Justice 132, 676, 699, 777, 885
---, Mrs. 595
  Roger B. 120, 595, 643
  Roger Brooke 712, 809
Taney Place 280
Taney Town Baptist Church 553
TANEYHILL, ---, Lt. 113
  G. L. 745
  G. Lane 746
  G. S. 745
  James 114
TANNER, Berry 218
Tannery 357
TANNEY, Hannah 231
TAPPER, ---, Capt. 792
TARBUTTON, W. A. 229
  William A. 231
Target Association of Baltimore County 817
TARR, Frederick C. 160
  H. J. C. 194
TASKER, --- 703
---, Col. 851
  B., Col. 424
  Benjamin 195, 704, 815, 848
TATE, D. M. 442, 445, 494
  David 38
  David M. 444
  James 101, 102
  James E. 456
TATEM, Benjamin 101
TATLOW, Joseph 310

TAYLEURE, Clifton W. 631, 688, 694
TAYLOR, --- 851
---, Capt. 300
---, Col. 923
---, Gen. 123, 124, 493, 650
---, Mrs. 594
---, President 744
Abraham 919, 920
Alonzo 693
B. F. 916, 922
Benjamin F. 161, 818, 917
Brian 920
Caleb S. 815
Charles A. 790
Charles F. 593, 600
Charles R. 465
David 122, 192, 193, 577
Edgar G. 161
Elizabeth 582
F. T. D. 266
Francis, Mrs. 879
G. K. 466
George B. 563
George G. 630
George W. 200
Henry 365, 368, 495, 564, 600, 631, 633, 887, 888, 889
Isaac 809, 814, 902
Jacob H. 576
Jacob J. 465
James 89, 248, 249
James B. 561
John 35, 74, 264, 734, 819, 921
John B. 742
John McLean 809
John, Capt. 44
Joseph 249, 471, 547, 549, 587
Joseph James 484
L. G. 249
Lawrence 919
Lemuel 84, 265, 266, 298, 459, 826
Levi 162, 189, 190
Louisa Maria (DASHIELL) 744
M. J., Mrs. 917
Marcellus K. 114
Martin 920
Mathew 252
R. A. 292, 439
R. Q. 828, 933
Richard 809
Robert 128, 188, 249, 262, 809, 923, 924, 934
Robert A. 600, 892
Robert F. 365
S. B. 193
Stephen B. 194
Steptoe B. 190
Talbot J. 821
Thomas 56, 112
Thurston M. 744
TAYLOR, W. W. 89, 316, 393, 523, 545
William 102, 103, 161, 208, 298, 545, 547, 628, 734
William H. 161, 809, 817
William W. 89, 456, 461, 470, 483, 809
William, Dr. 54
Zachary 846
Taylor, R. Q. & Co. 150
Taylor, Wilde & Co. 628
Taylor, William & Co. 102, 628
Taylor's Building 129, 142
Taylor's Choice 44, 920
Taylor's Mount 925
TCHUDY, Nicholas 809
TEACKLE, ---, Mr. 225
Emma (WILSON) 770
Margaret 743
St. George N. 809
St. George W. 743, 935
Thomas M. 770
TEAGUE, --- 568
Hillary 567
TEAKLE, J. B. 509
TEAL, F. D. 817
George McK. 855
George McKendre 489
Samuel W. 246
Teapot 432
TEGGES, Nicholas 191
TEGMEYER, John H. 187, 190, 210, 303
TEIPE, John 820
Telegram 638
Telegraph 643
Telegraph & Daily Advertiser 609
Temperance Advocate, The 637
Temperance Banner 628
Temperance Herald 616, 628
Temperance Temple 124, 141, 142, 145, 149, 152, 162, 787
Tempest Hill 275
TEMPLE, Benjamin L. 809
Temple Inn 703
TEMPLETON, George 506
Richard W. 814
TENANT, Thomas 187, 197, 214, 246, 316, 437, 438, 439, 470, 484, 577, 850
TENCH, Thomas 195
TENNANT, Boyce 809
Thomas 372, 425, 455, 809, 826
TENNENT, John 866
Tennessee Baptist Female College 564
TENNEY, A. G. 616
Catharine 400
TENSFIELD, John 189
Tenth District School Teachers 908
Tenth District School Trustees 908

Tenth District Teachers of Colored Schools 908
Teresian Nuns 598
Terra Cotta 342
Terrapin's Back 276
TERRY, John 518
M. J. 149
TESSIER, ---, Father 534
---, Rev. Father 236
---, Rev. Mr. 234
John 235
Tessier Street Colored Methodist Chapel 581
TEVIS, Joshua 864
Rebecca R. 864
Robert 860
TEWKSBURY, George D. 190
Texas 19, 30, 342, 347, 863, 876, 877, 882, 886
Texas Pacific Railroad 677
Thames Street 769
THAYER, N. P. 350
Nathaniel 809
The People's Gas-Light Co. 501
THELIN, W. T. 342
THEOBALD, Samuel 745
Thermia, ---, Bishop of 528
Thespian Assoc. 695
Third Baptist Church 559, 560
Third Church of the United Brethren 573
Third District School Trustees 834
Third District Teachers 834
Third District Teachers of Public Schools 834
Third English Lutheran Evangelical Church 569
Third English Reformed Church 572
Third Evangelical Church 590
Third German American Building Association 512
Third Mine Run 871
Third National Bank 400, 451, 466, 469, 489, 796
Third New Jerusalem Church 588
Third Presbyterian Church 548, 549
Third Reformed Church 572
Third Synagogue 588
Third Universalist Church 590
Thirdhaven Society of Friends 587
Thirteenth District School Teachers 936
Thirteenth District School Trustees 936
Thirteenth District Teachers of Colored Schools 936
Thistle Manufacturing Co. 410, 512
THOM, ---, Mr. 494
J. Pembroke 193

THOMAS, --- 136
---, Col. 884
---, Dr. 741
---, Mr. 500
A. G. 558
Abraham 454
Arthur G. 161
Azalia (HUSSEY) 500
D. 586
D. L. 249, 261
David E. 190, 577, 809
Douglas H. 489
E. L. 362
Ebenezer S. 819
Edward C. 193, 487
Eleanor 554
Elizabeth 773, 809
Evan 316, 321, 470, 766
Evan P. 463, 464
Evans 809
F. W. 628, 809
Francis 136, 195
Frank 145
George 253, 351
George F. 809
George P. 162, 190, 222, 456, 487, 488, 489
George T. 365
George W. 452
Isaiah 809
J. B. 241
J. C. 743
J. H. 125, 128, 365, 523
J. Hanson 128, 130, 137, 190, 365, 459, 697, 809, 851
J. Hanson, Mrs. 155
J. P. 809
J. R. 515
James 195, 581
James A. 189
James Carey 232, 604, 745, 838
James Carey, Mrs. 604
James H. 189
James P. 125, 126, 381
Jane 582
John 518, 519, 680, 741, 814, 850
John H. 604, 723
John H., Mrs. 604
John Hanson 115, 194
John L. 132, 162, 195, 494, 495, 497, 498
John W. 348
Joseph B. 241, 564
Joseph L. 241
Lambert 188, 192, 249, 582, 593
Luke 809
Mary Jane 582
Matilda L. (SEELEY) 498
Millard 301
O. H. 470
Owen 552

202

THOMAS, P. E. 244, 457, 458, 827
  P. F. 498, 699
  P. Francis 126
  Philip 734, 741, 742, 809
  Philip E. 315, 316, 317, 327, 330, 457, 458, 471, 588, 809, 826
  Philip Evan 318
  Philip F. 195
  Philip Francis 123, 716
  Philip Frank 497
  Philip J. 465
  Richard H. 469, 809
  Sarah 884
  Sterling 194, 381, 578, 809
  Stirling 469
  T. 742
  Thomas 55, 809
  Tristam 741
  William 100, 101, 103, 161, 311, 820
  William G. 124, 465, 595
  William J. 161
  Zarvona 135
Thomas, Joseph & Son 264
Thomas & Price 263
Thomas Viaduct 936
Thomas' Point 309
THOMPKINS, C. 103
THOMPSON, ---, Capt. 852
  ---, Dr. 834
  ---, Lt. 318
  ---, Miss 743
  A. 365
  Alexander 250
  Ann 459
  Arthur H. 585
  C. E. 191
  Charles 82
  Country 809
  Erastus 869
  Francis 351
  Frank 346
  George W. 161
  Gustavus A. 370
  Harry 809
  Henry 62, 437, 438, 439, 440, 470, 845, 850
  Henry A. 122, 288, 455, 485, 809, 826
  Hugh 83, 454, 679, 809
  I. D. 809
  J. Davis 880
  Jacob 847
  James 247, 311, 584, 757, 814
  James E. 636
  Jane 459, 676
  John 782, 784
  John A. 161, 190, 192, 200, 364, 465
  John D. 194
  John J. 459

THOMPSON, Joseph 166, 870
  Josias 250
  Mark C. W. 205
  Peter 459
  R. W. 138
  Rebecca 909
  Robert H. 820
  S. P. 441, 442, 494, 698
  Samuel 582, 741
  Samuel P. 441
  Samuel S. 161
  Solomon S. 161
  Thomas 459, 809
  W. T. 650
  William 101, 370, 464, 592, 728, 809
  William Silver 740
  William T. 628
Thompson & Bathurst 372
Thompson & Farish 372
Thompson & Walker 433
THOMSEN, J. J. 740
  J. J., Mrs. 604
  Laurence 234, 659
  Lawrence 471
THOMSON, Lawrence 464
  William 164
THORNBURG, David 482
  Joseph 238, 483, 809
THORNBURGH, George 247
THORNE, J. P. 191
  Thornton 342, 657
THORNTON, William H. 255
THORNWELL, J. H. 896
THORP, Joshua 252
Three Loggerheads 758, 759
Three Prong Branch 49
Three Tuns Hotel 321
Three Tuns Tavern 513
THROOP, J. V. N. 254
Thurlow 351
THURLOW, ---, Lord 709
THURSTON, H. Scott 222
TIBBALLS, William H. 202
TIBBS, William 223, 518, 920
Tidal Wave, The 641
Tide-Water Canal 314
TIDINGS, E. R. 899
TIDY, John B. 190
TIERNAN, Charles 234, 252, 253, 680, 850
  L. 433
  L. Ann 594
  L., Mrs. 595
  Luke 84, 86, 89, 120, 187, 188, 197, 207, 234, 235, 245, 250, 298, 303, 316, 393, 455, 456, 470, 488, 532, 594, 595, 826, 827
  Luke, Mrs. 594
  P. 237
  P. Ann S. 594
  P., Mrs. 595

Tiernan, Luke & Sons 293, 438
Tiernan, M. & P. & Co. 439
TIERS, Edward 657
TIFFANY, --- 252
---, Rev. Mr. 577
Andrew 262
Comfort 576, 809
G. P. 408
George B. 667
Henry 281, 440
Henry Otis 551
L. McL. 596
L. McLane 743, 745, 746
O. 674
O. C. 394, 439, 471
O. H. 579
Osmand C. 463
Osmond C. 464, 809
Otis 809
Tiffany, Duvall & Co. 854
Tigers 787
TILDEN, ---, Miss 687
Tilden Family 899
TILGHMAN, --- 698, 703
---, Capt. 114
Edward 710
Frisby 726, 845
James 118, 709
Lloyd 114
Louisa 909
Margaret 707
Margaret Ann 726
Matthew 75, 706, 707
Tench 452, 809, 845
Tilghman Family of Hope 717
Tilghman's Island 87
TILGMAN, Frisby 850
TILLARD, William H. 210
TILLE, Andreis 64
TILLINGHAST, George 433
John 433
TILLOTSON, B. M. 590
TILLYARD, ---, Mr. 681
TILYARD, C. S. 740
H. W. 809
William 320
TIMANUS, Charles 812, 896
Elizabeth W. 887
Hannah Wall 887
John 887
Luther 814
Timber Neck 49, 50, 59, 61
Timber Run 854
Times, The 629, 641
Times & Ledger 629, 630
TIMON, ---, Bishop 539
Timonium 14, 28, 30, 31, 347, 818,
    850, 883
TINGER, Charles 809
TINGES, A. H. 222
George W. 469

TINKER, C. A. 509
Charles A. 508, 509
TINNEN, James 887
TIPTON, Jonathan 519, 809
William 519
TISDALE, Israel 431
Ruth 431
TITENS, --- 673
Tivoli 887
TODD, ---, Gov. 147
Christopher 734, 741
Francis 863
James 48, 203
Lancelot 44
Richard 592
Thomas 54, 55, 818
Thomas B. 818, 927
William 814
Todd's Range 48, 49, 203
TODHUNTER, Joseph 252, 439, 463,
    464, 470
TODKILL, Anas 39
TOELLE, ---, Dr. 742
TOEPKEN, Jarard 261
TOFFLING, John H. 381
TOLL, B. 434
TOLLER, Walter 70
TOLLEY, ---, Mr. 47, 815
Delia 809
Edward 809
Elizabeth 920
Martha (HALL) 920
Mary 864, 920
Mary (GARRETTSON) 920
Sophia 920
Thomas 44, 45, 50, 223, 819, 920,
    924
Walter 70, 71, 72, 73, 819, 864, 909,
    910, 920, 921
Tolley Family 924
Tolley Farm 925
TOLLY, Walter 69, 778, 809
William 809
Tom's Brook 342
TOMAY, S. C. 903
TOME, Jacob 165, 368, 467, 488, 489
TOMKINS, Joseph G. 252
Tomora 805
TOMPKINS, John A. 604
John A., Mrs. 596
Phebe J. 229
R. G. 585
TONER, Charles 253
J. C. 193
J. M. 742
Michael 809
Samuel 245
Tongs, L. D. & Co. 839
TONRY, ---, Prof. 494
William P. 193, 495
Too's Marshes Light-house 310

204

TOOL, James 73
TOOLE, James 76
TORBIN, Thomas W. 630
TORMEY, Leonard J. 472, 938
TORNEY, John H. 161
TORRES, Francis 731
TORREY, Charles T. 809
TORRINGTON, Lida J. 927
TORSCH, John W. 191, 631, 675
TOTTLE, William A. 525
TOUCASA, Louis 592
TOUGH, John S. 194
TOUSARD, ---, Maj. 291
TOWER, James 809
 Lawrence 161
Tower Hill 463
TOWERS, James 298
 John 592
TOWNE, Benjamin 606
 Mary C. 596
TOWNER, John F. 190
TOWNSEND, ---, Rev. Mr. 902
 A. A. 641
 Granville S. 253, 348
 Joseph 62, 89, 170, 225, 244, 393, 483, 733
 L. L. 254
 Richard H. 893
 Robert 780
 Samuel 488
 Samuel P. 489
 Thomas J. 465
 Wilson 820, 927
Townsend, R. & Co. 255
Townsend, Whitely & Co. 410
TOWNSHEND, Joseph C. 488
 Samuel 488
TOWSER, John 911
Towson 812, 886, 893, 897, 901, 902, 906
TOWSON, --- 85, 88
 Charles 189, 191
 Charles S. 193
 E. 678
 Ezekiel 71, 72, 554, 809, 894, 895
 Nathan 84, 809, 895
 Ruth 809
 Thomas 265, 894
 William 554, 809, 903
Towson & Dulany's Valley Turnpike 894
Towson Family 894
Towson Guards 898, 903
Towson Lodge No. 79, I.O.O.F. 874, 896, 898, 902
Towson Street 769
Towson's Tavern 894, 895
Towsontown 16, 64, 137, 147, 165, 359, 749, 812, 814, 817, 874, 878, 886, 892, 896, 898, 899, 900, 902, 903, 904, 905, 907, 911

Towsontown Advocate 899
Towsontown Railroad 369, 815
Towsontown Riflemen 903
TOY, Isaac C. 244
 Isaac N. 393
 J. D. 616
 John D. 616, 809
 Joseph 809
 Mary 809
TRACEY, John 871
 Jonathan 814
 Joshua 855, 869
 Richard C. 815
 Thomas 877
 William H. 815
TRACY, Nicholas 814, 816
 Stephen 487
 William H. 869
Tracy's Landing 309
Traders' National Bank 451, 467, 469
Traders' Union Hall 560, 591
Trades Union 624
TRAIL, Louis W. 442
Transactions of Medical & Chirugical Faculty of Maryland 739
Transcript 622
Transquockin Canal Co. of Dorchester County 314
Trap Road 926
TRAPNELL, Philip 734, 741
Trappe Road 890
Traveller 631
TRAVERS, ---, Col. 211
 J. Henry 190
 John 439
 John H. 256
 John M. 194
 Robert M. 809
 William H. 194, 363, 366
 William R. 440, 695, 809
 William S. 364
TRAVIS, Samuel 107
Tray Run 342
TREADWAY, Richard 519
TREANOR, William 696
Treaverton Railroad 345
Tredegar Works 669
Tredyffrin Baptist Church 553
TREGO, William H. 809
TREGOTHA, Thomas 766
Trentham 841, 842, 858, 861, 862
Trenton 869
Trenton Chapel of the M.E. Church 869
TRESSEL, E. L. S. 570
Tribune 633
TRIMBLE, Hannah 809
 I. R. 358, 506
 Isaac 313, 318, 646, 809
 Isaac R. 130, 210

TRIMBLE, John 249, 393, 407, 459, 826, 827
  Thomas 780
  William 89, 170, 173, 187, 246, 809
Trimble, William's Wharf 311
Trinity Church 521, 681
Trinity Evangelical Lutheran Church 570
Trinity Lutheran Church 855
Trinity M.E. Church South 586
Trinity P.E. Church 522, 523, 674, 902, 904, 917
TRIPLET, John W. 812
TRIPLETT, ---, Mrs. 574
  John W. 817
Triplett's Alley 574
Tripolet's Wharf 432
TRIPPE, ---, Capt. 151
  A. C. 191
  Andrew C. 301
  Edward 300, 301
  James 809
  Levin 101
TROBLER, Henry 161
TROLDENIER, George 572
TROTTEN, Luke 53
  Thomas 246, 809
TROTTER, Robert 65
TROWBRIDGE, John 233
TROXELL, Philip N. 830
Troxell, Handy & Greer 426
TROXWELL, T. F. 466
True American, The 630
True Catholic, The 627, 647
True Christian, The 641
True Democrat, The 641
True Union, The 628, 630
TRUEMAN, --- 37
TRUITT, George F. 592
TRULEY, Hector 519
TRUMAN, Thomas 246, 815
Truman's Acquaintance 815
TRUST, Jacob 484, 890
TRUXTON, Thomas 293
TSCHEUBEUS, Francis X. 809
TSCHUDY, Nicholas 572
TUBBS, Barton 740
TUBMAN, Benjamin G. 488
TUCK, William H. 467
  William Hallam 717
TUCKER, ---, Admiral 923
  A. B. 809
  Charles 560
  E. 576
  Elizabeth Carroll 809
  George H. 241
  Henry R. 809
  J. T. 256
  James H. 161
  John A. 161
  John R. 927

TUCKER, Levi 560
  Wesley A. 367, 448
  William A. 452, 483
TUCKERMAN, ---, Mr. 654
TUCKETT, Harvey, Mrs. 691
TUDOR, Anna P. 230
  Sarah 604
TULL, Thomas J. 194
TULLY, Patrick T. 449
TUMBLINSON, William 809
Tunnelton 342
TUNSTALL, T. T. 880
Turf Register 751
Turk's Island 67
Turkey Point 309
TURNBAUGH, Jacob 869
TURNBULL, --- 759
  ---, Mr. 637, 759
  Alexander 547
  Alexander F. 320
  Alexander, Mrs. 604
  George 779
  H. C. 887, 902, 906
  Henry C. 546, 547, 828
  John 468
  Lawrence 624
Turnbull, Sweet & Co. 410
Turnbull Bros. 637
TURNER, --- 166
  ---, Mr. 217
  ---, Mrs. 872
  Andrew 872
  Charles 149
  Elizabeth (HUBER) 381
  Elizabeth Jane (BALDWIN) 458
  Ellen Rampley 872
  Emack 872
  Frederick S. 190, 194
  George W. 872
  H. F. 441
  H. M. 380
  J. C. 152
  J. J. 472, 487
  J. M. 123, 380
  J. Maybury 276
  J. S. 241
  Jacob 312
  James 819, 820, 871, 872, 873
  James Calder 872
  John 161
  John D. 809
  John L. 488, 813, 836
  John S. 813
  Joseph 188, 241, 249
  Joseph J. 189, 539
  Joshua 189, 240, 249, 463
  Joshua J. 189
  Joshua Mayberry 809
  L. 369
  Lewis 155, 370, 379, 380, 381, 488, 809, 820

TURNER, Lewis A. 155
Margaret 872
Margaret (BADER) 381
Martha 872
Martha (TURNER) 872
Mary Ann 872
Miranda Harris 872
Nathan 809
Rebecca 871
Robert 126, 193, 194, 469
S. E. 153
S. K., Mrs. 872
Samuel R. 252
Sarah (CALDER) 872, 873
T. B. H. 847
Thomas 748, 872
William 381, 488
William H. 190, 202, 615
William H. H. 249, 729
William W. 249
Zephaniah 458
Turner, Josiah & Co. 439
TURPIN, ---, Capt. 744
TURREAU, ---, Gen. 298
Turtle Creek 337
Tuscarora 342
Tuscarora Creek 402
Tusculum 612, 642
Tusculum Club 644
TUTTLE, ---, Mr. 630
---, Rev. Mr. 521
E. B. 601
William M. 809
William N. 624
TWAITS, --- 683
---, Mrs. 684
Twelfth District School Teachers 927
Twelfth District School Trustees 927
Twelfth District Teachers of Colored Schools 927
Twelfth Presbyterian Church 549
TWIFORD, A. E. 237
TWIGGS, ---, Gen. 134
TWINER, William 809
TWINING, ---, Capt. 311
Nathaniel 311
Twining & Vanhorn 312
Twining Vanhorn & Co. 311
Twinnall & Geroack 727
TYDINGS, E. R. 817, 880
TYLDEN, Marmaduke 416
William 416
TYLER, ---, Brig. Gen. 144
---, Dr. 741, 742
---, Gen. 145
Arthur W. 233
Charles 466, 809
E. B. 143, 493, 494, 495
J. 740

TYLER, John 122, 741
Nathaniel 637
Tyler, N. & Co. 637
TYSON, ---, Mr. 217, 367, 376
Abraham 772
Alex H. 189
Betsy 772
Dalby 772
Derrick 772
Elisha 89, 188, 197, 203, 245, 310, 375, 438, 484, 772, 809, 826
Elizabeth 772, 809
Enos 772
George 253, 772, 809
H. 550
H. G. 550
Hannah 772
Hannah Ann (WOOD) 772
Henry 210, 366, 772, 809, 888
Isaac 89, 245, 252, 393, 434, 438, 439, 456, 466, 470, 483, 771, 772, 773, 809
Isabella 596, 604
J. W., Mrs., Gen. 797
Jacob 772
James E. 440, 442, 488
James W. 368, 484, 772
Jesse 155, 298, 354, 458, 469, 483, 488, 599, 772, 773, 809
John 772
John S. 194, 737, 809
Margaret 809
Margaret (HOPKINS) 772
Martha E. 376
Mathias 311
Matthew 245
Matthias 772
Nathan 439, 442, 772, 809
Peter 772
Philip T. 253, 254, 809
Renier 772
Richard W. 772
Robert 441, 442, 444, 445, 494
Robert, Mrs. 596, 604
Sarah 772, 809
Tacey 772
Thomas 252, 298
William 470, 593
Tyson, Jacob & Son 439
Tyson, Jesse & Sons 438
Tyson & Anderson 432
Tyson Family 924
Tyson Mining Co. 512
Tyson Mining Co. of Baltimore City 854
Tyson's Chesapeake Iron-Furnace 926
TYTE, Charles 246
UBER, Carlton A. 161
UHLER, Andrew 867
Anna Maria (REESE) 656

207

UHLER, David 855
 Erasmus 246, 253, 484, 569, 572, 727
 George H. 656
 John C. 745
 John R. 161, 745, 746
 P. R. 664, 667
 Philip 188, 246, 569, 809
 Philip R. 13, 20, 233
 Philip Reese 656
 R. P. 665
 Servina 867
Uhler's Alley 51
Uhler's Run 51
UHLHORN, J. 809
 John 569
UHRIG, John 698
ULERY, E. G. 370, 847
 Eli G. 369
ULMAN, Alfred J. 841
 B. F. 747
 B. F., Mrs. 603
ULRICH, John 597
UMBAU, M. Herbert 809
UNDERDUE, James 568
UNDERWOOD, G. W. 877
 Thomas 252
 William C. 830
UNDUTCH, Nicholas 161
UNIACK, M. E. 292
Union 802, 900
Union Bank of Maryland 404, 450, 451, 798
Union Bethel Methodist Church 580
Union Bridge 355, 357, 855
Union Chapel of the M.E. Church 869
Union Club 147, 231, 771, 803
Union Colored Baptist Church 568
Union Company 301
Union Depot 345, 354, 355
Union District Telegraph Co. 509, 512
Union Dock 152
Union File Works 512
Union Fire Company 238, 240, 241, 242, 244, 245, 251, 261, 484
Union Fire Company of Washington 241
Union League Club 141
Union Lodge No. 50, Knights of Pythias 869
Union Machine-Shops 838
Union Manufacturing Co. 375, 393, 407, 820, 856
Union Musical Association 139
Union Orphan Asylum 154, 601
Union Oyster Co. 395, 512
Union Protestant Infirmary 154, 253, 744, 747

Union Railroad 182, 183, 353, 354, 355, 697, 702, 926, 928
Union Railroad & Tunnel 460
Union Relief Association of Baltimore 152
Union Riflemen 817
Union Society of the M.E. Church 581
Union Square 279
Union Square M.E. Church 577, 578, 579
Union State Central Committee of Md. 651
Union Town 311
Unionville 917
Unitarian Church 589
United Brethren 573
United Fire Company 241, 484
United Fire Department 242
United German Bank 468
United German Real Estate & Fire Insurance Co. of Baltimore 468
United Hose & Suction Company 253
United Hose & Suction Engine Company 241
United Sons of Towsontown Lodge, I.O.O.F. 903
United States Agricultural Society 885
United States Bank 853
United States Catholic Magazine 627
United States Coast Survey 288
United States Court Officers 729
United States General Insurance Co. 693
United States Hose Company 256
United States Hose Fire Company 242
United States Hotel 516
Univeristy of Maryland School of Medicine 748
Universalist Church 122, 127, 128, 152, 212, 590, 609
University of Maryland 644, 657, 698, 700, 701, 703, 708, 714, 719, 724, 735, 737, 739, 743, 744, 749, 750, 751, 753, 754, 755, 756, 770, 794, 796, 797, 798, 806, 808, 836, 878, 899, 915
UNKLES, C. R. 927
UPJOHN, ---, Mr. 521
Upper Back River Hundred 859
Upper Deer Creek Hundred 812
Upper Ellicott's Mills 425
Upper Falls 916, 922
Upper Marlborough 88
Upper Paper-Mill 816
Upper Potomac 818
Upperco 868
Uppercoe 854

UPPERCOE, Jesse 855
UPSHAW, Catherine 373
UPSHUR, Abel P. 556
  Arthur 719
  Rose 886
  Virginia 719
UPTON, Joshua 820
  Scott 809
Upton Court 49, 50
URNER, William 188
URQUHART, John E. 877
USHER, Thomas 432, 452, 455, 483
Usher, Abraham & Co. 432
UTIE, George 41
  Nathaniel 35, 41
UTYE, George 818
  Nathaniel 818
VABBE, Rud. 605
VACULA, V. 543
VAIL, ---, Mr. 504
  Alfred 505
  Horatio D. 281
VAIN, Edward 380
VALCK, Adrian 425, 433, 449, 452, 453
Valck, Adrian & Co. 372
VALENTINE, H. E. 597
  J. Henry 880
  William H. 250
VALIANT, Elizabeth 583
  John 582
  Mary Ann 583
  William H. 809
  William T. 193, 194, 199
  William Thomas 164, 200
VALITTE, G. Edmund 255
VALK, Adrian 482
VALLANDIGHAM, ---, Mr. 137
  C. L. 136, 142
Valley Falls 342
Valley of Jehosaphat 904
Valley Railroad 182, 805
Valley Railroad Co. of Virginia 183
VALOIS, Gustavus 161
VAN ANTWERP, ---, Rev. Dr. 891
  D. A. 931
VAN BIBBER, --- 809
  ---, Mr. 60
  A. 100, 728
  Abraham 102, 206, 452, 780, 809
  Andrew 407, 432
  Ann 866
  George D. 866
  I. 102
  Isaac 69, 70, 100, 196, 292, 407, 432, 452, 728, 809, 814
  J. 728
  John 596
  W. C. 596, 745, 915
  Washington 867

VAN BIBBER, William 866
VAN BOCKELIN, L. 523
VAN BOKKELEN, ---, Rev. Dr. 822
  L. 821
VAN BOKKELIN, L. 813
VAN BUREN, Martin 120, 122
VAN CHOATE, S. F. 509
VAN NESS, Eugene 809
VAN NOSTRAND, ---, Mr. 363
  Marshal 142, 880
  William 200
  William A. 140, 193, 200, 251
VAN RISWICK, John 359
VAN SCHALKUYCK, Alp. 236
  Aug. 236
Van Stamp & Suter 220
VAN WYCK, Stidman 253
  W. 678
  William 298, 454, 592, 679
Van Wyck & Morgan 438
VANCE, David 433
  Jacob 872
  Thomas 252
Vanclevesville 342
VANDERFORD, ---, Mr. 628
  Henry 627
VANDERHORST, John 263
  John H. 423
VANHACK, John 818
VANHOOK, ---, Mr. 896
VANHORN, Gabriel P. 312
  Gabriel Peterson 311
  J. W. 902
  John W. 898
  Peter P. 554
  Peter Pattersen 553
Vanhorn, Gabriel Peterson & Co. 311
VANS, William 118
VANSANT, ---, Mayor 468
  ---, Mr. 217
  Bettie 916
  J. 365, 508
  Joshua 123, 128, 137, 155, 165, 166, 178, 181, 187, 194, 195, 205, 222, 242, 247, 270, 365, 493, 497, 498, 694, 721, 729, 759, 870
  Joshua V. 809
  Joshua, Mrs. 155, 156, 809
  Mary Ann 809
  Nicholas 594
Vanville 311
VANZANT, Joshua 932
VASHON, Simon 70
VAUGHAN, A. S. 840
  Christopher 728
  George 809
  Gist 71
VAUGHEN, Gist 871
  William P. 161
VAUTIER, --- 676

VEASEY, Joseph 100
　Thomas 195
VEASY, --- 104
VEAZEY, George Ross 826
　I. Parker 191, 728
VEDDER, Charles 637
VEDITZ, Johanna 931
VEEDER, ---, Mrs. 271
VEES, Henry 469, 488
VEITH, Hermann 570
　John 534
VENABLE, Proctor A. 809
　Richard M. 449
Verdue, Karlognew, Pagen & Co. 102
VERNET, Horace 675
VERNON, ---, Admiral 905
---, Col. 498
　George W. F. 498
VEROT, Augustine 236
VERST, Augustine 822
VESSELS, ---, Mrs. 263
VICINANZA, Camillus 538
VICK, Eudora (HIGGINS) 749
VICKERS, B. A. 461, 462, 828
　B. Albert 193, 483
　Clement 301
　George R. 370, 809
　Joel 120, 299, 438, 461, 809
　Vickers Estate 280
VICKERY, H. T. 467
　Hazeltine G. 473
　Stephen 592
　William H. 191, 193, 484
VIDENKA, John 543
Vienna 897
Vienna Landing 310
Vigilant Fire Company 240, 241, 242, 249, 250, 258, 484
VIGILANTE, Sivius 538
VIGNEROUT, C. 544
VILLIGER, Burchard 536
VILMAR, ---, Prof. 852
VINCENT, --- 33
---, Gen. 793
　R. 917
　R., Mrs. 917
　Samuel 170, 174, 246
VINKLE, Columbus 261
VINSON, James 298
VINTER, Conrad 202
VINTON, R. S. 869, 875
　Robert S. 161
Virginia House 262
Virginia Midland Railroad 458
Visitor 646
VOCKE, Claas 195
　Class 471
VOEGELING, John 573
VOGELER, A. 740
VOGLE, Lewis 814, 870

VOGLE, Louis 761
VOGTMANN, ---, Rev. Mr. 543
VOIGHT, Lewis T. 625
VOLANDT, Christopher 809
VOLCK, --- 271, 826
　A. J. 675
VOLK, ---, Mr. 272
VOLLANDT, Frederick 809
　John M. 809
Volunteer Fire Department 483, 484
Volunteer Force Commissioned Officers, War 1861-1865 156, 157, 158, 159, 160, 161
VOLZ, H. 538
　Peter 468
VON BORRIES, Otto 161
VON DECRECG, Ida 625
VON FALKE, --- 657
VON HAGEN, Johan Caroline Martini 625
　Sigismund 161
VON HATTEN, Gerhard 250
VON HOLST, H. 233
VON KAPFF, ---, Mrs. 156
　B. J. 433
　Herman 471, 483
　J. B. 809
Von Kapff & Anspach 261, 433
Von Kapff & Brune 372, 438, 470
Von Kapft & Anspach 298
VON KEPROF, Frederick 902
VON KOERBER, Vincent E. 161
Von Knapp Property 834
VON LINGEN, A. 303
　G. A. 195, 441
　George A. 303, 304, 484
VON MARSDORF, Herman 161
VON MOLTKE, ---, Gen. 671
VON SCHILLING, Louis 161
VON SPRECHELSEN, George A. 262
VON SPRECKELSEN, George A. 548
VON WESSELY, Joseph 161
VONDERHORST, Catherine A. (KUEST) 930
　Henry R. 931
　J. H. 469
　Johanna (VEDITZ) 931
　John 597
　John H. 927, 930
VONDERSMITH, Daniel 855
　Peter 839
VOUCHER, ---, Mr. 82
Vulcan's Delight 424
WADE, Benjamin F. 499
　George W. 936
　John 575
Wadesville 342
WADHAMS, Edgar 236
WADSWORTH, ---, Col. 85, 86

WADSWORTH, John 911
WAESCHE, ---, Miss 595
  Frederick 252
WAGELIN, Charles M. 136
WAGGNER, G. 252
  Isaiah 935
WAGNER, ---, Dr. 605
  Basil 195, 383
  George 261
  Jacob 613, 810
  James J. 498
  James V. 127, 688
  John W. 836
WAGSTAFFE, Richard 757
WAIDNER, Jacob B. 502
WAILES, ---, Mr. 491
  Charles A. 490, 635, 810
  Hannah More (COLTON) 635
  William 497, 624
WAIN, George H. 161
WAINWRIGHT, James 244
  John 100
WAITE, William W. 161
Wakefield Valley 852
WALCOT, --- 693
---, Mr. 688
WALDRON, E. L. S. 855
  E. Q. S. 835
WALES, ---, Mr. 498
  William 498
WALK, Andrew 759
WALKER, --- 477, 651
---, Dr. 51, 57, 729
---, Rev. 810
  Agnes 803, 862
  Agnes Anna 864
  Ann 864
  Ann (CRADOCK) 841
  C. W. 253, 580
  Catharine 862
  Catherine (CRADOCK) 841
  Charles 71, 841, 860, 861, 862, 864, 865
  Charles Arthur 864
  Charles H. 252
  Charles W. 253, 810
  Daniel 871
  Elizabeth Hulse 864
  Francis A. 233
  George 50, 53, 55, 56, 803, 841, 862, 870
  George, Dr. 51
  Henry 810
  J. E. 693
  J. L. 768
  J. Wesley 810
  James 51, 53, 74, 729, 841, 842, 862, 872
  John 862, 873
  John Cradock 862
  John G. 816

WALKER, John George 864, 865
  John W. 254, 366, 814
  Joseph 128, 560, 814, 820
  Joseph E. 161
  Joshua 593
  Katharine (CRADOCK) 862
  Katherine (CRADOCK) 861
  Margaret 862, 864
  Mary 862
  Noah 364, 810
  P. G. 580
  P. H. 195, 834, 836, 837
  S. 678
  S. D. 393, 667
  Samuel 679
  Samuel D. 890
  Samuel H. 114
  Samuel P. 298
  Sibyl West 864
  Susanna A. 864
  Susannah 862
  Susannah (GARDNER) 841, 862
  T. C. 861
  Thomas 101
  Thomas C. 861, 862
  Thomas Cradock 841, 842, 862
Walker, Noah & Co. 129
Walker Family 858, 862, 865
WALL, ---, Miss 681
---, Mr. 681
---, Mrs. 681
  Daniel 841
  George 247, 433
  Jacob 247, 253, 576, 810
  Joshua 247
WALLACE, ---, Gen. 147, 148, 149, 150, 151, 633
  Catharine 583
  Charles 100, 101, 103
  James 162, 847
  Joseph W. 193
  Lewis 146
  Samuel 38
  William 810, 919
Wallace, Johnson, Muir & Co. 102
Wallace & Garrett 475
WALLACK, ---, Mrs. 694
  Henry 686
  J. 95, 269
  J. B. 811
  James 686, 694
  James W. 693, 696
WALLAHORN, Daniel 224
WALLAUER, George 571
WALLEY, Zedekiah 99
WALLIS, --- 723
---, Mr. 136, 699
  Philip 189
  S. Teackle 126, 128, 130, 166, 198, 200, 227, 624, 649, 655, 675, 676, 697, 714, 725, 743

WALLIS, Severn Teackle 137, 141, 194, 499, 631, 659, 698
WALLS, J. W. 745
  J. William 810
  William 254
WALMSLEY, Charles 531
  John S. 161
Walnut Street Theatre, Philadelphia 688
WALRAVEN, John 824
WALRUSLIES, John 759
WALSCHE, Frederick 298
WALSH, C. S. 680
  Charles S. 120
  H. H. 613
  J. Carroll 846
  Jacob 718
  John 247, 532
  John Carroll 44, 846, 923
  Margaret (YATES) 718
  Patrick 161
  R. 102
  Robert 168, 169, 235, 526, 532, 569, 648, 810
  T. Y. 255
  T. Yates 122, 192, 250, 499
  Thomas T. 189
  Thomas Yates 113, 189
  Thomas Yeates 810
  William J. 516
Walsh's Tanyard 518
WALTEMEYER, Charles 161
  Francis G. F. 161
  Jacob 194
WALTEMYER, F. 818
WALTER, ---, Mrs. 595
  Francis 673
  George 673
  George K. 440
  J. 236
  Jacob 810
  John H. 161
  Joseph 241
  Moses R. 841
  R. 466
  W. F. 478
  William Joseph 628
WALTERS, ---, Mr. 676, 677
  A. G. 825
  Charles E. 155
  Ellen (HARPER) 676
  Harry 346
  Henry 464, 676
  J. 101
  James D. 814
  Jane (THOMPSON) 676
  W. S. 440
  W. T. 302, 365, 674
  William H. 161
  William J. H. 449
  William T. 468, 675, 697, 698, 887
Walters, W. T. & Co. 662, 677
WALTHAM, Thomas 921
WALTON, George 74
  William B. 427
Walton & Ward 688
WALTZ, ---, Mr. 641
  E. B. 874, 905
  Peter 741
WAMPLER, ---, Mr. 218
  J. Lewis 197, 247
WAND, William 101
Wanderer 616
WANE, John 612
WANN, John 572
WANNALL, Jessie 633
WANNERWITCH, Frederick 820
WANSTEN, William 262
WANTLAND, Thomas E. 814
Wapping Street 554
WARD, --- 924
  ---, Mr. 58, 764
  B. C. 471
  Benjamin C. 659, 928
  Charles 343
  G. W. 458
  G. Washington 155
  George 759
  H. V. 695
  Hannah 45
  Henry 637
  J. Edward 820
  J. R. 828
  J. Robert 745
  John 816
  John H. 814
  Joseph 45, 263
  Owen 191, 193
  Samuel 45, 555
  Thomas 757, 837
  W. F. 579
  W. L. 579
  W. T. 576
  W. W. 579
  William 246, 712
  William F. 579
  William H. 205, 810
Ward's Methodist Chapel 868
WARDEN, James 810
WARDENBURG, W. F. 229
Warder, George A. & Co. 263
WARE, E. 192
  Elias 192, 194, 195
  Francis 72
  J. W. 846
  John F. W. 590
  Mary R. 893
  Nathaniel H. 810
  Robert G. 578
WARENDORF, Rosa 674
WARFIELD, ---, Capt. 652
  ---, Dr. 741, 783

WARFIELD, A. 734
Charles 470
Charles A. 736, 742
Charles Alex. 310
Charles Alexander 669, 740
D. 252
Daniel 440, 810
David 92, 809
Dennis 810
Eliza 669
George 303
George F. 187, 192, 252, 439, 458
Henry M. 125, 128, 130, 137, 141, 166, 194, 303, 358, 415, 440, 441, 442, 446, 847
Henry Mactier 446
Jesse 600
L. A. 161
Mrs., Dr. 596
Peregrine 741, 782
R. Emory 484, 640
William R. 222
Warfield's Church 120, 552, 584
Warfield's Meeting-House 591
Warfield's Mill 42
WARFORD, A. B. 346
WARING, Ann 878
Benjamin H. 847
George W. 372
WARNER, ---, Dr. 738
A. E. 192, 254
Adam G. 810
Andrew E. 92, 241, 254
E. A. 241
G. K. 911
George 84, 86, 89, 192, 195, 202, 207, 250, 316, 456, 457, 593, 667, 810, 819, 824, 826, 827
George C. 811
John Edward 161
Joseph E. 245
Joseph P. 245, 810
Michael 125, 142, 194, 199, 250, 458, 810, 811
Thomas 92, 246
William 188, 192, 246
William A. 246
William G. 246
WARRELL, ---, Mrs. 682
Warren 407, 876, 877, 881, 882, 901
WARREN, --- 684, 685
---, Admiral 87, 89, 106
---, Capt. 72
---, Mr. 686, 687
Ann 810
Edward 738, 752
George B. 390
Hester 811
John Borlaise 111, 112
Leander 810
Minton 233

WARREN, William 683, 810, 811
William H. 688
Warren & Wood 684, 688
Warren Baptist Church 559
Warren Cotton-Factory 408, 881
Warren Cotton-Mills 876
Warren Factory 142, 817, 882
Warren M.E. Church 882
Warren Manufacturing Co. 901
Warren Public School 901
Warren Riflemen 882
WARRICK, William 525
WARRING, C. 101
WARRINGTON, George 222
Harry 222
WARTMAN, John C. 814
Michael K. 813
Warwick Iron Co. 429
WASHBURN, H. H. 525
WASHBURNE, ---, Rev. Mr. 548
WASHINGTON, --- 37, 849
---, Gen. 80, 116, 255, 668, 780
---, Mrs. 82
Augustine 424
Frankie 810
George 72, 265, 266, 391, 398, 424, 905
George, Mrs. 743
Lawrence 391, 424, 905
Peter G. 506
Washington & Baltimore Canal Company 313
Washington and Alexandria Line 301
Washington College 223, 601, 802, 860, 862, 863, 899
Washington Constitution, The 627
Washington Cotton Manufacturing Co. 408, 840
Washington Factory 408, 880
Washington Fire Company 240, 241, 242, 484
Washington Fire Insurance Co. 488, 512
Washington Grove 342
Washington Hall 667, 695
Washington Hall Fair 508
Washington Hose Company 241, 253, 254, 258
Washington Junction 342
Washington Lodge of Odd-Fellows 369, 758
Washington Manufacturing Co. 407
Washington Medical College 737, 755, 786
Washington Mills 409
Washington Monument 138, 265, 266, 280, 521
Washington Place 664, 666
Washington Railroad 361
Washington Republic 612

Washington Road 896
Washington Square 89, 280
Washington Street 769
Washington Street Station M.P. Church 583
Washington Telegraph 616
Washington Turnpike 935, 937
Washington Union 620
Washington University 739, 751, 753, 754
Washington University at Baltimore 755
Washington University Hospital 738
Washington University of Baltimore 738, 752, 786
Washington University School of Medicine 738
Washingtonian Temperance Society 369
Watch House 557
WATCHMAN, John 255, 394
Watchman & Butts' Foundry 255
Watchman Fire Company 242, 255
WATER, ---, Mr. 849
Water Board 702
Water Department of Baltimore 886
Water Street 691, 759
Water's (Francis) Classical Seminary 233
Waterbury 342
Waterbury Station 358
Waterloo 354, 816
Waterloo Row 214
WATERMON, Jane 883
WATERS, Alexander 254
Andrew G., Mrs. 596
Charles E. 149
Charles E., Mrs. 596
Cyrus 879
E. G. 617, 746
Edward G. 139
Emily G. 596
F. E. 449
F. G. 576
Francis 226, 467, 581
George 246
Godfrey 921
H. 70
Henry 197
Hez. H. 450
Hezekiah 89, 168, 172, 238, 246, 461, 522, 592, 826, 827
James S. 205, 810
John 240, 241
John C. 922
Littleton 433
R. T. 889
Rebecca (ONION) 922
Richard 246, 810

WATERS, Somerset R. 810
Stephen 254
Thomas 100, 101
William H. 359
William S. 810
Wilson 741
Waters, Charles E. & Co. 149
Waters & Zacharie 433
Waters' Colored Methodist Chapel 581
Watersville 342
WATERTON, John 818
Joseph 818
WATKINGS, ---, Mr. 518
Francis 518
WATKINS, ---, Capt. 112
Charles 401
Francis 818
J. F. 365
J. M. 815, 903
J. Morris 902
Jame 39
John 922
John N. 810
John W. 129, 189, 729
John Wesley 189
Joshua 189
Nicholas 191
Thomas 749, 810
Virginia R. (OBER) 401
W. F. 600
Wilbur F. 522
William H. 161
William M. 161
WATKINSON, ---, Rev. Mr. 889
M. R. 562
W. R. 810
WATSON, --- 134
Elijah 255
Harrison 838
Henry 599
Hugh 161
John 361
Margaret 936
Robert 161, 593
T. 241
Thomas 92, 241
Thomas A. 810
William H. 113, 114, 133, 189, 194, 242, 251, 351, 810
William H., Mrs. 352
Watson, Henry Children's Aid Society of Baltimore 599, 602
Watson's Island 39
WATT, Jacob 247
John 253
Watt's Island 310
WATTERS, Godfrey 921
William 574
William J.H. 415
WATTS, ---, Capt. 89

WATTS, ---, Mr. 694
  Asbury 836
  C. 100
  D. B. 246
  Dickson 246
  John 552
  John H. C. 509
  John S. 253
  Nathaniel 836
  Philip 836
  Thomas 811
  Thomas B. 249
WAUGH, ---, Bishop 576, 577, 578, 580, 809, 929
  Beverly 582, 745
  J. W. 810
  John W. 813
  Waverly 595, 886, 887, 888, 889, 890
  Waverly Baptist Church 889
  Waverly Fire Department 888
  Waverly Gazette 837
  Waverly Hall 889
  Waverly Lodge 889, 834, 836, 903
  Waverly M.E. Church 889
  Waverly M.E. Colored Church 889
  Waverly Station-house Fire Company 818
WAY, A. J. H. 674, 675
  Joseph 733, 734
  Walter R. 161
WAYLAND, ---, Rev. Dr. 565
WAYNE, Henry N. 526
Waynesboro' 356, 357
WAYS, W. 95, 269
WAYSON, George W. 190
WEAKLY, E. A. 908
WEARY, John 252
  Peter 173
  Thomas 89
WEATHER, M. W. 855
  William F. 855
WEATHERBURN, John 70, 76, 246, 453, 456, 457, 520, 810
WEATHERBY, Jesse 101
WEATHERED, John 356
WEATHERS, Joseph 190, 194
WEAVER, --- 144
  D. C. 465
  George 253
  J. Harry 253, 264
  James E. 191
  John 462, 780
  John H. 138
  William H. 552
Weaver Family 852
WEBB, ---, Capt. 574
  ---, Mr. 184, 185, 261
  A. L. 362
  A. L. & Co. 132
  Augustus P. 487

WEBB, C. 365, 459
  Charles 155, 183, 184, 187, 189, 365, 368, 693
  Clarissa (LEGG) 183
  E. S. 153
  Francis I. D. 161
  George F. 466
  George F., Mrs. 604
  George W. 472
  Harrison H. 526
  Henry 828
  Henry W. 468
  Hester (COX) 185
  Jamar 194
  James 184, 193, 466, 488, 810
  Nelly 811
  W. H. 149
  W. P. 369, 828
  William 65
  William P. 370, 828
  William R. 828
Webb, Charles & James & Co. 184
Webb, Charles & Sons 184
WEBBER, H. A. 688
  William 600
WEBER, Charles 468, 489, 605
  W. F. 502
WEBSTER, ---, Sailing Master 91
  A. 585
  Augustus 617
  Daniel 122
  Edward H. 906
  Edwin H. 145, 497, 720
  Henry 193
  Henry W. 253, 483
  Isaac 38
  J. J. G. 271, 578, 837
  J. Lee 38
  James R. 229
  John 247
  John A. 810
  John Skinner 811
  Joseph 249
  M. 38
  Noah 224
  Richard 575
  T. 139
  Thomas W. 161
  W. Eugene 222
  William W. 188
  Wecker 655, 787
WEDERSTRANDT, John C. 77
WEDFORD, Henry 320
WEDGE, Simon 253
Wednesday Club 668, 674
WEECH, T. L. 578
WEEDEN, Lulu M. 870
Weekly American 610
Weekly Bulletin 635
Weekly Freeman 635
Weekly Gazette 633

Weekly Journal of Politics, Science & Literature 615
Weekly Times 641
WEEKS, B. 102
  John L. 155
Weemes Line 303
WEEMS, David 101
  G. W. 845
  John 877
  M. L. 135
  Mason L. 468
  Mason Locke 810
  Sarah 864
  Sarah Ann 877
  Sarah C. 865
  W. 102, 103
  William 101
  William M. 742
WEHR, Fred. 605
  Frederick 191, 468, 489
  H. 597
WEIL, J. 589
WEINBERGER, Levi 828
WEIR, John 173
Weisburg 27
WEISE, Felix 246
WEISEL, Daniel 600
WEISENFELD, B., Mrs. 603
  David 841
  M. 488
WEISENTHAL, Andrew 433, 809
  Charles F. 72, 810
  Charles Frederick 432
  Elizabeth 810
  Weisenthal & Coal 432
WEISENTHALL, ---, Dr. 733
  Andrew 732
  Charles Frederick 731
WEISER, Charles 343
  Lewis 161
WEISHAMPEL, J. F. 616, 630
WEISHAMPLE, J. F. 628
WEISHLER, ---, Mr. 568
Weiskittel, A. & Son 427
WEISKITTLE, Anton 468
WEISS, Frederick 280
WEISSNER, Frederick 927
WEITZELL, Henry 191
WELAND, D. C. 193
WELBY, Thomas J. 466
WELCH, A. 207
  Adam 207
  B. Allen 358
  E. A. 937
  John 263, 559, 758, 759, 810, 860
Welch's Adventure 49
WELD, Charles R. 590
  Thomas 531
WELFORD, R. T. 252
  Stevens W. 560
WELL, E. F. 550
WELLENER, Basil S. 430
  Elizabeth T. 430
WELLER, Elizabeth 866
  Joseph 813
WELLES, G. 156
Wellesley, ---, Marchioness of 821
  ---, Marquis of 708
WELLFORD, R. P. 252
WELLINGTON, --- 88
WELLMAN, William 840
WELLMORE, E. 675
Wellner & Beech 307
WELLS, --- 933
  ---, Mr. 60, 99
  Andrew H. 380
  Benjamin 71
  Bezaleel 863
  Charles 518
  Cyprian 239, 545, 572
  D. 95, 269
  Daniel 94, 267
  George 351, 574
  John 61, 262, 307, 741, 810, 922
  Joshua 810, 816, 892, 896
  Peter 189
  R. C. 190
  Rebecca (RISTEAU) 863
  Richard 191
  Richard C. 189
  Thomas 519, 584
Wells & McComas Monument 267, 281
Wells & McComas Riflemen 669
WELLSLEY, ---, Marchioness of 811
  Long, Mrs. 810
Wellwood Farm 854
WELSH, ---, Mr. 460, 634
  Adam 192, 250, 456, 457, 811
  Bartholomew T. 555
  Charles 395
  Charles A. 161
  George 74, 322, 779
  John 70, 555
  John W. 487
  Mary 395
  Robert S. 820
  Sarah E. 886
  Thomas J. 195, 820
  William 487, 894
  William H. 195, 487, 633, 650
  William O. 193
Welsh, Baker & Co. 633
Welsh Friends 883
Welsh Independent Church 590
WELTY, ---, Rev. Mr. 933
WELTZ, ---, Rev. Mr. 842
WEMPE, Henry 927
WENK, E. E. 489
WENTWORTH, Ella 630
WENTZ, John B. 191, 194, 231, 468
WERDEBAUGH, Henry J. 487

Werhagen D. & Groverman 298
Werner, Dresel & Co. 372
WESLEY, ---, Mr. 573
 Charles 582
 John 582
Wesley Chapel [M.E.] 579
Wesley M.E. Chapel 580, 909
Wesleyan Methodist Visitor 616
Wesleyan Repository & Religious Intelligencer 616
WEST, ---, Dr. 520
 ---, Miss 351
 ---, Mr. 860
 Charles 245
 Eli 810
 James 452, 455
 John 515
 Joseph 863
 L. B. 252
 Margaret 720
 Susannah (WALKER) 862
 Violetta (HOWARD) 863
 William 249, 519, 574, 720, 809, 810, 861, 862, 919
West Branch 870
West Branch of Gunpowder Falls 870
West Chester Junction 350
West End 342
West End Savings Association 512
West Hundred 812
West Point 865
West Point Chapel 855
West Point Military Academy 891
West River 634, 722, 756
West River Monthly Meeting 587
West River Society of Friends 587
West Street Chapel 584
WESTCOTT, John 428
 Mary 428
Wester Ogle 834, 835
WESTERMANN, N. 902
WESTERN, --- 693
Western Bank 406, 451
Western Branch Baptist Sunday-school 563
Western Cemetery 820
Western Continent, The 628, 649, 650, 651
Western Dispensary 748
Western Express 505
Western Female High School 227, 230, 601
Western Fountain 213
Western German Mission 578
Western Hose Company 256
Western Hose Fire Company 242
Western Hotel 261, 776
Western M.E. Chapel 580
Western Maryland Co. 344, 356, 357

Western Maryland Railroad 182, 183, 284, 318, 340, 345, 353, 354, 355, 356, 387, 626, 702, 815, 830, 831, 834, 841, 842, 851, 854, 857, 873, 928
Western Morse Telegraph Line 507
Western National Bank 389, 451, 462, 469
Western Refined 385
Western Run 517, 854, 857, 859, 863, 876, 883, 886
Western Run Parish 865, 866
Western Run Turnpike 876
Western Run Valley 30, 861, 862, 865
Western Scheutzen Park 517
Western Telegraph Co. 507
Western Union Telegraph Co. 504, 508, 512
Westham Granite Co. of Richmond 444
Westham Granite Quarries 669
Westliche Post 655
Westminster 42, 70, 344, 355, 357, 776, 866
Westminster Churchyard 645
Westminster Hall 703
Westminster Parish 862
Westminster Presbyterian Church 546, 547, 549, 937
Westminster Presbyterian Churchyard 271
Westminster Turnpike 854, 857, 865
Westover 743
Westphaelische Zeitung 625
WESTRICH, Charles 468
WESTWOOD, John H. 189
WETHERAL, James H. 898
WETHERALD, Esther 625
WETHERALL, ---, Miss 898
 May Bedel (PRESBURY) 425
 William 425
 William G. 425
WETHERBURN, John 117
WETHERED, Charles E. 155, 601
 John 130, 162, 195, 816, 828, 876
 L. 89
 Levin 461
 Lewin 393
 Lewyn 471
 Samuel 810, 828
Wethered Brothers 828
Wetheredsville 18, 369, 820, 821, 828, 829
WETHERELL, Henry 910, 920
WETHERSTEIN, John 927
Wetipquin Creek 744
WETSCHKY, Charles 161
WETTER, J. 842
Weverton 342
WEYER, Michael 246

WEYL, Charles 570, 811
WEYLER, J. F. 193
WEYMAN, ---, Bishop 581
 Robert 919
WHALEN, Stephen 190
WHARTMAN, John C. 813
 Michael 812
WHARTON, John O. 497, 498
 M. H. 565
WHATCOAT, ---, Bishop 576
 Whatcoat Cemetery 826
 Whatcoat Chapel 576
 Whatcoat M.E. Church 576
WHEAT, Edward 515
 Wheatfield Inn 514, 515
 Wheatland Grange No. 64, Patrons
  of Husbandry 832
WHEATLEY, John F. 810
 William F. 442
WHEATON, Edward 359
 Nathaniel 715
WHEDEN, James 484
WHEEDON, James 263
 James C. 162
 James H. 149
WHEELAN, ---, Bishop 529
 V. R. 540
WHEELEN, Hezekiah 742
WHEELER, ---, Lt. 656
 Belinda 867
 Benjamin 867, 884
 Benjamin F. 253
 Charity Ann 382
 Charles 534, 855
 Charles A. 193
 Ellen 867
 Francis J. 814
 H. Lizzie 908
 Henry W. 161
 J. D. 469, 472
 J. M. 855
 J. R. 575
 Jesse 246
 John 246, 814
 John M. 902
 Leonard 247
 Lewis H. 810, 898
 Michael 236
 Thomas 382
 William F. 855
 William T. 161
 Wheeler & Keech 906
 Wheeling 342
WHEELRIGHT, Jeremiah 488
WHEELWRIGHT, Jeremiah 810
 Jeremich 466
WHELAN, Catherine 810
 David 247
 M. J. 193
 Richard 810
 Thomas 190, 247, 256, 472, 488

WHELEN, Elizabeth L. 412
 Henry 412
WHETCROFT, William 76
WHETSON, William E. 465
Whetstone Neck 43
Whetstone Point 49, 50, 62, 73, 76,
 287, 290, 291, 422, 424, 849, 921
WHEY, John 568
Whig Club 607, 779
Whig Club Mob 778
Whig, The 612, 613, 646
WHILLDIN, ---, Capt. 348
WHIPPS, Benjamin 38
Whiskey Insurrection 668, 733
WHISTLER, G. W. 811
 George W. 810
WHITAKER, Frank 925
 George P. 424
 James 424
WHITCROFT, William 432
WHITE, ---, Bishop 915
 ---, Dr. 179, 741
 ---, Father 33
 ---, Misses 684
 ---, Mr. 179, 850
 ---, Mrs. 595
 ---, Rev. Dr. 835
 A. A. 745
 A. M. 466
 Abraham 192, 237, 532
 Alphonso A. 161
 C. J. 629
 Catherine 749
 Charles J. 534, 627
 Charles M. 886
 Charles T. 537
 Edward 741
 Edwin 899
 F. 369
 Francis 232, 345, 358, 441, 464, 488,
  600, 746, 810, 825, 932
 Francis, Mrs. 604
 Frank, Mrs. 596
 Galing 880
 Gideon 810
 H. 103, 439
 J. C. 89, 393, 735
 J. McKenney 415
 James 252
 Jerome 499
 John 65, 176, 188, 237, 493, 515,
  594, 595, 880
 John C. 175, 192, 495, 735
 John Campbell 86, 209, 734, 742,
  809, 824
 John H. 523
 John J. 880
 Joseph 251, 592, 810
 Miles 274, 465, 810
 Miles, Mrs. 604
 Orlando G. 190

218

WHITE, Rezin 247
Robert 749
S. 102, 103, 439
Sarah 594
Simon 592
Stephen 65
Stephen W. 346
Thomas 45, 65, 193, 407, 526, 915
W. A. 911
William 74
William C. 749
White, J. C. & Son 212
White, J. C. & Sons 439
White Buck & Hedrich 261
White Building 447
White Clay Creek 311
White Hall 347, 817, 836, 871, 872, 875, 889, 908, 913
White Haven 310
White Horse 514
White Marsh 703, 884
White Peruke 764
White Plains 382, 780
White Swan 513
White's Distillery 212
WHITEFIELD, --- 566
---, Mr. 544
---, Rev. Mr. 920
WHITEFORD, Charles E. 870
Hugh 742
James 189, 488
John 855
R. Lewis 488
Whitehall 30, 31
Whitehall Factory 408, 409, 836
Whitehall Mill 215
WHITEHEAD, James 520, 809
Whitelaw & Fenhagen 277
WHITELEY, B. 365
WHITELOCK, ---, Mr. 400
Anna 400
Elizabeth 400
George 399, 400, 856
Jane (WOOLSTON) 400
John 247
Margaret Sherwood 856
Mary 400
Sarah 399
Susan 400
William 400, 466, 484, 488, 489, 820
Whitelock, William & Co. 399
WHITELY, Benjamin 368, 459
W. I. 369
William S. 368
Whitemarsh Run 925
Whiteside & Cator 432
WHITESIDES, ---, Rev. Mr. 902
WHITEWRIGHT, William 390
WHITFIELD, ---, Archbishop 529, 530, 533, 541, 598

WHITFIELD, James 528, 534, 594, 811
WHITING, Adeline 722
James 484
WHITLOCK, --- 682
---, Mrs. 682
William 399
WHITMAN, Ezra 155, 162, 195, 640, 642, 847
Ezra R. 852
John H. 507
WHITNEY, Addison O. 790
Joseph C. 193
Milton 596, 810, 811
Milton, Mrs. 596
William D. 233
WHITRIDGE, Catharine C. (MORRIS) 756
H. L. 368
Helen 596
Horatio 810, 891
Horatio L. 440, 810
Horatio S. 441
John 755, 810, 825
John A. 482
Thomas 139, 288, 441, 464, 466, 470, 471, 484, 488, 577, 596
Thomas, Mrs. 596
William 502, 598, 745
WHITSON, David 465
David E. 139, 161, 202
Francis 155
WHITTAKER, Joseph 424
Nathaniel 402
Whittaker's Furnace 925
WHITTEMORE, G. H. 815
George H. 814
WHITTER, Anne E. 901
WHITTINGHAM, ---, Bishop 132, 137, 139, 521, 522, 523, 822, 837, 867, 888, 892
Richard 836
William R. 151
William Rollins 810
William Rollinson 521, 654
William Rollison 914
WHITTINGTON, J. 678
Joseph 886
WHITTLE, Charles N. 161
Samuel N. 161
WHITTLESAY, ---, Mr. 544
WHITTY, William H. 600
WHITWORTH, Abraham 575, 932
WHYTE, Thomas 193
William P. 723
William Pinkney 165, 181, 194, 195, 254, 903
Wichelhausen, H. D. & Co. 439
WICHELHAUSER, Jacob 372
WICKERHAM, William 240
WICKERSHAM, --- 193

WICKERSHAM, John 191, 938
W. 241
William 241, 251, 463
WIDERMAN, L. M. 815
WIEGEL, W. H. 150
William H. 161
William Henry 148
WIER, Elizabeth 915
WIERMAN, William 439
WIERS, Henry 872
WIES, August 927
WIESEL, Daniel 149
WIESENFELD, Moses 810
WIESENFIELD, Goody R. 149
M. 149
Michael 149
Wiesenfield & Co. 149
WIESENTHAL, Andrew 814
Charles 71
Charles Frederick 730
WIESENTHALL, ---, Dr. 568, 734
Andrew 731, 733
Charles Frederick 61
WIEST, Christopher 212
WIGFALL, Louis T. 810
WIGHT, Charles C. 229
George L. 659
John J. 878
Rezin 188
William J. 192
WIGHTMAN, Joseph W. 508
WIGMAN, H. 625
WIGNALL, Thomas 683
WIGNELL, ---, Mr. 682
James 118, 170, 810
Wignell & Reinagle 688
WIGWELL, William 35
WILBURN, B. R. 586
WILCOX, ---, Mr. 786
Henry 488
Theodore F. 466
Wilcox & White 674
WILDER, Levi 673
W. 889
Wilderness, Battle of 897
WILDEY, ---, Grand Master 760
Thomas 254, 269, 270, 279, 690, 758, 759, 760, 761, 810, 896
Wildey Monument 269, 279, 640, 761
Wildwood 400
WILEY, ---, Capt. 785
---, Mr. 354
George 77
John 810, 879, 911
John F. 194, 810
Luke 921
Samuel 191
Thomas 246
WILHELM, D. B. 838
Henry 161

WILHELM, P. F. 873
Samuel 810
WILISON, Charles 176
WILKENS, Edward 497
Louis 823
William 368, 810, 822, 823
WILKENS (WILKINS), Louis 423
Wilkens (Wilkins), William & Co. 423
Wilkens Avenue 820
Wilkes Street 769, 933
WILKINS, ---, Miss 595
Catharine (LORBACHER) 423
Christian 422
Edward 166, 498, 810, 847
H. 735, 742
Helen (SCHLUTER) 423
Henry 845
Joseph 481
Sophia (HEYER) 423
Sprigg, Mrs. 595
William 233, 368, 422, 423, 465, 810
Wilkins, William & Co. 822
Wilkins Avenue 871
WILKINSON, ---, Gen. 97
---, Mr. 106, 694
Basil M., Dr. 642
John 38
R. T. 255
Robert 77
Shubie, Capt. 810
Stephen 519
Stephen, Rev. 919
Thomas S. 205
Walter S. 195, 272, 446
William 71, 927
Wilkinson & Smith 238
Wilks Street M.E. Church 575
Wilks Street Methodist Church 574
WILL, William R. 237, 821
WILLARD, Solomon 317
WILLEMS, ---, Miss 682
WILLETT, ---, Col. 761
Charles S. 364
Willett Bell Encampment, No. 22 I.O.O.F. 874
William St. Independent Methodist Church 585
William Street M.E. Church 578
William Tell Building Association 512
WILLIAMS, --- 698, 769
---, Dr. 557, 699
---, Gen. 81
---, Mr. 658, 718
Amos 547
Amos A. 192
Anthony C. 161
B. H. 873
Barney 693, 694, 695
Benjamin 77, 205, 261, 312, 455
C. D. 324

WILLIAMS, Catharine 582
  Catharine (OWEN) 556
  Charles 432, 810
  Christopher 592
  Corinthia V. J. (READ) 556
  Cumberland 298
  E. Calvin 557
  E. G. 680
  Ebenezer 809
  Edward 161, 471, 556, 810
  Edward, Mrs. 594
  Eleanor (GITTINGS) 810
  Eleanor A. (GITTINGS) 718
  Elizabeth 582
  Elizabeth Bordley (HAWKINS) 717
  Frances 582
  G. H. 191, 484
  G. H., Mrs. 595
  G. Harlan 487, 488, 495
  G. Hawkins 810
  George 717, 820
  George H. 595, 723, 931
  George H., Mrs. 595
  George Harlan 720
  George Hawkins 665, 716, 717
  George May 718
  H. 303
  H. A. 694
  Henry 468, 604, 757
  Henry H. 810
  Herman 442
  J. 77, 102
  J. B. 631
  J. Savage, Mrs. 604
  J. T. 231
  J. W. M. 555, 565, 838
  J. W. N. 601
  James 84, 100, 188, 265, 266, 393, 471, 576, 592
  James F. 927
  James R. 582
  Jane S. 230
  Jno. W. M. 566
  John 161, 453, 596, 811, 830
  John A. 584
  John B. 187, 441, 635
  John F. 489
  John R. 616
  John S. 365, 440, 442
  John W. 246
  John W. M. 556
  Joseph 100, 264, 298
  Joshua B. 665
  Lloyd W. 720, 814, 896
  Luther 870
  Martha 810
  Mary 582
  N. 137
  N. F. 84, 298, 393, 439, 461
  Nathaniel 62, 98, 188, 193, 194, 393, 470, 497, 589, 729, 810

WILLIAMS, Nathaniel F. 84, 98, 120, 265, 266, 810
  Nathaniel H. 498
  Nathaniel S. 810
  O. H. 77, 82
  Otho H. 81, 452, 459, 497, 679, 698, 728
  Otho Holland 498, 810
  P. B. 667
  P. C. 596, 601, 743, 745
  Philip C. 746
  Robert 717
  Robert H. 830
  S. 103
  Samuel 463, 581
  Samuel M. 810
  Sarah 582
  Stephen 547, 548, 577, 810, 902
  Stillman 161
  T. 840
  Thomas 101, 394, 732
  Thomas E. 162
  Thomas M. 931
  Thomas P. 484
  Walter W. 522
  William 586
  William E. 845
  William J. 751, 810
  William T. 190
Williams, James & Co. 101
Williams, John & James Co. 262
Williams, L. & Co. 624
Williams Point 310
WILLIAMSON, ---, Mrs. 595
  Alex. S. 161
  Charles A. 810
  David 61, 192, 298, 483, 532, 594, 810, 826, 827
  George 188, 252, 740
  George W. 254
  J. D. 810
  Jane (PARKER) 662
  John 662
  Juliana 594
  Luke T. 141
  Sarah 660
  William 592
Williamson & Smith 261
Williamson's Hotel 740
Williamsport 318, 356
WILLIAR, H. D. 442
  H. R. 380
  William A. 456
WILLIARD, Julius 189
WILLIMSON, D. 237
WILLINGER, M. 468
WILLIS, ---, Mr. 925
  Henry 225, 239, 575
  John 817
  Solomon J. 255
  Thomas H. 255

WILLIS, William 392
WILLIT, Charles S. 465
WILLS, ---, Mr. 612
  J. Buchanan 817
  James 691
  John 505, 507, 508, 612, 635, 637
  Joshua 578
  R. H. 583
  Richard C. 161
  W. G. 593
  William H. 456
WILLSHIRE, James G. 738
WILLSON, Anna (MYER) 395
  F. S. 395
  Francis W. 810
  H. 103
WILMER, ---, Rev. Mr. 588
  Edward 522
  James J. 609
  James Jones 919, 920
  L. A. 617
  Lambert 617
  Simon 416, 522
  Skipwith 191
  Wilmer & Palmer 439
Wilmington 351
Wilmington & Smyrna Railroad Company 314
Wilmington & Susquehanna Railroad 348
Wilmington Road 130
WILMOT, --- 684
  ---, Mrs. 684
  John 810
  John G. 145, 193
  John T. 132
WILMOTT, Richard 519, 921
WILSON, --- 103, 104
  ---, Capt. 817
  ---, Dr. 744
  ---, Mr. 434, 440, 889
  ---, Rev. Mr. 933
  A. 509
  A. W. 586, 587, 636
  Alice 298
  Alicia Brewer 743
  Alicia Brewer (GRIFFITH) 743
  Ann 770
  Anne (CARSON) 770
  Anne R. 770
  Archibald 508
  Benjamin 120
  Charles A. 161
  Charles G. 370
  D. S. 456, 870, 887
  David 247, 248, 298, 617
  David R. 463, 484
  David S. 440, 483, 769, 770
  E. G. 302
  E., Miss 595
  E., Mrs. 595
WILSON, Edward 161
  Eliza M. 564
  Eliza McKim 770
  Emily Brewer 743
  Emma 770
  Ephraim 743
  F. 565
  Fayette 770
  Francis N. 810
  Francis W. 307
  Franklin 368, 555, 556, 562, 563, 564, 567, 568, 628, 630, 770, 830, 832, 838, 889
  G. G. 743
  Genie 908
  George 246, 809
  George H. 380
  George W. 922
  Gerrard 92
  Granville Oscar 431
  Greenbury 194
  Greenbury B. 810
  H. M. 576, 595, 743
  H. M., Mrs., Dr. 598
  H. P. C. 742, 743, 745, 937
  H. T. G. 739
  Hannah 770, 771
  Harry 936
  Henrietta (D'ARCY) 770
  Henrietta Chauncey 743
  Henry 76, 149, 194, 235, 727, 728
  Henry M. 745
  Henry Parke Custis 743
  Henry Parke Custus 743
  Henry R. 177, 770
  Isaac 161, 810
  Isaac G. 770
  Isabella 770
  J. 100
  J. E. 362
  J. G. 604
  J. M. 550
  J. P. 577
  J. S. 821
  J. W. 192, 365
  Jackson 813, 911
  James 84, 89, 175, 179, 187, 188, 209, 244, 316, 324, 393, 439, 440, 470, 556, 564, 769, 770, 809, 810, 811, 814, 824, 826, 827, 889, 892
  James G. 476, 769
  James H. 161
  James H., Mrs. 596
  James Hamilton 770
  James S. 465
  James Thomas 770
  James, Mrs. 556
  Jane 770
  Jane (STONEBURY) 769
  Jane S. 770

WILSON, John 188, 244, 246, 465, 484, 593, 757, 811
John Custis 743
John S. 821
John W. 140, 161, 193, 299, 810, 818
Joseph 38, 190
Joseph C. 288, 440, 576
Lewis 770
Luther 190, 810
Malcolm 161, 818
Malcomb 810
Margaret M. (MARRIOTT) 770
Maria (D'ARCY) 770
Martha 770
Mary (CRUSE) 770
Mary (KNOX) 770
Mary (SHIELDS) 769
Mary Anna 743
Mary B. 770
Mary Cruse 770
Mary E. 770
Mary F. 916
Mary Hollins (BOWLEY) 770
Mary L. 770
Melville 564, 770
Norval 586
Parke Custis 743
Peggy (CUSTIS) 743
Peter 380
Philip 120
Phoebe 398
Pierce Butler 852
R. J. 564
Robert 192, 463, 579, 810
Robert A. 161, 818
Robert Taylor 743
Robert Y. 810
Ruth (TISDALE) 431
S. A. 579, 826
S. F. 609
S. M. 586
Sallie (SKINNER) 770
Samuel 38, 89, 240, 241, 249, 251, 770
Samuel A. 579
Samuel J. 810
Stephen 82, 169, 452, 545, 547, 733, 810
Susan E. (SAVAGE) 743
T. H., Mrs. 595
T. Oswald 190
T., Mrs. 595
Thomas 343, 439, 440, 463, 466, 567, 593, 604, 614, 638, 698, 770, 810
Thomas J. 469, 484, 769, 770
Thomas R. 177
Virginia (APPLETON) 770
Virginia C. (ONION) 392
W. 162

WILSON, W. H. 586
W. W. 190
William 84, 89, 98, 170, 173, 188, 192, 194, 197, 201, 244, 246, 254, 271, 302, 393, 407, 432, 450, 455, 470, 482, 483, 545, 555, 556, 727, 734, 768, 769, 770, 771, 810, 892
William B. 476, 482, 770
William C. 770, 887
William G. 392
William Griffith 743
William K. 770
William Thomas 770
William W. 254
Young O. 587
Wilson, Colston & Co. 476, 769, 770
Wilson, J. B. & Co. 636
Wilson, Mullikin & Co. 439
Wilson, Thomas & Co. 614
Wilson, Thomas Fuel Giving Society 702
Wilson, Thomas Sanitarium for Children 604, 702
Wilson, William & Sons 438, 567, 769, 770, 828, 892
Wilson & Maris 769
Wilson & Perry 431
Wilson M.E. Church 917
Wilson's 354
Wilson's M.E. Church 904
Wilson's Slave Jail 144
WILSTORF, C. 469
WILT, Samuel 113
WILTON, B. 820
Winan's 354
Winan's M.E. Chapel 586
Winan's Shop 132
Winan's Wharf 90
WINANS, ---, Mr. 217, 322, 348
Julia 811
Ross 130, 132, 137, 194, 299, 319, 320, 321, 323, 328, 477, 810, 811, 847, 936
Thomas 181, 274, 299, 321, 810, 936
Thomas, Mrs. 593, 810
Winans & Co. 181
Winans Locomotive-Works 426
Winans M.E. Chapel 586
Winans Permanent Land & Loan Co. 512
Winans' Chapel 151, 548
Winans' Cigar Ship 299
Winans' Soup House 586
Winans' Yacht 299
Winchester 342
WINCHESTER, ---, Mr. 172
Alexander 547, 909
Ann (OWINGS) 862
David 265, 266, 298, 316, 439, 456, 469, 470, 811, 824

WINCHESTER, George 62, 120, 188, 195, 343, 782, 862
 J. 77
 J. Marshall 481
 Jacob 249
 James 194, 658, 729, 809, 810, 862
 Marshall 484
 Mary 909
 Richard 809
 Samuel 480, 811
 Sarah (OWINGS) 862
 Sarah A. (CARROLL) 909
 William 118, 169, 170, 449, 455, 456, 809
Winchester Baptists 554
WINDER, --- 85, 698
 ---, Gen. 91, 95, 96, 97
 ---, Gov. 87
 Charles H. 734, 810
 Charles S. 670, 810
 John H. 810
 Levin 75, 195, 809
 Richard B. 745
 W. 393
 William H. 84, 88, 92, 265, 266, 699, 711, 758, 810, 850
 William S. 819
Windmill Point 310
WINDOLF, Herman 605
Windsor 904, 905
WINEBERGER, J. S. 256
WINEBRENNER, Hannah 379
 P. Forney 379
WINEHOLT, Reuben H. 870
WINGATE, ---, Capt. 294
WINGMAN, Charles 298
WININGDER, Lewis 380
Winley's Forest 923
WINN, ---, Mr. 759
 John 254
Winnebrarians 902
WINNING, John 100, 519, 809
WINSLOW, C., Mrs. 604
 Caleb 745
 John 430
 Sallie 430
WINSTANDLEY, William H. 188
WINSTANLEY, W. H. 249
WINSTON, Cobb 933
WINTER, Amos 867
 C. F. 597
 Samuel 190
Winter Run 553
Winter's Run 311
Winter's Run Baptist Church 554
WINTERODE, George C. 836
WINTERS, Elisha 727
 Henry 250
 Henry W. 241
WINTHROP, ---, Mr. 652
 Robert C. 653

WIRGMAN, Charles 438
 O. P. 483
WIRT, --- 805
 ---, Mr. 641
 Henry 465
 William 120, 642, 644, 652, 679, 698, 712, 810
WIRTH, Joseph 542
WISCOTT, --- 104
WISE, ---, Miss 770
 ---, Mr. 271
 Ann (HUNTER) 875
 Annie 875
 Charles H. 875
 George D. 810
 Henry A. 122, 231
 John 120, 875
 John M. 819, 820
 Lavinia M. 875
 Miranda (HICKS) 875
 William 872, 875
WISEBOUGH, William L. 255
Wiseburg 817, 871, 874, 875
Wiseburg M.E. Church 875
WISEMAN, A. 740
WISNER, Jacob 369
 Noah 869
WISONG, W. A. 126, 478, 569
 William A. 153, 155, 194, 600, 602
WISSEL, Joseph 541
WITHERS, Charlotte (CALDER) 873
WITMAN, John H. 505, 810
WITMER, P. A. 231
WOELPER, George 89, 188
WOERNER, J. G. 929
WOLF, Alcaeus B. 241, 254
 Alonzo L. 469
 E. I. 569
 Edmond 487
 Edmund 194, 379, 466
 George W. 190
 I. 269
 J. 95
 Marcus 162, 380, 381, 810
 Marcus W. 467
 Samuel 250
 Sarah Mann (GEORGE) 467
Wolf & Slagle 379
WOLFE, Fr. E. S. 484
 T. R. 834
Wolfe Street 769
WOLFF, ---, Rev. Dr. 572
 Edward 365
 Jacob 516
WOLFORD, ---, Mr. 441
Wolftrap Light-house 310
WOLL, Jacob 576
WOLLMAN, Edward 161
WOLTHROP, John 498
Wolverham 858
WONDERLY, William S. 810

WOOD, --- 612
---, Dr. 741
---, Maj. 895
---, Mr. 164, 684, 685, 686, 687
---, Mrs. 684
C. S. 516
Gabriel 298
George 674
George J. P. 161
George M. D. 191
Gerard 741
Hannah (DAVIS) 772
Hannah Ann 772
James 772
James H. 190, 260
James M. 152
Jane 772
John 58, 380, 519
Nicholas L. 161, 163, 199, 200, 484, 485, 487
Priscilla (BACON) 772
Richard 772
Ruth (CLEMENT) 772
W. W. W. 359
William 38, 244, 504
William B. 683
William Maxwell 810
Wood & Oliphant 390
Wood Bridge 354
Wood Family 772
Woodall, William E. & Co. 303
Woodberry 15, 22, 215, 218, 245, 275, 347, 407, 410, 425, 507, 815, 834, 836, 837, 838, 887, 888, 889
Woodberry Baptist Church 838
Woodberry Factory 213, 817
Woodberry M.E. Church 888
Woodberry Mill 836
Woodberry Mills 275, 409
Woodberry News 815, 837
Woodbine 911
Woodbourne 623, 887
Woodburn 862, 865
WOODBURN, D. E. 484
Woodbury 886
WOODEN, J. 845
John 845
Wooden Horse 142
Woodensburg 854, 855
WOODHULL, Aaron 161
Max 141
Woodlawn 720
Woodlawn Cemetery 817, 839
Woodley 773, 774
WOODMASON, Charles 920
WOODS, ---, Mrs. 582
Charles L. 587
Henry 865
Hiram 359, 484, 488, 564, 565, 596, 810, 817, 839
Hiram, Mrs. 596

WOODS, Hudson 161
Mary Ann 583
R. C. 359
Wesley 582
William 197, 261
William M. 161, 190, 465
WOODSIDE, James 288
James D. 266
WOODSON, D. M. 560
Woodstock 20, 24, 342
Woodstock College 830, 833
Woodstock Station 833
WOODVILLE, William 480, 481, 810
Woodville, William & Son 481
WOODWARD, Anna V. 596
C. 190
E. T. J. 896
George P. 189, 190
John 574
R. F. 412
Thomas 53, 54, 758, 759
W. 523
William 125, 302, 412, 456, 462, 469, 484, 485, 596, 598
William W. 440
Woodward, Baldwin & Co. 412
Woodward, Baldwin & Norris 408, 412
Woodward, William & Co. 412
WOODWIN, William 380
WOODWORTH, Frederick 483
Samuel 642
Woodyard 351
WOODYEAR, Charles E. 139
E. G. 84
Edward 188
Edward G. 98, 188, 194, 758
WOODYEAR, Thomas 456
William E. 441, 442, 444, 489, 603
WOOL, ---, Gen. 140, 141, 650, 880
John E. 139
WOOLEN, Mary E. 477
Thomas 276
WOOLEY, Hannah 386
WOOLFORD, John 741
Levin 166
Levin R. 165
WOOLLEN, Robinson 249
Zachariah 188
WOOLLEY, ---, Col. 146, 147, 148, 149, 151
John 152, 810
WOOLSEY, George 70, 196
William 72, 101
WOOLSTON, Jane 400
Samuel S. 488
Stephen 400
WORKER, --- 201
Workingmen's Perpetual Building Association A of West End 512
Workington 743

World, The 640, 651
WORREL, Asenath (LOWE) 866
  Edward 740
  Thomas 866
WORRELL, ---, Dr. 741
  Thomas 251, 252, 299
WORSLEY, George Hughes 910, 919, 920
Worth 923
WORTHINGTON, --- 707
  ---, Judge 786
  ---, Mr. 217, 407, 463, 868
  A. B. 847
  Ann 858, 861, 862, 864
  Arterma 862
  Beale 640
  Benjamin I. 865, 866
  Benjamin J. 864
  C. 38
  Charles 120, 470, 741, 850, 862, 863, 864, 865
  Charlotte 864
  Comfort Dorsey 864
  Edward 855, 864, 866
  Edwin 864
  Elizabeth 864
  Elizabeth (HAMMOND) 832
  Elizabeth (RIDGELY) 862
  Ellen 864
  Garrett 864
  George 880
  George Fitzhugh 865, 879
  J. 38
  James 864
  John 733, 832, 842, 862, 864
  John G. 252
  John T. 816, 861, 865
  John T. H. 819, 862, 865
  John Tolley 819, 862, 864, 866
  John Tolly 865
  Kinsey 864
  Kittei 864
  Marcella (OWINGS) 832
  Martha 864
  Martha (GARRETTSON) 864
  Mary 864
  Mary (HAMMOND) 864
  Mary (TOLLEY) 864, 920
  Mary Ann 843, 862, 864
  N. B. 614, 846
  Nicholas 864
  Priscilla (BOND) 921
  R. J. 162, 903
  Rebecca 640
  Rezin 817
  Rezin Hammond 832
  Richard 355, 864
  Richard I. 855
  Rosetta 864
  Sallie 864

WORTHINGTON, Samuel 38, 70, 71, 810, 817, 819, 820, 857, 860, 862, 864, 865, 867, 876, 879, 894, 920
  Samuel W. 814, 880
  Sarah 862
  Sarah Hanson 862
  Susan 864
  Susan (JOHNS) 864, 865
  T. 103
  T. C. 815
  T. L. 880
  Thomas 62, 70, 103, 310, 810, 832, 862, 864
  Thomas C. 820, 830, 832
  Thomas Chew 832
  Vachel 864, 921
  W. G. D. 811, 850
  Walter 864, 865
  William 70, 858, 861, 862
  William G. D. 194
  Wilson 252
  Zachariah H. 819
  Worthington Family 858, 862
  Worthington Valley 18, 19, 28, 843, 854, 857, 862, 863
  Worthington's Mill 95
WORVER, Aaron 856
Wreath 616
WRENSHALL, J. C. 354
WRIGHT, Charles W. 161
  Clayton 810
  D. G. 191
  D. Girand 191
  D. Giraud 191
  E. K. 872
  Fanny 651
  Francis 818
  Frederick 817
  George F. 880
  Hendrick B. 504
  Henry S. 872
  J. P. 877
  J. Wesley, Mrs. 596
  James H. 820
  Jesse B. 241, 245
  Joel 189, 240, 241, 462
  John 817, 886, 902
  John N. 190, 193
  John S. 190
  Joseph H. 820
  Lizzie 156
  Lorenzo D. 190
  Louisa Turpin 744
  Luther 810
  Mary (HARRIS) 744
  Murrill S. 791
  Oliver B. 659
  R. E. 237
  Robert 195
  Robert Clinton 124, 810
  Robert S. 245

WRIGHT, Samuel 809
 Silas 504
 Solomon 709, 710
 William 920
 William H. D. C. 125
 William H. DeCoursey 810
Wright's Wharf 303
WRING, Thomas 298
WRIOTHESLEY, H. 814
WROTH, Henly 920
 Henry A. 442
 Peregrine 738
WUNDER, ---, Dr. 695
WUNDERMANN, Frederick 625
 Gottleib August 625
 John Philipp 625
WYATT, ---, Rev. Dr. 317, 521, 659
 Christopher B. 810
 F. 137
 James 810
 Thomas J. 521
 W. E. 902
 William 520
 William E. 589, 810
Wye Heights 718
WYER, ---, Rev. Mr. 565
WYEVILL, ---, Dr. 741
WYLIE, R. M. 441, 442
 R. N., Mrs. 604
 Robert 810, 848
WYMAN, John 810
 S. G. 887, 914
 Samuel G. 602, 698, 854, 937
 Samuel G., Mrs. 596
 William 471, 886, 887
Wyman, Appleton & Co. 854
Wyman, Samuel & Co. 854
WYNKOOP, ---, Dr. 732
 James 733, 809
WYNNE, James 628
 Mary Catherine, Mother 810
WYSONG, William A. 202, 599
WYVILL, Dorsey 741
Xaverian Brotherhood 938
Xaverian Brothers 826
Xaverian Brothers' School 536
Y.M.C.A. 636, 637, 668, 739
Y.M.C.A. Library 667
Y.M.C.A. of Woodberry 838
YANCY, William L. 113
YARDSLEY, William 100
YATES, George 48
 John 189
 John L. 189, 249
 Joseph 811
 Margaret 718
 T. 103
 Thomas 73, 76, 101, 103, 206, 452, 718, 811
 William H. 161
Yates & Campbell 433

Yates & Edmonson 433
Yates & Ligget 432
YEAGER, --- 300
YEAKLE, Virgie V. 916
YEARLEY, Joseph 575
 Thomas C. 938
YEARLY, Alexander 188, 593
 Thomas C. 472, 938
YEATES, George 811
 Georgia 927
 Henry P. P. 161
 John L. 189, 241
YEATON, William 70
YEISER, ---, Mr. 60
 Engelhard 452, 727
 Englehard 167, 173, 206, 208, 224, 238, 239, 520, 569
 Englehart 61
 Frederick 569, 572
Yeiser's Canal 61
YEISLEY, Jacob 153, 190
YEISSER, Englehard 172
YELLOT, Coleman 499
YELLOTT, --- 103
 ---, Associate Justice 903
 ---, Capt. 733
 ---, Judge 898, 904
 Charles M. 161
 Coleman 127, 131, 139, 193, 485, 811, 876, 896
 George 245, 625, 717, 811, 814, 903
 J. 102
 J. Israel 817
 Jeremiah 82, 101, 118, 162, 173, 291, 292, 298, 452, 521, 522, 592, 811, 823, 824, 904, 906, 910
 John 845, 904, 905, 906
 John I. 161, 820
Yellott, J. & Co. 102
YEO, ---, Mr. 919
 George 919
 John 918, 920
YERGER, E. M. 508, 624, 811
Yerger, E. M. & Co. 624
YERKES, ---, Rev. Mr. 902
 Stephen 720, 908
YINGLING, F. J. 856
 Joshua 488
 Nimrod 856
YMCA 525, 603
YMCA of Baltimore 557
YOAST, John 73
York 347
York County Academy 346
York Haven 343, 344, 347
York Haven Co. 343
York River Railroad 302
York Road 883, 888, 889, 890, 892, 902, 906, 907
York Road Railway 888, 903
York Spit Light-house 310

York Turnpike 871, 872, 875, 876, 881, 883, 886, 887, 888, 891, 893, 894, 895, 896, 898
York's Hope 918
YOUNG, ---, Dr. 741
---, Mr. 494, 635
---, Mrs. 264
A. B. 729
Ackerman J. 246
Alfred 841, 880
Amelia (FORNEY) 443
Ann S. (MC MURRAY) 776
Arabella 917
Benjamin 811
C. 686
C. E. 579
Charles 102
Edward 922
George 443
H. 252
Hugh 70, 79, 100, 101, 102, 392, 547, 779, 811
James 73, 164, 190, 191, 199, 200, 242, 251, 270, 484, 628, 630, 635, 811, 817
John 246, 741
John C. 161
John S. 188, 209
John Tully 73
Joseph 77, 254, 298
Mary A. (HILT) 443
McClintock 188, 254, 760
Micajah 776
Philemon 811
Rebecca 922
S. 921
Samuel 71, 298, 593, 741
Susan (SHOLL) 443
William 47, 74, 224, 443, 811, 814, 851, 921
William H. 190, 761
William S. 191, 415, 441, 442, 443, 445, 463, 487, 494
Young, H. & Co. 101, 102
Young, Hugh & Co. 101, 102
Young, Knox & Co. 101, 102
Young America 628
Young Catholics' Friends' Society 533, 601, 668
Young Idea, The 637
Young Ladies' Magazine 629
Young Men's Catholic Association Library 667
Young Men's Christian Association 154, 475
Young Men's Friend, The 637
Young Men's Journal, The 636
Young Men's Paper, The 650
Young Men's Society 613
YOUNGER, Hiram B. 161
YOUNKER, Francis 249
Youths' Athenaeum 625
YUNDLT, Leonard 592
YUNDT, Jacob 253
Z. 608
ZAHRAND, Carl 605
ZANTZINGER, Lewis 504
ZAWN, James J. 811
ZEHNER, John 820
ZEIGLER, George W. 693
ZELL, O. C. 821
  Oliver C. 502
  Oliver F. 448
  Peter 380
ZENNES, Jacob 821
ZEPP, Charles M. 884
  James A. 830
  Maria Louisa (BOSLEY) 884
ZEVELY, E. S. 636
ZIEGLER, Andrew 541
  W. K. 870
ZIMMER, Peter 542
ZIMMERMAN, ---, Mr. 696
  B. F. 190, 193, 252, 256
  Benjamin 830
  Benjamin F. 161
  Frederick 929
  G. H. 586, 855
  George A. 161
  George F. 256
  George H. 926
  George J. 153, 190, 256, 577
  J. W. 481
  Jacob C. 189
  John 576, 813
  Joshua 370, 820
  L. F. 570, 571
  Lydia A. 926
  Mary 926
ZINCK, Henry C. 886
Zion Church 524
Zion Church Graveyard 826
Zion German Lutheran Church 830
Zion Lutheran Church 569, 809
Zion School Library 667
Zion Tabernacle 580
Zion's Evangelical Lutheran Church 570
ZOLLER, John 149
Zoller & Little 383
ZOLLERS, Charles Henry 734
ZOLLICKOFFER, H. F. 442
ZOLLINGER, ---, Capt. 792
ZORAH, Henry 571
ZOUCK, H. J. 814
Zouck Family 869
Zoucksville 869
ZWANGER, John A. 811
ZWAROWITCH, Lewis 793

Other Heritage Books by Martha and Bill Reamy:

Erie County, New York Obituaries as Found in the Files of the Buffalo and Erie County Historical Society

Genealogical Abstracts from Biographical and Genealogical History of the State of Delaware, Volumes 1 and 2

History and Roster of Maryland Volunteers, War of 1861–1865: Index

Immigrant Ancestors of Marylanders, as Found in Local Histories

Pioneer Families of Orange County, New York

Records of St. Paul's Parish, [Baltimore, Maryland] Volumes 1 and 2

St. George's Parish Register [Harford County, Maryland], 1689–1793

St. James' Parish Registers, 1787–1815

St. Thomas' Parish Register, 1732–1850

The Index of Scharf's History of Baltimore City and County *[Maryland]*

Other Heritage Books by Martha Reamy:

1860 Census Baltimore City: Volume 1, 1st and 2nd Wards (Fells Point and Canton Waterfront Areas)

Abstracts of Carroll County Newspapers, 1831–1846
Marlene Bates and Martha Reamy

Abstracts of South Central Pennsylvania Newspapers: Volume 2, 1791–1795

Early Church Records of Chester County, Pennsylvania, Volume 2
Martha Reamy and Charlotte Meldrum

Early Families of Otsego County, New York, Volume 1

www.ingramcontent.com/pod-product-compliance
Lightning Source LLC
Chambersburg PA
CBHW071949160426
43198CB00011B/1608